Koreans in Japan

Koreans in Japan are a barely known minority, not only in the West but also within Japan itself. Their indistinguishable appearance from Japanese, their cultural literacy in Japanese society, and their fluency in the language make it all the more difficult to grasp the reality of complex social relations integral to this community. *Koreans in Japan* analyses both these relations and the particular conditions and constraints that Koreans face in Japanese society.

This book covers a wide range of topics pertaining to the everyday lives of Koreans in Japan. Subjects include intra-communal and inter-generational politics; women's self-expression; legal and social status in Japan; ethnic education; the history of Korean colonial displacement and postcolonial division under the Cold War; self-representation, and unstable identities. The volume reveals the highly resilient and diverse reality of Koreans in Japan, while simultaneously highlighting the fact that despite recent improvement, legal, social and economic constraints continue to exist in the lives of Koreans, in the form of state intervention, cultural mediation and personal internalization of the norms and values prevalent in Japanese society.

The contributions are written from a wide range of interdisciplinary perspectives, and from the perspective of insiders/outsiders. Up-to-date personal and archival investigation in this book provides a uniquely empathetic, yet theoretically sound, account of a previously invisible ethnic minority in Japan. This is a pioneering study which will fill a gap in existing literature for students and researchers in diverse fields such as Asian studies, politics, cultural studies, history, sociology, and anthropology.

Sonia Ryang was born in Japan to Korean parents. She is Assistant Professor of Anthropology at Johns Hopkins University, and author of *North Koreans in Japan: Language, Ideology, and Identity*.

RoutledgeCurzon Studies in Asia's Transformations
Edited by Mark Selden
Binghamton and Cornell Universities

The books in this series explore the political, social, economic and cultural consequences of Asia's twentieth-century transformations. The series emphasizes the tumultuous interplay of local, national, regional and global forces as Asia bids to become the hub of the world economy. While focusing on the contemporary, it also looks back to analyse the antecedents of Asia's contested rise.

The series comprises two strands:

RoutledgeCurzon Studies in Asia's Transformations is a forum for innovative new research intended for a high-level specialist readership, and the titles will be available in hardback only. Titles include:

1 The American Occupation of Japan and Okinawa
Literature and memory
Michael Molasky

2 Koreans in Japan
Critical voices from the margin
Edited by Sonia Ryang

Asia's Transformations aims to address the needs of students and teachers, and the titles will be published in hardback and paperback. Titles include:

Debating Human Rights
Critical essays from the United States and Asia
Edited by Peter Van Ness

Hong Kong's History
State and society under colonial rule
Edited by Tak-Wing Ngo

Japan's Comfort Women
Yuki Tanaka

Opium, Empire and the Global Political Economy
Carl A. Trocki

Chinese Society
Change, conflict and resistance
Edited by Elizabeth J. Perry and Mark Selden

Mao's Children in the New China
Voices from the red guard generation
Yarong Jiang and David Ashley

Koreans in Japan
Critical voices from the margin

Edited by Sonia Ryang

LONDON AND NEW YORK

First published 2000
by Routledge
2 Park Square, Milton Park, Abingdon, Oxon, OX14 4RN

Transferred to Digital Printing 2005

Simultaneously published in the USA and Canada
by Routledge
270 Madison Ave, New York NY 10016

Reprinted 2001 (twice)

RoutledgeCurzon is an imprint of the Taylor & Francis Group

© 2000 Sonia Ryang for selection and editorial material; individual contributors, their contributions

Typeset in Times by
Curran Publishing Services Ltd

All rights reserved. No part of this book may be reprinted or reproduced or utilised in any form or by any electronic, mechanical, or other means, now known or hereafter invented, including photocopying and recording, or in any information storage or retrieval system, without permission in writing from the publishers.

British Library Cataloguing in Publication Data
A catalogue record for this book is available
from the British Library

Library of Congress Cataloging in Publication Data
Koreans in Japan: critical voices from the margin / edited by Sonia Ryang.
   240 pp. 23.4 x 15.6 cm. – (Routledge studies in Asia's transformations)
   Includes bibliographical references and index
   1. Koreans – Japan – History. 2. Japan – Ethnic relations.
   I. Ryang, Sonia. II. Series.
   DS832.7.K6K66 2000
   952'.004957–dc21   99–39943
                                                                   CIP

ISBN 0-415-37939-3

Contents

Contributors		vii
Note to the reader		ix
Acknowledgements		x
	Introduction: resident Koreans in Japan SONIA RYANG	1
1	The politics of legal status: the equation of nationality with ethnonational identity CHIKAKO KASHIWAZAKI	13
2	The North Korean homeland of Koreans in Japan SONIA RYANG	32
3	Political correctness, postcoloniality and the self-representation of "Koreanness" in Japan KOICHI IWABUCHI	55
4	Mothers write Ikaino MELISSA WENDER	74
5	Reading against the bourgeois and national bodies: transcultural body-politics in Yu Miri's textual representations LISA YONEYAMA	103
6	Cultural identity in the work of Yi Yang-ji CAROL HAYES	119
7	Korean ethnic schools in occupied Japan, 1945–52 HIROMITSU INOKUCHI	140
8	Korean children, textbooks, and educational practices in Japanese primary schools ERIKO AOKI	157

9 Kids between nations: ethnic classes in the construction
  of Korean identities in Japanese public schools 175
  JEFFRY T. HESTER

10 Ordinary (Korean) Japanese 197
   JOHN LIE

   Bibliography 208
   Index 226

Contributors

Eriko Aoki is professor of anthropology at Suzuka International University in Japan. She obtained her Ph.D. in anthropology from the Australian National University, and is the author of English and Japanese articles on eastern Indonesia and gender, among other subjects. Her recent publications include "The Case of Pwloin Statues" in James J. Fox (ed.), *To Speak in Pairs: Essays on Ritual Languages of Eastern Indonesia*. She has widely participated in the community-level exchange with Korean residents and writes on the topics of Koreans and other minorities in Japan.

Carol Hayes is a lecturer in Japanese at the Department of East Asian Studies, University of Durham, UK. She obtained a Ph.D. in Japanese literature from the University of Sydney. She has published articles on cultural identity in contemporary Japanese fiction and modern Japanese poetry, particularly the work of Hagiwara Sakutarō. She is currently researching cultural identity in the literature of a number of Koreans resident in Japan: Li Hoe-Sŏng, Yi Yang-ji, Yu Miri and in the films of Sai Yōichi.

Jeffry T. Hester received his Ph.D. in sociocultural anthropology from the University of California, Berkeley and is assistant professor of anthropology at Kansai Gaidai University, Osaka.

Hiromitsu Inokuchi received his Ph.D. from the University of Wisconsin, Madison, and currently teaches at the University of East Asia, Shimonoseki, Japan. His dissertation, "US Middle School Students' Discourses on Japan: A Study of Politics of Representation," analyzes the languages used by US students when writing and talking about Japan. He is a sociologist of culture and education, and has published articles on ideology and education, textbook controversy in Japan, and the identity formation of resident Koreans.

Koichi Iwabuchi teaches media and cultural studies at the International Christian University, Tokyo. He completed his Ph.D. at the University of Western Sydney, Nepean, in 1999. His articles have been published in English, Japanese, and Chinese, in journals including *Communal/Plural: Journal of Transnational and Cross-cultural Studies* and *Sekai*. His forthcoming work includes "Becoming Culturally Proximate: A/Scent of Japanese Idol Dramas in Taiwan" (in Brian Moeran (ed.), *Asian Media and Advertising*, 1999, London: Curzon Press), and a book tentatively entitled *Returning to Asia: Japan in the Cultural Dynamics of Globalization, Localization and Asianization*.

Chikako Kashiwazaki received a Ph.D. in sociology from Brown University and teaches at Sophia University in Japan. Her dissertation examined stability and change in Japanese nationality and citizenship laws from a comparative-historical perspective. Her articles are published in *Research in Political Sociology* and *International Journal of Comparative Sociology*. She is currently conducting research on the historical dynamics of citizenship and nationality, immigration and ethnicity, and nationalism.

John Lie is professor of sociology and head of the Department of Sociology at the University of Illinois at Urbana–Champaign. His recent writings on Japan include *Sociology of Contemporary Japan* (special issue of *Current Sociology* vol. 44 no. 1, 1996), and a forthcoming book tentatively entitled *Multiethnic Japan*.

Sonia Ryang is assistant professor of anthropology at Johns Hopkins University. Born and raised in Japan, she obtained her Ph.D. in social anthropology from Cambridge University, England. She is the author of *North Koreans in Japan: Language, Ideology, and Identity* (Westview Press, 1997). Her forthcoming work is entitled *After Benedict: Rethinking Japan as Anthropological Other*.

Melissa Wender received her Ph.D. from the University of Chicago. She is assistant professor in the department of German, Russian, and East Asian Languages and Literatures at Bates College. Her dissertation was on literature by Koreans in Japan from the mid-1960s to the present. Her particular interest is in the intersection of gender, ethnicity, and nationality in resident Koreans' literary narratives of identity, and in the way that these literary texts are both influenced by and bear upon political discourses. She has also begun to translate some of the work she discusses in her dissertation, and hopes to publish a collection of stories by resident Koreans in the near future. Her other research interests include the literature and culture of other minorities in Japan and depictions of family, class, and nation in contemporary Japanese popular culture.

Lisa Yoneyama is associate professor of cultural studies and Japanese studies at Literature Department, University of California, San Diego. She was born in Illinois, USA, and raised in Kyoto, Japan. She obtained a Ph.D. in anthropology from Stanford University, and is the author of *Hiroshima Traces: Time, Space, and the Dialectics of Memory*, published by the University of California Press.

Note to the reader

1 In this book the transliteration of Japanese words follows the conventional Japanese romanization system. Macrons have been put on words and names that are not familiar to western readers. For example, Tokyo does not have macrons, but Chūō kōron does.
2 The transliteration of Korean words does not always follow the McCune-Reischauer system. Some words are transliterated following the North Korean version of their pronunciation. Diacritics are used to distinguish some vowels. For example, chosŏn and minjujuŭi take diacritics.
3 The transliteration of names of Korean people usually takes a hyphen between the two syllables of the first name. However, where the individuals themselves use a Japanized version of their name, the hyphen is omitted. For example, Yi Yang-ji is given in the Korean form, but Yu Miri is in the Japanized form. In unspecifiable cases, the convention used is to transliterate Korean names using Korean pronunciation.
4 The Western convention of placing given names before family names has been used for the chapter authors. The East Asian convention of giving the family name first is used for the individuals and authors quoted and discussed in the text, unless the individual herself or himself has a specific preference for the alternative.
5 Japanese and Korean names of institutions are written with the first letter of the first word capitalized without italicization; all other foreign names and words are italicized in lower case throughout. For example, Buraku kaihō dōmei takes the former form and *zainichi* the latter.
6 Esoteric place names such as Ikaino have been given an initial capital. The frequently mentioned state names *chōsen* (Korea) and *kankoku* (ROK) are treated as general names, and hence are not capitalized but are italicized, as in *chōsenjin* and *kankokujin* (Korean or Koreans). Where the name of an individual is used as the title of a book or an essay, these are dealt with arbitrarily. For example, the form *Yuhi* has been adopted in preference to *Yu-hi*.
7 When Korean words are used, but denote the user's reading them in Japanese, the transliteration follows Japanese romanization, as in *Ikaino taryon*, instead of *Ikaino t'aryŏng*.
8 The names of the two states in the Korean peninsula, the Democratic People's Republic of Korea and the Republic of Korea, are at times abbreviated as DPRK and ROK. These are also referred to as North Korea and South Korea respectively.
9 Government documents and newspaper articles are listed separately, with their titles first, in the bibliography. Some journal articles that do not bear the individual author's name are also listed with the title.

Acknowledgements

I wish to thank all the individuals who contributed to this volume, and who put up with my often demanding requests and deadlines. I wish also to acknowledge Mark Selden, the series editor for Routledge, and Victoria Smith, senior project editor for Routledge; without their help this book would not have been born. The manuscript greatly benefited from the illuminating comments of anonymous reviewers for Routledge, for which I am grateful. Final reading of the manuscript took place in Johns Hopkins Hospital neonatal intensive care unit where my daughter was staying at the time of writing this acknowledgement. I am grateful to the Johns Hopkins medical staff who gave me the space to work, and to my colleagues and students in the Department of Anthropology, Johns Hopkins University, who supported me throughout this very difficult period. Most importantly, I wish to thank my daughter whose courage and strength kept me going. I wish also to thank Susan Curran whose editorial work greatly improved the book.

Grateful thanks are due to Chong Ch'u-wŏl for permitting the inclusion in its entirety of her poem "Kimch'i" in chapter 4, Kōdansha for permitting the quotations from the *Collected Works of Yi Yang-ji* and *Yuhi* in chapter 6, and Kyōikyu Shuppan for permitting the quotations from its textbooks in chapter 8.

Sonia Ryang

Introduction
Resident Koreans in Japan

Sonia Ryang

Despite the political and economic importance of both Japan and Korea to western nations whose economies are ever more closely bound up with Asia, and who have fought major twentieth-century wars in the region, academic investigations into Japanese and Korean societies have not yet reached the level where they provide much direct insight into the current social, economic, and political problems confronting the US and other western societies. Often Japanese society is viewed as exotic or different, or at best relevant only in terms of management style. However, study of this society is a rich field which can offer many case studies relevant to western societies. Relevant perspectives include the experience in Japan of racial segregation, ethnic discrimination and the systemic violation of human rights of minority peoples; and internal debate and mutual critique of minority groups themselves, and the power relations within such communities. These issues cross gender and class boundaries.

By introducing Koreans living in Japan as long-term foreign residents, this collection invites readers to compare their conditions, perceptions, and movements with those of minorities and oppressed peoples in the west and elsewhere. The formation and transformation of ethnic identity and cultural diversity are concerns Koreans in Japan share with many other minority groups in contemporary societies. In locating the experiences of resident Koreans in Japan within the parameters of marginalized and colonized peoples, this book offers fresh insight into, and analysis of, the colonial and postcolonial experience of a people who are hardly known in the west.[1]

Historical background

Japan colonized Korea for three and a half decades from 1910 to 1945, incorporating Koreans and other Asians within its expansive empire. According to Peter Duus, Japanese colonization of Korea was based on "mimesis" of western imperialism. Duus also points out, though, that "however much Japanese practices of imperialist domination resembled those of the Western powers, it should be remembered that the Japanese arrived at them by a quite different historical route and under quite different historical circumstances" (Duus 1995: 425).

Japan itself was subject to western encroachment in the mid-nineteenth century. Its empire-building coincided with, rather than followed, its attempts at modern nation-building after the 1868 restoration of imperial order under the Meiji emperor. For example, when Japan opened Korea to the world outside the traditional Sino-centric realm as a result of the western-style unequal treaty between Japan and Korea signed in 1876, Japan was still under the extraterritoriality of the western powers as a result of the US gunboat diplomacy of 1853. Indeed, even before its economy had been significantly modernized, and even before Japan had extricated itself from the unequal treaties which it had signed with the western powers, Japan was already starting to appear as a potential imperialist power in the eyes of its Asian neighbors including Korea (see Norman 1973).

Japanese expansion was initially confined to its periphery. It began with East Asia, gradually extending to Southeast Asia and the Pacific. Culturally – more controversially speaking, "racially" – Japan's empire centered on East Asian people sharing common practices and traditions such as wet-rice cultivation, Confucian heritage, the Chinese characters in the written language, and international relations constructed around a Sino-centric tributary system. In contrast to many other colonialisms, Japanese colonizers in East Asia could not readily be distinguished physically from those they colonized. The Japanese in Korea, Taiwan, Okinawa, Manchuria, and elsewhere sought simultaneously to establish their own privileged position and to assimilate colonized peoples through the imposition of the Japanese language and education system. Issues of assimilation thus remained essential, yet controversial and rife with internal contradictions, since after all, the empire-building was underpinned by multiethnic reality.

From the start, Koreans fiercely resisted colonial rule. Anarchists and communists as well as some conservative nationalists not only inaugurated resistance movements in Korea, but also collaborated with revolutionaries in Japan, China, Manchuria, and elsewhere. Koreans were particularly active in the labor movement and in communist party activities in Japan up to the mid-1930s, when the left was brutally suppressed. In Manchuria, nationalistic Korean communists, including Kim Il Sung, initiated armed resistance, building on shifting alliances with Chinese or Soviet communists (Wada 1992). In Korea proper, anti-Japanese resistance surged as early as 1919 despite tight Japanese military and political controls.

Following mobilization for the fifteen-year war starting with Japan's aggression in China (1931–45), renewed efforts were made to turn Koreans into imperial subjects (see Kashiwazaki in this volume). By the early 1940s, the Japanese rulers in the colony were deploying a slogan *naisenittai*, literally, Korea and Japan forming one body. The then governor-general Minami Jirō stated that Japanese and Koreans must form "one body" blending their "blood and flesh" together, and claimed, "Korea is not a colony [since it is part of Japan]. If anybody were to call Korea a colony, beat them up" (quoted in Miyata 1985: 165–6).

Prior to this, in 1939, as part of a general campaign to turn Koreans into the emperor's subjects the Japanese government-general imposed new strictures on the household registration of Koreans in the peninsula. The policy – *sōshikaimei*

– forced a great many Koreans to adopt Japanese-style names and abandon their Korean names. It clashed with the incest taboo which had been Korean custom since the time of Yi dynasty (1392–1910) and which prevented Koreans from marrying a person of the same clan. Traditionally, Korean women did not adopt their husband's name after marriage, since adopting their husband's clan name was seen – albeit in retrospect and only in a formal sense – as tantamount to marrying a person of the same clan. Furthermore, reflecting the internal contradiction of the logic of colonial assimilation, even under *sōshikaimei* the distinction between Japanese and Korean ancestry was maintained. For example Koreans were forbidden to move their household registry to Japan proper. This worked as a device to keep Koreans secondary to Japanese in terms of membership of the empire. More importantly, it proved to be crucial in the postwar establishment of the nationality of Koreans in Japan, as we shall see.[2]

Miyata Setsuko suggests that *sōshikaimei* was preparation for the full conscription of Korean males as the emperor's soldiers, which was the ultimate goal of the *naisenittai* campaign (Miyata 1992). Indeed, following *sōshikaimei*, conscription was applied to Korean men starting from 1943. A total of 257,404 Korean men were drafted into the Japanese army (civilian component inclusive) and 106,782 into the navy (Tsuboe 1949: 23). Many lost their lives by fighting as Japanese soldiers. After the war, twenty-three Koreans were executed as Japanese war criminals and 125 served postwar sentences as war criminals (Utsumi 1991: 71). Hundreds and thousands of Korean men were taken to mines and construction sites in Japan and elsewhere as labor recruits during the war. From 1939 to December 1944, a total of 634,093 male Koreans were brought to Japan to supplement the labor force in various sectors: 320,148 worked in coal mining, 61,409 in metal mining, 129,664 in construction and civil engineering, and 122,872 in manufacturing and machine industries (Kim Yŏng-dal 1991: 35). Workers were subjected to slave labor, and many were injured, and in some cases killed, in the work place by accident, malnutrition, and maltreatment. Many Korean women were forced into prostitution for the army as "comfort women" and taken as far away as Southeast Asia and the Pacific fronts, where many died or were killed in the final months of the war.[3]

All these actions were carried out with the rhetoric of Japan and Korea forming one body, but the reality was different. Koreans were discriminated against in the mines and other labor sites, receiving less payment and a harder workload than Japanese workers (see e.g. Pak Kyŏng-sik 1992). In the military, Koreans were viewed with suspicion owing to their incompetence arising from a lack of comprehension of the Japanese language (Miyata 1985: ch. 3). A complete conversion of Koreans into the emperor's subjects was after all impossible, insofar as seemingly multiethnic slogans such as "the Great East Asia Coprosperity Sphere" fundamentally stood on the premise of maintaining the racio-ethnic superiority of Japanese. Not surprisingly, the majority of Koreans emerged from the colonial experience with deep-rooted anger toward Japan and fierce patriotism and nationalism.

When the war ended, there were more than two million Koreans living in

Japan. Many rushed back home to Korea, only to find their home country divided. The north had been placed within the Soviet sphere, the south in the US zone. The situation moved inexorably toward civil war and international conflict, with the declaration of separate states in the north and the south in 1948, and the Korean War in 1950. After three years of war, Korea's partition was complete, resulting in the creation of two antagonistic regimes out of a single historically unified region.[4]

Of two million Koreans in Japan, some 600,000 remained throughout the postwar turmoil. Uncertain about Korea's future, or prevented from returning immediately to their homes in the peninsula, they formed an expatriate community, extremely anti-Japanese and nationalistic, but with their allegiances split between the two different regimes in the peninsula.

During the colonial period, Koreans were classified as Japanese citizens and enjoyed certain citizenship rights. Korean males in Japan, like their Japanese counterparts, could vote and be elected to public office, and indeed several were so elected. In December 1945, Koreans lost their voting rights. In 1947 they had to register as resident aliens in Japan under the Alien Registration Law. In 1950 the Japanese Nationality Law was established on the basis of the patrilineal parentage principle, thereby excluding Koreans. Those whose household registry was not found in Japan proper lost Japanese nationality. The earlier practice of keeping the household registry of Koreans in Korea created a criterion for drawing the boundary of Japanese citizenship.

In 1945, when the Allied occupation of Japan started, Koreans in Japan were liberated people; by 1952, when the occupation ended, they were stateless people with few civil rights and extreme insecurity of residential status. The San Francisco Peace Treaty of 1952 guaranteed Korean independence from Japan, but the treaty and Japanese post-independence policy simultaneously deprived Koreans resident in Japan of Japanese citizenship (Kashiwazaki in this volume). With this, Koreans lost the rights of political participation as well as occupational and educational opportunities which were dependent on Japanese citizenship, including the licensing of certain businesses, national health insurance, and social security. They also lost war veterans' pensions and war bereavement pensions, national income benefits, and the right of overseas travel (owing to their lack of Japanese or any other passports), to cite but a few examples. They received a renewable visa-like status and were subjected to tight surveillance, required to be fingerprinted and to carry a registration certificate at all times, and they faced the possibility of deportation to North or South Korea, despite the lack of Japanese diplomatic relations with either Korea prior to 1965.

The 1965 South Korea–Japan normalization of diplomatic relations enabled Koreans in Japan to obtain the right of permanent residence on condition that they apply for South Korean nationality. This arrangement restructured expatriate political power relations: faced with this choice, many Korean residents, including some who had previously supported North Korea, applied for South Korean nationality. Those who remained stateless, approximately 250,000 out of 640,000 in 1974 (Lee 1981: 144–5), had no civil status or overseas travel document until the early 1980s, that is, for more than three decades after Korea's liberation.

Expatriate politics

The first three decades of the postcolonial life of Koreans in Japan were dominated by Cold War tensions. Koreans viewed the partition of their homeland as the outrageous outcome of colonial rule and postcolonial foreign intervention. Many regarded Korea's partition and their sojourn in Japan as temporary, and focused on the resolution of national and international political issues concerning the Korean homeland. Although living in Japan, many Korean residents envisioned no long-term future for themselves in Japan.

Despite the fact that some 98 percent of resident Koreans in Japan originated from the south of Korea, supporters of North Korea were initially more numerous and better organized than those supporting South Korea. This is because the most politically radical and anti-Japanese Koreans, prior to and during the war, were communists active in the independence struggle. The release of some well-known Korean communists from prison in Tokyo in October 1945 also strengthened left leadership in the expatriate movement. Supporters of South Korea emerged as the right wing of the expatriate community.

The first Korean leftist organization, the League of Koreans (organized in October 1945), was suppressed by Japanese and occupation authorities in 1949, following the closure of Korean schools which had mushroomed in the immediate postwar years (see Inokuchi in this volume). Chongryun, the left-wing organization that followed the league (founded in May 1955), reinforced ties between the North Korean government and Japan-resident Koreans and rebuilt Korean schools. Initially, Chongryun enjoyed broad support, strengthened by its provision of education facilities. Although Chongryun's 150 schools, ranging from primary, junior high, and senior high schools to a university, received no formal accreditation from the Japanese Ministry of Education, many resident Koreans supported Chongryun and sent their children to its schools to receive a (North) Korean style education (Ryang 1997). Even some parents who opted for South Korean nationality after 1965 paid to keep their children in Chongryun schools rather than send them to Japanese public schools.

In the 1950s and 1960s, colonial memories of the first generation penetrated every nook and cranny of social and family life. Social bonds were strong in Korean neighborhoods, marked by ethnic food, customs, mutual help arrangements, and pride in the face of poverty and discrimination. Many, especially first-generation residents, continued to hope for an eventual homecoming to Korea. All faced the problem of survival in a harsh environment.

In the 1970s and 1980s profound changes took place in the lives of Koreans in Japan. Although continuing to face discrimination, including exclusion from voting entitlements, restrictions on overseas travel, statelessness, and occupational and educational discrimination, they nevertheless shared in the long economic boom that made Japan an economic power and assured near-full employment. Some individuals prospered through ownership of restaurants, pachinko parlors, and money-lending businesses. Many Korean neighborhoods began to dissolve, with the exodus of young people to Japanese middle-class residential areas. Those that remained enjoyed improved housing and sanitary conditions, and tended to blend with Japanese neighborhoods.

Important changes in the legal position also affected Korean residents. Ratification of the International Covenants on Human Rights (1979) and the United Nations Refugee Convention (1981) required the Japanese government to improve the status of Korean residents by granting permanent residence and providing re-entry permits for overseas travel to nearly all Korean residents without the prerequisite possession of South Korean nationality.[5]

By the 1980s, Japan-born resident Koreans were numerically dominant over the Korea-born. Speaking native Japanese, attending Japanese schools, watching Japanese television and films, in many instances working for Japanese firms, and with some passing as Japanese, it is not surprising that the primary cultural identity for many became that of the Japanese. In this milieu, the homeland-oriented politics of the first generation no longer dominated. Nor did the two opposing political organizations, Chongryun supporting North Korea and Mindan supporting South Korea, structure public opinion among Korean residents. The North Korea-supporting Chongryun became a minority group within Koreans in Japan, to some extent because of the democratization and subsequent stability of South Korea, but more significantly because of the better integration of Koreans into Japanese society (see Ryang in this volume for a discussion of Chongryun Koreans). For example, about 90 percent of Korean children in Japan today learn at Japanese schools (see Aoki and Hester in this volume). More personal and less organized forms of micro politics and cultural concerns gained momentum, paralleling changes characteristic of Japanese society in the post-Cold War era (see Wender in this volume). Intra-communal critical concerns multiplied, with respect to such issues as gender relations, gerontocracy and ageism, class differentiation, and antagonisms based on political difference. Like people elsewhere, Koreans in Japan are divided by politics, gender, class, occupation, education, age, and status. Young people became interested in identity politics, not from the angle of the north–south binary opposition, but with an eye to questioning their future in Japan. Many now actively debate ethnic identity, diaspora politics, and integration in, or autonomy from, Japanese society.

With the passage of time, the number of Koreans willing and able to naturalize as Japanese increased. In the 1950s, less than 2,500 a year became naturalized, many of whom were Japanese women who married Korean men. The number increased to 3,600 per year in the years 1960–6 (Morita 1996: 119), 4,700 per year in the 1970s, and 5,400 per year in the 1980s. In 1997 alone 9,678 were naturalized (*Asahi shinbun*, 4 April 1998). In the 1990s it has become far easier to obtain Japanese citizenship.[6] Intermarriages between Koreans and Japanese have steadily increased. In 1973, 50.6 percent of the total number of marriages involving Koreans were Korean-to-Korean marriages; in 1994, only 17.5 percent were Korean-to-Korean marriages, with the rest being marriages between Korean and Japanese (81.7 percent) and between Korean and other nationals (0.8 percent) (calculated from Kim Yŏng-dal 1996: 179). In addition, after the 1988 liberalization of overseas travel of South Koreans, there was an increase in so-called newcomers from South Korea. Many obtain employment in family businesses run by resident Koreans, and many intermarry. The current total number of Koreans in Japan – estimated around 650,000 – includes these new immigrants, who further complicate the internal constitution of the community.

The majority of resident Koreans in Japan today look toward a future in Japan for themselves and their children, not a return to a Korean homeland. More and more Korean residents, whether or not they choose to become naturalized Japanese citizens or to marry Japanese, recognize that, for better or for worse, Japan is their home. This volume provides glimpses into the daily lives, hopes, and identities of these Koreans.

Highlighting internal debates

How, then, do resident Koreans in Japan perceive themselves? Their self-representation takes diverse forms including such media as literary, autobiographical, and social-scientific writing, performing and visual arts, historical studies, theatre and film. Theirs is not merely self-representation but engagement with the ongoing perspectives of both Korean residents and Japanese. It includes the critique of what they regard as facile or false identification as resident Korean, and much that is pessimistically accepted by the community as being inevitable. This volume introduces highlights from the literary and art worlds of Koreans as a means of exploring their self-examination and critically assessing the limits and possibilities of their oeuvres. Koichi Iwabuchi writes about a recent hit movie about Koreans and other ethnic minorities in Japan produced by resident Korean filmmakers. Iwabuchi introduces the diverse power relations pertaining to the production, distribution, and response to the film, showing that nothing can be explained in simple terms of ethnic conflict or essentialized ethnic identity. He vividly describes the volatile intersection between the intention and motivation of self-projecting agencies, and intervention by commercialism, political correctness, and other factors in contemporary Japanese media.

Carol Hayes, Melissa Wender, and Lisa Yoneyama focus on women writers among resident Koreans. Korean literature in Japan was written predominantly from a male perspective prior to the 1970s, but the new generation of women authors does not necessarily write from the vantage point of patriarchy and nationalism. Their subjectivities often consciously or unconsciously comment on patriarchal social relations dominant in the Korean community, from side angles. Precisely because they interrogate patriarchal nationalism, their work has often spurred reactions among resident Korean readers, while women writers themselves are far from in agreement in terms of their self-positioning *vis-à-vis* such entities as nation, homeland, and family, as these essays reveal.

Writing about two local women authors in Ikaino, Osaka, the area known as Korea town, Melissa Wender examines the complex web of personal and collective politics where women often discover themselves to be empowered by "creolized" impure language and by the female body that engages in working and laboring (i.e. producing and reproducing). Wender herself writes experimentally in her essay, in search of a new form of mutual understanding and sharing of emotion between subject and author, weaving into a rich text her personal encounters with her women writers as well as other writers and civil rights activists in the vicinity of Ikaino. She raises important questions concerning the participation of Koreans in grassroots-level politics.

Carol Hayes and Lisa Yoneyama deal with nationally acclaimed resident Korean female authors in Japan, Yi Yang-ji and Yu Miri. The nation, ethnicity, and "Korea" are perceived in very different form by those two young Japan-born authors, not only in comparison to the earlier generation of predominantly male Korean authors, but also from each other. While Yi struggled to come to terms with her Korean origins through a series of painful journeys of self-examination, about which she wrote in her award-winning, yet traumatic *Yuhi*, Yu's "Korea" remains in the realm of the "unsaid" in her likewise award-winning, equally traumatic, family saga. Yi's vision certainly problematizes nation and the state, but Yū is more individual and personal, focusing on the shaky grounds of modern family relations and ambiguous sexuality. In her analysis of Yu's texts, Yoneyama takes a multilayered approach, reading the very absence of the reference to the national homeland, so pervasive in Korean literature in Japan, as a sign of Yu's effort to subvert the fixation of identities. Both Hayes and Yoneyama tell us of the personal struggles of these women as they try to carve out niches in order to find their own writing position and a space called home and homeland.

The concept of home is closely juxtaposed with the notion of homeland in my chapter, focusing on the vision of North Korea as home to those Korean residents who identify themselves as North Korea's overseas nationals. This chapter should be paired with Chikako Kashiwazaki's chapter on citizenship and the legal status of Koreans in Japan. Both chapters touch issues of civil membership of a nation-state, which Kashiwazaki explores through the systemic examination of changing legal relations, and I explore by looking at the political identification adopted by the agents themselves, resident Koreans. The Kashiwazaki chapter is a critique not only of changing features of Japan's discriminatory system of citizenship and naturalization, but also of the nationalist-essentialist approaches historically taken by Korean expatriate organizations themselves, including Chongryun and Mindan. My chapter addresses the personal realm that emerged in reaction to the homeland-bound politics of the North Korea-supporting Chongryun, especially among its younger generations. I point to the illusions of those who identify North Korea as home while simultaneously invoking the need to build their home in Japan.

The question of identity in general, and national and ethnic identity in particular requires not just the identification of the subject with a specific space as home, but also the examination of the processes of production and reproduction of such an identity. In this, education assumes a crucial role given that in modern societies mass education necessarily takes the form of national education. The struggle over non-national education, such as Korean ethnic education within Japan's nation-state boundaries, usually is subjected to both persistent obstacles from authoritarian pressure and micro politics at the grassroots level. Hiromitsu Inokuchi, Eriko Aoki, and Jeffry Hester discuss relevant issues in this area. Given that education is one of the most powerful state vehicles for preparing children ideologically as national subjects, all three authors inquire into the scope and nature of Japanese nationalist domination in the learning and socialization processes of resident Korean children who attend Japanese schools.[7]

Inokuchi assesses the historical impact of Korean education, beginning with the Allied occupation of Japan (1945–52), and focusing on the April 1948 incidents of violent suppression of Korean schools in Osaka and Kobe by the Allied authorities. He lays bare the historical origins of the structural marginalization of Korean education through the decision by Japanese educational authorities to disqualify and exclude it from the realm of public education. Inokuchi's historical background introduces the contemporary context of Korean education in Osaka, which Aoki and Hester both develop with their first-hand insight into the educational process through case studies conducted in separate locations in Osaka. The Hester chapter is an account of the micro-dynamics of Korean teachers, children, and parents, who try to render Korean education and identity meaningful through extra-curricular classes for primary school pupils. Hester's ethnography draws on his study of a Korean class located within, but supplementary to, Japanese public primary education, and he invites his readers to experience fascinating moments of learning how to be "Korean." Aoki offers a close study of the school textbooks used in Osaka primary public education. She spells out how even well-intended efforts by Japanese educational authorities often result in excluding Korean children from the classrooms of Japanese schools, due to the fundamentally nation-centered pedagogical principle enforced by the Ministry of Education. We see in these essays that Japanese education, even in the most "Korea-conscious" location of Osaka, which has the highest density in Japan of Korean residents, still leaves much to be achieved to convey the ethnic-conscious and self-empowering orientation that Korean children require to attain dignity and self-assurance in Japanese society.

Concluding this volume, John Lie writes about the identity of Koreans in Japan. Polemically using the term "Korean Japanese," one that is usually not deployed by Korean residents themselves, Lie probes the possibility of creating new identities for Koreans in Japan, that transcend existing finite frameworks. Revisiting the area of literary self-expression by leading "Korean Japanese" authors, Lie reminds the reader that no identity can exist one-dimensionally, and the identity of Koreans in Japan is no exception, since "personal narratives resist simple, reductionist, and essentialist characterizations."

What unifies the diverse subject matter of this volume is the sympathetic, yet critical, angle each chapter assumes. Each in its own way not only adds to existing studies pertaining to Koreans in Japan, but also assesses the debates internal to the Korean community. In this way the authors actively engage with the resident Korean politics of ethnic identity, and the intra-ethnic effort to create alternative niches in Japanese society, and between Japanese and Korean societies and cultures. On balance, this volume emphasizes the margin of the margin in introducing a selection of Korean residents. It focuses on children, women, and a demonized political minority, those who profess loyalty to North Korea, since a glimpse of the most marginalized can often lend clarity to the picture of a larger entity enveloping them: that is, the world of resident Koreans and the wider Japanese society. And voices from the margin can provide urgent criticism of the dominant powers: hence the subtitle, *critical voices from the margin*.

The voices and perspectives the volume introduces are diverse. Some are politically committed to North Korea or South Korea; others indifferent. Some are emotionally deeply tied to the fatherland, Korea; others locate themselves squarely within Japanese society. What cuts across all those resident Koreans is that wherever they stand, they stand ambiguously. In the world of Koreans in Japan, there are no clear-cut north–south boundaries or Japan–Korea borders which can provide them with a permanent location. Their identities are perpetually ambiguous, torn between the nation-states of Japan and Korea, between the two halves of the Korean peninsula, and between the ideals of the older Korea-born generation and the reality of younger generations born in Japan and experiencing contemporary Japanese life with no experience in Korea.

Koreans in Japan are a little-known minority in western discourse.[8] Compared to such mainstream minorities such as Jews in the west, African-Americans in the US, and Commonwealth immigrants in the UK, Koreans in Japan, like the Chinese in Indonesia or Nepalese workers in South Korea, for example, have been largely invisible minorities to the west. In this setting – itself a reflection of the western domination of the business of constructing minorities – Koreans in Japan seem almost irrelevant. However, the range of experience explored in this volume, of the discrimination Koreans face in Japan, and of Koreans to find scope for self-expression and a means of self-empowerment in Japan, can offer a significant meeting point for different groups of marginalized peoples. Koreans in Japan have faced, and continue to face and respond to, diverse forms of discrimination. Their experience in grappling with human rights violation and social injustice, as well as intra-communal political diversity, is relevant to others' experiences in the west and beyond.

Similarly, just as we learn from observing the debate internal to the Afro-American community (e.g. Patterson 1997), we can learn from internal debates within the Korean community in Japan. Among the questions that minority studies can fruitfully address are how marginalized groups such as women and children within the minority group can find a means of self-empowerment and critical edge to speak against the dominant current, what kind of effects the transition from patriarchal nationalism to personally-oriented politics can produce, and how class differentiation influences power relations within the community.

As among African-Americans, we find ethnic absolutism among Koreans in Japan, privileging an essentialized notion of being "Korean" (see Gilroy 1993). As among Korean-Americans, we find Koreans in Japan involved in complex and at times acrimonious multiethnic relations in Japan: for example, as employers of Southeast Asian immigrant workers, or newcomers from the Korean peninsula itself. Such a picture creates for Koreans in Japan a keen need to adjust and readjust their ethnic orientation, with reference to the changes in their own economic position and social status. (On Korean-Americans, see Abelmann and Lie 1995.) Like diasporic Chinese, we find Koreans making attempts to form transnational identities (Ong and Nonini 1997). We find difficulty and pain, happiness and joy among Koreans in Japan whose lives we now unfold to the reader, as they are found among all peoples. In unfolding these experiences, we hope to open the way to understanding the human condition of Koreans and other minorities in Japan and beyond.

Notes

1 In this Introduction, the terms "resident Koreans" and "Koreans in Japan" are used interchangeably. Norma Field's 1993 article first introduced the term "resident Koreans" (Field 1993). Since then, it has become widely used to denote Korean residents in Japan.
2 *Sōshikaimei* was met with diverse reactions from within Japan proper. Some felt that it would damage the "Japanese national body," *kokutai*, while others worried that there would be no method clearly to distinguish Koreans from Japanese (Miyata 1992: 96–102; for *kokutai*, see Gluck 1985: ch. 5). To be precise, the legalization of *sōshikaimei* took place in 1939, while the actual name-changing started from February 1940. Before the deadline of August 10, about 80 percent of Koreans in the peninsula changed their names into Japanese-style names, while 20 percent retained their Korean names, but followed the Japanese household registration form, unifying the married-in women's name with that of the household head (Yang T'ae-ho 1992: 125–6). For more details, see Miyata, Kim, and Yang (1992).
3 The issue of "comfort women" or *jūgunianfu*, has been actively debated in Korean and Japanese milieus in the 1990s. Women writers of Korea and Japan have been active in a range of documentation, including interviews with the former "comfort women" and former Japanese soldiers (for example, Yun *et al.* 1992; Nishino 1992; Suzuki 1992). More recently, feminists of Japan and Korea have developed a sophisticated discussion which goes beyond a mere exposition of the horrific sufferings of those women, and critically reflects on the male-centric logic of modern nation-building and colonialism, on the one hand, and the patriarchal and nationalistic historiography of postcolonial nation-rebuilding, on the other. (See Ueno 1998; see also Ryang 1998.) However, this comes with a caveat: transcending of nation-state boundaries has different consequences for the former colonizer and for the colonized, including the issues pertaining to the state-level postwar compensation (see my comment on Ueno in Ryang forthcoming).
4 See Cumings (1981, 1990, and 1997: chs. 4 and 5) for a detailed study of complex situation between the end of the Second World War and the outbreak of the Korean War.
5 A re-entry permit does not solve all problems involved with overseas trips. It entails obtaining a visa prior to travel, and comes with many other restrictions. While Japanese passports can easily be renewed at consulates overseas, the renewal of a re-entry permit is not guaranteed and is subject to the consul-general's arbitrary discretion. In a word, it never works as a passport to Japan. For a report presented to the United Nations, see Association Fighting for the Acquisition of the Human Rights of Koreans in Japan (1979).
6 Unlike US citizenship which is given to all individuals who are born on the US soil, the *only* way that Koreans in Japan can obtain Japanese citizenship is through naturalization. Although Japanese naturalization has become a simpler procedure in the last decade, it nevertheless presupposes a national conversion. Resident Koreans should be given the option to take Japanese nationality as part of the compensation

for the past colonial rule, and should not have to go through submission to the state-imposed system of naturalization, since the majority of Koreans live in Japan as a result of the past colonial relations. Japanese society in general appears unwilling to accept "non-Japanese" as Japanese citizens, and stigma is still attached to naturalization from both the Korean and the Japanese perspectives. Therefore, the majority of naturalized persons remain silent about their Korean heritage. In this sense, it is difficult to call those who are naturalized "Korean-Japanese," the term that is not translatable in the current Japanese vocabulary and perhaps would not be accepted by resident Koreans at large (but see Lie in this volume).

7 There is no specific chapter on Korean children who attend Korean schools in Japan in this volume. For a study in this area, see Ryang (1997).

8 The existing literature on Koreans in Japan written in English is not extensive. Wagner (1951), Mitchell (1967), Lee and De Vos (1981), Weiner (1989), and Weiner (1994) are the most frequently-quoted sources. These are mostly historical studies, with sociological and some anthropological insights as in Lee and De Vos (1981). Collections such as Weiner (1997) and Maher and Macdonald (1995) have relevant essays.

1 The politics of legal status
The equation of nationality with ethnonational identity

Chikako Kashiwazaki

The exclusion of Koreans from Japanese citizenry is often understood as a continuation of the Japanese state policy from the colonial period. The conception of the imperial community as an ethnically homogeneous "family-nation" with the emperor as the head had no place for non-Japanese people except as assimilated imperial subjects with complete loyalty to the emperor. Similarly, postwar Japan maintains a strict naturalization system that demands from applicants a high degree of assimilation into Japanese society and culture. The continuity in the principle of "assimilation or exclusion," however, does not fully account for the postwar system of nationality regulation or the attitude of Koreans toward Japanese nationality.

The purpose of this chapter is to consider an historical process by which interactions between political actors generated an equation between the concept of nationality and ethnonational identity, or the notion of national essence, in postwar Japan. Recent legal changes in Western European states in dealing with resident aliens show a trend towards extending a range of citizenship rights to long-term resident aliens, and widening access to nationality for non-citizen immigrants. The Japanese case stands in contrast to this trend, in that the restrictive regulation of nationality has persisted for decades despite the presence of 600,000 to 700,000 Koreans as resident aliens ever since the end of the Second World War.

In both colonial and postwar periods, membership in the Japanese state was simultaneously linked with the issues of assimilation, the state's domestic and international security concerns, and loyalty to a specific political community. The relationship among these factors, however, changed after 1945. The analysis in this chapter draws attention to different aspects of Japanese state interests to identify the sources of restrictive nationality law and regulations. The chapter also tries to show how the equation between nationality and national essence held by the government and immigration authorities of Japan was, ironically, shared by the majority of resident aliens, notably Koreans, who were divided into pro-South Korean and pro-North Korean groups, reflecting the partition of the Korean peninsula in 1945.

The rest of the chapter is divided into four parts. The first section offers a comparative perspective by reviewing changes in the relationship between nationality and citizenship in Western Europe and the role played by the state.

The second section examines Japanese colonial rule of Korea, with a focus on the interplay between assimilation policies and the state's security concerns. The third section discusses the reorganization of nationality and citizenship during the Allied occupation of Japan. The final section traces the way in which the concept of nationality came to be perceived as national essence and as such rejected by Koreans in Japan, and considers historical ramifications concerning the legal regulation of nationality.

Nationality, citizenship, and state interests

Nationality is here understood as formal membership in a state in the sense of international law. In scholarly works as well as in ordinary English usage of the term, "citizenship" is usually used interchangeably with the term "nationality." For the analysis in this chapter, citizenship is treated as conceptually distinct from nationality and is defined as a bundle of rights and duties the state confers or imposes upon individuals.

Nationality by definition entails one's unconditional right to enter the state's territories and the right to diplomatic protection while residing in another country. Although it is now usually taken for granted that full citizenship corresponds to nationality, historically this rarely was the case. Even in societies that we now call democratic, full citizenship used to be typically limited to male property owners before the introduction of universal suffrage. Often in colonial empires, colonized subjects were attributed nationality of the "mother country" but were not granted full citizenship. A solid association between nationality as membership in a state and full citizenship is a relatively new phenomenon which emerged after the First World War. Two processes were conducive to a gradual equation of nationality and citizenship within the boundaries of a national state: democratization characterized by increased demand for civil rights and equal opportunities, on the one hand, and the reorganization of international relations due to rising nationalisms in the dominated regions of the world, on the other. It was the post-Second World War decolonization which made the national state form the most legitimate boundaries of sovereignty. National state membership thus became a primary basis for the differentiation of legal status within state territories, drawing a distinction between citizens/nationals and non-citizens/non-nationals.

The changing legal status of resident aliens in Western Europe in recent decades marks another development in the relationship between nationality and citizenship. The settlement of immigrants and their families in Western European countries led to the extension of a range of "partial" citizenship rights to resident aliens. Tomas Hammar categorizes the new group of non-citizens as "denizens," who have permanent resident status and enjoy extensive civil and social citizenship rights, if not electoral rights on the national level (Hammar 1990: 12–15). With the increase in denizens, legal changes in nationality laws occurred in recent years, particularly in countries where the transmission of nationality followed the principle of *jus sanguinis* (by parentage). These changes include the establishment or broadening of the categories of second-generation immigrants who enjoy a legal claim to nationality (Germany and Sweden), and greater tolerance for dual nationality (Switzerland and the Netherlands) (Bauböck 1994: 33; Çinar 1994; Soysal 1994: 26–7).[1]

The concept of state interests helps account for the emergence of denizens and the lowering barrier to acquiring nationality among second- and third-generation immigrants. States play a central role in the matter of nationality because the right to determine who can be a citizen largely and ultimately rests on the sovereignty of the state. The state is here conceptualized as "a set of organizations invested with the authority to make binding decisions for people and organizations juridically located in a particular territory" (Rueschemeyer and Evans 1985: 46–7). My discussion assumes that states may formulate and pursue goals which are not simply reflective of the demands or interests of social groups or classes (Skocpol 1985: 9) regarding, in the present discussion, the issues of nationality and citizenship. However, the state is not always internally coherent, nor is it ruled by a single ideology, and it is possible that officials at different levels and in different institutions of a state may have contradicting interests.

State interests in several areas are considered relevant to the present discussion. First, any state has interests in defining the populations subject to its rule and in creating some unity among them. If the population is ethnically heterogeneous, then the articulation of unity may involve an inclusion of all ethnic groups, an exclusion (or expulsion) of some groups, or else a creation of tiered membership. Second, states are interested in applying standard rules over their territories for effectively extracting resources and monitoring the activities of residents. Third, states are concerned about domestic and international security, namely any political and military threat to their effective rule. For this reason states aim to cultivate among their members loyalty to the state, or primary allegiance over any other political entity. Fourth, cultural and ideological dimensions also comprise state interests. The prevailing understanding of nationhood among state managers may shape policy formulation. The importance of projecting its image as a democratic state, for instance, would make a state responsive to international legal norms.

Given state interests in internal social order and external security, the presence of a large group of resident aliens poses potential problems to a state if, for instance, the marginalization of immigrants leads to social and political unrest. The encouragement of return migration is one option. If it is not feasible, the state would likely seek some form of incorporation of the immigrants into society through the extension of citizenship rights in return for civil obligation. Once the flow of return migration diminished in the mid-1970s, immigrant-receiving countries in Western Europe turned increasingly toward incorporation (Soysal 1994). In some cases, a redefinition of state interests seems to be under way. For instance, discretionary naturalization in Germany has been regarded as a restrictive system because it includes "public interest" as a criterion.[2] However, the Ministry of Interior has assumed since 1991 that there is a public interest in the naturalization of long-term residents and young foreigners living in Germany (Çinar 1994: 53).

States' incorporation regimes in turn provide immigrants with a framework within which they articulate their demands. With prolonged stays and the development of social relations in their country of residence, immigrants themselves are likely to develop a greater interest in expanding the range of citizenship rights within the host society. As a result of the interactions between states and immigrant groups in Western Europe, the acquisition of nationality by immigrants is increasingly understood as a point on a continuum of legal status from "aliens" to "denizens" and then to "full citizens," while the symbolic significance attached to membership in a national state is to some extent attenuated (Çinar 1994; van den Bedem 1994). It should be noted, however, that this trend toward readjusting the concept of nationality does not necessarily separate it from full citizenship. In most countries, in other words, the possession of nationality remains a precondition for enjoying full citizenship.[3]

European experiences thus suggest progressive legal incorporation of permanently settled immigrants into citizenry. If the key in this process is the transition of immigrants from sojourners to permanent settlers in the host society, the case of Japan demands explanation. The settlement of Korean migrants in Japan occurred much earlier than that of major immigrant groups in Europe today, and yet Japanese nationality regulation has changed little. In the area of *partial* citizenship, the legal status of long-term resident foreigners has gradually improved over time, and scholars have applied the concept of denizenship to Koreans in Japan (Kajita 1996; Kondō 1996). Nevertheless, greater disjunction remains between "denizens" and "full citizens" in Japan than is typically the case in Euope.

The ideology of Japanese ethnic homogeneity appears to be a likely factor explaining the restrictive access to Japanese nationality. However, state interests are multidimensional, as discussed above. One might ask, referring to European experiences, whether Japanese state managers might not find it beneficial to turn resident Koreans into Japanese citizens, so as to reduce the tension arising from intergroup relations in society. Further analysis is required of the construction of nationality-based differentiation in legal status.

Japan's colonial rule

In Japan today the concept of nationality rigidly remains, and denotes symbolic membership in the Japanese nationhood as defined by culture, descent, or the ideologically-charged metaphor of one large household. We shall trace aspects of Japan's colonial rule of Korea to see how elements of the postwar conception of Japanese nationality historically took shape. A close relationship between the Japanese state's security concerns and assimilation policies is key. Historical legacies of Japan's colonial rule were later to influence the identities of resident Koreans.

Compared with postwar Japan, the ethnically heterogeneous composition of populations was much more obvious and widely recognized in the Japanese colonial empire. Politicians, military officers, academics, and commentators expressed a variety of conceptions of the imperial community, which contained contradictory doctrines such as the multiethnic origin of the Japanese, common descent with Koreans, the Japanese as one family descending from a single lineage, the emperor's nation, and the racial brotherhood and union of all Asians as culminated in the idea of the Great East Asia Coprosperity Sphere (Oguma 1995). Informed by these diverse visions of the political community as well as by European models of colonial rule, Japanese state managers attempted to forge some unity among diverse imperial subjects, including the Koreans, towards the effective government. Accordingly, colonial policies exhibited a complex interplay between assimilation and separation, and unification and division of colonized subjects and the colonizing population.

A brief reflection on the term "assimilation" is necessary. While its meaning is multidimensional, two broad categories may be identified in colonial policies: legal-institutional assimilation and cultural assimilation. The former involves the extension of the institutions of the "mother country" to colonies. This aspect of assimilation facilitates the equalization of citizenship rights and duties to some degree, due to its tendency toward the equal treatment of subjects. Cultural assimilation denotes approximating the colonized to the colonizer through education and acculturation in terms of language, religion, lifestyle, and symbols of the empire. Assimilation in Japanese colonialism had distinct characteristics in its cultural components. In European colonialism, cultural assimilation was for the most part a project of "civilizing" the colonized people through the dissemination of Western culture. In the case of Japan, cultural assimilation was closely linked to the issue of national security, as discussed below. Assimilation policies demanded "spiritual" assimilation, centered on loyalty and allegiance to the Japanese emperor, from the colonized population at large.

Upon Japan's colonization of Korea in 1910, Koreans were attributed Japanese nationality, but remained second-class subjects in many respects and were differentiated from Japanese regarding citizenship rights and duties. Incompatibilities between indigenous customs and traditions and Japanese laws also slowed legal assimilation. Yet some degree of legal assimilation was effective for social control and security measures. By incorporating colonial subjects into a common legal-institutional framework, the imperial state gained an effective means of surveillance and control. Cultural assimilation was also useful for social control, because greater subjective identification with the empire made anti-colonial movements less likely. Since the Japanese imperial state faced persistent anti-colonial, independent movements among Koreans throughout the colonial period (Mitchell 1967: chs 2, 4, and 5; Weiner 1994: ch. 5), the state's security concerns shaped the ways in which legal-institutional assimilation and cultural assimilation were played out.

The household registration system is one example where some degree of legal assimilation, in this case the standardization of registries, served the purpose of consolidating colonial rule.[4] In Korea, Japanese administrators initiated the reorganization of the existing Korean household registry in 1909, in preparation for the official annexation a year later. The police played a major role in compiling the new registry (Yoshida 1993). The Korean household registry was gradually modified into the Japanese model during the colonial period. This is discussed in more detail later in the chapter.

Household registries served as a legal underpinning for the distinction between "Japanese proper" and colonial subjects. The former had their household register in Japan, while the latter had theirs in the colonies, regardless of their place of residence. It was not permissible to move the register from the colony to the metropole or *vice versa*. (This was to influence the postwar establishment of the nationality of Koreans and some Japanese.) In effect, household registries could be used as a device for marking the status of the colonized.

Conscription is a case in point. The military obligation law of 1927 stated that "those to whom the household registration law is applicable" were subject to conscription. Koreans, regardless of their place of residence, were excluded because the Korean household registry was governed by a special law of the government-general of Korea, separate from the law applied to Japan proper. Since military duty requires a high level of loyalty to the state, the government maintained the practice of having only "Japanese proper" serve in the army until the early 1940s. Household registries were therefore useful as an identifier of eligibility in that they delineated "proper" Japanese from the rest (Tashiro, Yoshida, and Hayashida 1969: 3–5; Tanaka 1974: 82–9).

There were nevertheless some tendencies toward equal treatment of imperial subjects in terms of rights and duties. While voting rights were not extended to colonies, colonial subjects residing on the Japanese home islands participated in national and local elections after universal male suffrage was established in 1925. For instance, 16,170 Koreans, or 45 percent of the total eligible Korean voters, cast their votes for the 1932 election (Chee 1983: 83). Between 1929 and 1943, a total of 200 Korean candidacies were registered in national and local elections, of which thirty-two were successful, though only one person was elected to the House of Representatives (Tanaka 1974: 76; Weiner 1994: 147–50; Matsuda 1995: 102ff.).

There were Koreans moving to Japan from the early period of the colonial rule by the Japanese. A small number of Korean workers and street vendors were found in Japan following the opening of Korea by the 1876 treaty with Japan (Yamawaki 1994). After the formal annexation of Korea by Japan in 1910, labor migration increased in size. The national census of 1920 recorded approximately 40,000 Koreans, the number increasing in 1930 to 420,000 and in 1940, 1,240,000 approximately (Morita 1968: 66). Koreans were concentrated in urban, industrial areas. The degree of settlement is, however, not easy to determine: some stayed in Japan for decades, while others were short-term migrant workers, frequently traveling between the colony and metropolis.

Far from the rhetoric of inclusion and appeal to common descent, there was a clear differentiation between Japanese and Koreans in economic positions as well as culture. Prejudice and mistrust against non-Japanese on the part of the Japanese culminated in the massacre of Koreans and Chinese in the aftermath of the Great Kantō Earthquake of 1923 (Weiner 1989: ch. 6). The incident prompted state officials actively to promote assimilation, particularly of cultural and spiritual kinds.

Under the slogan of *naisenyūwa*, or conciliation of Japanese and Koreans, the government in the 1920s provided financial assistance to mutual-aid associations, the representative of which was Sōaikai, or mutual care association (Weiner 1994: 156–7). Official support for these associations was intended to counter the growth of radical political movements among Koreans. Since early in the colonial era, Korean students in Japan organized themselves for the cause of national liberation (ibid: 14–21). In the 1920s, Korean communist organizations were among the major targets for the government's campaign to eradicate left-wing movements (Mitchell 1967: 48–58). Sōaikai came to be used, for instance, for the purpose of strikebreaking (Weiner 1994: 156).

In the mid-1930s, "conciliation" organizations were restructured and integrated into a nation-wide network known as Kyōwakai, or harmonization association, under the auspices of the social affairs bureau of the Ministry of Home Affairs. One of the central tasks of the Kyōwakai programs was the "cultivation of a sense of being an imperial subject," which was to be accomplished "through the inculcation of filial piety, loyalty, morality, a fuller appreciation of Japan's international position, and the spirit of work and co-operation" (Weiner 1994: 164). Although Kyōwakai was publicly represented as a welfare agency, it increasingly served as a means of social control. During the Pacific War, every Korean laborer automatically became a Kyōwakai member when he came to Japan to work (Mitchell 1967: 82).

On the Korean peninsula, the use of assimilation for social control took an extreme form under the *kōminka* drive from the late 1930s, which was a policy to turn Koreans into the emperor's people, or *kōmin*. *Kōminka*, or making Koreans into *kōmin*, demanded of colonized subjects complete loyalty to the emperor and was implemented in the areas of military, education, and the household registration system.

One of the important programs of *kōminka* was *sōshikaimei*, or to have Koreans change their names into Japanese names and be registered in the Japanese-style household registry. The household registers in the colony, though in some respects "Japanized," had still followed the Korean traditional method of leaving the maiden name of married women. For example, one register could have more than one family name; that of the household head, usually a bread-earning male, that of his wife and possibly, that of his mother or his daughter-in-law, depending on the structure of the family. After *sōshikaimei* in 1940, all members of one household came to be registered under one family name, that of the household head. The new rule thus followed the Japanese convention stipulated soon after the Meiji Restoration, or the restoration of the imperial order, in 1868.

In *sōshikaimei* legal and cultural assimilation merged together. The need to unify Korean households under the imperial order, so as to turn Koreans into full-fledged imperial subjects, was behind the program (see Miyata, Kim, and Yang 1992). It was closely related with human resource mobilization for war, including the governor-general's plan to introduce conscription in Korea (implemented in 1944). As a rationale for the implementation of *sōshikaimei*, a Home Ministry's document stated that it would have been unbearable had the emperor's army included persons named "Kim" or "Li" (Miyata, Kim, and Yang 1992: 40). The retention of Korean names was equated with the retention of Korean identity and hence, evidence of insufficient identification with, and loyalty to, the Japanese empire.

The adoption of Japanese names by Koreans under *sōshikaimei* meant that their ethnic identity became less obvious than before. The proposal of this program by the government general in Korea initially seemed to generate concerns in the central government about the anticipated difficulty in making distinctions between the two peoples. The role of separate household registries was again significant, because Koreans were still differentiated from Japanese by the location of their household register (Miyata 1990: 59).

In the last year of the Second World War, the imposition of heavy burdens on Koreans for war effort led the Japanese metropolitan government to take further steps toward legal-institutional assimilation and the equalization of political rights. In December 1944, the Cabinet decided to permit Koreans residing on Japanese home islands to transfer their household registers from the Korean to the Japanese registry under certain conditions (Oguma 1998: 442-9; Ōnuma 1980a: 200). The election law was amended in 1945 to extend suffrage to colonies with a tax payment condition, though the law was never implemented owing to Japan's defeat in the war. Because Japanese rule ended shortly after the implementation of *kōminka* programs, assimilation of Koreans into Japanese remained an ambivalent half-project. Meanwhile, the inferiority of Koreans continued to be widely seen as unquestionable among Japanese, from the authorities to the grassroots level (see for example, Weiner 1989).

Postwar reorganization of nationality and citizenship

Japan faced a labor shortage with the outbreak of the Pacific War in 1941, and Koreans were brought to construction and production sites in Japan and elsewhere.[5] These were mostly men, but many women were also taken as workers, and in some cases as prostitutes for the army (e.g. Yun *et al.* 1992; Nishino 1992). By the time the war ended, the number of Koreans in Japan is said to have been approximately two million (see Morita 1996: 156–7). The majority of those who had been forcibly brought to Japan were repatriated upon the end of the war, while those who had more or less settled in Japan stayed on. The latter were estimated at about 590,000 in 1948 (Wagner 1951: 95). Their hope of return was further shattered as their homeland was partitioned between the Soviet-occupied north and the US-occupied south, and as the subsequent Korean War (1950–3) consolidated the division.[6] The legal status of these Koreans remaining in Japan was central to the postwar reorganization of Japanese nationality and citizenship.

During the Allied occupation of Japan between 1945 and 1952, Koreans in Japan were technically still Japanese nationals in the absence of an international arrangement of their nationality status. The attitude of the Supreme Commander for the Allied Powers (SCAP) was to treat them as "liberated people" only to the extent permitted from the point of view of security, in accordance with the 1945 initial directive from Washington (Onuma 1978: 95). In the context of the prevailing left-wing tendencies both in Japan and on the Korean peninsula, the SCAP's priority gradually shifted from democratization to the economic recovery of Japan and the maintenance of social order. From the beginning of 1946, the SCAP's intelligence section began to identify the Koreans as "illegal elements" or "disturbing elements" (Kobayashi 1994: 170). The Japanese Home Ministry and the police reported on incidents that involved Koreans and reinforced the US agency's negative perception of them. From 1948 onwards, the SCAP associated the political activities of Koreans more specifically with communism (ibid.; see also Inokuchi in this volume).

The Japanese government manipulated the ambiguity of the nationality status of former colonial subjects. In the domain of criminal jurisdiction, the Japanese government continued treating Koreans as "Japanese nationals" since it facilitated better security and social control. In other domains the same concerns led the government to treat Koreans as effectively foreigners, and to restrict their citizenship rights. The denial of their rights as Japanese nationals was most evident in the alien registration system, which is discussed later in the chapter.

A major curtailment also occurred in terms of political rights. The fear of the impact of left-leaning Koreans as a voting bloc spread among Diet members and government officials (Mizuno 1996 and 1997). In December 1945, the Diet passed legislation that suspended the voting rights of those who were "not subject to the household registration law." Thus, the separation based on the location of household registries, a system institutionalized under colonialism, continued to serve as the method of drawing the boundaries between "Japanese proper" and colonized subjects.

During the occupation period, an overall restrictive system of nationality regulation was instituted as a result of the combined effect of three legal arrangements: the creation of an immigration control system; the continuation of *jus sanguinis* and strict naturalization criteria; and the uniform loss of Japanese nationality by ex-colonial subjects.

The postwar immigration control system was instituted in the period between 1947 and 1952. The Alien Registration Law of 1947 stipulated that the Koreans should be regarded as aliens for the purpose of the application of this law. An additional clause further required the non-Japanese residing in Japan to register as aliens. A Japanese government report addressed to the SCAP in 1949 asserted that forced repatriation of "undesirable foreigners" was applicable to Koreans who violated provisions in the Alien Registration Law, regardless of the length of their stay in Japan (Onuma 1979d: 101–3). Since the law regarded Koreans as aliens, it was possible for the Japanese government to propose the "repatriation" of persons who technically still possessed Japanese nationality (see also Ryang in this volume).

From the SCAP's point of view, the Alien Registration Law and other related ordinances fell short of constituting a comprehensive immigration control system. Accordingly, the Immigration Control Order was announced in 1951. It was designed to control travelers into and out of Japan and to regulate their residential status, and was never meant to be sufficient to deal with the former colonial subjects who had resided in Japan for years. When the San Francisco Peace Treaty went into effect in 1952, the 1951 order was officially applied to Koreans, though long-term residents were exempted from applying for a visa (Ōnuma 1980a: 246–9).

Meanwhile in 1950, the revised Nationality Law came into effect, which retained the patrilineal *jus sanguinis* principle. The SCAP had no objection to the continuitation of *jus sanguinis*. This was to be expected because both *jus sanguinis* and *jus soli* (nationality attribution by birthplace) were legitimate principles in light of international legal norms (Ōnuma 1980b: 283). Consequently, American-style immigration control, originally designed for a country with *jus soli*, was combined with the system of strict *jus sanguinis*. This made it difficult for non-citizen immigrants and residents to acquire Japanese nationality.

The last major legal arrangement was the settlement of the nationality status of ex-colonial subjects. Throughout the occupation period, the Japanese government maintained that the issue of nationality should be settled by a peace treaty. As has been discussed, however, the Japanese government contradicted its own official stance by depriving former imperial subjects of important components of their citizenship rights such as voting rights, while denying them access to privileges given to other foreigners in Japan, including the Allied personnel.

The nationality status of Koreans was further complicated owing to the partition of the Korean peninsula into two separate states in 1948. Both Korean states defined their citizens by criteria based on descent. The 1948 Nationality Law of South Korea adopted the principle of *jus sanguinis* and therefore regarded overseas Koreans as its nationals. In accordance with the 1949 Overseas Nationals Registration Law, Mindan, a Korean organization in Japan (see below), was entrusted with the process of registering Koreans in Japan. North Korea did not have a nationality law until 1963, though the citizen certificate system of 1946 employed Korean descent as a criterion for membership of the state (Ōnuma 1980a: 217–25). In the absence of diplomatic relations, however, there was no official recognition of Korean nationality on the part of the Japanese government until 1965, when Japan restored diplomatic relations only with South Korea.

Initially, Japanese government officials had been prepared to give Korean residents some kind of option rights regarding Japanese nationality. An important policy change occurred when the Japanese government learned that the SCAP did not specifically require an option right clause for nationality to be included in the San Francisco Peace Treaty.[7] While the stipulation of option rights would have obliged the Japanese state to accept the choices made by Korean individuals, its absence allowed the state selectively to permit naturalization in a discretionary manner (Ōnuma 1980a: 254–6; Matsumoto 1988).

On 19 April 1952, nine days before the San Francisco Peace Treaty went into effect, the Japanese government issued circular no. 438, which stipulated the *uniform loss* of Japanese nationality by Koreans and Taiwanese as a result of the Peace Treaty, regardless of their place of residence. The criterion used was again household registry: those who had their household register in colonies lost Japanese nationality even if they lived in Japan. Furthermore, the circular notice explicitly stated that Koreans and Taiwanese were required to go through the process of naturalization just as other foreigners were, if they wished to acquire Japanese nationality (Ōnuma 1979a: 296–7).

The Japanese government measure did not follow contemporary international legal norms about preventing statelessness upon territorial transfers; those persons who had not acquired a new nationality were made practically stateless. The unilateral settlement of the issue of nationality was justified by the assumption that the San Francisco Peace Treaty, to which no Korean government was a signatory power, implied a consensus about the change in nationalities. The logic was that since the treaty ensured the end of Japanese control over Korean territory, Koreans were now independent and hence, no longer Japanese nationals. The 1961 Supreme Court ruling upheld this official view, even though some legal scholars have expressed dissenting views.[8]

The creation of the overall restrictive regime on nationality, however, did not occur in a teleological manner. For one thing, *jus sanguinis* as a rule of nationality law was merely a continuation from the previous law. The institution of the immigration control system was guided by the SCAP as part of legal institution-building under the occupation. Tight border control was also in line with the SCAP's interest in combating the spread of communism. Even the settlement of nationality was originally not intended to produce the effect that it did. Only at a later stage did the Japanese state seize the opportunity to move against international norms regarding statelessness and to stipulate the uniform loss of Japanese nationality by ex-colonial subjects. The decision reflected the Japanese government's contention that having ethnic minorities among Japanese nationals was problematic, and that many Koreans were anti-Japanese and should not be included as citizens without a test.

The period between 1945 and 1952 had some parallel with the colonial period regarding the relationship between the Japanese state and the Koreans. In both periods, concerns for social order and security shaped Japanese state policies. The use of the household registry as an identifier of non-Japanese also reveals institutional continuity between pre- and postwar years.

However, an important change occurred in the relationship between nationality and citizenship. In the colonial period, Koreans experienced inequality in citizenship status owing to the status of the colonized, despite their having common nationality status. In the postwar period, the nationality status justified their inequality and exclusion. The latter system was based on the logic of the national state: equality in citizenship depends on common nationality. Because of the loss of Japanese nationality, Korean veterans were not to be entitled to pension and other benefits; Korean civil servants in Japan had to apply for naturalization, or risk unemployment. Koreans came to be excluded from state and other public qualifications owing to their not having Japanese nationality.

Nationality and nationalism

In the period of turmoil after Japan's defeat in the Second World War, Koreans in Japan held to the attitude which Ōnuma Yasuaki called *kikokushugi*, or repatriationism (1979a: 270). In other words, the general consensus among them was that they would return to the homeland before long and their stay in Japan was only temporary.

Following the liberation, Koreans formed the League of Koreans in October 1945, with the repatriation of all the Koreans to Korea as its main slogan. The league initially attracted 1.5 million members (Ōnuma 1980a: 241 n87). The league's leadership consisted mainly of leftists who had been arrested in the 1930s and were released after the war. The anti-communists formed their own organization, the Association of Koreans in Japan, or Mindan in abbreviation, on a much lesser scale.[9]

The league was not a North Korean organization – the North Korean state did not yet exist in 1945 – to the extent that Mindan was not a South Korean organization. For example, the league initially had its branch office in Seoul and defined itself as an interim organization to facilitate repatriation. It is important to note that the partition of Korea into the Soviet-governed north and the US-governed south was widely regarded as a temporary measure until the anticipated reunification of Korea. Although the majority of Koreans in Japan came originally from the southern provinces, they opted for the League of Koreans, partly because they regarded the partition as only short-term and hence, did not see the leftist turn of the league as an exclusive loyalty toward the northern half. In addition, the northern regime was more popular than the southern counterpart (Ryang 1997: 79–84; Ryang in this volume).

However, with the rising tension on the peninsula between the separate regimes, which culminated in the Korean War from 1950 to 1953, division of the homeland was eventually reflected in the Korean expatriate community. Nevertheless, both rightist and leftist organizations had common grounds: they were adamantly anti-Japanese and anti-colonial, nationalist and "repatriationist." In other words, neither had any agenda covering the eventual settlement of Koreans in Japan. From this perspective, they both rejected the idea of retaining Japanese nationality, which was an embodied memory of the colonial past.

In 1947, in accordance with the Alien Registration Law, the household registers of Koreans were removed from the colonial registry and placed in alien registration. Unlike the household register, which is basically an open document, the alien registration is a closed record. A person who is registered under this does not have access to the original record, which is kept in a Japanese local government office. All she or he can see is her or his own certificate, which used to be a small book and now is a plastic card. Only the local government office in charge *and* the police authorities have access to the original record of the registered. Koreans now had to renew their residential status every four years, carry the certificate in person at all times, produce it upon police request, and produce fingerprinting each time they registered. (The law has since changed.)

What mattered for Korean organizations, however, was not the duty and penalty entailed in the alien registration itself: they were willing to accept these if they provided a ground for establishing that Koreans in Japan were no longer Japanese nationals. What mattered to them instead was the record of "nationality" column of the alien registration certificate.

As Ōnuma clarifies, the nationality record of the certificate, although it says "nationality," or *kokuseki*, does not formally establish the nationality of the certificate holder, since it is ultimately the Japanese internal record (Ōnuma 1980a: 229). When Koreans were first registered in the alien registration, their nationality was recorded as "*chōsen*," denoting that the person originated from the Korean peninsula. In 1949 the South Korean government demanded that the Japanese government use "*kankoku*," the Republic of Korea, instead of *chōsen*. However, a mere record of *kankoku* did not fully certify that the holder was a South Korean national. In 1950 the Japanese justice minister stated that given the lack of diplomatic relations between Japan and the Korean peninsula, it did not matter for one's legal status at all if the record was *chōsen* or *kankoku*. In other words, neither denoted nationality in the eyes of the Japanese authority (Ryang 1997: 222).

Nevertheless, the focal point of both leftist and rightist Korean nationalists became the choice of term in the alien registration certificate. *Kankoku* was equated with South Korean nationality and *chōsen* with North Korean nationality. Following the South Korean request of 1949, those Koreans who wanted to make their "nationality" explicitly South Korean tried to re-register themselves under *kankoku* in their alien registration. Regardless of their support either of north or south, Korean organizations on both sides saw this record as more than a legal convenience or functionality.

What was originally seen as a temporary partition was, year after year, looking increasingly permanent. In 1948 separate states were established on the peninsula with antagonizing ideological leadership, under the direct influence of the Cold War. In 1950 the civil war started, which in the three years of its duration produced a total of 760,000 dead or missing in the south and 2.7 million casualties and refugees in the north (Rekishigaku kenkyūkai 1990: 120). By the time the Korean War ended in 1953, the division among Koreans in Japan was irreconcilable, as they were now supporters of two regimes that had committed a considerable number of atrocities and much violence upon each other.

By the mid-1950s, the power relation internal to Korean nationalism in Japan was rearranged. Following the league's suppression in 1949 by the Occupation authorities, the leftist group eventually formed a new organization, the General Association of Korean Residents in Japan, or Chongryun in abbreviation, clearly upholding North Korea as its homeland and defining Koreans in Japan as North Korea's overseas nationals (see Ryang in this volume). Mindan's link to South Korea was also strengthened, owing to the lack of official representation of South Korea in Japan until the normalization treaty of 1965.

The Japan–South Korea normalization treaty of 1965 opened another dimension to the nationality issue of Koreans in Japan: it acknowledged South Korean nationality. While South Korean nationality holders were eligible to apply for permanent resident status, the supporters of Chongryun and North Korea were not (see below and Ryang in this volume). Already in the 1960s, the prospects for the repatriation of Koreans in Japan were becoming uncertain as their residence in Japan dragged on.[10] Nevertheless, the basic stance toward the concept of nationality held by Mindan and the league first, and then Chongryun, remained the same: presupposing national essence to lie behind the concept of nationality. In part reflecting this, the number of naturalizations remained low among Koreans in Japan until recent decades. For example, fewer than 2,500 Koreans per year were naturalized in the 1950s, as compared with an annual average of 4,700 in the 1970s and 5,400 in the 1980s (Kim Yŏng-dal 1990: 7).[11]

For the Japanese Ministry of Justice, the regulation of nationality with the principle of *jus sanguinis* and strict naturalization rules assumed a specific function after 1952. The immediate target group was the Koreans, and the nationality law was anticipated to prevent their easy access to Japanese nationality.

Investigations of applicants for naturalization followed the administrative guidance issued by the Ministry of Justice. According to "criteria for granting naturalization" dated 1958, the political orientation of individual applicants weighed heavily in consideration. For example, members of the Communist Party and the North Korea-supporting Chongryun were not allowed to naturalize.[12] These criteria also insisted on the adoption of Japanese culture and convention to a considerable extent. They stipulated that permission not be granted to a person "who cannot be considered fully assimilated into Japanese society regarding lifestyle and in other aspects" or a person "who lives in special residential areas such as the Korean neighborhood" (Kim Yŏng-dal 1990: 222–8). Based on this principle, and reminiscent of *sōshikaimei* during the colonial period, applicants for naturalization were expected to adopt a name suitable for a Japanese. Although there was no legal enforcement of the adoption of a Japanese name, in practice it formed part of conditions for naturalization (see Inaba 1975).

Naturalization goes hand in hand with household registration. Whoever is registered in the Japanese household registry is a Japanese national. Japanese nationality is then transmitted through the registry to the next generation. In order to prevent undesirable persons from becoming Japanese, officials showed interest not only in tightening naturalization criteria but also in preventing fraud in the documentation for household registration. In the words of Tashiro Aritsugu, a Justice Ministry official in 1969:

> I think the work on naturalization is extremely important for the state. We allow only those foreigners with good conduct to be naturalized. But if household registration were "mere formality," foreigners would choose to use false documents to obtain the status of Japanese, instead of going through cumbersome naturalization. That would be ridiculous [in my view] ... We should consider household registry as an integral part of the overall institution of the state.
>
> (Tashiro 1969: 10–11; my translation)

He emphasized that making one mistake in the household register would be detrimental (1969: 7). Once nationality and full citizenship are granted, the Japanese state has less capacity to control former resident aliens, being no longer able to exercise the option of deportation as the ultimate measure for maintaining national security. According to this reasoning, a politicized national minority group *with full citizenship* could pose an even greater problem of security and control than when its members remained foreigners. Here we see the legacy of the pattern developed during Japan's colonial era. From the point of view of the Japanese state, a high degree of assimilation alone could solve the problem of security. Becoming culturally and spiritually Japanese was therefore considered a precondition for naturalization.

The logic behind the naturalization system fitted well with the prevailing postwar conception of Japanese nationhood. During Japan's colonial expansion, the multiethnic origin of the Japanese nation was recognized and even celebrated. After Japan's defeat in war, in contrast, academics and popular writers portrayed Japan as an island-nation inhabited by homogeneous people. A newly defined role of the emperor as a non-political, symbolic status also contributed to the vision of Japanese nationhood as culturally integrated under the emperor. The peaking of the discourse on Japanese cultural uniqueness, or *nihonjinron*, in the 1970s at once culminated in, and was a reinforcing factor to, the perception of a homogeneous Japanese society. Little room was left for fostering alternative visions of an ethnically diverse society (Oguma 1995: 339–45; Yoshino 1992: ch. 2).

Government officials in general shared the prevailing postwar conception of homogeneous Japan articulated in the society, and attached symbolic cultural and ethnic meanings to nationality. It does not follow, however, that officials aimed at preserving the "purity" of ethnic Japanese, as conceptualized in terms of a blood association. The goal of maintaining the alleged ethnic homogeneity of Japanese nationals was attainable so long as non-citizens who obtained Japanese nationality were sufficiently assimilated and did not affect existing homogeneity.

By the mid-1960s, it was becoming increasingly clear that resident Koreans were a permanent feature of Japanese society. Like Western European states, the Japanese state showed interest in the incorporation of immigrants, because the presence of a non-citizen national minority group was a source of constant security concerns. Three times between 1965 and 1967, the Justice Ministry issued an article on naturalization in a government publication, encouraging naturalization and offering detailed explanations of its procedures. For instance, the 1967 article emphasized that naturalization was not particularly difficult, contrary to what many people seemed to believe (Kim Yŏng-dal 1990: 21). Nevertheless, the channel for naturalization was maintained narrow and strict because government officials had little intention of sacrificing security and assimilation standards for the sake of boosting the number of naturalizations. They had therefore two motivations that were at odds with each other: the long-term goal of the incorporation of immigrants through assimilation, and the maintenance of preventive measures for potential security problems.

Owing to both the attitude of dominant Korean organizations and the Japanese nationality criteria based on *jus sanguinis* and restrictive naturalization, approximately 600,000 Koreans continued living in Japan as resident aliens. Since the Japanese state maintained the bifurcation of legal status based on nationality, Koreans in Japan received poor legal protection and enjoyed few social citizenship rights throughout the 1970s.

The 1980s and early 1990s saw a change in the level of legal protection and the range of citizenship rights enjoyed by permanent resident aliens. In 1979 the Japanese government ratified the two International Covenants on Human Rights, and in 1981, the UN Refugee Convention. In order to comply with these conventions, which require equal treatment of nationals and non-citizens in the area of social citizenship rights, the Japanese government was compelled to revise existing laws (Ōnuma 1992: 520–1). Among the social rights that were extended to resident aliens by the mid-1980s were access to public sector housing and housing loans, child care allowances, the national pension plan, and the national health care plan (Ogawa 1985: 47; Tanaka 1991: 140–3).[13] The gate to public sector employment widened, albeit slowly, while nationality-based eligibility restriction is being disputed.[14]

The ratification of international conventions also brought about an improvement in the residential status of Koreans in Japan. The aforementioned 1965 treaty between South Korea and Japan allowed those who had obtained South Korean nationality to apply for permanent residence in Japan, which entailed both greater residential security and wider social insurance entitlements than before. However, there were those who did not opt for South Korean nationality and this 1965-type permanent residence, notably those associated with Chongryun. In 1981, when legislation concerning the admission of refugees became necessary, the Japanese Diet passed revisions to the Immigration Control Law to create a new permanent resident status to cover the remaining former colonial subjects and their descendants. In 1991, all permanent resident statuses were unified under the name of "special permanent residence", with more security and wider rights. The alien registration system was also reformed. In the mid-1980s refusal to be fingerprinted for registration peaked despite the risk and penalty. Reflecting pressures from various quarters, fingerprinting was replaced with an alternative system of identity check in the early 1990s.

By the 1990s, the internal constitution of Korean communities in Japan had gone through important changes. No longer were first generation immigrants presiding over the community: the vast majority of Koreans in Japan were Japan-born. Intermarriage between Koreans and Japanese increased.[15] The old "repatriationism" became almost non-existent. Many continue to be interested in the situation on the Korean peninsula including the prospect of reunification, but they have little wish to join either north or south in actuality (see Ryang 1997: ch. 6).

Throughout the 1980s and the 1990s, the resident Korean groups and their supporters who pushed for the extension of citizenship rights, including voting entitlements and other civil and social rights, developed a basic stance that is best reflected in the term *teijūgaikokujin*, or permanently settled *foreigners*. They focused exclusively on the improvement of the status of Koreans as denizens, in Hammar's formulation (discussed earlier). In this sense, the assumption of Chongryun and Mindan regarding Japanese nationality remains intact, that is, the ultimate rejection of it.

Compared with the 1970s, resident Koreans today enjoy a wider range of citizenship rights. Yet in spite of – or in some ways because of – the greater opportunity to be integrated into Japanese society, many Korean opinion leaders have reiterated their negative evaluation of acquiring Japanese nationality.[16] In their view, the challenge for the Korean community is to retain ethnic identity and cultural heritage while securing the equality of rights and opportunity as residents in Japanese society. They consider naturalization, under the current system, as unhelpful for this objective, because of the strong pressure for assimilation into Japanese society. Consequently, new social movements among Koreans, couched in human rights and the residential conception of citizenship rights, have in recent years included little demand for dual nationality or easier naturalization.

Nevertheless, the number of naturalized Koreans is steadily increasing: naturalization by Koreans reached 10,000 in 1995 (*Hōmunenkan* 1996). The attitude of the authorities is also showing some flexibility. For instance, in his essay in 1996 an official in charge of naturalization wrote:

> [I]t goes without saying that sharing the same nationality does not require people to have homogeneous culture and lifestyles.... Only when naturalized persons become able to say "I am a Japanese of such and such origin" without hiding their previous nationality will Japanese society be said to have internationalized from within.
>
> (Hara 1996: 6; my translation)

This remark reveals a contrast with Tashiro's remark in the 1960s (quoted earlier). It also reflects the understanding among officials that, given the trend in Western countries, outright insistence on assimilation would negatively affect the image of the Japanese state in the international community.

Conclusion

The equation between nationality and ethnonational identity in postwar Japan persisted because nationality remained linked closely with the issues of assimilation, loyalty, and national security. The equation was maintained and reproduced through the interactions between the Japanese state and Korean organizations in Japan. What is distinctive in comparative perspective is that neither the Japanese state nor Korean organizations sought an easing of access to Japanese nationality.

The present study cautions against assuming an unchanging view of Japan, such as an organic "family-nation," as a determinant of the historical development of the legal system in Japan. The notion of exclusion alone does not explain why and how the concept of nationality was related to the mechanisms of exclusion of Koreans in the postwar period, but not in the colonial period. The transformation of Japan into a national state in the postwar period, and the conditions and attitudes of Koreans in Japan in this period, were key to the development of the restrictive nationality regulation.

Because full citizenship as well as the unconditional right to the state territory is associated with nationality, the acquisition of Japanese nationality is potentially a favorable option, if it is reasonably accessible, for a number of Koreans in Japan. It would become an even more attractive option if the equation between nationality and ethnonational identity were substantially weakened.

Acknowledgements

The author would like to thank Sonia Ryang and Erin Chung for their helpful comments and suggestions on earlier drafts.

Notes

1 The overall portrayal of the trend in Western Europe here inevitably conceals internal diversity. Countries have differed in the manner and extent to which different components of citizenship rights are extended to resident aliens, as well as in the conditions under which immigrants of the second- and subsequent generations acquire nationality. Britain is an exception in that major immigrant groups have had full citizenship in Britain by virtue of being British subjects; restriction on the right to abode constitutes the primary barrier to enjoying full citizenship (Dummett and Nicol 1990).
2 Researchers have portrayed Germany as a classic case where an ethnically exclusive conception of nationhood gave support to restrictive nationality regulation (Brubaker 1992; Castles and Miller 1993).
3 Again, the British case is an anomaly due to the poor fit between nationality and full citizenship.
4 The Japanese household registration established in the Meiji period (1868–1912) was not only a registration of the population with household as a unit, but also a self-policing institution which held a household head responsible for the law-abiding and good behavior of members in the unit. It was used effectively for taxation, conscription, and other civil and legal control of the population.
5 The issue of the wartime labor mobilization forced on Koreans is widely documented and studied in Japan by both Korean and Japanese authors: to cite only a few, Pak, Yamada, and Yang (1993) and Hayashi (1989).
6 For a detailed study of postwar Korea until the outbreak of the Korean War, see Cumings (1981), and for the Korean War, Halliday and Cumings (1988).
7 In the matter of nationality settlements, the overall SCAP approach was characterized by non-intervention. The SCAP held the view that changes in nationality should not be imposed by the occupation forces, but should instead be settled between the relevant parties (Ōnuma 1980a: 245). Kim T'ae-gi's recent study shows that the Japanese Ministry of Foreign Affairs had a plan, as early as in 1949, to deprive all Koreans of Japanese nationality in due course (Kim T'ae-gi 1997: 611–14).
8 Ōnuma Yasuaki questions the constitutionality of the one-sided forfeiture of Japanese nationality by Koreans residing in Japan (Ōnuma 1979a). The 1952 treaty did not have any reference to the establishment of the nationality of Koreans. His study

The politics of legal status   31

argues that for both legal and humanitarian reasons, the exclusion of Koreans from Japanese nationality was unfounded (see Ōnuma 1979a, 1979b, 1979c, 1980a, 1980b, and 1980c).

9 The league received support from between 60 and 90 percent of Koreans in Japan (Ōnuma 1980a: 241 n87).
10 Repatriation to North Korea was opened in 1959. See Ryang in this volume for more details.
11 The majority of the naturalized persons in the 1950s were Japanese women who used to be married to Korean men, as well their children; they had lost Japanese nationality in 1952.
12 This document was included as an appendix to the Justice Ministry's internal circular note on "Guidelines for Processing Applications for Naturalization" issued in 1962 (Kim Yŏng-dal 1990: 204–29). Updated guidelines exist but are not publicly available.
13 However, Korean veterans who served in the Japanese armed forces have continued to be excluded from compensations based on the 1952 Act for the families of the dead, disabled, and wounded in war.
14 The basis of this exclusion is the official guideline set in 1953 by the cabinet legislation bureau, according to which Japanese nationality was required of anyone occupying a position that involves "an exercise of public authority or the formation of public will" (Tanaka 1985: 37). Since the government and courts have interpreted this phrase broadly, non-citizens have been virtually excluded from public sector jobs. For instance, the total number of non-citizens formally employed as public school teachers was only about thirty as of 1985 (Tanaka 1985: 40). The validity of the practice has increasingly been contested, and several local governments in recent years began to hire non-citizens, albeit on a limited scale and with restriction on promotions.
15 By the mid-1980s, Koreans in Japan were more likely to marry a Japanese national than another Korean (*Konintōkei* 1987).
16 The orientation of second-generation Korean intellectuals is reflected in the following remarks by Kim Kyŏng-dŭk, who won a legal battle and became the first non-citizen judicial trainee in 1978, and then the first non-citizen certified lawyer in Japan.

> Even if a system of as-of-right nationality acquisition were instituted, it would only result in 'assimilationistic' acquisition just as in the case of naturalization, in the absence of a secure legal and institutional framework that would enable us to live as *kanminzoku* or *chōsenminzoku* (ethnic Koreans).
> ("Teijūgaikokujin nokosareta mondai" 1990: 114)

2 The North Korean homeland of Koreans in Japan

Sonia Ryang

With the recent outbreak of news of famine and social and economic stagnation in North Korea, it may come as a surprise to learn that there are Koreans who identify the north as their homeland. This is all the more surprising considering that these Koreans live in Japan. The North Korean homeland continues to exist in the minds of a significant group of Koreans in Japan, across several generations, assuming different forms and meanings in changing historical contexts.

These Koreans are affiliated with Chongryun, a North Korea-supporting organization in Japan. This chapter explores the concept of home found among Chongryun Koreans. We shall see that the discourse of North Korea as a home away from home, that is, from Japan in which they actually live, paradoxically expresses the homelessness through which those Koreans live.[1]

The chapter first traces the historical process by which the post-Korean War repatriation of Koreans from Japan to North Korea became possible. It examines the subsequent opening of the channels for Koreans in Japan to visit North Korea in the 1980s: this was a critical event defining and redefining the concept of "North Korea as home." It then turns to the internal analysis of the discourse of home and its meaning for those Koreans who regard themselves as "North Korea's overseas nationals." Not only do I try to render their perception of North Korea intelligible, but I also critically engage with such a perception in and against the situation in which they find themselves.

Repatriation to North Korea

For two decades after the end of the Second World War, the legal status of Koreans in Japan was peculiar. They were migrants remaining in Japan after the end of the Japanese colonial rule of Korea. On the one hand, they were no longer Japanese citizens owing to the forfeiture of their Japanese nationality as an effect of the 1952 San Francisco Peace Treaty between the Japanese and US governments (see Kashiwazaki in this volume). On the other hand, owing to complications in the Korean peninsula, notably the partition into the US-governed south and the Soviet- and Chinese-backed north, there was no unified homeland with which they could identify immediately after the war.

It was only in 1965 that Japan and South Korea resumed diplomatic relations, while Japan continues not to recognize North Korea today. This means that until 1965, there was no state within which residence, let alone citizenship, of Koreans in Japan could clearly have been established.[2] Legal precedents prior to 1965 in Japanese courts show that there was no unified solution for defining the nationality of Korean residents in Japan. Some held the view that they were South Korean citizens, while others saw the possibility of North Korean citizenship. Yet others deemed it possible potentially to hold dual nationality of Japan and either Korean government.[3]

During the two decades prior to the 1965 treaty, the South Korean government maintained that matters pertaining to Koreans in Japan fell under the responsibility of the Japanese government. For example, it refused to accept Korean residents in Japan who had been convicted to deportation. Owing to this refusal, they had to be accommodated in relocation camps in southwestern Japan for years (Tatsumi 1966). Like Japanese Nationality Law, South Korean Nationality Law was based on the principle of patrilineal parentage, rather than place of birth or matrilineal parentage (Ōnuma 1980a: 225). From this perspective it could be argued that Koreans in Japan whose patrilineal origin was in South Korea were potentially South Korean citizens. But in practice, the South Korean government did little to facilitate repatriation for Koreans who had remained in Japan. Prior to the 1965 treaty between Japan and South Korea, it was the North Korean government that acknowledged that Koreans in Japan were North Korean nationals and encouraged their repatriation to the north, as we shall see below.

The repatriation of Koreans from Japan to Korea was not new: during the years immediately following the Second World War, the majority out of 2.4 million Koreans were repatriated, leaving a little less than 650,000 in Japan as of 1946 (Tsuboi 1957: 12). Of all the repatriates in this period, only a handful went back to northern Korea, the reason being that the predominant majority came originally from southern provinces. Of the 650,000 left in Japan in 1946, according to the authorities, 9,701 applied to return to northern Korea, while 514,060 applied to return to the south, with the remainder not applying for repatriation (Inoue 1956: 2).

Repatriation seemed a "natural" solution for most Koreans in Japan, as well as for the Japanese government. Under Japanese colonial rule, tens of thousands of Koreans had come to Japan for better job opportunities. They were mostly seasonal workers, and few contemplated permanent settlement in Japan. Thousands more Koreans had been forcibly taken to Japan during the war as home-front workers. With the end of the war, those workers lost their source of income and had no choice but to return to Korea. During the period of the postwar turmoil, both Occupation authorities and the Japanese government had no clear policy other than repatriating Koreans to Korea; no serious consideration was entertained to enabling them to stay on in Japan (see Lee and De Vos 1981: ch. 3).

With the outbreak of the Korean War in 1950, the traffic between Japan and the peninsula became difficult, and repatriation of Koreans from Japan to southern Korea stopped. Instead, reflecting socio-economic instability in the advent of the war, thousands of Koreans began migrating illegally to Japan. In 1948, Japanese police arrested 7,978 illegal immigrants from Korea and in 1949, 8,302 (Nyūkoku kanrikyoku 1964: 14–15). At any rate, the war's outbreak trapped about 650,000 Koreans within the Japanese archipelago.

After the truce in 1953, in 1954 the North Korean Foreign Ministry publicized a communiqué declaring its intention to enter into normal diplomatic relations with Japan. This was repeated in February 1955 through another communiqué. Although nothing substantial came from these North Korean initiatives in terms of diplomatic relations, they initiated irregular, but real, contacts between Japan and North Korea in the area concerning the repatriation of the remaining nationals on each other's soil.

In 1954 the Japan Red Cross telegraphed the North Korean Red Cross a message requesting the sending back of the Japanese nationals remaining in North Korea to Japan. The Japan Red Cross suggested that it would be possible to repatriate Koreans in Japan to North Korea in exchange for the repatriation of Japanese nationals (Chang Myŏng-su 1995b: 97). This was the beginning of discussion of repatriation of Koreans to North Korea. Things moved slowly, however: although thirty-six Japanese nationals were repatriated from North Korea in 1956, the reverse repatriation of Koreans did not take place at that stage.

In 1958 the North Korean premier Kim Il Sung officially stated that the North Korean state would welcome the repatriation of Koreans from Japan (1972: 4). He repeated the same statement in January 1959, referring to repatriation as the "sacred right and humanitarian need" of Koreans in Japan "to come back to the bosom of their own fatherland, in search of a decent living" (1972: 5). In 1958, a group of Koreans living in Kawasaki city near Tokyo sent a letter to the North Korean government requesting repatriation to the north. Supported by Japanese communists and other sympathizers, this opened a popular campaign demanding repatriation to the north by Koreans in Japan (Zainihon chōsenjin sōrengōkai 1989: 29).

As was briefly mentioned by Kim Il Sung, the main reason for the Korean exodus from Japan was poverty. Surveys by Koreans themselves, the Japan Red Cross, and the immigration authorities report likewise (Inoue 1956; Kim Byŏng-sik 1959a and 1959b; Seikatsujittai chōsadan 1959a and 1959b; Nyūkoku kanrikyoku 1976: 53–5). Although Japan entered a long-lasting boom following the Korean War, Koreans for the most part were not beneficiaries until much later. Occasional news on North Korea and its Soviet-backed post-Korean War economic reconstruction gave Koreans in Japan a ray of hope. In 1957, the North Korean government started to send an education fund to Korean schools in Japan, which was taken as a proof of the powerful growth of the North Korean economy.

North Korea's economic growth was not the only factor. It was a time of patriotic zeal in the form of postcolonial nationalism among Koreans in Japan. Many Koreans in Japan, from the end of the Second World War until the 1950s, looked toward the north rather than the south as an embodiment of national independence. The record of the anti-Japanese guerrilla fight claimed by Kim Il Sung exceeded the American-educated and American-backed southern premier

Syngman Rhee in terms of eligibility as a national leader. As of early 1955, Japanese police authorities estimated that about 90 percent of Koreans in Japan supported North Korea (Hiroyama 1955: 10).

At that time, few Koreans foresaw the possibility of a long-term stay in Japan and many, especially the first generation, for whom the memory of colonial oppression was still alive, assumed that before long Korea would be reunified and Koreans in Japan would join the new independent Korean nation. To look to North Korea as their homeland did not, therefore, exclude the possibility eventually of returning to South Korea, in the eyes especially of the first generation, whose memory of native places in the south was contiguous with the northern soil. As for the young Koreans in Japan, North Korea offered an opportunity. For many gifted young men and women, career prospects in Japan were grim owing to Japan's racist exclusion of Koreans from job opportunities. Under such conditions, it was not illogical for parents to entertain the hope that their children would achieve a brilliant future in North Korea.

With the mediation of the International Red Cross, in August 1959 the North Korean Red Cross and the Japan Red Cross agreed on repatriating Koreans from Japan to North Korea on a voluntary basis. In December 1959, a Soviet-built boat entered Niigata, a port in central Japan on the Japan Sea coast, with a large cloth banner across its body, saying "We welcome the repatriation of Koreans from Japan!" This was met with an enthusiastic welcome by Koreans in Japan who filled an otherwise deserted small port.

"A great exodus from capitalism to socialism"

In order to understand the desire to be repatriated to the north held by many Koreans in Japan in the mid-1950s, it is important to bear in mind the shift in ethnic politics at that time, which resulted in the emergence of the pro-North Korean Chongryun from the ranks of Korean leftists in Japan. Following the end of the war, the Korean community in Japan saw the emergence of two ethnic organizations, the leftist League of Koreans and the rightist Association of Koreans in Japan, abbreviated as Mindan. Owing to its close ties with the Japanese communists, the league was suppressed in 1948 by Occupation authorities, while by the time the Korean War ended in 1953, Koreans were clearly split into two antagonistic groups, pro-north and pro-south. The remnants of the league were now organized around the underground organization Minjŏn. Despite their allegiance to opposing regimes in the peninsula, both Minjŏn and Mindan were characterized by their driving nationalism, looking toward the eventual reunification of Korea and the repatriation of all Koreans from Japan (see Kashiwazaki and Inokuchi in this volume).

The nationalists in Minjŏn, however, were frustrated: since the dissolution of the League of Koreans, they had no choice other than to rely on the Japanese Communist Party which was not suppressed and controlled Minjŏn's decision-making. The party at that time insisted on an international united front of Koreans and Japanese for the achievement of the Japanese revolution. While Korean nationalists were on the lookout to end intervention by Japanese communists, the aforementioned North Korean communiqués were announced in 1954 and 1955. This gave Korean nationalists grounds to sever ties with the party, as their involvement with the anticipated Japanese revolution would upset the North Korean effort to enter diplomatic relations with the Japanese government of the day. On the basis of this logic, Korean nationalists pulled out of the Japanese Communist Party, and in May 1955 Minjŏn re-emerged as the general association of Korean residents in Japan, or Chongryun in the Korean abbreviation.

Chongryun upheld as its organizational principle safeguarding the honor of North Korea, the homeland, and being lawful in all its activities in Japan. The repatriation zeal has to be seen in conjunction with Chongryun's goal of unifying all Korean forces in Japan and its self-definition as a North Korean organization based in Japan, working for the prosperity of the homeland and its people, not an organization of Koreans in Japan with an eye to their future well-being in Japan. This is because at the time of Chongryun's foundation many first-generation Koreans still hoped and expected the repatriation to happen for themselves and their families. Therefore, participation in Japanese society was irrelevant except as a means to that end. Chongryun is not an anti-Japanese organization: on the contrary, it has consistently remained indifferent to Japanese politics. Although it informs its members and affiliates of the Japanese state's discrimination against Koreans, especially Chongryun Koreans, and Japan's non-recognition of North Korean sovereignty, Chongryun is more interested in consciousness-raising of its members through the school education system and other ideological apparatuses for achieving devotion to North Korea as the sole and authentic homeland of Koreans in Japan (see Ryang 1997).

Chongryun constructed a nation-wide organizational web extending to every Japanese prefecture. It built more than 150 Korean schools including nursery school, primary, middle, and high schools, a college, and a graduate school for which North Korean funds were provided, while Korean families in Japan provided their own payments in support of their ethnic schools.[4] The school education system was crucial in creating a pedagogical mechanism for reproducing a discourse and ideology which upheld North Korea as the authentic homeland for Koreans in Japan. Chongryun's system of school education teaches students to look up to North Korea as their homeland and Kim Il Sung as their national leader.

Apart from schools, Chongryun established a credit union and an insurance company. It organized performing art companies and sports teams. In all these activities, it upheld North Korea as the only legitimate homeland for all Koreans in Japan. It strongly identified with the future of Koreans in Japan taking place on the soil of the Korean peninsula, which it believed should be reunified under the North Korean initiative. It thus shifted the ideological focus of leftist Koreans away from a commitment to the international communist cause at the expense of nationalism, to the full-fledged nationalist cause devoted to North Korea and the future repatriation of Koreans in Japan to a unified Korea.

The opening of repatriation to North Korea in 1959 was a great victory for

Chongryun. Chongryun's publications carried the news under headings such as "A great national exodus from capitalism to socialism," "Our glorious fatherland calls compatriots," and "Motherly bosom of our fatherland, the paradise on earth" (*Ŏmŏnichoguk ŭi p'um, chisangragwŏn*).5 The initial reactions of repatriates were positive. The following are excerpts from the letters of high-school and middle-school students who were enrolled in Chongryun's Tokyo Korea junior and senior high school at the time of repatriation.

From Song Jong-ch'ŏl of Namp'o revolutionary school of the bereaved 6:42 a.m. on December 23 [1959] – "Look! Our fatherland is here!" With this voice, we, all 976 repatriates on deck, felt overwhelmed. . . . We cried and smiled, the tears and smiles that no one in this world has ever seen. . . . We participated in the New Year's festival at Kim Il Sung University. The university students entertained us with a wonderful reception. . . . On January 2, 1960, we watched a play "Brothers" (by Han Sŏl-ya). Dear friends, I had the honor of shaking hands with our Leader [Kim Il Sung]. . . . Seven of us [repatriated students] had this honor. Everyone was too moved to utter a word. . . . You must all come here to the fatherland as soon as possible to receive such an honor. . . . Looking forward to our reunion in Pyongyang. Long live the Democratic People's Republic of Korea! Long live the Workers' Party of Korea! Long live our respected and beloved leader Marshal Kim Il Sung!
(Song Jong-ch'ŏl 1960: 31–3)

From Ku Wŏn-ho of Pyongyang medical school Dear teachers and friends! I wish first of all to report to you that . . . today I met our great leader Marshal Kim Il Sung and had the honor to talk with him for one and a half-hours. . . . The leader asked every one of us about our family and living conditions.

[The author entered North Korea from its northwestern border via China after his participation in an international youth festival in Vienna in August 1959.] Through the train windows we saw the Yalu River, the fatherland's landscape, numerous cranes, and high-rising apartment buildings. When the train arrived at Sinŭiju, thousands of students were waiting on the platform and greeted us chanting "Welcome Korean students from Japan." I could not hold back my tears. I felt I had finally come back to my own homeland. . . . Under the special care of the government and the party, it has been officially decided that I would attend the Pyongyang medical school, following my wishes. I send my handshake to you, my teachers and friends, who are struggling to achieve the repatriation of all Koreans.
(Ku Wŏn-ho 1960: 34–42)

From Pak Sun-ja of Haeju city We went to see the house in which our family is going to live. . . . Inside there are two *ondol* rooms.6 There are wardrobe, radio, mirror, portrait of Marshal Kim Il Sung, writing desk and hangers. In the kitchen is a stove that is used for cooking as well as for *ondol* heating. There are two rice cookers, basket and jars, etc. Inside a jar, rice is already stored. Also, soy sauce, bean curd, salt, oil, and *kimch'i* are already there. In the sideboard, there are cups and saucers, cutlery, coffeepot and other crockery, and serving bottles. We could not have dreamt of buying these things in Japan. In a word, the house has everything we need to start living right from this moment. This is all thanks to our leader Marshal Kim Il Sung, our party, and our government. (The author was a first year middle school pupil [13 years old] when she was repatriated [with her family].)

(Pak Sun-ja 1960: 23–4)

In these letters we can perceive the writers' hope for North Korea's development, their own future lives in North Korea, and their appreciation of being welcomed as citizens of North Korea.[7]

Since the overwhelming majority of Koreans in Japan came from the southern provinces, strictly speaking their moving to North Korea was not a repatriation, considering that the north and the south had become separate states, albeit born out of what was regarded as one nation. It is precisely here that the term repatriation, *kwiguk*, and the act of using this term come to bear political meaning. It is interesting to note that the Japan Red Cross used the term *hikiage* which can be translated as repatriation but also as evacuation or withdrawal; the South Korea supporters in Japan, that is, the opponents of the repatriation to the north, who are mainly affiliated to Mindan, called it *puksong*, sending [the people] to the north. While *hikiage* implies a movement back to the original and normal point – as if it was not normal, and hence not acceptable, for Koreans to be in Japan – "sending" implies certain forcibleness such as deportation, as if repatriates were sent to North Korea against their will. Chongryun maintained *kwiguk*, repatriation.[8] Although it was technically not a repatriation in terms of the place of the origin, as long as Chongryun Koreans called North Korea their "motherly homeland," their exodus out of Japan could be legitimately regarded as repatriation.

In December 1959, during the first month of the repatriation, 2,942 persons moved to North Korea, which was followed by 48,956 in 1960 and 22,201 in 1961. Up until 1967 a total of 88,611 had been repatriated (Kōseishō engokyoku 1968). The repatriation peaked in 1960 to 1961, following the April 19 uprising in South Korea, which overthrew the Syngman Rhee government and conveyed a sense that South Korea would soon collapse, forecasting to many the imminent reunification of Korea. After four years of discontinuity from 1967, due to the Japan Red Cross's insistence that there were no longer enough volunteers to keep the route open, the repatriation was reopened in 1971, but on a much smaller scale. By 1976 a total of 92,749 had been repatriated, including about 6,600 Japanese nationals (Kōseisho engokyoku 1968: 691); in 1984 the total reached 93,339, recording a meager increase for twelve years (*Kyoto shinbun* 29 May 1994). The repatriation route is still open today, but the number of repatriates is almost non-existent, while the route is proving to be more useful for the flow of goods between Japan and North Korea.

The reason for the decline in number of repatriates by the mid-1960s is closely connected to the changing relations among South Korean, North Korean, and Japanese governments. After the rise of Park Jung Hee to presidential power, South Korea quickly pushed negotiations with Japan over the colonial settlement. As stated earlier, in 1965 Japan and South Korea entered full diplomatic relations, one of the results of this being the acknowledgement of South Korean nationality and the issuance of Japanese permanent residence to the holders of South Korean nationality.

For Koreans who had been confined in Japan with no valid travel document, let alone official nationality, this was an attractive option. Many opted for it, thereby effectively ending their relation to Chongryun. At the height of the Cold War, the option for South Korea automatically canceled the affiliation with Chongryun and North Korea. For those who opted for South Korean nationality and Japanese permanent residence, it became possible to claim wider welfare and social benefits in Japan. More importantly, they could now travel abroad. While repatriation to North Korea was one-way journey, having South Korean nationality enabled Koreans to visit their family in the south. In 1967 alone, 14,310 South Korean nationals obtained a re-entry permit to Japan (which indicates that they were Koreans in Japan who had acquired South Korean nationality after 1965) while none of the 1,831 repatriates to North Korea in the same year had any prospect of re-visiting their families in Japan (calculated from *Shutsunyūkoku kanri tōkeinenpō* and Kōseishō engokyoku 1968).

By the time the 1965 treaty was ratified, the zeal for the repatriation to the north had waned. Already two decades had passed since the end of the war. Those Koreans who had been born in Japan in 1945 had reached adulthood, while many third-generation Koreans had been born. The stalemate in the Cold War showed every sign of prolonging partition of the peninsula, while life in Japan was becoming more permanent, and less hard, for Koreans. Repatriates from Japan were left confined in North Korea with no hope for reunion with their families and friends in Japan, while those who were left in Japan had little information on the everyday lives of their repatriated family members, apart from the official portrayal in Chongryun's publications and superficial letters they rarely received from North Korea. It was only in the 1980s that a significant change was brought to this situation.

From repatriation to visits

In 1979 Japan joined the International Covenants on Human Rights and in 1982, the UN Refugee Convention. One of the implications of this was to enable Koreans – mainly Chongryun-affiliated Koreans – who had no travel document and no secure residential status inside Japan to travel abroad. In 1981, the Japanese Ministry of Justice institutionalized the issuance of re-entry permits to Japan for Koreans who did not have South Korean nationality.[9] In 1982, a permanent residence order was issued in order to improve the precarious residential status of those Koreans (see Kashiwazaki in this volume).[10]

This change increased the instances of travel abroad by Chongryun Koreans. In 1969 only six Korean persons without South Korean nationality traveled abroad from Japan, which was followed by twenty seven re-entrants to Japan in 1971, most of whom were Chongryun delegates to North Korea (*Shutsunyūkoku kanri tōkeinenpō*). In 1979, the year of Japan's joining the International Covenant, a total of 2,579 Koreans without South Korean nationality obtained re-entry permits and traveled outside Japan. Of 2,579, 2,033 left via Niigata, most likely aboard a North Korean ship visiting North Korea. (The number of repatriates was already small by then.) From 1980 onwards travel abroad by Chongryun Koreans and other Koreans without South Korean nationality steadily increased. In 1980 the number was 4,273, which increased to 9,070 in 1986. In 1989 and the early 1990s the number remained close to the 15,000 range (*Shutsunyūkoku kanri tōkeinenpō*).

Although not all of these were visiting North Korea, considering that North Korean ships usually entered Niigata port, we can have a rough sense of the number of Chongryun visitors to North Korea by tracing the figure attached to this port. In 1980, 3,765 non-South Korean Koreans traveled from Japan via Niigata. The figure stays within the range of 3,300 to 3,500 up until 1985, increases to 3,851 in 1986, then to 4,532 in 1987, 3,953 in 1988, 5,246 in 1989 – the year when the 13th International Youth and Students Festival was held in Pyongyang and many Chongryun volunteers visited North Korea – 4,392 in 1990, 4,686 in 1991, 5,067 in 1992 – the year of Kim Il Sung's 80th birthday – 3,344 in 1993, and 4,249 in 1994: the year of Kim Il Sung's death. All in all, it appears that between 1979 and 1994 a yearly average of 3,898 Koreans left Japan via Niigata, and that most of these Koreans were Chongryun Koreans visiting North Korea (calculated from *Shutsunyūkoku kanri tōkeinenpō*).

Who were those visitors to North Korea? Many were participants in student delegations from Chongryun's Korean schools in Japan. Since 1980 Chongryun's Korea University, for example, formally included a North Korean study trip in its curriculum. Some majors required six to twelve months' study in North Korea. Others were teachers and activists of Chongryun, who were required to take re-education courses in Pyongyang. Yet others were visiting their repatriated families in North Korea. The standard reunion trip lasted two weeks. The cost was very small initially: around 60,000 yen in the early 1980s, including meals, accommodation, sightseeing, and "guided" visits to the repatriated.

According to Chongryun's official publication, between August 1979 and October 1997, 300 group reunion boat trips were made (*Chosŏn sinbo* 17 October 1997). The Soviet-built ship was replaced by the North-Korean built *Mangyŏngbong* in the 1970s. It took the *Mangyŏngbong* fifty hours to sail between Niigata and Wŏnsan, North Korea's eastern central port. In the late 1970s a larger North Korean-built ship, the *Samjiyŏn*, reduced the sailing time to thirty-six hours. Chongryun donors funded the technologically superior *Mangyŏngbong 92* in 1992, which runs between the Japanese and North Korean coasts in twenty-eight hours (*Chosŏn sinbo* 17 October 1997). Reflecting the end of the Cold War, North Korea has considerably eased its closed-country policy. North Korea and Japan are now connected by flights via Beijing and a few direct charter flights are also available. Not only Koreans in Japan, but also a few Japanese, take holiday tours to North Korea by air. Such routes provide Japanese and other foreign journalists with opportunities to visit North Korea with Chongryun's mediation without having to go through official channels (see e.g. Sekigawa 1992).[11]

In 1984 I visited North Korea as a reporter for *Chosŏn sinbo*, the Korean-language daily newspaper of Chongryun, accompanying reunion visitors. The case I quote below is useful in understanding the early reaction of the reunion visitors from Japan, and provides a point of reference for the more recent perception of North Korea by Chongryun Koreans which is discussed in the following section.

Yu-ja (a pseudonym for a Japanese-resident Korean woman) has three older brothers who were repatriated in 1962. She was a little girl when her brothers left for North Korea.[12] Her mother, wanting to have a daughter, had waited nearly ten years before she gave birth to Yu-ja. Her family had always been well-off and the reason for her brothers' repatriation was not financial: it was more about her parents' wishes to enable their sons to achieve a good career. The two older sons graduated from a medical school in Pyongyang, while the youngest became a pharmacologist.

Their repatriation was motivated by another factor: recovery of national identity. Yu-ja's family lives in one of the southernmost provinces in Japan, where no Korean school existed at the time of her brothers' repatriation. Her brothers went to Japanese schools. When the oldest brother reached the final year of high school, her parents decided to do something to heighten their national consciousness. One possible option was to send them to Korea University in Tokyo, but the older sons wanted to be medical doctors and Korea University does not have a medical school. Hence, repatriation seemed an ideal solution. Three sons went to North Korea when a neighboring family was repatriated: since the parents chose to remain in Japan, and since the sons were eighteen, fifteen, and thirteen years old, they had to be accompanied by adults. Yu-ja's parents hoped that they would shortly join their sons in the peninsula. They never did, mainly because their business did very well in the subsequent decades and they felt their sons would be better off if they could economically back up their livelihood from Japan. From an early stage it was no secret to the parents that things were tight in North Korea, because they deciphered modest mentions made in their sons' letters. Needless to say, it was a painful option not to live with their sons and not even to be able to see them for an indefinite period of time.

Twenty-two years had passed since the sons had seen their baby sister. Yu-ja had then only been three; now she was a twenty-five-year-old woman. The brothers rejoiced, proudly repeating to me, "Look how beautiful our sister is!" I agreed unreservedly. But for Yu-ja, things were different. For her, the memory of her older brothers was vague: she had been too young to remember much about them. She later confided to me that although it was fantastic to have met her brothers, it was more important for her to have visited the homeland. Yu-ja had studied at Korean schools. After her graduation from a Korean high school, which had been set up locally since her brothers' repatriation, she had become an employee of a Korean credit union of Chongryun, where she had been active in youth league activities. (All Chongryun credit union branches have a North-Korean style youth league organization.) She said that the homeland was where her brothers were raised and in this sense, her brothers were part of the homeland. She was very proud of her brothers' achievements, but was equally thankful for the homeland that had given them such an opportunity.

Her learning at the Korean school enabled her to identify her feelings with Chongryun's official discourse about North Korea, representing it as "motherly bosom," ŏmŏni p'um. In this sense, her personal feelings toward her brothers had a peculiar bearing on her absorbing Chongryun's collective identity, that is, the identity of overseas nationals of North Korea. In other words, for her, memory of the repatriated brothers merged with her longing for the homeland, the bosom to which Koreans in Japan should be able eventually to return. She said that the reason why she felt so at home with her brothers whom she had not met for more than twenty years was because she had met them in the homeland, the home for overseas nationals of North Korea, a space which she had dreamed about in the classroom, listening to her teachers and reading textbooks. To visit North Korea was to visit the memory of her own childhood in Korean schools and the content of what she had learned there. In North Korea, there were many references that created nostalgia in her mind: big socialist slogan panels atop the buildings, Korean People's Army officers in uniforms, pseudo-Bauhaus architecture in urban areas, a barren but unspoiled landscape, orderly citizens, vast streets with no cars and so on were the images to which she had been exposed since her primary-school days.

Yu-ja's reaction was by and large typical of young people who had been educated in Chongryun schools, calling North Korea their homeland and longing to visit it. It is true that many found North Korea was not a paradise on earth. The lack of material goods and the low living standard of their repatriated families and friends concerned many. Nevertheless, in the early 1980s immediately following the opening of the family reunion route, Chongryun Koreans responded sympathetically to North Korea's conditions and the difficulties it faced, trying to see positive sides and disregarding negative sides: in a word, identifying North Korea as their homeland and taking pride in its achievements. Such a stance existed back to back with their ambivalence toward Japan. "Japan is where we live, but the home where our mind resides is North Korea": that was what they had been taught at schools and that was also what the reality in Japanese society brought home to them, by way of various ethnic and social discriminations. This had a consequence of drawing their affection away from Japan, although the ambivalent relation with Japanese society undeniably persisted.

In addition, in the initial stage of family reunion visits, North Korean officials were careful and considerate in conducting tours for the visitors from Japan. Hotel rooms and meals were prepared with precision, and a relatively high standard of service was maintained. When the visitors from Japan were invited to their repatriated family's home or apartment, the party granted the family new furnishing and better food, including sugar and rice cakes, fruits and wine, which were not usually available for ordinary residents of North Korea. There was a happy coincidence between the eagerness and sympathy of the Chongryun visitors and the attitude of the North Korean authorities. In the 1990s, however, things became complex in multiple directions.

North Korea: a home for Koreans?

The world has known for some time that the economy of North Korea has not been performing as gigantically as it was in the 1960s, when Soviet and Chinese aid reached it regularly. It has also known that Kim Il Sung's reign increasingly drew suspicion, with the designation of Kim's own son as successor. But it was only recently that the facts of North Korea's crises were perceived as "real" – and not as the enemy propaganda – by Chongryun Koreans. In part this is owing to the fact that the recent crises were associated with bad weather: a natural calamity beyond the human control, including that of the "Great Leader." This rationale made it possible for Chongryun's official publications to report North Korea's economic disaster without hinting at the incompetence of the leadership.

In addition, Japan's mainstream media has started to send first-hand reports about North Korea's situation. (This may reflect North Korea's partial opening in the 1990s, including the flight routes, as stated in the earlier section.) Following massive floods in two consecutive years, 1995 and 1996, a dry summer accompanied by typhoon damage in 1997 devastated the North Korean agriculture and food situation. The *per capita* daily grain ration fell to 100 grams, from 700 grams in 1997. The ration distribution became intermittent (*Asahi shinbun* 23 July 1997). A Japanese journalist reported that owing to the increasing deaths by starvation and undernourishment, funerals were allowed only to be small scale and in the evening, attended by the immediate family alone (*Asahi shinbun* 25 August 1997). As the poverty and lack of food intensified, there were reports that crimes related to this situation were on the increase, from petty theft to organized gang robbery, often involving murder (RENK henshūbu 1997).

Along with these stories, detailed information on repatriates is reaching Koreans in Japan through various channels, including defectors to the south (Chang Myŏng-su 1995a). Recently a Korean woman in Japan, Pak Ch'un-sŏn, a sister of a man whom she believed to have been executed in a North Korean concentration camp, denounced the North Korean government, demanding a clear explanation about her brother's death and the return of his remains (Pak Ch'un-sŏn 1994). Her brother had been repatriated in 1962, when he had been active as a top star in Chongryun's performing arts company. He had been assigned to the Japanese-language broadcasting service in Pyongyang. Mrs Pak had used to listen to her brother's voice on the radio, but it vanished from the air from 1978. She later learned that her brother had been shot in 1985 in a concentration camp, having been accused of spying (*Osaka shinbun* 3 August 1994). This and other stories are increasingly heard in the Japanese media.

The wider access to North Korean information comes with other changing conditions pertaining to Koreans in Japan. Their legal status and social positions have improved in the 1990s. Most have been granted permanent residence in Japan. In 1992 their permanent residence status was upgraded, giving them better access to civil rights (see note 10). Their economic situation is also better, reflecting Japan's long-term economic growth. Their generational profile has also changed: no longer is the first generation the decision-maker; no longer is the repatriation of all Koreans the collective ideal. Younger generations, even those enrolled in Chongryun schools, are natives of Japan and Japanese culture. Disillusioned or simply uninterested, with the end of the Cold War many Chongryun Koreans, including some of the most committed, left the organization. Some are speaking against Chongryun or are becoming doubtful about North Korea's future. In this picture, North Korea should prove to be increasingly foreign for Chongryun Koreans. In the rest of this section, I shall explore parameters of the discourse of "North Korea as home" which, paradoxically, cannot be ruled out hurriedly despite the adverse situation surrounding North Korea and Chongryun. On the basis of the interviews conducted in 1992 to 1994, with more recent interviews in 1996 and 1997, I present below two young Chongryun Koreans and their views toward North Korea.[13]

Mrs Chang (a pseudonym) is a second-generation resident of Japan, born and raised in a city in rural Japan. A mother of two sons, she was 40 years old in 1997. Her retired father-in-law lives with her family. He was a lifelong major donor to Chongryun, and a key person in securing the organization's finance. Mrs Chang, who was educated in Japanese schools, switched to a Korean school in the final year of high school. She later studied in Chongryun's Korea University:

> For the first time in my life I felt at home with my environment and myself in Korea University. It was the first time that I was totally surrounded by Koreans, only Koreans. Of course, it took time. Those students who had studied in Korean schools since they were children were very different from me: they were tough, I thought, and very competent in expressing what they thought. I could not follow my university courses in the beginning [owing to a lack of proficiency in the Korean language]. After four years of hard work, I felt I was one of them, a competent Korean, an overseas national of our fatherland.

In her senior year in 1980, she visited North Korea with her classmates. She regards the visit as one of the most significant events in her life.

> I was moved beyond reason. All those things that we heard in lectures were there in front of me. I found individuals I met in the fatherland . . . how shall I say . . . pure and hard working. I thought they were all trying to do something for their own country – our country, *uri nara*. I should try harder to join

in their effort, I thought. When I think about it, I was rather simplistic. But, sometimes, simplicity becomes more significant than we think it might be. It still influences me – I mean, the freshness of my unspoiled feelings.

So far, there is much that resonates with Yu-ja's experience in 1984. However, as Mrs Chang goes on referring to today's Chongryun, her perspective becomes complicated. She knows, for example, the details about payments that Chongryun Koreans have to make in order to ensure the safety and well-being of their repatriated families in North Korea. She also knows that it is possible to invite the repatriated family over to Japan in exchange for a substantial sum paid to the North Korean office in charge.

Multiple sources tell me that it costs around two million yen to facilitate a week's visit to Japan by a repatriate. So for a month's stay, it would cost the inviting family eight million yen (approximately $61,500 at the 1998 exchange rate of $1: 130 yen). Needless to say, few families can afford this. I have been told that a request to move one's repatriated family to Pyongyang, where living conditions are better, requires payment of about four million yen. No one, however, is clear who is actually paid: the payment is assumed to be sent through Chongryun's relevant offices, the details of which cannot be known.

With Kim Il Sung's death in July 1994 and his son Kim Jong Il's subsequent succession to the supreme power in North Korea, Chongryun Koreans are facing increasing insecurity about the future of the organization on the one hand, and an increasing distancing from the organization on the other. This is because many of them do not necessarily trust or even know much about Kim Jong Il, as compared with his father. Mrs Chang is no exception. She feels disappointment about the father–son succession, as well as the lack of any visible improvement in North Korea's economic recovery after the son's succession. I have earlier mentioned that the "natural" cause for the recent economic crises in North Korea rendered it possible for Chongryun Koreans easily to recognize North Korea's difficulties. The rhetoric of "natural calamity" works to enable Chongryun and North Korean authorities to rationalize the disaster, avoiding political responsibility. Although many first-generation Chongryun Koreans take this rationalization at face value, younger Chongryun Koreans, including Mrs Chang, are more skeptical:

> It is a complicated matter. We know *uri nara* [our country] is experiencing difficulty lately. We'd like to – I think, we must – help our fatherland recover from the current hardship. But, I am not satisfied with the way it is done – by extracting money from those of us who happen to have our family members repatriated and furthermore, who happen to be able to afford a demanding amount of payment. If *uri choguk* [our fatherland] was an attractive homeland for us all – as I found it on my first visit – I think we'd all be more than willing to pay. Even people without resources would squeeze something out; we'd go without a meal or two to help our fatherland. The problem is that we no longer find it that way, yet a more difficult problem is that we *want* it to be better. We cannot ignore it or desert it, I mean, at least my family cannot.

Dilemma seeps through her words. She has no one repatriated in her natal family, but several of her in-laws are living in Pyongyang. Her children are enrolled in a Chongryun school and she wishes things to improve in North Korea. Is North Korea, after all, her home, albeit in a spiritual sense?

> I'd say yes. But, this "yes" is qualified. I feel for it [North Korea]. I feel for it a lot, deeply and truly. Why . . . Isn't it because I personally have recovered my national identity after being exposed to Chongryun's Korean education? Isn't it because I feel my personal dignity was restored in Korea University? When I was studying at Japanese high school, I was a servile person, not able to stand up for my own opinion. I knew I was an outsider. I knew I was rejected by my Japanese peers and Japanese society as a whole. It is important, yes indeed important, that I got to know *uri nara* [i.e. North Korea] as my fatherland. In this sense, perhaps, *choguk* [the fatherland] is my home, if not the real home in which I live, but a home in my mind that I can return to with affection and fond memories. And this is why I feel so painful to hear recent news about its hardship and critical of the incompetence of North Korea's leadership and Chongryun cadres.

Unlike Yu-ja, who had very few critical edges to her perception of North Korea, Mrs Chang's opinion is based on sober reflection on the recent collapse of North Korean economy. She is also critical of the way Chongryun conducts organizational matters, demanding money of its members and supporters. Nevertheless, her "home in her mind" remains in a space called North Korea. Also evident is an interesting separation between North Korean leadership, politics and economy on the one hand, and North Korea as a space, imaginary homeland or indeed, imaginary home, on the other.[14]

Similar perceptions are found in the words of a Chongryun schoolteacher, who has been teaching for twelve years since his graduation from Korea University. Jin-su (a pseudonym), who is single and has no repatriated family, visits North Korea more or less regularly, either leading the school tours or for teacher re-education courses. The most recent visit was in 1997.

> It was reinvigorating to have been in the fatherland. There I can forget about little worries that I have to deal with in everyday life in Japan. I don't have to be on the rush-hour train, I don't have to cook my meals, I don't have to behave as a "Korean" since everyone else is also Korean. I feel my mind cleansed in the air of the fatherland. I don't know why, but I feel purified there. It's like being in an oasis. The fatherland gives me new life.

Is visiting North Korea same as going home?[15]

> Yes, it is. Japan is where I live and I know I will *not* be repatriated to the fatherland to live. But, Japan is never my home in a wholesome sense. Japanese society would never accept me, a Chongryun teacher. If I were to

quit this job, I'd have nothing to do, I'd be left with no qualification, and I'd have to settle for degrading jobs such as a day laborer – yes, just like our fathers did in the past. In other words, we would be brought back to something similar to our colonial past if we were to leave Chongryun and join Japanese society. In our fatherland, I [feel I] behave differently. I become more proud of myself as a patriotic teacher overseas. I even walk and speak differently, with more dignity, more confidence, and more life. I experience self-transformation there.

Given that Jin-su and other Chongryun teachers and officers are usually given cadre treatment while in North Korea, being accommodated in Chongryun-donated recreation centers with full maid service in isolation from the daily reality of North Korea, is not Jin-su idealizing North Korea? How much does he know of the recent famine and other crises there?

I do, and I am seriously worried about the future of our fatherland. When I first visited the fatherland in my senior year, I did not feel any worry or, yes, responsibility toward the fatherland. I was happy, enjoying the visit. And, I was not concerned with the fatherland's future as my own business. Now that I've been teaching about the fatherland for more than a decade, I have come to identify myself more closely with the fatherland. In this sense, recent news about food shortage and social unrest worries me a lot. I get especially annoyed when I think about the power wielding of the cadres who do nothing but exploit the population. The same attitude can be found among Chongryun cadres, too. I lose sleep over this.

Jin-su, as a full-time employee of Chongryun and especially, as a teacher who educates younger Koreans to follow North Korea, employs a more romanticized language referring to North Korea as home. Mrs Chang on the other hand expresses a balanced view, carefully choosing her words and scrupulously qualifying her answers. Nevertheless, both are in agreement in regarding North Korea as their genuine home rather than Japan. In the final section of this chapter, I shall assess their views against a more critical perception of the discourse of "North Korea as home."

Home lost, home gained

In ordinary language, as well as in the academic language of anthropology or cultural studies, the concept of home is becoming increasingly important. In inversion to, or correlation with, the intensifying isolation of individuals from society and the break-up of old communities, associated with modernity, the desire for home is beginning to be understood not only as legitimate but also as a project meriting serious study. In this century, where we have witnessed and continue to witness the violent displacement of peoples from their native communities, by war, famine, natural calamity, labor migration, racial segregation, colonial uprooting, political persecution and so on, we cannot, indeed, not talk about home. Some have identified homelessness as a general condition in modernity (Arendt 1966; Weil 1978), while others point out that the uncritical acceptance of the nation form as a dominant territorialization of our time creates homelessness for migrants, immigrants, and stateless people (Balibar 1991a). Homelessness is as old as human history, as can be seen in the history of the Jewish diaspora (see Safran 1991), but the twentieth-century homelessness takes a clear form of "statelessness" owing to the world's division according to nation-state boundaries as the norm (Xenos 1993: 423). In this domination of the nation-states in classifying peoples, those without their homeland to return to or their national state to identify with, are categorically and emotionally homeless. It is no coincidence that Chongryun Koreans have no passports. They have no homeland government to look to for protection in the case of emergency. In the world's map of nation-states, Chongryun Koreans are stateless, and hence, homeless.

Measured against this homelessness, how can we assess their identifying North Korea as their home? The first thing that comes to mind is their marginal status in Japan. In her article dealing with Asian-American theater in Los Angeles, Dorinne Kondo writes that home is "that which we cannot not want" and it is more so for "people on the margin" (1996: 97). She continues:

> [Home] stands for a safe place, where there is no need to explain oneself to outsiders; it stands for community; more problematically, it can elicit a nostalgia for a past golden age that never was, a nostalgia that elides exclusion, power relations, and difference. Motifs of "home" animate works by peoples in diaspora, often peoples of color, who may have no permanent home; people on the margins, such as gays and lesbians, for whom home was rarely, if ever, safe; and women and children, for whom the "haven" of home can be a site of violence and oppression.
>
> (Kondo 1996: 97)

"Nostalgia for a past golden age that never was" approaches very closely Chongryun Koreans' relation to North Korea when they think of it as their home. As stated in relation to Yu-ja, and also in Mrs Chang's and Jin-su's words, North Korea is a space which they have invested with their personal past, particularly childhood and youthful memories and dreams. As such it is a site where they can be "Koreans" without being singled out as someone who is not Japanese, as Jin-su put it, and where they recover self-dignity away from sense of self-loss they experience in Japanese society, as Mrs Chang said. In other words, the ultimate marginality of Chongryun Koreans in Japan maintains in part their identification of North Korea as a space in which they feel at home. In the sense that Michel de Certeau suggests, Chongryun Koreans as "users" made North Korea into a space that is a product of their everyday practice of appropriation or "use," a practice that turns a non-identifiable place into identifiable space (de Certeau 1984: xiii–xv). It also resembles what Anthony Giddens suggests in distinguishing place and space, place being "the physical settings of social activity as situated

The North Korean homeland 49

geographically," while in conditions of modernity, space is increasingly being dislocated from place, in that space no longer presupposes its close association with time and immediate reality (Giddens 1990: 18–19). North Korea as home in this sense denotes a space, while Japan remains a place.[16]

Chongryun Koreans know that they will never be accepted in Japanese society, once they go outside the symbolic boundaries of Chongryun. This has not so much to do with their cultural literacy in Japanese society: they can speak Japanese fluently and behave just like the Japanese. They may even feel attached to Japan: many Chongryun Koreans know that they will continue to live in Japan, not in North Korea. But, their Chongryun-given qualifications would be useless and their Chongryun-related work experience would be irrelevant, if they were to seek careers in the Japanese sectors. Chongryun schools lack government recognition. Hence, Chongryun teachers could not teach in Japanese schools. Chongryun high school graduates do not qualify to take the entrance examinations for the Japanese state universities. A Chongryun journalist would be a mere ideologue outside Chongryun boundaries. A Chongryun artist would be a propagandist outside the boundaries. Whenever the Japanese media is loaded with North-Korea bashing – be it the nuclear plant issue or the nepotistic leader succession, the bombing of a South Korean aircraft or the suspected kidnapping of Japanese by North Korean agents – Chongryun schoolgirls wearing Korean-style uniforms are a soft target for harassment and attack by right-wingers and other Japanese. Thus, Chongryun boundaries – largely symbolic but at times real – are, for its members, the end of their home and the beginning of the exclusion from Japanese society. Where Japan is a nation-state that is not their home, their "home" in Japan is the Chongryun community, existing as an extension of their spiritual home, North Korea.

Thus far, I have been oblivious of the distinction between "home" and "homeland." Here I wish to introduce this distinction to the case of Chongryun Koreans, for a more critical understanding of their concept of "North Korea as home." Building on Hannah Arendt's notion of "home" as the product of political life (Arendt 1966), Nicholas Xenos suggests the definition of home and homeland as follows:

> Homelands are places that are unchanging and to which one must return, no matter how hostile they may be to the returnee. Homes can be made and remade, if there is a space for them.
>
> (Xenos 1993: 427)

In the modern nation-state system, the crisis of homelessness occurs not because people have lost their homeland, but because they have lost a possibility of building a home in a new space, without submitting to the cultural and *national* assimilation system which usually humiliates non-nationals (Xenos 1993: 427). North Korea was a homeland for the first generation; for the second generation, it is a home, rather than a homeland, if we take Xenos's distinction as a working model. Scores of Chongryun Koreans I have interviewed since

1992, across gender and generations, stated that they would not apply for North Korean citizenship and nationality in the event of Japan–North Korea diplomatic normalization. Some said they would take South Korean nationality, and many others said they would apply for Japanese nationality. In other words, in the 1990s even those who would readily employ the rhetoric of "North Korea as home" viewed their personal future in Japan. Although they see no possibility of making Japan a new home, the fact remains, and the memory entails, that they were born and grew up there, will create a family and will die there. What else can this be, if it cannot be a home?

"North Korea as home" is a double-sided notion and as such, it involves double standards and self-illusion. Chongryun Koreans can register facts about North Korea, including negative ones, and be critical about its government and leadership, while keeping North Korea as their "oasis." At the same time, if first-generation Chongryun Koreans had North Korea as their homeland, Japan-born Chongryun Koreans have no homeland: neither Japan nor North Korea is their homeland. It becomes understandable, then, why since the late 1960s repatriation to North Korea has no longer been an attraction, while even after the opening of the visiting route to North Korea in the 1980s, Japan-born Chongryun Koreans never entertain the possibility of "returning" to North Korea. This is in contrast to, for example, the second-generation Cuban-American Antonio Maceo Brigade, who wanted to join the Cuban revolution in Cuba (see Torres 1995).

Although the marginality of Chongryun Koreans in Japanese society is compensated for by an imaginary "home" in North Korea, they are, in the most direct sense, outsiders in North Korea. Chongryun Koreans do not hold North Korean nationality or legal citizenship there. A difference, I must emphasize, exists between Chongryun Koreans and North Koreans in North Korea. For example, when I visited North Korea as a Chongryun journalist in the mid-1980s, my party supervisor always ensured that I be constantly reminded of my lack of a proper Korean accent and rich revolutionary vocabulary. Chongryun Koreans learn at school the Korean language as used in North Korea, but since they use Korean only at school and speak Japanese at home, their skill is far from comparable to that of North Koreans. All in all, Chongryun Koreans are culturally better-versed in Japan; the stern fact remains that North Korea, which may be "home" in their mind, is a foreign land for them in all practical senses.

Chongryun Koreans' daily lives are full of negotiation between Japan and North Korea, possible homes and impossible homelands. Now that the real North Korea is known to be a place offering little hope – indeed, now that it stands in disarray – an imaginary home North Korea can ironically be embellished, that is, a space that exists in a different realm from its real crisis. Borrowing from Chongryun's old metaphor, it is precisely because everyone knows that North Korea is no longer "a paradise on earth," and more importantly, because everyone knows that they will not have to go back and live there, it is romanticized as a paradise and oasis, as in Jin-su's remarks. This is in parallel to what James Clifford calls a distinction between a nationalist critical longing and the actual nation-building (1994: 307): although Chongryun Koreans are longing for a nation-state entity to identify themselves with, they do not easily surrender to the possibility of merging in North Korea as actual citizens. As has been shown, repatriation has long ceased to be an option. The same, however, goes for Chongryun Koreans' relation to Japan: they resist the possibility of naturalization and of becoming Japanese citizens. Thus, they seem to exist halfway in and out of both North Korea and Japan.

If, as Jonathan Rutherford suggests, "home is where we speak from" (1990: 24), and if, as Stuart Hall suggests, "we cannot speak for very long . . . about 'one experience, one identity,' without acknowledging . . . [its] ruptures and discontinuities" (1990: 225), it would be legitimate to see Chongryun Koreans as having two homes, both real or both imaginary, oscillating between the two, and choosing to speak from one or the other. They see North Korea as home when they speak from their native land which is oasis, cradle, or the place where they cleanse their mind; they see Japan as their home from where they speak about their marginalized existence, their exclusion, and their ambivalent and contradictory identity.

How should we assess this split perception between Japan and North Korea? Should we celebrate this as the appropriation of a metaphorical home by self-empowering agency despite the marginalized position of Koreans in Japan: another case of the victimhood glorified by the victims themselves? My contention is negative to such an approach. Merely to invest the hitherto oppressed social minority with a new power of appropriation amounts only to replicating the oppression by reinterpreting it into something positive: "although they are marginalized, they have the strength of rationalizing their marginalization." Such an intellectual exercise would do nothing but preserve the existing power structure, be it within Chongryun's organizational boundaries or in Japanese society at large. Chongryun Koreans did not awake to North Korea's dire economic situation until much later than did the western understanding. Why this time lag? Jin-su, and to some degree Mrs Chang, call North Korea home away from home, while they are fully aware that they will continue to live in Japan. Why this self-illusion?

This is not to deny Chongryun Koreans the imaginary homeland of North Korea. However, it *is* to assert that they are entitled as much to such a home as to fuller participation in Japanese society. As long as their life in Japan, with their cultural marginalization and second-class citizenship, necessitates the daily negotiation between the two homes, they remain, paradoxically, homeless in a double sense. For of their two homes, neither is viable in terms of residential security and full-fledged civil and national membership. And if so, the reality of double homelessness needs to be recognized. For Chongryun Koreans to achieve a better future in Japan, to escape temporarily and occasionally to the imaginary oasis of North Korea can only be passive and conservative at best, and counterproductive at worst. It cannot bring about a radical transformation and improvement in their everyday life. Rather than celebrating their North Korean homeland, or perhaps in combination with such a celebration, their Japanese home needs to be built into a tangible reality, from where they can speak, insisting on their social and civil rights and claiming everything to which they believe they are entitled. In other words, "home" here is not the oasis that they arrive at from across the ocean, in order to breathe and recuperate, but the place that they themselves build, through their sweat and struggle, in order to live and continue to live. Such an option will be a short-cut for emancipation and full participation in Japanese society, their other home: be it imaginary or real.

Acknowledgements

I am grateful to Mark Selden, Victoria Smith, Charles Armstrong, Richard Grinker, and Chikako Kashiwazaki for their helpful comments and criticisms. A shorter version of this paper was read in a speaker series at the Center for Korean Studies, University of California, Berkeley. I benefited from the fruitful discussion which followed my talk. The interviews are taken from my fieldwork in Japan, funded by the Toyota Foundation, to whom I am very grateful. Finally, I wish to thank Chongryun Koreans who supported and cooperated with my research.

Notes

1 This chapter does not deal with non-Chongryun Koreans in Japan. For views of South Korea as the homeland, as against North Korea as the homeland, see for example Hayes in this volume on Yi Yang-ji.
2 The Japanese Immigration Control Law, passed in October 1951, was hurriedly established under the Allied occupation following the war's end. The law was intended to cover movements in and out of Japanese ports and as such, it was not meant to deal with Koreans and other former colonial subjects such as the Taiwanese, who had been in residence in Japan since before the end of the war, let alone to deal with their children and grandchildren who had been born in Japan (see Ōnuma 1980a: 246–8). Following the 1952 treaty between the USA and Japan, by which Koreans officially lost their Japanese nationality, the 1951 law was automatically applied to them as if they were temporary residents or even visitors in Japan (see Kashiwazaki in this volume).
3 Although the Japanese government at that time considered that the *lex domicilii* proper for Koreans in Japan was that of South Korea (Narige 1964a), this stance was not always followed by court procedures. Some held the view that, at least for those originally coming from northern Korea, North Korean private law could have been applied. Since the North Korean law was not known, the second proper law would be that of Japan (Narige 1964b; Tameike 1959). Others followed the government stance (Kuwata 1959 and 1960), while yet others regarded it proper to consider other factors including individuals' wishes as to which state they associated with, regardless of their provincial origins (Akiba 1960; Egawa and Sawaki 1958; Hayata 1965).
4 The initial North Korean fund was used to build the new lecture hall of Korea University, managed by Chongryun. The fund stopped coming from around the 1980s, reflecting North Korea's economic difficulties. However, the moral and economic impact of the initial fund was deeply appreciated by Koreans in Japan. For Chongryun's education system, see Ryang (1997: chs 1 and 2).
5 The translation of *choguk*, the term North Koreans and Chongryun use to denote the homeland, is strictly speaking a gendered term, fatherland, and not motherland. I use "fatherland" where appropriate in the text despite its sexist connotation, to maintain consistency with the original.

The North Korean homeland 53

6 *Ondol* is a heating system traditional to Korea. A stove in the kitchen is designed to send the heat to the space between the ground and the stone floor, so as not to waste the heat when cooking is done.
7 I am not saying that *all* the repatriates shared the same degree of national pride. Recently revealed news on the early repatriates is full of grim stories. See the later section of the chapter.
8 Chang Myŏng-su, who has had a long-term involvement with the repatriation campaign, points out that the Japan Red Cross documents show the racist attitude held by them toward Koreans in Japan. In a word, the Japanese authorities including the Red Cross wanted to get rid of "trouble-makers" and an "economic burden": labels associated with Koreans in the 1950s and the 1960s (Chang Myŏng-su 1995b). An extensive collection of documents related to the North Korean repatriation can be found in Kim and Takayanagi (1995).
9 We can identify this group of Koreans by the official recording method of Japanese government papers: they are classified under *chōsen*, denoting the Korean peninsula, but not denoting any nationality. This, however, does not mean that we can equate the non-South Korean Koreans with Chongryun-affiliated Koreans, and the holders of South Korean nationality with Chongryun's opponents. Legal status, in other words, does not overlap with political affiliation or lack of it. It also needs to be emphasized that the re-entry permit issued by the Japanese Ministry of Justice has never been established as conferring an automatic "right to return" to where one lives, even after Japan joined the Covenants. It in principle remains a matter that is ultimately at the mercy of the justice minister (Okamoto 1990: 34–5).
10 In 1992 all the Korean permanent residents in Japan, regardless of whether they held permanent residence as a result of the 1965 treaty, or the 1982-type of permanent residence, were unified under the category "special permanent resident." The older permanent residence status enforced the deportation of Koreans who received a prison sentence of one year or longer; the new permanent residence status extended this limit up to seven years or longer. Before 1992, when the permanent residence of Koreans had not been upgraded to enable them to enjoy wider civil rights in Japan, each Korean person had to petition (albeit nominally) the justice minister asking permission to come back to Japan each time they traveled outside Japan.
11 According to a Chongryun officer, these routes, although not officially closed, have made much narrower than before by the North Korean authorities, owing to the recent economic and environmental crises in North Korea.
12 Individual circumstances, including all names, have been modified to a sufficient extent to conceal the identity of interviewees in order to protect their privacy.
13 The interpretation offered below differs for first-generation Koreans who retain memories of their native place in the Korean peninsula. Many first-generation Chongryun activists told me that they did not find it difficult to perceive North Korea as an extension of their homeland in the south. Although obviously southern towns and villages they left decades ago for Japan would have no similarity to North Korea today, the fact that they stand on soil directly connected to the home in which they were born and grew up is understood to be very significant for them. Japan-born younger generations do not experience this raw sense of homecoming when they visit North Korea. A parallel case of generational difference upon returning to the homeland can be found among Palestinian refugees of the West Bank (see Bisharat 1997), while the opposite case of one-and-a-half and second generations identifying the homeland that the first generation abandoned can be found among Cuban-American radicals (see Torres 1995).
14 Mrs Chang's words remind me of Salman Rushdie's experience of finding Bombay, and especially his father's house, exactly as he had imagined upon his visit. It was connected to his having been looking at an old photo of his father's house (Rushdie

1981: 9–10). After all, imagination always presupposes memory and other prior information, as in the cases of Yu-ja and Mrs Chang.

15 Interviews with these two individuals were carried out mainly in Japanese. At times, I used the expression *furusato*, native place, phrasing it as "is visiting North Korea something like returning to *furusato*?" At other times, I used *ie* or *uchi*, meaning "house" or "home" in Japanese, saying "is visiting North Korea something like returning home?" Jin-su and other more politically oriented Chongryun Koreans used the Korean word for native place, *kohyang*, perhaps because of their exposure to Korean as teacher or organizational activist.

16 I am grateful to Han Geon-Soo and Philip Taylor for drawing my attention to de Certeau.

3 Political correctness, postcoloniality, and the self-representation of "Koreanness" in Japan

Koichi Iwabuchi

No nation is pure or homogeneous in terms of race, ethnicity and culture. Any nation contains cultural difference within its boundary. This difference is, however, often forgotten in the discursive representation of the nation as a racially and culturally homogeneous entity. As Stuart Hall argues, "a nation is not only a political entity but something which produces meanings – a system of cultural representation" (1992: 292). Likewise, Japan's national identity is produced and reproduced by discursive strategies, rather than by a reality itself (Iwabuchi 1994). No one would deny, for example, that since the colonization of Korea in 1910, if not before, resident Koreans have been found in Japan, and about 700,000 of them continue to live in Japan today.[1] Their existence, however, has not been acknowledged as constitutive of Japan, its society and culture, in either Japanese official discourse or the media. The Japanese media have tended to represent resident Koreans as irrelevant to Japanese national life, by neglecting them altogether, or representing them in such a manner that they are confined to a space of eternal victimhood: victims of Japan's past colonialism. Resident Koreans had to be forgotten or somehow completely separated from the ongoing process of constructing modern Japan in order to imagine Japan as a monoracial nation, an imagining which necessitated a clear break from the colonialist past: resident Koreans are neither *in* nor *of* Japan.

This chapter explores an emerging alternative to the Japanese media representation of resident Koreans through the analysis of a popular 1993 comedy film, *Tsuki wa dotchini deteiru* (Where is the Moon?, hereafter referred to as *Moon*). *Moon* was written, directed, and produced by resident Koreans, who attempt by means of self-representation to go beyond both invisibility and the role of victim given to them in the Japanese media. The film marked an important historical, postcolonial turn in terms of the media representation of resident Koreans. Precisely because of its challenge against the conventional representation of resident Koreans in Japan, *Moon* achieved the first commercial success for a Korea-related film in Japan, and was enthusiastically received by Japanese viewers as well as resident Koreans. The film posed, moreover, a double critique in the sense that it drew our attention to the silence on the subject of resident Koreans by the Japanese media, and at the same time raised serious questions which tended to be neglected in the self-representation by resident Koreans, such as intra-ethnic social relations among resident Koreans themselves and inter-ethnic relations between resident Koreans, Japanese, and other non-Japanese residents in Japan in the 1990s. In this way, *Moon* articulated the beginning of a deconstruction of an essentialized Korean subject – a subject who was voiceless and had only the face of the oppressed – by representing impure Korean identities and their ambivalent existence in Japan.

Though groundbreaking in this regard, *Moon* nevertheless has its limitations. It contains, like all media texts, complications, ambiguity, and contradictions. *Moon* at once empowers and solicits the co-optation by the represented – Koreans – of reproducing unequal power relations. Crucial for the latter point is the manner in which it opened a way for comfortable Japanese consumption of a new stereotype, of self-sufficient resident Koreans who are no longer concerned with Japan's colonialist past. Giving insufficient attention to intra-ethnic differences and to the historical memory of resident Koreans, a significant factor in its Japanese context, *Moon* risks producing a new representative image of resident Koreans which renders Japan's colonial responsibilities irrelevant. However, these limitations of *Moon* are related as much to the position of the Japanese media consumers who are keen on erasing and absorbing (and hence, "Japanizing") cultural others, as to the film's textuality, as we shall see in the following.

"I hate Koreans, but I like you": beyond taboo and invisible presence

Moon is a comedy about the everyday life of a resident Korean taxi driver, Ch'ung-nam, or Tadao as his name is pronounced in Japanese. (I will use Tadao in future, since the protagonist is called this in the film.) The story is an adaptation of Yang Sŏg-il's autobiographical novel, *Takushī kyōsōkyoku* (Taxi Crazy Rhapsody, 1981). The film revolves around Tadao's experiences of living in Japan as a resident Korean in the 1990s: inter-ethnic and inter-racial romance, work relationships, family life, and his personal reflections on them. Sai Yōichi, a resident Korean director, was so excited by Yang's novel that he had been determined to produce a film since its publication in 1981, but the project took twelve years. All major production houses were reluctant to be involved with a Korea-related film. Their reluctance reflects a Japanese media convention, by which resident Koreans are predominantly dealt with either as a taboo or as tragic victims of Japanese colonialism. Neither of these alternatives lend themselves to a desirable market product (see Nomura 1996). The legend also has it that Korea-related films had never attracted a wide audience in Japan's media market. Some production houses asked the director to make the protagonist Japanese character. In addition, *Moon's* liberal use of *sabetsuyōgo* (discriminatory words) caused great difficulty for the Japanese film industry. Even after *Moon's* box-office success, it was a problem for Japanese free-to-air TV stations to broadcast the film (*Asahi shinbun*, evening edition, 18 March 1994). The question is to what extent the media industry was genuinely concerned over the use of discriminatory words: rather, the problem seems to have been the film's "Koreanness." Hesitation and tacit resistance among Japanese mass media, particularly audiovisual media, manifested their role in gatekeeping Japan's desire to forget its colonialist past and to imagine "Japan" as a racially homogeneous nation.

One reason it has become taboo to feature resident Koreans on mass media is to avoid possible criticism and denunciation by the minority group that is represented. This concern for rather hypocritical political correctness began in the late 1960s in response to a denunciation strategy adopted by Buraku kaihō dōmei (Buraku Liberation League), a political organization of the largest minority group, Burakumin, who are the descendants of outcasts in the premodern Japan. Denunciation has been useful and necessary in limiting the circulation of derogatory words and negative depictions of minority groups. It has undoubtedly had some positive effect in dissipating negative images of marginalized groups. Japanese media are, however, little concerned with political change or reform. One unfortunate outcome of this well-intentioned move of minority groups is excessive self-censorship of Japanese mass media, particularly in the television. Fear of denunciation has led to a generalized avoidance of issues relating to ethnic and other minorities, rather than searching for alternative, more democratic representation. As a result the minority groups, including resident Koreans, have seldom been represented on television.

Chōsenjin (Korean), for example, is not a discriminatory word in itself, but its use has been self-censored by the mass media because it was used in a derogatory way in conjunction with ethnic discrimination against Koreans. *Chōsen*, originally the name of an ancient Korean state, was resurrected by the Japanese colonial government when the country was annexed. *Chōsenjin*, the term referring to the people in the colony Korea, took on the connotations of inferiority through the reports of Japanese journalism (see Weiner 1989). In those, *chōsenjin* were an incorrigible mob; they were filthy, uncivilized, and violent; they cheated, polluted, and caused trouble, and so on. It was as *chōsenjin* that the image of Koreans was constructed in Japanese popular discourse as unruly people with criminal tendencies. The censorship of discriminatory language in the manual of media correctness in postwar Japan is therefore a curious inversion of this one-sided colonial media coverage, an attempt to cope with a historical problem of the media's own creation.

Needless to say, social and ethnic discrimination directed against resident Koreans is not simply internal to the media representation. It exists on a societal level, from governmental discourse down to the everyday life of ordinary citizens. Nevertheless, it is true that the media plays a constitutive role in reproducing the discrimination and stigma that resident Koreans bear. In conjunction with the lack of proper historical education concerning its colonial past in the postwar Japanese school curriculum, media silence about resident Koreans and the name *chōsen*, far from providing the viewers with correctives, became an effective accomplice for the Japanese state's obliteration of its colonial past. If, as Pierre Bourdieu argued, the limit of language is the limit of politics (1991), the absence of reference to Korea or *chōsen* placed a grave limitation on the Japanese viewers' imagination of, and hence relation to, those resident Koreans who may simply be their neighbors or classmates (see Nomura 1996).

The invisible presence of Koreans in Japan is a social effect produced by the media representation of resident Koreans: the existence of resident Koreans in Japan is apparent but, on the individual level, difference remains unrecognized. To avoid racial discrimination, many resident Koreans are hiding their descent by using Japanese names as they were forced to do under Japanese colonial rule. Owing to the physical similarity between Japanese and resident Koreans, it is almost impossible to distinguish between the two by appearance. Unlike blacks, their bodily difference never "implodes" in Japanese eyes. In the mass media as well as in everyday life, Japanese people encounter Koreans without knowing that they are of Korean descent. Because of the difficulty of being employed in more mainstream occupations such as large companies, many resident Koreans enter the sport and entertainment world. With a small number of exceptions, they also hide their Korean origin. The most prominent example was the professional wrestler, Rikidōzan. In the late 1950s and 1960s, he became a national hero because he fought against American wrestlers, at that time symbols of Japan's old enemy and present master. There were rumors of his origin, but it was only after his death that his Korean descent was exposed (Hwang Min-gi 1992).

Moon tries to deconstruct these reified images, and the invisible presence of resident Koreans in which the everyday life of "Koreans-next-door" is totally missing. The film was a phenomenal box-office success as a Korea-related film, and won most of the prestigious film awards in Japan in 1993. (A sequel to *Moon* is under consideration.) This popularity was quite unexpected by the Japanese film industry, but the commercial success of *Moon* was precisely because of its challenging and mocking of the Japanese media's superficial practices of political correctness, which had stiffened the segregation between Japanese and resident Koreans. The film was acclaimed for liberating the Japanese film world and its audiences from this suffocating situation by unmasking – not concealing – the existence of Korea-related derogatory words and racist attitudes in the everyday lives and minds of Japanese. For example, a Japanese punch-drunk taxi driver, a co-worker of Tadao, repeatedly tells him "I hate Koreans but I like you, Chūsan" (*Chōsenjin wa kirai dakedo Chūsan wa sukida*) ("Chū" is a Japanese pronunciation of "Ch'ung," the protagonist's name). A provocative and deliberate recourse to the derogatory term, *chōsenjin*, is used here to bring home to the Japanese audience their indifference and reluctance to learn about resident Koreans. The function of *chōsenjin* parallels the positive use of the term "black" in African-American politics. Using one's own name, a name slandered and defamed by one's oppressors, proved to be an effective weapon in reminding them of their wrongdoing. *Moon* radically destabilizes the complacency that "ordinary" Japanese feel in accommodating their daily encounter with individual resident Koreans, and invokes the dominant racist images Japanese have of faceless resident Koreans.

The film also caricatures the superficial liberal stance of Japanese who seem knowledgeable and sympathetic to resident Koreans. A tipsy young male customer

PC, postcoloniality, and self-representation 59

turns the conversation to the issue of resident Koreans in Japan after noticing Tadao's ID plate. On the one hand, the customer reads Tadao's family name in its Japanese reading "Ga" and conspicuously sticks with it, even after Tadao tells him that its correct Korean form is "Kang." On the other hand, the customer brings up the topic of "*zainichi kankokuchōsenjin mondai*" (issues related to resident South and North Koreans in Japan). Expressing the issue in this way, signaling the complexity of the question of North and South Korean affiliation among resident Koreans in Japan, rather than using *chōsenjin* (Korean) *mondai* or *kankokujin* (South Korean) *mondai*, conveys to the viewer the impression that the customer wants to display his political awareness to the Korean driver. His subsequent conversation, however, reveals his shallowness and insensitivity, when he describes his visit to his resident Korean friend's house as a child:

(T: Tadao, C: customer)

> C: His grandma spoke to me in damned thick Korean. I really felt sorry to see my Korean friend hang down his head, 'cause, you know, he was embarrassed.
> T: Since she lived in Japan, she should have spoken Japanese, shouldn't she?
> C: Yeah, you think so too, Mr Ga?
> T: Of course.

The customer then introduces the issue of "comfort women" (the Korean women who were forced into prostitution for the Japanese military during the war), but he casually dismisses the issue, saying that they were just prostitutes anyway and it happened before he was born, as if, therefore, it is none of his business. Tadao, for his part, remains nonchalant and pretends to be ignorant of the issue. The customer – indifferent to Tadao's response – continues further to reveal his ignorance and acceptance of the stereotypical image of Korean criminality and tendency to violence.

> C : I am trying to read as much about *kankokuchōsen mondai* as possible. The Los Angeles riots were really terrifying. I was amazed to see Koreans so enthusiastically shooting guns.
> T: Indeed, it was terrifying.
> C: Maybe that's what Korean power is all about, isn't it? I wanna experience it myself some day.
> T: Yes, me too.
> C: Maybe I should go to Seoul soon.
> T: I would like to go with you. Please be my guide (laughter).

When the cab reaches the destination, however, the customer dashes off without paying. Tadao, after a long chase, catches the customer. Outraged and exhausted, Tadao nevertheless does not even touch him, takes money from his purse, gives him the exact amount of change, and says loudly "Thank you very much." The customer, now intimidated, groveling and begging not to be hurt, still addresses him as "Mr Ga." Tadao for his part spews out all his grudges against him by kicking a rubbish bin.

We are reminded here how Japanese political correctness is superficial – using a correct name categorizing Korean issues in Japan but not bothering to use a correct personal name for Tadao – and how Japanese have not tried seriously to confront resident Koreans as individuals. Often those Japanese who appear to act and speak in a politically correct manner, and who appear sympathetic with resident Koreans, do not in fact fully understand the extent of difficulties resident Koreans face in their everyday lives. In the final instance, they avoid any confrontation with them. In other words, although they may be able to identify the Korean issue as an onlooker, they are not even aware that they themselves share time and space with resident Koreans. Ironically, "Koreanness" for those "politically correct" Japanese citizens, personified by the customer in *Moon*, is merely a reified public image and as such, is as much dehumanizing as outright discrimination against Koreans. Someone who actually says "I hate Koreans" – just like Tadao's alcoholic co-worker – is in a sense more sincere and easier to deal with, because s/he is at least directly candid about his/her prejudice.

Tadao's behavior to the customer is a reminder of the vulnerable position in which resident Koreans are placed in Japan. Tadao, a foreign national, is constrained from attacking against a Japanese national by the possibility of harsh penalties, including deportation. Tadao's actions also suggest that he does not want to owe anything to the Japanese, who are here represented in the hypocritical and deceitful figure of the customer. In this way, the film is as much a critique of the obliteration of the individual humanity of resident Koreans from Japanese society, as a depiction of the everyday life of resident Koreans themselves.

From political correctness to postcoloniality

Moon also rejects the dogmatic discourse of Japanese intellectuals and activists condemning Japan's neglect of its war responsibility and racial discrimination against Koreans. Although this self-critical attitude is sincere and should not be dismissed cynically, these obsessive attacks on Japan's colonialist past and racist present tend to reinforce the image of resident Koreans as weak victims. Lee Seijaku (1997), a third-generation resident Korean in Japan, for example, wrote about her experience of such constraints. When she spoke against this one-sided view in a symposium, Japanese participants condemned her for lacking sympathy with "real" victims and for therefore having been assimilated into Japan. As she attends élite schools, her relatively privileged position deprives her of "authenticity" in being a resident Korean in Japan. Her problem exemplifies Iain Chambers' observation:

> The corollary that seals this logic and finally condemns the subordinate to the eternal role of 'authenticity' is that success is suspect: it automatically

suggests a sell-out. . . . Expression and representation are compelled to support the collective burden and unity of a presumed representation.
(Chambers 1994: 38)

While acknowledging the existence of harsh discrimination against resident Koreans in Japan, Lee is frustrated that her subjectivity is entirely contained within the faceless collective category of repressed resident Koreans.

Moon is not the first film produced by resident Koreans in Japan, but its attempt to go beyond the representation of resident Koreans as victims marks a sharp difference from other self-representations of resident Koreans, which have tended to focus on the suffering of resident Koreans from the dual tragedies of Japan's past colonialism and the subsequent partition of their motherland into north and south. In 1989, for example, *Yun no machi* (The Town of Yun) was produced by another resident Korean director, Kim U-sŏng. Both directors, Sai Yōichi and Kim U-sŏng, aimed to produce a film of the "real" lives of resident Koreans which goes beyond a reified image of resident Koreans as victims. The crucial difference between *Moon* and *Yun* and the two directors can be seen in terms of their conceptions of the realism of representing resident Koreans, a difference which seems to have much to do with the popularity of the films. It is suggestive in this respect that Kim was also interested in producing a film based upon the original novel of *Moon*, but eventually gave up the attempt, in the recognition that the novel did not suit his directing style (Sai *et al.* 1994: 42). His realism, as we see it in *Yun*, tends to stress the hardships Koreans in Japan face in their everyday lives. In *Yun*, the director seeks to represent a Korean reality by using a real third-generation resident Korean woman as a heroine, so that her performance in the film reflects her own identity issue (Kim U-sŏng 1994). *Yun* is a story about the marriage of the third-generation resident Korean woman and a Japanese man, focusing on the issues of ethnic discrimination, nationality and naturalization, and the unification of the two Korean states by following up the process of their marriage. Despite the director's intention of depicting the heroine's personal world, the collective hardship of resident Koreans pervades *Yun* to the extent that it overshadows the representation of personalities and everyday life (Ochi 1994).

In contrast, most of the cast of *Moon* are Japanese, including the actor who plays Tadao. The director never thought that using resident Koreans was necessary. Instead he followed the standard practice of audition and selected actors on merit, and most of them were Japanese. The story of *Moon* focuses on the multifaceted experience of the everyday life of resident Koreans. Consequently, it rejects the fixed assumption that Korea-related texts can only deal with Japanese colonization, harsh discrimination, and the agony that resident Koreans face. In *Moon*, we see not only the uneven encounters between resident Koreans and Japanese, but also those between resident Koreans and other ethnic minorities. This is exemplified in the love affair between Tadao and a Filipina bar hostess, Connie, who works for a bar owned by Tadao's mother. The presence of Tadao's mother in the film also allows for the depiction of the intergenerational relationship among resident Koreans. All of these issues are comically depicted through Tadao's apolitical, detached, but well-balanced eyes. *Moon*'s realism is based not on the political consciousness of its protagonists or the political correctness of the director, but on the self-relativizing witty representation of the everyday lives of "ordinary" resident Koreans. Its characters are not totally indifferent to politics, but are not overcommitted to nationalistic ideology. They know very well how to live as resident Koreans in Japan, sometimes ironically laughing at themselves and at other times embracing their ethnic heritage. By rejecting the "bargain sale" of the history of suffering and tragedy of resident Koreans, as the director Sai Yōichi put it (1994), the ambivalence that resident Koreans experience in their everyday lives is depicted in a more nuanced manner in *Moon* than in *Yun*.

Moon's opening scene is a wedding banquet in which the conflict between two resident Korean groups, one identifying with North Korea and the other with the south, is represented not as a political conflict but as part of daily reality. A middle-aged male guest who identifies himself with South Korea repeatedly complains to the banquet presenter that there are too many speeches by supporters of North Korea. It is an exaggerated caricature of Korean ethnic politics in Japan, which is a life-and-death issue for the older generation, but is nothing but conventional routine for the younger generation such as Tadao. We see this when Tadao attempts to seduce women with the line "Let's unite our bodies for the sake of the unification of the two Koreas." Thus, Tadao appropriates the politically charged term, "the reunification of Korea," for his personal game, rather than for ethno-national politics. *Moon* shows us the multiple levels of relations to the homeland politics held by resident Koreans in Japan.

The suffering of Koreans by Japanese colonialism is also used as a topic for Tadao to arouse the interest of a Filipina bar hostess, Connie. He lies that his brothers were killed in the war to solicit her sympathy. His attempt to exploit their shared minority status by proposing that he and Connie unite to form solidarity between the oppressed is cut short by Connie, who directly faces Tadao and says, "You are seducing me, aren't you?" In this way, the film unfolds the world of resident Koreans where politics is in everyday life and everyday life is full of "political" jokes. Because of the script's mocking tone, the satire becomes more effective and, in a way, it becomes a more serious critique of the monolithic labeling of resident Koreans as victims.

In paying attention to inter-generational relations within Korean communities, the film depicts Tadao's mother as tough but typically overcaring. She has Kim Il Sung's portrait in her apartment and sends goods and cash to her repatriated family in North Korea. While the love affair between Tadao and Connie – between a Japan-born Korean man and an Osaka-accented Filipina woman – represents a new phase of Japan's multiethnic reality, Tadao's mother's opposition to their relationship is attributed to her concern for ethnic "purity." She insists that Tadao marry a Korean: a typical attitude of first-generation parents. But the film shows that this is hardly likely. Tadao is not interested in getting married at all and especially not to a Korean, an attitude that is becoming increasingly common among younger-generation resident Koreans in Japan.

Such self-relativizing moments depicted in *Moon* reflects a shift in resident Koreans' identification with their homeland. As can be seen in the case of Tadao and his mother, the divide between the older and younger generations has become too wide to be accommodated in a simple picture. Older generations experienced colonialism, the Second World War, the Korean War, and economic hardship during and after the war. These hardships cultivated a dream of homecoming, which became more and more unrealistic as time passed by. The subsequent partition of Korea and the self-alienation policy of the organizations of Korean communities in Japan (see Ryang 1992) emphasized their links with Korean origins and fostered their image of a putative Korean ethnic identity. This has long shaped the form of political and cultural self-expression of Korean communities in Japan: resident Koreans dealt with themes and stories of ethno-nationalism, with the dream of returning to the homeland on the one hand, and the image of national traitors who go through humiliating processes of assimilation and naturalization, hiding their ethnic origin, a negative "double" of the former, on the other.

Younger generations do not necessarily feel that the Korean peninsula is their homeland any longer (see e.g. Field 1993; Takeda, Kang, and Katō 1995). Their permanent residence in Japan has become an undeniable fact. Since the early 1980s, they have displayed more affirmative views of their own hybridity, and a search for a third way "looking neither to naturalization, which would require them to abandon their ethnicity, nor to returning to a divided or even a unified homeland" (Field 1993: 646). The crucial question concerning their national/cultural identity is how they can accommodate, as Werner Sollors (1986) puts it, both their "descent" and "consent" or, in the words of Paul Gilroy (1990), it is not only "where we are from" but "where we are at" that matters.

In the self-representation of resident Koreans in Japan, "where you are at" has tended predominantly to be constituted by the discursive act of fostering one's homeland in their consciousness. As Ien Ang argues concerning the Chinese diaspora, "the adversity of 'where you are at' produces the cultivation of a lost 'where you're from'" (1994: 10). However, the attachment of older generations to the homeland has been disturbed by the unequivocal differences between resident Koreans in Japan and Koreans in Korea. In Korea, overseas Koreans tend to be regarded as inauthentic Koreans. Given especially the ambivalent sentiment that Korea still retains toward Japan's past colonial rule, resident Koreans from Japan are particularly looked at with suspicion. The self divided between "Japan" and "Korea" has been a main theme for the cultural expressions of resident Koreans in Japan, but their in-betweenness tended to be negatively represented in terms of lacking authenticity as either Korean or Japanese (see Yi Yang-ji depicted in Hayes in this volume). This is a situation in which "the question of 'where you're from' is made to overwhelm the reality of 'where you're at', the politics of diaspora becomes a disempowering rather than an empowering one, a hindrance to 'identity' rather than an enabling principle" (Ang 1994: 15).

It is this imprisonment within "where resident Koreans are from" that *Moon* tries to overcome by depicting an ambivalent "reality" of "where resident Koreans are at." It is not simply represented by self-reflexively making fun of the way in which a history of suffering is always used as a linchpin of Korean identity in Japan. *Moon* also elucidates the relatively privileged position and "Japanized" ethnic identity of resident Koreans, by juxtaposing resident Koreans with other ethnic minorities who came to Japan only recently. For example, Tadao's mother, the owner of a nightclub, is rather proud of her achievement as a proprietor and complains about the laziness and "foreignness" of Filipina bar hostesses. She preaches to her Filipina employees, referring to the hardship to which she has been subjected to as a resident Korean in order to achieve a success in Japan. However, her story is met with giggles and indifference. For Filipina bar hostesses, she is employer, boss, and exploiter. She repeatedly reminds the hostesses of the difference between them and herself in terms of their acquired level of knowledge of Japanese culture. "In Japan, do as Japanese do"; "Don't you know the Japanese saying 'Blood is thicker than water'?"; "This is a Japanese custom, you Filipina would never understand." This indicates that resident Koreans in Japan have become more "Japanese" than other newcomers. It also suggests a double standard of resident Koreans in deploying their ethnicity to Japanese and to other less powerful ethnic minorities. *Moon* exposes how resident Koreans, inescapably "contaminated" by Japanese culture, reproduce the same discriminatory attitudes they have suffered from in their dealings with other ethnic minorities. This becomes clear when the mother quarrels with Connie over her relationship with Tadao. When Connie fiercely strikes back, the mother finally throws out the fatal words to Connie, "Go back to your own country!" Her outburst is followed by a moment of self-reflection as she remembers the same insulting phrase uttered by Japanese to herself in the past.

Moon's rejection of self-victimizing, and its strategy to represent the ambivalent existence of "ordinary" resident Koreans in Japan, offer the possibility of overcoming the framework of rigid opposition between the colonized and the colonizer. The construction of Korean-as-victim deters both resident Koreans and Japanese from engaging seriously with the cultural differences of resident Koreans in terms of their diasporic experiences, by confining the relationship between Japanese and resident Koreans to a binary opposition of oppressor and oppressed. The unfortunate by-product of Japanese political correctness, revolving around the two poles – the suppression of the existence of resident Koreans in Japan and the obsession with the story of oppressed resident Koreans – has tended to discourage engagement with the other PC, postcoloniality within Japan. Although the meaning and theoretical connotations of "post" in postcolonial have attracted much criticism in terms of the sweeping generalization of diverse colonial experiences, ahistorical erasure of the lingering colonial legacy, and the obscuring of the uneven power relations between the dominant and the dominated (e.g. McClintock 1992; Shohat 1992), "postcolonial" here is not meant in an ahistorical sense of severing any connections with the past. Rather it articulates a historically embedded attempt to "re-read the very binary form in which the colonial encounter has for so long itself been represented" when such a binary form no longer empowers the struggle of the (former) colonized (Hall 1996a: 247).

This is an attempt by resident Koreans to rethink the history of Japanese colonialism by attending to the multifarious ways in which they have negotiated the oppression in colonial and postcolonial Japan. It is their attempt to deconstruct the notion of an essential Korean subject by attending to the hitherto neglected complexity and diversity among resident Koreans. *Moon* tries to engage the fact of hybridity, of "*zainichi*" (residing in Japan) as "*a priori* impure identity." In other words, the film treats the in-betweenness or improper "Japaneseness" as well as incomplete "Koreanness" as an unambiguous fact. The film liberates resident Koreans from the burden of history, which imposed on them the Manichean oppositioning. The film allows a subtle escape from the tyranny of collective memory to a more nuanced subjectivity, but one which is nevertheless embedded within history. It opens a way for "thinking the cultural consequences of the colonizing process diasporically, in non-original ways – that is, through rather than around hybridity" (Hall 1996a: 251).

The productive potential of "post" in postcolonial does not lie simply in its celebratory articulation of an ambiguous, hybrid subject, either. Rather it is to turn our attention to a new configuration of power relations and identity politics which can no longer adequately be represented by a clearly-demarcated opposition between the colonizer and the colonized. For the case of resident Koreans in Japan, this emerging conjuncture is also marked by the shifting material conditions of resident Koreans, the diversifying sense of identification with Korea and Japan among resident Koreans, and the comparatively advantageous position of resident Koreans *vis-à-vis* the newcomers among ethnic minorities, the influx of which has been facilitated by global capitalism. At the same time, the emerging postcolonial engagement of resident Koreans in Japan, does not erase what it precedes. It is undoubtedly over-determined by Japanese colonialism. However, in the new conjuncture, lingering uneven power relations between the dominant and the dominated are also articulated in different ways. A postcolonial turn which we can discern in *Moon* is accompanied by new, emergent political questions and criticisms.

Japanese consumption of Korean self-representation

One of the strongest criticisms of *Moon* was of its lack of a feminist perspective and the masculinist deployment of the stereotypical images of Filipinas. Connie is depicted as a sturdy and self-confident Filipina bar hostess who has worked in Japan since she was fifteen years old. Her fluent Japanese in the Osaka dialect, combined with a foreign accent, also marks her strong personality. Tadao has a relationship with her, but keeps on neglecting her proposal that they move together to the Philippines. Sex, lies, and escape (and a bit of violence in the final instance) characterize Tadao's involvement with Connie. Chŏng Yŏng-he, a second-generation female resident Korean scholar in Japan, denounces the film from the perspective of minority feminism as second-rate masculinist and racist: the hero's dependency on, and exploitative relation with, a Filipino bar hostess appears to be no different from other Japanese films (1994b). Li Sang-t'e, a male resident Korean commentator, criticizes the film makers for slyly having tried to deconstruct a reified image of resident Koreans in Japan by exploiting another reified image, that of Filipinos (1993). Ann Kaneko is also critical of the representation of the Filipina hostess in the film:

> Despite the efforts of the film's Korean-Japanese makers at tackling the larger issues of race relations in Japan, especially dealing with the situation of Korean-Japanese, their own limited vision of Filipina women prompts them to present a rather stereotypical view of them, no different than the images produced by their Japanese counterparts. Although it is a harder look and is less patronizing, Moreno's character [Connie] is still the caricatured, streetwise, and determined hostess, quite adept at using people to get her way.
> (Kaneko 1995: 68)

The director, Sai Yōichi, justified the use of a Filipina by saying that the character was based upon a close interview with an actual Filipina hostess. He acknowledged that he was very conscious of the stereotypical image of Filipinos but concluded from his research that the most appropriate character for the partner of a bawdy Korean was still a "cheerful, and optimistic" Filipina (Sai 1993). His defense seems to be based upon his conviction that a Filipina hostess, like other members of ethnic minorities in Japan, is not just a weak victim but a strong-minded person. In this regard, Connie's character in *Moon* differs from the typical Japanese representations of Filipinos. Nevertheless, it remains an open question whether *Moon*'s depiction of Connie reproduces another stereotype of Filipina women in Japan.

Sai also confesses that a Filipina character was not his first choice. Writing the scenario of the protagonist's love affairs, which do not appear in Yang Sŏg-il's original novel, he first tried to use a Korean female character as a partner for Tadao. However, he felt he could not produce a subtle and satiric love story by using a Korean couple, because such a story would tend to be clouded by the history of the hardship of resident Koreans, as was the case with *Yun*. He admitted that the script would overly reflect his own experiences of romantic relationships, which did not escape the image of national suffering, and that Tadao would look too heroic a figure for a protagonist of a love comedy, if his partner were to be cast as a resident Korean (Sai 1994; Sai *et al.* 1994).

This reminds us that the original novel retains a more critical perspective on Japanese historical and social discrimination against resident Koreans, by depicting the emotional conflicts of a resident Korean taxi driver. In the film, however, the owner of the taxi company is changed from Japanese to a resident Korean and the conflictual relationship between Japanese and resident Koreans fades away. This is not to say that the film should have dealt with serious issues, as more orthodox critics would argue. However, the very existence of some

PC, postcoloniality, and self-representation 67

issues which were left out in the process of producing a comedy seems to articulate the limitations of *Moon*. Even if the message of *Moon* is the denial of any politicized message in its text (Sai 1993), it cannot entirely be free from a politics of representation, which the textual absence evokes.

In relation to this, it should be remembered that *Moon*'s self-reflexive text can be received without discomfort by some Japanese audiences who have a desire, whether overt or covert, to forget and suppress memories of Japanese colonial rule and its brutal invasion of other parts of Asia. The film was easily consumed by Japanese viewers as a funny inside story about resident Koreans. As An Une (An Une *et al.* 1994) points out, a Japanese film such as *Gakiteikoku* (The Empire of Kids, Izutsu Kazuyuki, director, 1981), deals more radically with racial discrimination and derogatory language against resident Koreans. It is a story about Japanese and resident Korean delinquent high school students in the Osaka region. This film, An argues, did not attract much attention because it was produced by a Japanese crew. The very fact that *Moon* is produced entirely by resident Koreans gives license to Japanese viewers comfortably to enjoy what is happening in the Korean community, because it is a story of another world which has little to do with the Japanese themselves.

Likewise, many resident Korean intellectuals and activists expressed a sense of anger and frustration with the Japanese acclamation of *Moon*. Li Sang-t'e, for example, wrote that there were neither fresh insights nor an empowering message in this film for resident Koreans (1993). According to Li, the mere use of some provocative phrases such as "I hate Koreans" and the exposure of trivial details of the everyday life of resident Koreans which had not been known by many Japanese, do not contribute to deconstructing the already reified image of resident Koreans in Japan. Chŏng Yŏng-he (1994a) also expressed her frustration by saying that the film did not properly capture the reality of Korean communities in Japan, a reality which was much more exciting and diverse. According to Chŏng, the film simply exploits the ignorance of Japanese audiences about resident Koreans in Japan. She argues that "it is something like a bullied person finally attaining the status of entertainer by performing as a clown" (1994a: 7). Chŏng, in another article, warns of the possibility of ethnic minorities collaborating in the reproduction of existing power relations between the dominant and the dominated by acting as a "commissioned" speaker of the latter (1996). *Moon* is still the kind of text that the dominant Japanese can allow, because a resident Korean who does not care much about Japan's colonial past can easily be chosen as a new representative, "token" figure of resident Koreans in Japan (Spivak and Gunew 1993: 194–5).

Moon's success caused some popular magazines to run feature stories about resident Koreans in Japan. In these texts, young streetwise figures are shown as the new types of resident Koreans in Japan. *Spa!*, a popular weekly magazine for youth, for example, had a feature story, "Tōshindai no zainichi chōsenjin" (Unwrapping the reality of resident Koreans in Japan) (10 November 1993). It shows two pictures of a young female third-generation resident Korean: one in Korean ethnic dress and with a serious face, and the other in casual jeans and sweater with a smile. The article quotes a Japanese person who saw the pictures commenting that she did not look different from Japanese. Although the article might aim to multiply the images of resident Koreans in Japan, the dichotomized representation in the two pictures connotes that the "true" picture of resident Koreans is the one which she is not in ethnic dress, as though the visible differences of resident Koreans are false and perhaps, undesirable. The article featured the producer of *Moon*, Li Bong-u, who was characterized as a representative of third-generation resident Koreans in Japan:

> Li Bong-u is one of the jaunty third-generation resident Koreans, whose lifestyle is characterized by the new, innovative view that "we do not care about the thirty-six-year long Japanese colonial rule. What is most important is my life of here and now."
> ("Tōshindai no zainichi chōsenjin," 10 November 1993: 121)

Echoing this stance of the producer, *Moon* successfully destabilizes the fixed image of resident Koreans in Japan as victims, but produces a new stereotypical image of "hybrid" resident Koreans as nonchalant, apolitical youth.

The issue of tokenism reminds us of the significance of articulating "where you are from" in the Japanese context, because its defeat in the Second World War allowed Japan to escape any serious confrontation with decolonization and its aftermath in the former colonies. The articulation of the impure Korean subject in the postwar Japan must accompany the critical examination of the colonial past, because there is always a danger that the "post" of postcolonial masks the issue of Japanese war responsibility, and the difference of resident Koreans is so easily forgotten. It can be argued that mainstream Japanese only appreciate the superficial and stale representation of Korean lives and feel a sense of "fresh surprise" from *Moon*, as if they had so far had nothing to do with the Korean community in Japan and had totally forgotten the historical origins of the resident Korean communities in Japanese colonialism (Chŏng 1994b: 7). The ahistorical reception of *Moon* by Japanese audiences seems to be indicative of their refusal seriously to confront resident Koreans as "others." It renders the film a defense for Japan's achievement of internationalization and its tolerance for multiculturalism, which postulates a clearly demarcated cultural hierarchy and leaves unchallenged the hegemonic position of the dominant group, the Japanese.

From the Japanese side, the existence of resident Koreans does not bother them as long as they are like "us." It is often the case when the descent of a fellow resident Korean is revealed or confessed, that Japanese react in an assimilationist way, saying "Never mind your descent. I think you are completely Japanese." Nomura Susumu points out that most Japanese people do not understand that the acknowledgement of their sameness with the Japanese is offensive to resident Koreans. A woman whose mother is a first-generation resident Korean told Nomura that she wanted her friends to listen seriously to her confession and acknowledge her difference as the base of their friendship (Nomura 1996: 73).

The lack of sensitivity on the part of the Japanese to the cultural difference of resident Koreans in Japan has much in common with Japanese colonial ideology. It is often pointed out that the Japanese capacity for assimilating foreign cultures has been extended to race and ethnicity to justify the Japanese colonization of Korea and Taiwan in the first part of the twentieth century (Oguma 1995; Iwabuchi 1998). One of the ideologies of colonial rule was *dōbundōso* (common culture, common ancestry) which emphasized a common origin for Japanese and Koreans in ancient times. According to this ideology, it was not only "natural" for the two nations to merge together, but also Japanese colonialism was regarded as superior to, and less racist than, the Western equivalent, because Japan was generous enough to allow other races the honor of becoming Japanese. The benevolence of the "Japanization" of Koreans and their exclusion as an inferior other were the two sides of the same coin. In the colonial Korea, Koreans were forced to speak Japanese and to adopt Japanese names, for example. In this way, Japanization meant the extermination of all visible "Koreanness."

It should be emphasized that the rigidity of the Japanese policy of the assimilation of its colonial subjects did not necessarily mean that the policy, or its ideology, was effective. The cultural consequences of Japanese colonialism, as with any other colonialism, were very complicated and contradictory in terms of domination and resistance. To what extent Koreans were "Japanized" and what the assimilation exactly meant are highly debatable questions, which are beyond the scope of this chapter. However, what seems less debatable is the prevalent attitude of the Japanese toward the cultural difference of the colonized: for Koreans to become Japanese, it was held, they had to forget or suppress their descent and history. All visible cultural differences had to be erased, in other words. As Tessa Morris-Suzuki (1995) argues, "assimilation became a matter of amnesia" in Japan, but we should conceive this amnesia as having dual meaning: to forget where Koreans are originally from and to suppress the ambivalence and the incompleteness of Japanese assimilation policy.

Japanese insensitivity to the cultural difference of Koreans in Japan is thus also marked by the desire to negate the inevitable failure and incomplete project of Japanizing Koreans. If, in modern Japan, amnesia has been essential for others to be allowed to become Japanese, we can destabilize the assimilationist desire by narrating resident Koreans' colonial experiences as a constitutive part of modern Japan. It is to reveal "the many ways in which colonization was never simply external to the societies of the imperial metropolis" (Hall 1996a: 246). Japanese society itself has been deeply carved by Japanese colonization and its aftermath. If an ahistorical representation of "where you are at" makes resident Koreans "almost the same," it is the recontextualization of the history of "where you're from" that marks them as "not quite" existent in Japan (Bhabha 1994).

The issue of tokenism, on the other hand, has something to do with the insufficient attention the film pays to internal differences within the Korean communities in Japan. The debate between the politics of essentialism and diversity within an ethnic minority group is not unique to resident Koreans in Japan. In the United States and Britain, for example, the counter-strategy against dominant stereotypes of blacks has been forged by reversing stereotypes and replacing positive images for negative ones (Hall 1997). This is a "strategic use of a positive essentialism in a scrupulously visible political interest" (Spivak 1987: 205). Here a new meaning of blackness is sought, but at the cost of blurring internal diversity. Blackness as a collective identity swallows differences of gender, sexuality, and class. Hall argues that this stage of devoting creative energy exclusively to "strategic essentialism" is over:

> Films are not necessarily good because black people make them. They are not necessarily "right-on" by virtue of the fact that they deal with the black experience. Once you enter the politics of the end of the essential black subject you are plunged headlong into the maelstrom of a continuously contingent, unguaranteed, political argument and debate: a critical politics, a politics of criticism. You can no longer conduct black politics through the strategy of a simple set of reversals, putting in the place of the bad old essential white subject, the new essentially good black subject.
>
> (Hall 1996b: 444)

The strategy of reversing stereotypes and replacing bad with good challenges the negative stereotypes, but it neither subverts the latter nor displaces them, since it does not undermine the binaries on which the construction of cultural and racial Other is based (Hall 1997). In another article, while acknowledging the significance of strategic essentialism, Hall proposes that "it is to the diversity, not the homogeneity, of black experience that we must now give our undivided creative attention" (1996c: 473). In *Moon*, the subversiveness of the hybridity of resident Koreans is confined to going beyond the reified perception of their "place" in Japan, a problem which can be articulated by a generational divide among first-, second-, third-, and fourth-generation Koreans. A strategic deployment of hybridity in *Moon* makes it possible for resident Koreans, and for that matter other non-Korean audiences, to realize that there may be a space that exists between the binary opposition between two "pure" identities, "Koreanness" and "Japaneseness." Strategic hybridity in *Moon* is a necessary detour to advance from a reified essentialism which does not well articulate a number of different options and forms of everyday life that can accommodate diasporic transculturation of "Koreanness." However, it is a thorough commitment to multiple differences within resident Koreans – not only internal generational differences which *Moon* cannot properly confront, but also differences of gender, class, and sexuality – that is required to deconstruct an essentialized resident Korean subject. As a third-generation Korean female writer Kyō Nobuko argues:

> Both the image of resident Koreans represented in *Moon* which may be fresh to many Japanese and the popular image which is not represented in the film are only stereotypes of resident Koreans in Japan. I really want to resist either image being imposed on me.
>
> (Kyō 1994: 182)

No matter how differently an image is represented, the singularity of the new image of resident Koreans evoked by *Moon* easily leads to another reinforcement of the one-dimensional image of the Korean subject in Japan, one that cannot accommodate the individuality of resident Koreans.

Towards a postcolonial coalition

The criticism of *Moon* shows the difficulty of reconciling two interrelated poles – overdetermination by Japanese colonialism and multiple differences within resident Koreans – in the postcolonial politics of representation. It is also a question of how to deploy strategically two modes of subjectivities: a rigidly demarcated (neo)colonial subject and an ambivalent, hybrid postcolonial subject. By posing these new questions, *Moon* certainly opened a new era in the politics of representation, where there is neither an essentialized Korean subject nor a politically guaranteed representation: any representation of resident Koreans in Japan can no longer escape political debate and criticism. Furthermore, *Moon*'s significance goes beyond theoretical issues. No other film has ever empowered (young) resident Koreans to affirm their impure, hybrid Koreanness in Japan *vis-à-vis* older generations and other ethnic minorities. No other film has forced Japanese to realize the existence of invisible resident Koreans in Japan. No other film has ever spurred such heated discussion, criticism and, in the long run, communication between and among resident Koreans and Japanese.

Since *Moon*, several independent resident Korean directors have produced films which are more sensitive to various kinds of difference and more engaged with history than *Moon*. *Osaka Story* (1996), for example, subtly deals with the complexities of intertwined differences, though there is no explicit political message in the text. It is a documentary about the director's family. The director, Nakada Tōichi, a naturalized Korean-Japanese, has a Korean father and a Japanese mother. He tries to take a fresh view of his family and his personal history by documenting the family discord caused by his domineering father, who has a concubinary family in South Korea. The generational gap between the director and his father is a main theme, but the film also deals with other differences within the family: the history of the relations between Korea and Japan, between the Korean ethnic community and Osaka regional culture, naturalization, relations internal to the family, and the homosexuality of the director.

In 1997, a four-hour-long documentary film about resident Koreans in Japan, *Zainichi* (Oh Duk Soo, director), was completed. The film production was funded by donations from resident Korean and Japanese supporters. The film is divided into two parts. The first part covers the postwar history of Japan from the resident Koreans' point of view. It is a history of the political struggle and economic difficulty which most first and second generations experienced. The second part consists of the personal stories of six Korean individual – one first-generation, two second-generation, and three third-generation – all of whom have tried hard to make Japan their place of residence while not forgetting their place of origin. Although the relatively short and superficial footage of third-generation youths shows the ambivalent feelings the second-generation male director has towards the third generation, the film tries to balance "where you are from" and "where you are at" by showing that its subjects wish to make Japan another home without forgetting and concealing "where they are from."

Moon also caused Japanese media to deal with the issue of resident Koreans, and to question an exclusive Japanese national identity more than before. Nuanced forms of resident Koreans' self-representation would have a certain effect on mainstream Japanese society by revealing the fictionality of "Japaneseness" from within and by deconstructing the exclusive equation of Japanese language, nationality, and ethnicity. This would therefore open the way to a more inclusive notion of citizenship in Japan (see Katō *et al.* 1990; Field 1993; Kim U-sŏng 1994; Takeda, Kang, and Katō 1995).

However, it should be emphasized that not too many expectations should be placed on resident Koreans playing a crucial role in changing the existing meaning of "being Japanese." As Japanese consumption of *Moon* suggested, the issue at stake here is less the speaking position of resident Koreans than the reception of the Japanese. The relationship between the speaking positions of resident Koreans and the listening positions of Japanese is always already asymmetrical and over-determined by Japan's colonial history. Identities of resident Koreans, no matter how they are represented in multiple and positively ambivalent ways, are always constructed under unequal and oppressive relations. Without realizing this, some "progressive" intellectuals and activists often naively express their hope that resident Koreans will declare in public that they are "Japanese" (e.g. Nishibe *et al.* 1996: 41). For them this would be the most effective way in which the hermetically sealed Japanese essentialist national identity would be deconstructed by an impure Japanese. Although no doubt deconstructive, this also conceals why resident Koreans in Japan have long been reluctant to accept the humiliating experiences of the naturalization process, such as the requirement of adopting a Japanese name and the secret investigation of their life by the police. It is not just a matter of personal identification but a structural discriminatory obstacle that has long deterred resident Koreans from becoming Japanese. Without changing this structural discrimination, a facile inclusion and celebration of impure Japanese contributes to the reproduction of concentric assimilation. The existence of resident Koreans would expand the meaning of Japaneseness but would not change its core.

This is a process of reproducing a "self-confirming other" (Spivak 1988), a narrative to which the majority are eager to listen, in order to learn not about the interrogated subject, but about self. By the act of listening to Koreans, the Japanese can indulge their curiosity for the problem as it reflects themselves: "Japan." What is more disturbing with this process, however, is that the Japanese do not realize that they are safely shifting the responsibility for fighting against racial discrimination and the burden of representation onto the ethnic minority (Chŏng Yŏng-he 1996). It commonly happens that the ethnic minority is asked what the majority should do. In a TV discussion program about resident Koreans in Japan (*Asamade namaterebi*, TV Asahi, 26

September 1997), a resident Korean female discussant pointed out the political nature of the term *zainichi kankokuchōsenjin*, which, as mentioned before, takes the politically divided Korean peninsula for granted and emphasizes the nation-state boundaries. The Japanese male presenter, who seemed to know little about resident Koreans and was therefore supposed to represent "ordinary" Japanese audiences, somewhat hysterically said to her, "If we are told such a thing by you Koreans, we do not know what we should do. Please tell me what we should call you." By refusing to think, avoiding the initiative, and wishing that the discriminated would speak for themselves, he demonstrated a standard Japanese response when confronted with the issue of racial discrimination. It is as if it were the responsibility of the ethnic minority to educate the majority on how to deal with them.

As a Japanese myself, I cannot help but think that what is most imperative is for the Japanese to relieve resident Koreans of the burden of postcolonial engagement by considering what they can do, together with resident Koreans, to deconstruct an exclusive notion of "the Japanese" and "the Koreans." As Ella Shohat and Robert Stam argue: "Relatively privileged people have many possible roles besides wallowing in self-regarding guilt: they can fight racism in their own milieu, work to restructure power, serve as spies and allies for marginalized people" (1994: 345). The invitation of *Moon* to join the postcolonial politics of representation is not addressed to resident Koreans alone. The message is similarly sent to Japanese, by calling for "intercommunal coalitions joined in shared struggles" (Shohat and Stam 1994: 347). Whether such coalitions can be formed depends largely upon how Japanese people respond to the invitation.

Note

1 In this chapter, I use the term "resident Koreans" for people of Korean descent who permanently reside in Japan. Since the majority of such people, though they may be up to fourth-generation residents, do not take up Japanese nationality, I do not use the term Korean-Japanese.

4 Mothers write Ikaino

Melissa Wender

Panic coursed through my veins. I rifled through my bags one last time, but no wallet. It was 9 o'clock at night, and I was in the apartment of Chong Ch'u-wŏl, a writer I had come to Osaka to see. We'd just come back from the public bath. Maybe I'd dropped it, I thought, in the coffee shop where we'd spent several hours talking, or on the street, or in the dressing room of the bathhouse. Chong and her husband and son devised a search plan. The first stop the next morning was the coffee shop: at any rate, we all wanted coffee. To my great relief, the wallet, its contents untouched, lay on the floor beneath the table where we'd sat.

For some reason, this incident sticks in my mind as my real introduction to Ikaino, the Korean neighborhood in Osaka, although by this time I'd already read a good deal about the place and had been there for several days. I'd even been given tours of the area by three people, including Chong. Perhaps it's because Ikaino appears in the writings of Koreans in Japan as a place in which crises (of a good deal more severity than mine) are an integral part of daily life. Or maybe it was that the heat, long hard conversation with Chong and another writer, Kim Ch'ang-saeng, and my efforts to comprehend the drunken but sincere words of Chong's husband had made me feel foggy-headed. As Chong and her family rushed to my aid, I had the sense for the first time that I was actually doing something in Ikaino, rather than simply observing others' lives.

My initial curiosity about Koreans in Japan derived from what I learned during my first stay in Japan in 1986. I read in the English-language newspapers that Koreans protesting the Alien Registration Law, which required them to register as foreigners, give fingerprints, and carry at all times a card certifying their registration, were engaging in civil disobedience, refusing to have their prints taken. Though I had studied Japanese history at a reputable (but, in retrospect, conservative) US institution of higher education, I didn't know that there was a large community of Koreans in Japan or why they were there. When I had been led by the hand by my homestay mother to register as an alien, I had given my prints without a second thought.

In part as a result of my concern with such discrimination in Japan, I began to learn Korean, and eventually spent time in Seoul. In graduate school I found myself on the south side of Chicago, in a neighborhood supposedly well-integrated. It didn't seem to be so to me. Increasingly I found myself thinking about minority communities. After taking a Japanese language class in which we read works by minority writers, I decided to conduct research on the literature of resident Koreans.[1]

In that class, I first read Chong Ch'u-wŏl. In this chapter, I will discuss her work and that of another Korean woman writer based in Osaka, Kim Ch'angsaeng. These women have used Ikaino to various ends in their works: as background, as a metaphor, as a character. They stress material aspects of existence in this Korean neighborhood, focusing in particular on the experiences of women. In their work, the concrete, the bodily, the local, the margin, Koreanness, and women's lives are woven into an intricate web.

Much of their work appeared in the 1980s, and I read it as entrenched in the discourse of the *chiikiundō* (local, or community movement) of which the anti-fingerprinting movement I read about in 1986 was a crucial part. This is the best-known of movements by resident Koreans, and one of the more successful: the fingerprinting requirement was repealed for permanent residents (most of whom are Koreans) in 1992. The protests against this law attracted international attention, including the support of well-known figures like Jesse Jackson. Yet although in one sense it was a mass movement, actual resistance took place at local government offices, where foreigners registered. In addition, many of the movement's leaders were engaged in community-building efforts, and justified their actions within this context, as part of a struggle to wrest power from the controlling state and put it into the hands of local communities.

In the 1980s, Japan's status as an economic superpower became an incontrovertible fact. The decade simultaneously saw major shifts in the structure of global capitalism, which, many have argued, gave rise to what we know as postmodern cultural forms (Harvey 1990). As elsewhere, the question of whether the world had indeed entered a postmodern era and whether a modernist public sphere was viable in such a time drew the attention of scholars in Japan (Miyoshi and Harootunian 1989).

Some of the most salient features of the new stage of capitalism, sometimes called "disorganized" capitalism, are flexible "just-in-time production," globalization (including a division of labor across rather than within nations), and decentralization. The postmodern cultural forms seen as concomitant with these economic changes are characterized by fragmentation and an emphasis on difference, and a schizophrenia of sorts, in which, in the words of Fredric Jameson, "the interlocking syntagmatic series of signifiers which constitutes an utterance or a meaning" breaks down (Harvey 1990; quoted from Jameson 1995: 26).[2]

Many have observed that such economic and cultural shifts – as well as "space-time compression," the feeling of time being faster and distances closer, which we experience as a result of new technologies that have helped to bring about these shifts – have left many people groping for their bearings in the world. Thus, the argument goes, there is a renewed interest in place. We find increased correlation of spatial positioning and identity, particularly among feminists, postcolonial peoples, and minorities, who play with notions of the home, the margin, the local.[3] Some critics, such as David Harvey, have characterized the emphasis on region, place, and otherness in politics as reactionary in their nostalgia and desire for stability; others, notably Doreen Massey in a criticism of Harvey, have proposed that it is possible to perceive of place in a more dynamic manner, with an identity that "is always formed by the juxtaposition and co-presence... of particular sets of interrelations... [and] a proportion of the social interrelations will be wider than and go beyond the area being referred to in any particular context as a place" (Massey 1994: 168–9).

The renewed interest in local community among Koreans in Japan concatenates with this global trend, and when I began this research, I thought that my main conclusion would center on precisely such issues. However, the longer I have pondered the literature of Chong Ch'u-wŏl and Kim Ch'ang-saeng and texts from the anti-fingerprinting movement, the more I have begun to feel that to make only such an (albeit satisfying) argument would be a great mistake. The dialectic between the fictional realm and the arena of grassroots politics is complex and sometimes messy; resident Koreans used these discourses to form identities, that are in turn of course complex and messy. One of my objectives in this essay will be to delineate and decipher that jumble and, in so doing, to explore the ways in which the literary and political acts of Korean individuals have transfigured the Japanese social landscape.

In 1973, the name "Ikaino" disappeared from the map of Osaka, split up and renamed as parts of Ikuno ward (*ku*). The oldest and largest Korean neighborhood in Japan, however, was not so easily excised from the consciousness of its residents. The popular first-generation poet Kim Si-jong memorialized it in his "Ikaino shishū" (Ikaino poems):

> Everyone knows it yet
> It's not on the map
> It's not on the map so
> It's not Japan
> It's not Japan so
> It might as well vanish
> It doesn't matter so
> We do as we please.
> (Kim Si-jong 1975: 184)[4]

Legend has it that Koreans began to settle in Ikaino with the beginning of the construction of the Hirano Canal in 1923 (Kim Ch'ang-saeng 1985: 16). More likely, however, Koreans settled in what became known as Ikaino because of the preponderance of small and mid-size factories there (Song Yŏn-ok 1993: 58–63). A ferry began running between Chejudo, an island off the southern tip of Korea, and Osaka in 1922; Chejudo had been hit particularly hard by Japanese colonial rule, and by 1934 nearly a quarter of its population had headed to Japan in search of work (Song Yŏn-ok 1993: 55–6). Contemporary accounts describe living conditions as wretched (Kim Ch'ang-saeng 1985: 13–14).

Resident Koreans did not benefit from Japan's postwar economic growth to the same extent as the majority of Japanese residents. In the 1950s, boom years for the Japanese economy, Koreans faced unemployment rates of up to 80 percent (Yang Yŏng-hu 1994: 178). In the 1960s and the 1970s, they continued to lag behind Japanese economically. Even in the 1980s, legal discrimination persisted and poverty had not vanished: in 1986, 42.6 percent of Korean families in Ikunoku received public assistance (Song Yŏn-ok 1993: 80). Still, Ikaino was not the slum that it once had been.

Relative economic equity with Japanese, as well as the passage of time, meant that as in the rest of Japan, Koreans in Ikaino were becoming assimilated. The vast majority were Japan-born and spoke little or no Korean, attended Japanese public schools, and, even with *kimch'i* sold so nearby, ate predominantly Japanese food. At precisely this moment when the culture that bound Koreans in Ikaino together was threatening to disappear, the women writers I discuss in this chapter held up the "ghetto" as their primary referent for Korean identity. But what was that community? Why was their Ikaino inhabited particularly by women who not only retained markers of Korean culture such as eating Korean foods and using Korean names, but spoke an accented and creoled Japanese, and even practiced shamanistic religious practices from Chejudo? Does this merely represent an attempt to find a form of affiliation that is not national but is firmly ethnic? If so, why employ Ikaino to talk about these women, and why these women to speak of Ikaino?

It will be helpful to locate the discussion of Ikaino and local communities within a debate over resident Korean identity which surfaced at roughly the same time. For the first time, some began to argue that there was a "third way," a way of life involving neither assimilation nor returning to Korea (Field 1993: 646). Three camps of Koreans were identified: those with *dōkashikō* (inclination toward assimilation), *sokokushikō* (inclination toward the homeland, even if they did not plan to return there), and *zainichishikō* (much like the "third way;" the literal meaning of *zainichi* is "residing in Japan") (Yun Kŏn-ch'a 1992: 238). To the participants in this conversation, assimilation was simply not an option, and it was thus the other two camps that received their attention. These men (they are all men) argued in lofty language which of these stances was better, as if one way or the other reflected a more honest way of being Korean.

The divide between them is particularly prominent in a 1985 debate opposing "*zainichi* as method" to "*zainichi* as fact." Kang Sang-jung, the proponent of the former, places emphasis on the fact that unlike other "minorities" in Japan, resident Koreans have a homeland. In fact, he sees the position of "straddling the national border" between Japan and Korea as the most significant aspect of their existence. He refers to this as their duality. This duality, he argues, compels them to orient themselves toward the homeland (whose history their own fate depends upon). In addition, because it places them outside the system of modern nation-states, it enables them to see the pitfalls of "Japanese-style modernization" (and potentially a Korean modernization modeling itself after Japan's) and puts them in a unique position to critique such modernity and its concomitant national ideologies. In order for resident Koreans to be capable of such critique, however, they need to maintain a certain distance from Japan's "value system" and thus to assert their place as "marginal" rather than fight for the right to be integrated into the national community (Kang Sang-jung 1988).

Yang T'ae-ho, in contrast, believes that Kang, in his effort to stress this concept of duality, "attempts to make a method out of [resident Koreans'] foreignness." Yang sees it as dangerous because it reinforces the equation of ethnicity with nationhood. Yang stresses that it is not entirely accurate to call resident Koreans foreigners, thus implicitly questioning the determination of Japaneseness or foreignness based on "blood." He fundamentally disagrees with Kang's sense that resident Koreans are "straddling the national border," that their lives are as tied to the fate of the Korean peninsula as Kang claims. He calls for recognition of "*zainichi* as fact." For better or worse, he contends, most resident Koreans have made and will continue to make Japan their home, and this needs to be acknowledged, even if it seems as though it will lead to the eventual dissolution of the community as they assimilate. The emphasis therefore needs to be placed on finding common grounds with – and, the suggestion is, fighting for the same rights as – other members of Japanese society. Even if this struggle stresses Koreans' right to the same treatment as Japanese residents based on a common humanity, the process need not necessarily entail sacrificing a sense of their identity as ethnically Korean (Yang T'ae-ho 1988).

The distinction between the positions has often been characterized as a generational one, the *sokokushikō* gradually giving way to the *zainichishikō*. For the most part, literature has been evaluated in a political manner, and divided, like people themselves, into these camps. An increasing inclination toward the *zainichishikō* in literature is also generally seen as reflection of a generational shift. In this scheme, the literature of Ikaino, focused on a place within Japan, would serve as evidence of this fact.

Yang T'ae-ho was a member of Mintōren (Minzoku sabetsu to tatakau renmei, the league to fight ethnic/national discrimination), an umbrella organization of resident Korean civil rights groups. While Mintōren did not initiate the anti-fingerprinting struggle, it did play a central role in disseminating information and bringing together "refusers" (as they were called) from various regions of the country. Yang T'ae-ho in fact participated in the anti-fingerprinting movement. Even though Mindan and Chongryun, the organizations affiliated respectively with the South and North Korean governments, spoke out in support of refusers, the philosophy of the movement as a whole locates it staunchly within the "*zainichi* as fact" camp.

Other scholars have argued that the effect of Japan's postwar economic development, and of the "high growth economy" on resident Koreans is as responsible for the shift to *zainichishikō*. Although Koreans did not reap benefits equal to Japanese, many grew richer, and all were influenced by social changes spawned by the country's new-found affluence, such as so-called "my-home-ism," intense competition in education, and the declining birth rate (Mun Kyŏng-su 1996). Japanese civil activists had begun to focus their sights on local issues in the late 1960s; by the mid-1970s, a small number of resident Koreans began to do so as well. Only in the middle to late 1980s, however, when Japan had become a major player in the global economy and laborers flowed to Japan from the Middle East, South America, and Asia (including South Korea), do we find the peak of the local movement among Koreans. This influx of foreigners who had quite a different relationship to Japan from resident Koreans – who were not at all assimilated and made for a much more visibly diverse community – no doubt contributed to resident Koreans' increasing tendency to recognize the degree to which they had a stake in Japanese social and political life. This gave them the courage to participate in the anti-fingerprinting struggle and to assert that Ikaino was their home. We can thus see the increased inclination toward *zainichishikō* (and sometimes toward assimilation) as tied to Japan's particular experience of the transformation of global capitalism.

As I stressed at the outset, however, I see resident Koreans' "turn to the local" not as simply a reflection of, or reaction to, particular experiences of disorganized capitalism and/or postmodernism, but rather as entrenched in many different discourses at the same time. Let me now begin to unravel the internal dynamics within, and dialectical relationships between, texts focusing on the local. Since it was literature that lured me in to this subject in the first place, I will begin my analysis looking at works by Chong Ch'u-wŏl, and end with those of Kim Ch'ang-saeng. Between these I will sandwich my discussion of the anti-fingerprinting movement, focusing on the case of a prominent (male) refuser and community activist from Ikaino.

Resident Koreans today are more likely to flee Ikaino than to gravitate toward it, but in 1960, at age sixteen, unable to find employment after graduating from middle school, Chong Ch'u-wŏl ran away to Ikaino. The Koreans who gathered at her family home in Kyūshū, in southern Japan, had often talked about the neighborhood, and both of her parents had lived there when young. Her first job was for a Korean-run clothing manufacturer; the employees lived on the first floor and worked on the second. She was provided with meals and tickets to the public bath, but she made so little money that it took her two years to earn enough to visit her parents. Later she worked pasting heels on shoes (and wrote a memorable poem about her experience of growing light-headed on the glue); for many years, she ran a bar. Today she is in semi-retirement, writes when she can, and spends much of her time helping to raise several young grandchildren.

Both in print and in person, Chong tells these and other details of her personal history with candor. She began writing poetry while working in Ikaino's small factories, and as Norma Field has recounted, she would often write in the bathroom: the only place where she could find peace. The tale of Chong's move from the country to the city, and of her creating art amidst hardship has immense power, yet what is most distinctive about her work is rather her persistence in showing how her own life is entwined with those of the various people with whom she has come into contact, and how their lives are together entrenched in broader histories. If modern Japanese fiction has tended to border on autobiography, her work comes closer to ethnography.[5]

The particular community at the center of her work is that of Ikaino, and especially women in Ikaino. From the 1970s onward, she depicts the repetitions of daily life, maintained within the home and by women. Women are thus granted respect for their role in the reproduction of Koreanness. Food is of particular importance in this regard:

> When morning comes
> To the waves of tiles
> The woman takes out *kimch'i* from the jar
> And cuts it, chop chop
> As from long long ago
> Women have always done, day after day
> The green smell
> Of a clump of soil in the field
> Of garlic
> The white leaves, dyed with red hot pepper
> Crimson *kimch'i*
> Even for her mouth-rinsing son
> Her gum-chewing daughter
> The *kimch'i* on the table
> Even then
> Incites an appetite
> Dyeing them crimson
> To their stomachs
> The sting! Dyeing also
> The woman's fingers, crimson
> When morning comes chop chop
> From the point of the knife
> She cuts in the hometown
> "C'mon guys,
> Time to get up!"
> (Reprinted from her 1971 collection in Chong
> 1984: 86–7; Chong 1987: 113–14)[6]

Here the less literal reproduction of the *furusato* (translated here as the hometown, but which could also mean homeland) "day after day, from long long ago" is linked to food. And food, which produces the odors associated with Koreans in stereotypes of them by Japanese, is turned into lush imagery of reproduction and desire: *kimch'i* crimson like blood, the green smell of soil and garlic, *kimch'i* stimulating appetite, which, as in English, can also signal desire.

Yet if the bloody images here are linked with the giving and maintaining of life through food, they are also violent: we hear and then see the chopping of the knife; we feel the woman's fingers sting. The reproduction of culture, at least on this embodied level, is a fraught matter; as that of human beings, it is inherently painful. These aspects of the poem seem implanted in a cyclical, productive space and time, like the folkloric chronotope described by Mikhail Bakhtin (1981), yet the presence of gum-chewing and mouth-rinsing children situates the action of the poem firmly in the present. The final line (literally "wake up!") can be read as a clarion call to the reader – and perhaps the narrator herself – to snap out of a reverie.

In an essay contemporary with this poem, published in 1973, Chong credits first-generation women with giving life to Ikaino by creating the market at its heart, setting up shops and tables selling Korean goods to ensure that they could "pass on to their children all the Korea that they possessed – the flavors, the customs, the conventions." If they had "fended off persecution with [their strong] bodies," however, it was a "strength that almost appears to be stupidity" which enabled them to do so (Chong 1986: 174).[7]

In this and other essays and stories also originally published in the early 1970s, the traditions of Chejudo shamanism provide a source of seemingly superhuman strength for these women. In one story, she says, "women who give of themselves as mothers, wives, daughters, women of Haeng-ja's generation, when they have been sapped of inner strength, recharged their power by tying themselves to the gods and to the spirits" (Chong 1986: 119–20). She even calls shamanism the only orgasmic ecstasy that these women will experience (Chong 1986: 124). In addition, she repeatedly utters the phrase *saniittai* (three statuses, one body; referring to the dead, the living, and the Korean woman being rolled into one), mentions the transmigration of souls, and juxtaposes her own pregnancies with the death of others, intimating just such transmigration. In so doing, she evokes a pre-, or perhaps anti-, modern time, linking birth with death, and biological with cultural reproduction.

If exploring shamanism allows her to find value in what has been debased as feminine, she is simultaneously blunt in her criticism of the Ikaino women's dependence on shamans. For example, she tells of her mother-in-law, who is dying from Parkinson's disease and yet demands that Chong call a shaman (again) despite the high price and the fact that the shaman herself admits that some people simply will not get better (Chong 1986: 179). She likens the habit of first-generation women in Ikaino of hiring shamans to the gambling engaged in by men, a sign of their desperate hope for a better life (Chong 1986: 202). They did not have the ability to control the course of their own lives, and their illiteracy left them no choice but to grasp for the help of gods (Chong 1986: 211).

In Chong's work, women's efforts to propagate Koreanness – and the strength that empowers them in this task – cannot be understood apart not only from such religious notions but from their role in the material reproduction of human bodies. As we saw in the *kimch'i* poem, she stresses both cultural and material functions of food. The interlacing of the cultural and the biological in her literature, however, is most palpable in her portrayal of motherhood.

I suggested earlier that much of her writing verges on anthropology. In one piece that very much fits this description, "Waga aisuru chōsen no onnatachi" (The Korean Women I So Love), published first in 1974, the act of giving and sustaining life is at the core of the connections she makes between her own experiences and those of other women in her community, and thus in her interest in relating their stories:

> In Ikunoku, Osaka, where I live, there are sixty thousand resident Koreans.
>
> Let us suppose that ten thousand of those people are women who are related by their very flesh to the transmigration of souls. My days, those of these ten thousand women, are exhausted by the unrewarded love that is motherhood, by the manners of mothering. But we have no regrets.
>
> . . . Men are born from women's bellies; for this reason alone, women embrace men with their mothering, and therein protect the normalcy of the everyday.
>
> In Japan, these women's preservation of normalcy in the everyday becomes, in a word, beauty.
>
> (Chong 1986: 9)

The tone of this passage, in the opening few pages, is literary. Here and in the conclusion we find a plenitude of emotion and the aesthetic. Large assumptions such as whether all women really embrace their role as mothers are left unexamined. The series of flesh, transmigration, mothering, and preservation of the everyday, somehow results in "her days" being not similar to, but the same as, those of ten thousand other Korean women who are mothers.

The body of the text, however, tells the stories of seven women in a voice which is more matter of fact, even ethnographic. We learn of Yŏng-hwa, whose husband drinks himself into a stupor every night and becomes violent. She understands that his days of high-pressured but repetitive labor with dangerous machines, which turn him into a human vegetable, cause him to act this way. Her comprehension does not lead her to be passive, however: "When her husband, consumed by alcohol, begins to hit and scream, Yŏng-hwa isn't silent. She believes that hitting back and screaming back are an expression of fondness" (Chong 1986: 10).

In most of these tales, economic strain is a major cause of hardship. We hear of a woman buried by a cruel system of money-lending prevalent among women in the Korean community, with interest of nearly 100 percent; a pregnant young woman doing piecework in a cramped apartment so that her husband can participate in grassroots activism; a woman whose husband was born in Japan but lived in Chejudo for some time and is thus technically an illegal alien and can only work under the table. Chong sometimes refers directly to the way that Japanese capitalism affects these people: the woman with the activist husband, Chong notes, thinks that "it is difficult for the grass to exercise the subjectivity of grass in Japan, which overflows with commodities" (Chong 1986: 20).

In her closing passage, Chong asserts that one thing has the power to turn these women's lives, which are indeed tragedies, into "divine comedies." That one thing is their speech (*kotoba*) (Chong 1986: 23). She praises the humor, the roughness, the crudeness, the bluntness of their words, their intonation and timing. So too the unique blend of Korean and Japanese, the masterful analogies, the jests. She cites one woman: "Try making my life into a novel. You'll win the Nobel Prize for sure!" This language, she opines, enables them to turn sadness into laughter, and to "weave together the everyday" (Chong 1986: 24).

Ultimately, she declares that these women's speech is the true art of the people. What a contrast, she remarks, with the dignified words of a Japanese writer upon learning that his hunger strike urging commutation of the death sentence imposed on South Korean poet of the people, Kim Chi-ha, had achieved its goal. Of course it's better that they protest, she goes on, but have they ever thought about why it is impossible for women like me to act as they do? Have they ever thought about the relationship between Japan and Korea and why people like me are here? (Chong 1986: 24–5). She closes:

> I imagine that of the approximately ten thousand Korean women in Ikunoku, fewer than half know Kim Chi-ha's name. For this I love these Korean women, heroines of divine comedies yet to be written.
> (Chong 1986: 25)

Chong does sometimes slip into a romanticization of these women's suffering. Beautiful, yes, but trapped, as we see in her references to domestic violence. On one occasion, she describes women as putting up with their husband's beatings because their maternal nature allows them to be giving enough to let men be the humans, that is to say, to express their pain of "the life of *zainichi* [residing in Japan], with no exits, no escape" (Chong 1986: 117). Elsewhere she describes her own husband's violence as the most direct form of communication (Chong 1986: 195). I doubt that humor and generosity can obviate the physical and psychic pain of abuse.

It may have been radical to assert that it was the power and mothering of Korean women that assured the continuation of Korean culture, but at what cost? Such a perspective, in which women's positive qualities are linked so closely with their biology, like certain types of feminism in the United States, is "in danger of solidifying an important bulwark for sexist oppression: the belief in an innate 'womanhood' to which we must all adhere lest we be deemed either inferior or not 'true' women" (Alcoff 1988: 414). In this case, it does not even seem feminist: maternal nurturing will condemn them to a lifetime of suffering.

Chong published three books between 1984 and 1987, the latter two by Tokyo presses. This might be unremarkable for some writers, but she had published only one book before this, in 1971, and has issued nothing since, although when I met with her in 1997, she had a manuscript being looked at by a publisher. These books for the most part contained material that had been printed previously, but it bears noting that her work was considered worthy of attention at this precise moment.

The burgeoning of the anti-fingerprinting movement clearly not only contributed to the success of her work but served as an impetus for it. Each of her books from these years touches upon the matter. *Saran he/aishite imasu* (*Sarang hae/* I Love You, 1987), gathers essays she wrote for two journals put out by the labor unions of local government employees actively participating in the movement; *Ikaino taryon* (Ikaino Lament, 1986) includes the transcription of a talk she gave at a national conference of one of these unions. Even the earliest collection,

Ikaino/onna/ai/uta (Ikaino/Woman/Love/Poems, 1984) contains a poem addressing the fingerprinting system and resident Koreans' use of Japanese names.[8] In 1985, Chong herself refused to be fingerprinted. Within less than a year, however, she gave her prints "of her own will." The police threatened her with losing the bar she ran, and so, in order to "protect her family," she conceded (Chong 1987: 185–8). She nonetheless continued to write and speak out against the system.

Rather than delving into texts directly considering only the fingerprinting system, however, I wish to examine a piece which explores issues that form the intellectual underpinnings to resident Koreans' objection to this requirement of the Alien Registration Law. In a 1985 story (essay?) entitled "Mun Konbun ŏmŏni no ningo" (Mun Kon-bun *Ŏmŏni*'s Apple), we find further development of themes from Chong's earlier work: references to the fleshly connection of mothers to the transmigration of souls, the setting of Ikaino, old women's masterful speech. Yet what sets it apart is the degree to which she draws these together to contemplate the relationship of the individual, and particularly female, body in space and language with the politics and history of the nation-state. This theme lies at the base of the anti-fingerprinting movement because the system, designed by the Japanese nation-state during the colonial period, kept Koreans in check not only by holding written records of their presence, but by marking their beings with material proof of their bodies.

The story begins with a discussion of Korean apples. There are two sorts, the narrator tells us: *sagwa*, the commercially cultivated type, and *nŭnggŭm*, the wild and smaller variety. And then, she says, there is something in the "fluent Japanese" of first-generation Korean immigrants, something superior to even the *nŭnggŭm*: the *ningo* (Chong 1985: 15). *Ningo* is technically a mispronunciation of *ringo*, the Japanese word for apple. However, in Chong's story there is no mispronunciation, only "living language" (Chong 1985: 16). Living language, or *seikatsugo*, more literally the language of daily life, is not mistaken, but "delicious" (Chong 1985: 14), for it bears the traces of history:

> The taste of the *ningo*, only guessed at when biting into the western breed of apple known as a *sagwa*, is the taste of passion of the aged immigrants, already waiting only to vanish, a clear taste, clear after being filtered through their flesh.
>
> (Chong 1985: 14–15)

The text then jumps immediately to a poem entitled "Ningo," which begins "I bite the flesh of an apple/The dripping blood/So clear" and ends with the lines "Apples/One basket a hundred yen/Get your apples here!" At the start, the shift in tone to poetry is minimal, since the prose itself is poetic, breaking sentences in the middle as if they are lines of poetry, or adding commas to break sentences into the rhythm of a verse, but by the end of the poem itself the language is not "poetic" *per se*, but that of Osaka dialect, words no longer about, but rather in, living language.

Chong is not the only nor the first to include the living language of first-generation Koreans in her work; nor is she the first to play with form. Other resident Korean writers have done likewise in a desire to twist the Japanese language and literary tradition into shapes of their very own. For example, Ri Kaisei, in his Akutagawa-award-winning story *Kinuta o utsu onna* (The Woman Who Fulled Clothes; Ri Kaisei [Li Hoe-sŭng] 1972), infuses the common *shishōsetsu* (I-novel, or personal narrative, a form associated with Japan's modernity, and in which perspective is for the most part limited to a single point of view) with elements of the Korean *sinse t'aryŏng*, a form of lamentation of life linked with both the Korean storytelling tradition and shamanism.[9] The writers' motivation was founded in the conception that language (and by association, literature) structures and limits the way we think. The Japanese language was the language of the colonizer, and its words for Koreans and their culture were all imbued with negative nuances. To incorporate living language (oral, not written, that is) was to make visible the control that had been wrought by written Japanese, by the treaties granting them control over Korean land and treatises affirming that Koreans were backward and dirty.

The living language inhabiting the pages of second-generation writers' works is characteristically the language of the first generation, and often of their parents and parents' friends. In Chong's case, that language is almost always that of women, and this story is no exception. Of particular importance is that by repeating certain phrases throughout the narrative, she develops a sense of the "home" as the site of the living language. For example, after a query about the meaning of language for Korean women, she says:

> After having parted [once] with language, my encounter with true language began.
> In the home, there was the language of everyday life.
> (Chong 1985: 16)

In describing what she means by this language of everyday life, she speaks of the language her parents used at home and the similar language her children now use (Chong 1985: 16) and cites the speech of the women in the neighboring homes (Chong 1985: 17).

It is not coincidental that the people in whom she finds vital language are women, and the site where she locates it is the gendered space of the home. We have seen that a perception of women as more bound to their biological existence than men is consistent throughout Chong's work. The home (*ie*), although manipulated so often by the abstraction of the Japanese state that it is permeated by it, is nonetheless also the place of material reproduction of bodies: of eating, of birth, of nurturing. Like language itself, it serves as the location for twisting that very abstraction. In Chong's words:

> I couldn't see the meaning in writing poetry, that is the meaning of words . . .
> At some point I had been programmed to become of the kind nature

(/sex) that is the mother, unable even to stand on the side of the people and say "Death to those who use words!"

The personal histories of *zainichi*, the painful history which is the very history of Japan, the stormy conditions, which women's history could not even begin to grasp, was perhaps a history of human resistance within that deepest place, the home, but even though they did not understand doing so to be Confucian, they cared warmly for the men they lived with and the sons they popped out, and as they rubbed their bodies, and put their hands together in prayer, Korean women, who had hoped for their good health just for a single day, just for that day, while they killed themselves, for these resident Korean women, what meaning could words, could language, have?

I decided to live my poetry with my flesh.

How painful to write poems on one's body.

(Chong 1985: 15)

The resistance here is fleshly, however, in speech and not in writing. She has just mentioned that the comment "Death to those who use words!" is from a farming woman in Narita, where a large struggle developed against the building of Tokyo International Airport, which had led the government to push farmers off the land. Many students, members of a strong and violent New Left, joined this movement, and this statement is undoubtedly a response to their hyper-intellectualizing their actions. The implication is that this sort of abstract understanding of oppression, men's intellectualism, has no use for women, ensconced in the material world by virtue of the fact that they give birth.

Yet Chong says that writing "on her body," was painful, and she sounds regretful that she has been "programmed" to be so kind, so we begin to get the sense that she also feels that writing can be, or perhaps should be, important. The rest of the story indeed explains how she came back to writing, and argues that even writing from the home can serve as resistance. This shift in her thought is most apparent when talks about writing again after a decade of near silence. In 1984, 4,000 copies of a collection of her poems, *Ikaino/onna/ai/uta* (Ikaino/Woman/Love/Poems), were released by a small publisher. The incident she credits with spurring her to write this book draws attention to the political nature of her writing. She could not simply stand by and watch, she affirms, "the epoch-making event of Chun Doo-hwan's visit to Japan and the emperor's apology" (Chong 1985: 17), that is to say, the first visit of a Korean president to Japan since the war and the apology of the emperor for the colonization of Korea.

In addition, several times she refers this act as a "solitary rebellion," Osaka she designates as the "periphery" of the "state" (*kokka*, a compound composed of the characters for country and house/home/family), and her "home" (or house or family) she calls the "deepest part of the periphery." (Chong 1985: 17). "Solitary rebellion" was the term used again and again to describe the act of the first fingerprint refuser in 1980, before the broader movement emerged. Tellingly, the covers of the volume feature vastly enlarged fingerprints, sky blue and lime green on an off-white background. Which better confirms my unique existence, she teases, my fingerprint or my poems? Even a home in the hinterlands, she declares, can be a site for political action. Not such a revelation, perhaps, to those of us living in the United States today, but certainly not a common thing for a resident Korean woman to assert. What is evident here is that writing achieves politicality through recognizing that personal histories (in cyclical time) are what form the grander narrative of the history of nations (linear time).[10]

In the culmination to the first section, she has a revelation. When she reads her poetry aloud, she feels that the rhythm her parents gave her has permeated her Japanese (Chong 1985: 19). Earlier she had mentioned having felt shame at her parents' speech when she was a child; yet now she knows that "the memory of that shame . . . was proof that I have lived, and to lose that memory would be to deny my very existence" (Chong 1985: 16). She says that she has found meaning in writing poetry: "The poems I write," she says, "are proof that (I/we) lived in Japan" (Chong 1985: 19). Two points are crucial here. First, she comes to see both the memory of feeling ashamed and the process of overcoming that shame as part of who she is (her history), and second, she determines that the meaning of writing poetry (history) lies in the context in which it is heard/transmitted, notably from generation to generation. The latter point is even more evident in the second half of the story, to which I now turn.

In this section, entitled "My encounter with *ningo*," we (and Chong herself) are at last introduced to the *ŏmŏni*, or mother, of the title.[11] Last fall, she tells us, the morning after reading her poetry in a mixed-genre performance, she received a phone call from a friend who had come to hear her. Her mother, who learned to write by attending middle school at night, also writes poetry, and would like to meet Chong, the friend tells her. Thirty minutes later, Chong's encounter with this woman begins.

I pointed out earlier that Chong sometimes incorporates elements of ethnography into her work, but as is manifest in the passage about apples, it might be more accurate to say (at least in this story) that she blends multiple genres. In this story, she uses structure and style strategically to enable her to explicate her vision of the relationship between space, gender, language, and history. She intersperses analytical prose, lyrical prose, stream of consciousness, poetry, story-like dialogue, and even a transcription of a tape of Mun reminiscing about her life.

The first part of the story is limited to Chong's voices: poet, explicator of her own work, anthropologist (she records multiple examples of typical creoled speech); in the second half, she cedes the title of poet to Mun Kon-bun, and becomes annotator. We hear also from Mun's daughters, and others they run across. We read a poem of Mun's, we read Chong's interpretation and reaction, we hear of how they agree to meet weekly, of more poems and more interpretations, and of further meetings and further reactions. Finally, she asks Mun if she will speak about her life, and the transcription she provides, Chong notes, was performed by a bedridden friend. The piece ends with a final poem by Mun, and a final interpretation and emotional reflection by Chong. The effect is a web of conversations, and the shift performs the function of leading readers to see that the act we have been undertaking is not passive, but an active and integral part of the making of meaning. The multiplicity of voices is resonant with the Bakhtinian notion of the novel as composed of diverse language (Bakhtin 1981).

Let me provide a simple example, one I have chosen for obvious reasons:

> the *ningo* that permeates her [Mun's] life and that of my own mother is proof of their humanity.

"On fingerprinting" by Mun Kon-bun

> They said, you're Japanese.
> They said, stop being Korean.
> I came by boat.
> When raising my children
> I wore a *kimono*.
> To rent a house
> I wore a *kimono*.
> I put my *chŏgori*
> away in the dresser.
> I will give my fingerprints
> for alien registration.
> I'll make my children give theirs.
> But,
> I don't want to make my grandchildren give theirs.

Every Friday when we part, I give Mun *ŏmŏni* homework.
    She did this poem for homework, too.
    "Mother keeps going around to all of her daughters' houses, saying, teach me history, teach me history. I think she's even having indigestion. Do you suppose she really should study history properly after all?"
    It was just about then that I got the call from my friend.
    "No, I think *ŏmŏni* is just fine the way she is. All she needs to do is to put her life into poems without worrying too much," I answered.

(Chong 1985: 26)

In just a half a page, we see the voice shifting from Chong's analytical voice, to Mun's poem, to a descriptive tone from Chong, to Mun's daughter and Chong in conversation on the telephone. Much is lost in translation here: we do not feel the difference in texture of written and oral, or formal and informal, language, nor do we see that the poem is littered with mistakes, including one which turns "alien" into "monster." Nonetheless we get a feel for the rapidity with which such fluctuations in tone occur. This pace is not unique to this passage.

Takeuchi Yasuhiro, who published an analysis of the story a few months later in the literary journal in which it originally appeared, indeed calls upon notions from Bakhtin to make rather grand conclusions. The "polyphonic" character of the narration, he argues, enables this story to "overcome differences between Japanese and Koreans" without "dissolving the problems," by which he presumably means unresolved historical and political issues (Takeuchi 1985: 19). How could this be? I am not confident that merely granting oneself the ability to imagine the abstract other could bring about such an effect. Even the more specific point that the Japanese language is constituted by Koreans in Japan as well as by Japanese probably does not have such expansive ramifications. However, as Takeuchi suggests, this work does stand apart from the majority of fiction in Japanese, in that it proposes a new form of "linguistic action," one that affirms the possibility of communication with others even in a consumer society where most "so-called literature has transformed into mere entertainment" (Takeuchi 1985: 19–20).

Saussure's discussion of linguistics, he tells us, precludes any consideration of *parole* (individual utterance or speech act) and *langage* (language-speech, or perhaps living language), focusing rather on the system of language, or *langue*. Bakhtin, on the other hand, urged that *parole* should be at the center of any philosophy of language, and that "the principle organizing all utterances, all expressions is not internal but external, that is in the social milieu which surrounds the individual" (Takeuchi 1985: 21).[12] We have seen that Chong Ch'u-wŏl's work places its emphasis on the importance of the utterance of individuals (in the form of living language), and that it is intensely novelistic in the sense that Bakhtin used the word. It is inhabited by many different voices, thereby monopolizing the fact that language is on "the borderline between oneself and the other" (Bakhtin 1981: 293), that it is "overpopulated with the intentions of others" (ibid.: 294). It accents the "dialogic" character of communication, to borrow another term from Bakhtin (1981). To elaborate, it points to the fact that its meanings are necessarily imbedded in an ongoing social process, that it too is "living" and will attain new meanings each time it is read. Therefore, Takeuchi stresses, as did Bakhtin, and would I, that language and literature must be studied in its sociohistorical context.

I have drawn extensively from Takeuchi's reference to Bakhtin not only because I agree with some of what he says, but because he is part of the context necessary for understanding Chong Ch'u-wŏl's texts. He also helps to locate her place *vis-à-vis* Japanese literature and not just resident Korean identity. As he tells us, in Japan at the time of the writing of his essay, 1985, the effects of structuralism (based on Saussure) had led critics far away from actually thinking about what literary works specifically do. Marxists were stuck in old theories of culture as superstructure, and others bandied about theories of poststructuralism and postmodernism as if they were designer clothing.[13]

Aside from the presence of a strong old-school Marxist camp, the sight is not unfamiliar. I raise Takeuchi's point that Chong's work poses an alternative to structuralist (and poststructuralist) notions of language, which is my concern, too. I have consistently referred to the "I" in this piece as Chong (Takeuchi does not) because I want to reject a poststructuralist tendency to refer to the narrator of an ostensibly non-fiction text as being somehow unrelated to the living being of the same name. Rather than placing emphasis on the fact that the "I" in the text who authored *Chong Ch'u-wŏl's Collected Poems* cannot be identical to (or even an identical reflection of) that living, breathing human body who originally wrote the words constituting the book of the same title sold in the "real," material, world, I want to stress the fact that the multiple voices in the text (the "I"s) and the ranges of forms of expression that she uses in her daily life all emerge from a single, biological being who (sometimes) goes by the name Chong Ch'u-wŏl. People reading this and other pieces with this name on them have written to her, visited her at the bar she used to run, and (as in this text), called her up on the telephone. Her writings function intertextually within broader discourses about Koreans in Japan and about Japanese literature, and their circulation in turn changes the way that she lives (and the conversations she has) from day to day.

Based on such observations about her texts, it seems fair to say that her vision of Ikaino and of the home approaches the re-imagining of place provided by Doreen Massey, one that acknowledges not only its dynamism but its connections with other places. Part of the objection of people like David Harvey to place-based politics, Massey contends, is that they confound them with place-bound politics, and that they thus see them as never being able to counter the oppressive power of global capitalism (Massey 1994: 167). We see in Chong, however, that her focus on the local and on women does not prevent her from understanding the way that global capitalism holds us down, or believing that class-based politics are also important.

Yet at times she aestheticizes motherhood and Koreanness to a degree I find vexing. This is no less true in this story than in her earlier works. The final poem in "Mun Kon-bun *Ŏmŏni*'s Apple," in fact, is one by Mun recalling the safety and connection she felt snuggling under her mother's skirts as she worked. The poem ends simply, "That mother's child has become a mother/Now I have become an old grandma" (Chong 1985: 30). Chong accepts, even builds upon, Mun's nostalgic portrayal of the mother-child relationship. She sees the skirt connecting Mun and her mother as Mun's "own maternal nature," and perceives the last lines to indicate Mun's perception of the smallness of each of us "in the cycle of transmigration and reincarnation" (ibid.).

In addition, we remember, in this story she called the flavor of the uncultivated, oddly shaped apple, whose flavor is reflected in the speech of first-generation women, "clear." Here and elsewhere, resident Korean women, and in particular first-generation women, most of whom are illiterate or only semi-literate, occupy a distinctive position in her formulation of the margin. Why should Mun be held back from learning about history? I feel as though I am hearing familiar old binaries, women and nature and oral language pitted against men and culture and written language: not to mention proletariat vs. the rest, colonized (Koreans) vs. colonizers (Japanese), the former being pure, the latter, corrupted.

Is motherhood the only vehicle through which we can understand others' pain, through which supra-national affiliation can be forged? Or only minorities (or immigrants or formerly colonized peoples)? Can women only contribute to the

Mothers write Ikaino 91

lessening of others' oppression through reproduction? Is written language only valuable when it approximates the oral? For all these shortcomings, to affirm that the margins (women/the home and Ikaino) are important and to say that the simple acts of resident Korean women's lives are beautiful did turn on its head the dominant ideology. Even within the discourse on resident Korean identity, the attempt to integrate women's experience, and to link it with the more properly historical, was distinctive.

We have seen that the *chiikiundō* (local community movement) and anti-fingerprinting struggle are an important context to Chong Ch'u-wŏl's literature. Like these movements, she finds inspiration in the idea that people can live more humanely if they respect people's differences, and identify with, and pour energy into, local communities. Not all fingerprint refusers, however, shared Chong's concern with the particular plight of women, although more women participated than had in any such movement in the past. From its very beginnings women were prominent in the struggle. Approximately half of the first thirty refusers from September 1980 to February 1983 were female ("Hitosashiyubi no jiyū" henshūiinkai 1984: 232).

Several of the earliest women refusers were from Osaka, and formed an organization called "Shimon ōnatsu seido ni hantaisuru naze naze shimon? onnatachi no kai" (Why Fingerprints, Why? Women Against the Fingerprinting System). One of the members, Pak Ae-ja, in the founding statement for the group, defines her anti-fingerprinting stance as based on the same principles as her opposition to Japanese family registration laws: both systems are examples of the excessive control of people by the state. Hence she refuses to enter her name or her children's in her husband's family registry. He is Japanese: and Japanese law requires women to take their husband's name and become part of his family. In Korea, women's fate is equally bad: they are not even considered worthy of taking the man's name or being put into his family records. In both cases, children are entered only in the man's family's register and "belong" to him. "My children belong to me," she says, and she thus refuses to enter them in his registry ("Hitosashiyubi no jiyū' henshūiinkai 1984: 93). She further inveighs against the ways that these systems have been used in the modern nation-states of Japan and South Korea to discriminate against people by caste or place of origin (ibid.: 93–5). She perceives the Japanese system of managing its populace – going online as she wrote – as worthy of the concern of not only resident Koreans, but all members of the Japanese community (ibid.: 96).

While her feminist views were decidedly not mainstream, this essay found its way into a book sometimes called the "bible" of anti-Alien Registration Law activism, the 1984 *Hitosashiyubi no jiyū* (Freedom for the Index Finger). Another woman activist who contributed to this volume, Yang Yŏng-ja, uses gatherings of refusers as a forum to speak out (sing out, actually) about the oppression of women within resident Korean life. Her earliest memories, she reveals, are of her father beating her mother. When she performed a song about this violence at gatherings of Alien Registration Law protestors, however, several other Koreans castigated her, she recalls, arguing that men had done what they could, given the circumstances. They never blame the men, only Japanese imperialism, she bemoans ("Hitosashiyubi no jiyū" henshūiinkai 1984: 69–71). Unlike Chong Ch'u-wŏl, she speaks bitterly of the image of "'strong, kind, powerful maternalism . . . forced upon these women on the lowest rungs of society" (ibid.: 72). Resident Korean women should use the movement as "training" for expressing their pain, their sadness, their hopes. "Freedom is not one's own," she declares, "until one feels it for oneself" (ibid.: 73).

It is no doubt a distinctive feature of this movement that women like these were able to manipulate it to their own ends. In all likelihood, the local character of the struggle made it easier for them to do so. Although the relative success of the struggle (the fingerprinting requirement was repealed in 1992, but only for permanent residents) was at least in part dependent on the ability of the umbrella group Mintōren, the founders of whom were mostly Christian, to mobilize Christians worldwide, the real power of this struggle nonetheless came from the collaboration between resident Koreans and Japanese living in the same regions. The act of alien registration, including fingerprinting, took place at the office of local government, at city, town, or ward offices. The first Japanese to join in were employees of those local government offices, who first garnered the support of their union branches and eventually that of local officials (mayors, for instance) against the Ministry of Justice, the body controlling immigration and alien registration. In addition, the fact that many refusers were already active in community-building efforts when they engaged in civil disobedience made it easier for them to organize, and more difficult for the courts to paint them as criminals.

The case of one such community worker, Kim Dŏk-hwan, who was (and is) based in Ikaino, is illustrative for us here. In May of 1985, the same year as "Mun Kon-bun Ŏmŏni's Apple," Kim Dŏk-hwan refused to give his prints at the Ikuno ward office. While he was not a member of Mintōren, he was a Christian, and he did work for a community center run by his local church. Osaka, like several other local governments, however, was refusing to cooperate with Ministry of Justice demands, and he did not at first face prosecution. However, after he refused to appear for questioning at the local police office, he was arrested. (Kim Dŏk-hwan shi no gaitōhōsaiban o shiensuru kai [hereafter Kim o shiensuru kai] 1990: 184–5).

He was brought to trial in March 1987. He used the time granted him in the courtroom to make a case not only against the specific law, but more generally for the inclusion of resident Koreans within Japanese society, particularly at the level of the local community. To this end, he described his own experience of poverty and prejudice, relating it to the broader exclusion of Koreans in Japan over history. He argued that the fingerprinting system was the legacy of a blatantly racist colonial system of control, one adjusted rather than eliminated in the postwar period (Kim o shiensuru kai 1990: 203–7).

Kim clearly did not see legal changes as sufficient to provide resident Koreans an atmosphere in which they could live with dignity. Hence he sees his involvement with the *chiikiundō* (community movement) as part and parcel with his efforts to eradicate discriminatory laws. His interest in this movement began when in 1977 he began teaching at an *ŏmŏnihakkyo* (literally, mothers' school), where first-generation women came to learn to read and write Japanese. It was run by the Osaka Seiwa church, which he attended. In 1978, he had joined in the struggle against housing discrimination in Ikunoku, in 1979 he was appointed manager of the Ikuno local action committee (which was formed by a coalition of eight area churches), and in 1982 he began working full time heading the Seiwa community center. The *ŏmŏnihakkyo*, he reports, is "not only a place to learn to read and write, but a support for these women in their lives, or, in the terms we use today, a site of community" (Kim o shiensuru kai 1990: 250).

His first efforts in the community, he says, were depressing. Ikuno had a higher rate of juvenile delinquency than other Osaka wards, and 70 percent of the cases of youth misconduct involved Koreans; yet not a single Korean group was included in the ward office's list of organizations working on social issues. In addition, despite the fact that one quarter of the population of the ward was Korean, and one of the elementary schools 85 percent Korean, not a single Korean parent was an official in the PTA (Kim o shiensuru kai 1990: 38). When he became head of the Seiwa community center, his main objective, he says, was to facilitate *deai*, or "encounters." He stresses that this word is at the very core of his activism, that the coexistence of Koreans and Japanese in Japanese society depends upon it (ibid.: 40). To this end, the Seiwa center ran a nursery school, as did Korean churches elsewhere in Japan.

Perhaps its (and thus Kim Dŏk-hwan's) most successful endeavor, however, is one unique to that locale: the Ikuno national/ethnic (i.e. Korean) cultural festival (*Ikuno minzoku bunkasai*) – featuring music, food, dancing, games, and so on – held each fall since 1983. In his trial, Kim Dŏk-hwan reports that initially, he had a lot of difficulty garnering support for this event, both from Koreans, who were strongly divided into camps affiliated with the two respective governments of the peninsula, and Japanese, who at first did not want to let them use schoolyards or public parks (Kim o shiensuru kai 1990: 41–3). The police had a hard time believing that this was a cultural festival and not a political demonstration, and did not want to supply the permit they needed for a parade through the streets; the parade was delayed to allow a "purifying" by the local shrine scheduled to go first (ibid.: 43). In the end, however, the event went on, and since then, not only have schools offered their space, but local Japanese people have even begun to contribute money for the event (ibid.: 44).[14]

Some people did continue to find the open display of Korean culture to be an obstruction to the creation of community. Kim Dŏk-hwan argues, however, that this rather is a step toward true "internationalization" (Kim o shiensuru kai 1990: 277). It still was a move in the direction of coexistence (one buzzword of the movement), for in order for Koreans to be full participants in a community, they needed to have pride in themselves. At the time he founded the cultural festival, many resident Koreans had become aware of their identity in negative ways, that is to say through discrimination and poverty. He and other community activists proposed that in order for children to gain a more positive view of Koreanness, they needed to be exposed to "culture." Thus culture began to emerge as a nexus which resident Koreans used to form their identities.

I went to this festival with Kim Ch'ang-saeng in 1997, and she told me that she had been nearly every year. Her work bears the influence of both the community movement and Chong Ch'u-wŏl's literary world. She professes that she was so moved by reading Chong that while she couldn't get her own copy of her first collection of poetry, she transcribed a borrowed copy word for word into her notebook (Pae Jang-jin *et al.* 1987: 77). She then went on to articulate her own Ikaino in the essays in *Watashino Ikaino* (My Ikaino), published in 1982, and "Akai mi" (The Red Fruit), a 1987 short story. Kim is a friend of Chong's, and their work shares many themes, but her writing is more critical of women's oppression and more direct in proposing ways they might overcome it. Stylistically it differs as well. At times searingly funny, its rendering of the details of life, work, and death in language is somewhat simpler than Chong's, all accented with dialogue in Ikaino dialect. Her writing thus evokes a gritty reality not always visible in Chong's.

The figure of Kim Ch'ang-saeng's bitter mother looms large in *My Ikaino*. Two essays in particular trace Kim's attempts to come to terms with her mother. One of these pieces, published originally in 1977, is the story of her mother's death. Unlike the writing of most earlier resident Korean writers, there is no resplendent maternal sentiment here. In one passage, we find a perspective rare in its frankness. She watches as her sister-in-law bathes her invalid mother:

> It was a cruel sight. Would I have to gaze upon the hole from which I was born as my mother had once yelled at my brother that he must do [when he was changing her diaper]? Her pubic hair all fallen out, it was the hole from which I was born that gazed at me. From between my sister-in-law's legs [who stands above her as she lies on her futon], she had trapped me, and would not look away. I'm being tested. This mother was testing her own daughter.
>
> (Kim 1982: 35–6)

The mother is not passive; the very body of this naked woman is transformed from that which is gazed upon and has violence done to it, to that which does the looking and inflicts the violence. Indeed, at every turn, her mother is cursing her children. Kim Ch'ang-saeng says that as a child she had rejected everything about her mother: her Koreanness, her poverty, her lack of education. She yearned for a mother who would make her a lunch to take to school; she was jealous of the very Japanese word for mother. While she could cry for the fate of the Korean people she read about in books, she says, not so for her own mother; she spoke filthy Korean (Kim 1982: 36).

She tells us that only when she transferred from a Japanese school to Korean school, run by Chongryun, the North Korea-affiliated organization, and began to learn Korean did her feelings for her mother begin to soften (Kim 1982: 36–7).

From the early seventies, many had stressed learning the Korean language as the key to attaining Korean identity. While clearly no resident Korean was ever going to recover true Koreanness (or become the same as a Korean-born Korean) by virtue of learning Korean, it is important to acknowledge that learning the language has provided a great number of people with a sense of empowerment (e.g. Yong Yo Yi 1995).

By the time of this essay, Kim Ch'ang-saeng had come to see her mother's life and death as similar to that of many other first-generation Korean immigrants, and "the dark days [her] mother, born in 1907, had led as the very history of [her] homeland, Korea" (Kim 1982: 41). By the publication of a second essay reflecting on her mother's death four years later, she even embraces the ways she is similar to her mother (Kim 1982: 49). She now imagines listening to her mother's ceaseless complaining not with the thought "not again," but with eager ears. It now seems to her a plaintive cry for "the life she tried to but was never able to live" (Kim 1982: 56).

If she saw her mother's history as much the same as other first-generation Koreans, she indicates that her mother saw her suffering rather as the result of "a bad fate" (Kim 1982: 42). Not long after, she wonders if her mother's life might have been different if she had not been illiterate. Would written language alone have accorded her the perspective necessary to see how her own life was the consequence of that broader history? In the next essay, she says of her mother that her illiteracy meant that she was "never, in her whole life, able to look at herself objectively" (Kim 1982: 49). She thus avers that written language gives people the capacity to perceive themselves abstractly as units in world history. For all her acuity at transcribing dialogue, then, Kim's work evaluates the written more positively than Chong's. She in particular finds useful the separation from self that writing permits, perhaps because it remains as an object after the fact as opposed to disappearing into air, as does speech.

Kim's works more directly express the notion that literacy is a practical tool not only for personal affirmation but for social change. In a 1980 essay, she tells of teaching at the ŏmŏnihakkyo in the Seiwa church in Ikaino. Before she began teaching there, she had seen a sign for the class, and simply assumed that the women were learning to write Korean. She peeked in one day, and to her great surprise, it was Japanese. Then again, she muses, "In Ikaino, empty theories have no meaning" (Kim 1982: 113). The women are most proud of being able to read the station names on the train and, ironically, being able to write their names when filling out documents for alien registration. Learning to read and write had helped the women to be practical in a quite different way, however: it gave them the confidence to protest against housing discrimination in Ikaino, to speak out against the Japanese state (Kim 1985: 23).

If her conceptions of language diverge from those we saw in Chong, so too does her Ikaino. She claims it as her "homeland" but it has taken her a while to be able to do so with a sense of peace (Kim 1985: 61). In a discussion in 1987, she observes that her view of Ikaino is quite different from Chong's. When someone credits Chong with developing the notion that Ikaino is Korea, Kim responds:

> Ikaino is Korea, all right, but for me, that's not enough. The *Ŏmŏni* are sure strong and they sure raised us well through that era. . . . But can't we get beyond that somehow? That's what I think we should be focusing on now.
>
> (quoted in Pae Jang-jin *et al.* 1987: 77)

She further suggests that the difference between their approaches is a result of the fact that she had grown up in Ikaino and wanted to run away, while Chong (whom she sees as having an internal sense of herself as Korean) had come in search of a Korean "community" to run away to, a place where she could just be Korean (Pae Jang-jin *et al.* 1987: 77).

Whatever the reasons, Kim's Ikaino is not a romanticized margin, but a place rent by conflict. Political differences sometimes bring members of the community to spar. She tells the story of a woman who reports that while in South Korea as a student, she was raped by an intelligence agent interrogating her for anti-government activism. As a demonstration in her support, one woman shopkeeper brings her Chinese medicine, but the South Korea-affiliated Mindan women's group says she has no proof, and calls her a whore (Kim 1982: 76–7). Nonetheless, she believes that if Korean reunification is to come from anywhere, it must come from Ikaino. In Ikaino, unlike Korea itself, those supporting the North and those affiliated with the South live side by side and must deal with each other on a daily basis simply to go on with their lives (Kim 1982: 82–3). She thus seems to find hope that the recognition of conflict will impel people to acknowledge the necessity for change.

In addition, the daily life of mothering and working in Ikaino, which seems only a pleasure in Chong, is oppressive here. In the first essay on her mother's death, she describes with painstaking detail the moments after she has heard that her mother has died:

> With tears streaming down my face, I put another load of dirty clothes in to the washing machine, ran upstairs, took the clothes in from the line and folded them. I was angry at myself. I was angry at this stupid busy life which deprived me of even the time to cry. I had thought before that when the time came that my mother died, I would leave my daughter with my husband and go hide away somewhere. But in the reality of my daily life, even the death of my mother is dissolved into the habits of everyday life. All my time, minced and cooked. Even when I tell myself "my mother's died, I have no home and no embrace to return to," my hands move on their own. My daughter is fussing and crying, and I change her diaper. I stuff a change of clothes in a bag. When my husband finally comes home and I tell him, he brushes me off, telling me not to lie. I guess my tears had dried and my expression was blank.
>
> (Kim 1982: 38)

The contrast with Chong is striking. The rushed tempo of her life, the mindless repetition, afford her not even the opportunity to mourn, never mind to protest. Elsewhere, in a manic, almost manifesto-like essay in which she describes her busy life working and raising a child, she calls daily life a "massive mechanism" (Kim 1982: 89). "I want to go to the mountains! I want to read a book!" she cries (ibid.). Unlike Chong, then, she is not speaking "from" the home or Ikaino as abstract border, but within the very trenches that are borders under conflict.

She imagines an escape from this misery. She finds it not with knowledge attained not from fellow resident Korean women (who tell her to have children young, and to put up with whatever comes), but from reading books. After talking of her despair, her tone shifts suddenly and she quotes Ibsen's Nora and a Japanese feminist, whose words, she says, "saved" her (Kim 1982: 88–91). Waiting and forbearing should not be women's only virtues, she argues, "let's use that [notion] back against men. In our very day to day lives, let's develop the will to change." She finally concludes, "my reunification of the homeland lies on the same faraway line of the horizon where women's lives and their sex are fused into one" (Kim 1982: 93). The personal is made political here in a manner consonant with 1970s US feminism. If this is also romanticization of a sort, it is patently divergent from the ideas we saw in Chong. Women's attainment of written language is not a positive thing merely because it allows them to communicate what they have to say, but because it enables them to hear the voices of people outside the small community in which they live. The act of reading is preeminent here in a new way.

In her 1987 "Akai mi" (The Red Fruit), Kim further affirms writing and female sexuality in a complex text weaving a narrative of a Korean woman character's oppression (including rape) by her husband and his complicit mother and her eventual divorce, her childhood shame over being Korean and fantasies of being Japanese, with the childlike fantasy world of her own daughter. Her narrative is rich, laden with imagery of childbearing (seeds, fruit, apples) and of transmigration (circles, a crematorium, ashes, Buddhist chants). In addition, her own experience of rape (by her husband) and unfulfilling masturbation are contrasted with the possibility of hope that her daughter will find sexual satisfaction through her acquisition of literacy in Korean:

> On the next exposed page, the boxes were filled with apples. The Korean "o"s – written darkly with a practice pencil – the strength left over from writing the circle made a line extend beyond it. The measured boxes were filled with mismatched apples that hadn't been pruned.
> Would they possibly ever ripen?
>
> (Kim 1987: 276)

Within the lines escaping their bounds, the escape from the uniformity of the circles of Korean letters lies the opportunity, perhaps, for an escape from the circularity of Buddhist transmigration and the repetition of oppression of women.

The fact that Kim builds on symbols and imagery from Chong's writing makes it easy enough to contrast the two writers. We might identify Chong's romanticization of orality and repetitive cycles of childbearing and culture (or more spiritually put, the transmigration of souls), as almost anti-modern, and Kim's grasping the power of the written and of progress as affirming the linear time of history and a Habermasian positive valuation of the modern. Likewise, we might assume that Chong is, in the manner of much "postcolonial" theory, hoping to fight colonialism by rejecting all that is tainted by association with the colonial, including rationality and narratives of progress, and that Kim is engaging in a more classic modernist "nationalist" sort of anti-colonialism that merely hopes to overturn the balance of power (after all, it is Korean and not Japanese her daughter is learning).

If this is true, they nonetheless both find value in the community (particularly of women) in Ikaino. Kim volunteers as a teacher in that community, and talks about being happy to live in a place where there are other Koreans, in a place overflowing with Korean language, food, and culture. The bodily also has a prominent place in Kim's work, although more often it is the body dissatisfied: one exhausted, pained, sexually frustrated. For Kim, the critical task is not only to find the positive in what it is already in Ikaino and Korean culture, but to acknowledge what is bad as well so that everyone's quality of life may be bettered. In the round-table discussion quoted above, she says that she has been reading a collection by African-American writers, and has found striking the way that they all talk about the support of the "community." In her reading, what they dread is not so much discrimination or lack of education, but "severing themselves from the traditions of their race/people" (Pae Jang-jin *et al*. 1987: 78). As simple as this notion may be, we must remember that even as these works were being published, ideas affirming the importance not of identification with Japan but of affiliation with the homeland (such as the "*zainichi* as method" argument) still held great power for people, and that even within the "*zainichi* as fact" camp, feminist voices had barely begun to be heard.

When I first decided to consider Ikaino literature and the anti-fingerprinting movement, I anticipated that they would neatly fit into my preconceived notion of what "*zainichi* as fact" was all about. I thought that they would simply show how resident Koreans had used identification with the local regions where they lived to enable them to perceive their identity as residents in Japan without forcing them to identify with the Japanese state. The essential objective of the anti-fingerprinting movement is to deny the modern nation-state system (in the form of Japan) the ability to control individuals, to make people into abstract units, and to instead assert the right to determine individual identities apart from such a system. Kim Dŏk-hwan's narrative was one of many such individual stories to make that point. To stress, as Chong and Kim do, the importance of the daily experience of being female in Ikaino seems to teach a similar lesson. Clearly they find a subjectivity in spaces seen as somehow not entirely controlled by Japanese language and ideology. Their portrayal of first-generation women provides an antidote to the exoticization found, for example, in a 1987 collection of photographs, *Onnatachi no Ikaino* (*Women's Ikaino*), in which the photographer says, "The women, more than the men, were people of an alien culture" (Ōta

1987: 131). It also challenges the sexism of earlier male authors' romanticization of their mothers' forbearance. When I met them, I felt that writing had empowered them both.

I suggested at the beginning of this essay that their philosophies of writing (found in both form and content) were interlaced with the very turn to the local. It is perhaps easier to see in Chong's case how this is so, as she rejects standardized written speech in favor of "living language" just as the community movement attempts to establish a life of dignity outside the control of the centralized state. In addition, her stress on the production of meaning within the writer–reader relationship seems a response to the increasing commodification of literature. Her concept of the margin, if at times nationalistic, ultimately seems a broader appeal against the homogenization of culture and the oppression of minority voices in Japan. By 1987, she was calling for collaboration not only with the labor unions of local governments, but with other minorities: Okinawans, Burakumin, and Ainu (Chong 1987: 246). When I spoke with her in the summer of 1996, she told me that for her, Ikaino was wherever oppressed people are found. She said she wanted her next book to be about the Filipina women she had met while working in a pachinko parlor in the countryside outside Tokyo. "The deepest part of the periphery," it seems, is no longer populated only by Koreans.

Kim's work, on the other hand, while it does contain a good dose of dialogue in Osaka dialect (and thus makes good use of Bakhtinian dialogism), still finds meaning in using the standard language and literary form of the Japanese nation to argue against the ideology implicit in them. Her stress on reading works of long-dead authors appeals to a different sort of relationship between reader and writer, but still one no less opposed to the mere consumption of texts. Kim Ch'ang-saeng also lives betwixt (and sometimes clings to) vestiges of nationalism: her family still works in the North Korea-affiliated organization, and she did not hide her delight that I spoke Korean and loved Korean food. Yet she is more openly critical of Korean women's oppression of other Korean women. It makes no difference if feminist ideas come from the west or even from Japan. Her Korean culture is one creatively assembled of those elements she finds useful. Much the same might be said of the women activists I cited.

Even the community movement, associated so closely with the idea of *zainichishikō*, which taught older women to write Japanese, the language they needed for practical purposes, believed that Koreans should identify with Korean "culture." Therein lay the purpose of events like the Ikuno ethnic festival. It might rather have proposed ways for them to find value in the culture which was theirs to begin with, a culture which is an amalgam of Korean and Japanese, a culture borne of the history of Koreans in Japan. The anti-fingerprinting struggle likewise did not argue (as perhaps it might have) that not only the requirements of the Alien Registration Law, but the fact that people from Japan's former colonies had not been granted the choice of Japanese citizenship, was utterly unjust. Even today, when a great number of resident Koreans become Japanese citizens each year, when people whose parents or grandparents naturalized have earned the right to use Korean names, and when there are significant movements fighting for Koreans' rights to be employed in management positions in local government and to vote in local elections, hardly a soul is to be heard arguing that former colonial immigrants and their descendants should be offered the choice of becoming Japanese citizens. And ten years ago, at the height of the anti-fingerprinting movement, this was all the more the case.

Perhaps I have been too critical, stressing the *de facto* nationalism of cultural activities or learning Korean language rather than acknowledging the ideology of multiculturalism put forward here. It is evident that the conceptions of the local proposed by these authors and activists are not simply reactionary nationalism, nor conservative postmodernism, ascribing to the notion that what happens in their local area cannot be understood via the rubric of a metanarrative such as that of global capitalism. Each of these individuals tries to depict the dialectic between the local and the global, both materially and in terms of discourse. Less thoughtful entreaties for coexistence (in Japan as in the US) tend to rely on the assumption that there are people who hold culturally distinct identities. Joan Scott proposes that a genuine multiculturalism would perceive identities as relational, historically defined, and engaged in an "ongoing process of differentiation, relentless in its repetition, but also . . . subject to redefinition, resistance and change" (Scott 1995: 11). I sense here increasing inclination to characterize both resident Koreanness and Japaneseness in this manner.

It is important to realize that in the 1980s, and even now, Japanese society has had trouble getting its head around even the more ordinary version of multiculturalism. There has been great resistance to seeing resident Koreans as "Korean-Japanese," that is to say, Japanese of Korean descent, even though (by American standards of ethnicity) of course many such people exist. "Go home" letters sent to fingerprint refusers attest to this fact; how can someone go home to a place s/he has never been? All this is on top of the fact that discrimination in housing, employment, and government benefits persists. It thus takes a great deal of courage, or, some would say, foolhardiness, to propose making that leap to identifying oneself primarily as one who belongs in Japan, the ultimate sign of which would be to become a Japanese citizen. Until Japan's wartime history is taught in a way that explains and justifies resident Koreans' presence in Japan by acknowledging the fact that it was Japan's colonial policy which forced them to come in the first place, no such view even has soil from which to sprout. Even then, there is no guarantee that people will become accepting of such notions.

Teaching directly about the facts of colonialism and the history of Koreans in Japan may help, but it is not sufficient. A true commitment to history, that is to say, to the future, is surely evoked not only through abstract and logical understanding of the world, but also through a complex and sometimes contradictory emotional one. The role of literature in this respect cannot be overstated, and for this reason I have integrated a reading of resident Korean literature into my own history.

Mothers write Ikaino 101

I want to believe that some day both resident Koreans and the Japanese among whom they live will come to accept a view of the world that finds liberation and dignity in an honest and emotional engagement with history rather than in clinging to simplistic cultural nationalism. I am left hoping that I, as a different sort of foreigner with a different but nonetheless powerful connection with the place called Japan, will be able to contribute to a necessarily ongoing effort to achieve that goal.

Acknowledgements

I want to thank Norma Field and Sonia Ryang for their critical acumen and emotional support, Chong Ch'u-wŏl and Kim Ch'ang-saeng for opening their hearts (and mouths) for this odd foreigner, and lastly, Song Yŏn-ok for making me feel that I had family in Osaka.

I would also like to acknowledge the Fulbright Commission, without whose funding for dissertation research this paper could never have been written.

Notes

1 Throughout this essay I use the terms "Korean in Japan" and "resident Korean" interchangeably. The latter I have borrowed from Norma Field (1993).
2 I have given a simplified description of postmodernism for reasons of space. Two indispensable texts arguing the connection between changes in capitalism and shifts in cultural expression are Harvey (1990) and Jameson (1995). One more essential piece is Massey's criticism. See Massey (1994: 212–48).
3 I find Caren Kaplan's account of this trend particularly helpful. See Kaplan (1996: 143–87).
4 This and all translations which appear in this essay are my own. A slightly longer selection from this poem is included in Suzuki and Oiwa (1996: 182–3).
5 I think here of recent anthropological work in a conversational style, and particularly that by feminists, such as those included in Behar and Gordon (1995).
6 I have not been able to locate this first collection, but the fifth section of *Ikaino/Woman/Love/Poems*, is composed of selections from that book (Chong 1984: 86–164).
7 Kim Si-jong, the male poet whom I quoted earlier, similarly characterizes women of Ikaino. He observes that because they have the responsibility of appeasing the hunger of their families, and the stomach is an "incredible thing," "The women are strong, oh yes. Exceptionally so" (Kim Si-jong 1975: 184–5).
8 A translation of this poem appears in Leza Lowitz and Miyuki Aoyama (1995: 40–3) (under the title "Two Names").
9 Ri expressed to me that he prefers to be referred to by the Japanese pronunciation of his name, Ri Kaisei, which he calls his pen name, in distinction to his Korean name, Li Hoe-sŏng.
10 Julia Kristeva's "Women's Time" and Mikhail Bakhtin's "Forms of Time and of the Chronotope in the Novel" were helpful to me in making this distinction (Kristeva 1986).
11 *Ŏmŏni*, which means mother, is a term used in Korean to speak of any woman who has had children.
12 The English translation of the work cited here, *Marxism and the Philosophy of Language*, is actually credited to V. N. Volosinov (1986), although it has been widely

assumed to be Bakhtin's work. The Japanese translation of the work lists the author as Bakhtin.
13 Karatani Kojin's *Gendai bungaku no kigen* (The Origins of Modern Japanese Literature), first published in book form in 1980 in Japanese, is a preeminent example of literary criticism with strong poststructuralist/postmodernist influences. See Karatani (1993).
14 The scholars Tani Tomio (1996) and Harajiri Hideki (1997), both of whom have done fieldwork in Ikaino, report that there is relatively little contact between local Japanese and Korean groups. They also note the presence of somewhat exclusionary associations of members of Japanese families who have lived in the area since before the influx of both Koreans and Japanese from other parts of the country in the early modern era.

5 Reading against the bourgeois and national bodies

Transcultural body-politics in Yu Miri's textual representations

Lisa Yoneyama

The nineties has witnessed a kind of renaissance of *zainichi* Korean writers, that is, Korean national writers who were born, raised and continue to reside in Japan as permanent resident aliens.[1] Within the Japanese literary establishment, a number of Korean-Japanese writers – many of whom wrote in both Korean and Japanese languages – have won high acclaim since the time of Japanese colonial rule over Korea. For many decades, the legacy of the early twentieth-century proletarian writers' transnational networks in East Asia, and the dominant leftist concerns of the postwar Japanese literary establishment, have fostered readerships responsive to *zainichi* Korean writers' Marxist critiques of the Japanese monarchical system and their advocacy of anti-colonialism, anti-racism, and other progressive political agenda. Yet the distinct feature of the *zainichi* Korean writers' popularity in the nineties is the remarkable prominence of women's literary engagements as novelists, critics, columnists, and journal editors. Earlier *zainichi* Korean writers' activities were not necessarily perceived as creating a cultural trend that would impact mainstream society, in part because they limited their engagements to writing fiction and to the immediate literary and political circle. In contrast, Yu Miri, the writer I wish to explore in this paper, and other women authors who have gained increasing visibility in Japanese society in the last ten years or so, have been writing in a variety of genres and are widely involved in different sectors of the culture industry, including fashion magazines and television talk shows.

In general, *zainichi* Korean writers' works have been constituted as a terrain over which the forces of colonial history, law, politics, and culture intersect in complex and overlapping ways. The choice of using the Korean or Japanese readings of authors' names, the adoption of monolingual or bilingual writing, the genre selected for their works: all these have historically been tied to the positions adopted *vis-à-vis* mainstream Japanese society, one's family and community, gender, the two Korean regimes, organizational affiliations, and one's primary location of residency and politics. The questions that inevitably accompany such choices are also intimately linked to the strategies of criticism and forms of insubordination and/or resistance embraced by the authors. In the writings of such renowned male authors as Li Hoe-sŏng, the central figure among the postwar *zainichi* writers who was awarded with the 1972 Akutagawa award, the tropes of "homeland" (*sokoku*), "ethnos" (*minzoku*), and the unification (*tōitsu*) of the two regimes, always loomed large in the protagonist's/narrator's psychology as a utopian site of longing and yet impossible return. The desire to redeem and reunite the "homeland" often paralleled the frustrations of ethnically minoritized individuals in the stories who have not found a "home," a site of comfort, belonging, and patriarchal order. Works by others such as Kim Hak-yŏng also dredged deeply into the protagonists' anxieties and the instability of their social being, their emasculated state and their linguistic and national ambiguities.[2] The agonizing conditions are understood to have derived from the protagonists' inability to establish themselves as successful subjects within Japan's capitalist economy and the nationalized political sphere, because of the racism and discrimination which *zainichi* Koreans face in Japan.

Critics have pointed out that, while similarly probing the question of "being different" in Japanese society, the works of the women writers who have achieved commercial success in recent years and received wide popular attention tend not only to foreground women as their main protagonists; they also divert from earlier writings in their treatment of everyday social relations and their positions *vis-à-vis* the two nations. As a professional writer, mother, and a pachinko parlor owner, Sŏng Mi-ja, for instance, writes about women's struggles over and within one's residence and workplace. At the same time, Sŏng perceives her writings to be a kind of collective message delivered from the second to third generation of *zainichi* Korean women (Sŏng 1995). Kyō Nobuko, who was awarded a non-fiction literary prize in the late eighties, delineates the structural impediments that *zainichi* face in the society, but through portrayals of the mundane and intimate relationships between the writer and her Japanese husband, with second-generation parents, neighbors, classmates, and colleagues (Kyō 1987). Furthermore, Kyō and other writers such as Pak Kyŏng-nam deliberately attempt to confound the binary oppositions between the Koreans as passive victims and the Japanese as a unidimensionally oppressive collectivity.[3] Still other writers such as Yi Yang-ji, who died shortly after receiving the Akutagawa award, complicate the Korean diaspora's relationship to the national language and community.[4]

A number of important questions need to be raised about what appears to be a new cultural trend. Most crucially, the national attention to these writers as well as their commercial and critical success must be juxtaposed to the society's overall inattention to the legal and socio-economic disprivileges and discrimination which many *zainichi* continue to face on a daily basis. While the naturalization/nationalization process increasingly allows diversity in forms (unconventional Japanese surnames and so on), the so-called "nationality requirement" (*kokusekijōkō*) virtually excludes non-nationals from employment in the public sectors (public schools, public hospitals, the local police force and so on) which offer relatively stable job conditions.

It is also important to investigate the effect of the prominence of these writers – and their feminine gender in particular – within the context of the official multicultural policy of Japan's so-called "internationalization," or *kokusaika*. The way the officially sponsored "internationalization" operates in this context can be likened to the way multiculturalism works in the liberal and transnational corporate discourses. Sociologist Avery Gordon argued that, rather than promoting radical structural transformations, the mechanism of inclusion of diverse population into the liberal political sphere and the transnationally operating capitalism is working as what she called "diversity management": that is, a way of domesticating the presence of differences and their potential threats to the *status quo*.[5] In this particular respect, one needs to be especially vigilant when identifying in these popularized writings distinct absence of the urgent desire to reclaim "ethnos" or even "homeland" as the imagined origin and the telos of nationalist consciousness.[6] Have the questions of racial and ethnic discrimination, and the material historicity of Korean diaspora become secondary for them? Like disloyal daughters of the colonized, who forsake their fathers and male siblings, have these women writers ceased to see the significance of addressing the injustice and oppression that arise from their ethnic and national identifications?

In this paper, I am particularly interested in exploring the works of Yu Miri, one of the most popularized *zainichi* Korean writers of the nineties. While equally concerned with the above questions, I am also intrigued by the consistent focus in Yu's textual representations on the theme of dysfunctional family and unconventional sexuality as the central site of literary scrutiny. Use of family plots in a semi-autobiographical form is in itself not at all unique to Yu. The failure to erect the familyhood idealized by the modern bourgeois society has often been posited by many *zainichi* writers as an allegory for the tragic history of Korean nationhood ruined by Japanese colonialism.[7] The distinctiveness of Yu's works lies instead in the relentless decentering of the patriarchal authority and sexualization of female plots. Moreover, in contrast to those writings that, through their scrutiny of the "failed" family forms, unintentionally reintroduce that which is lacking as that which needs to be longed for and restored, Yu's textual representations consistently refuse to posit family and home as the objects of desire for communal recuperation. What is at stake in breaking down the family-er terms in which the ethnic Koreans' everyday lifeworld has thus far been portrayed?

Born in 1968 in a prefecture nearby Tokyo as a second-generation *zainichi* South Korean, Yu began writing dramas when she was sixteen. Her decorated career as a professional writer, however, was preceded by a rough adolescence: the author was bullied at school, ran away from home, and attempted suicide a number of times. After having performed as a stage actress for a theater group called Tokyo Kid Brothers, Yu established another group, Seishun Gogatsutō (Youthful May Party) in 1988. In 1993 she became the youngest individual to receive a Kishida Kunio theatrical drama award for her *Sakana no matsuri* (The Fish Festival) (Yu 1993). Three years later in 1996, her *Furuhausu* (Fullhouse/The Full House) received double awards: the Noma literary novice award and the Izumi Kyōka literary award. In 1997 Yu was awarded the Akutagawa award for her story, "Kazoku shinema" (The Family Cinema) (Yu 1997a). The author's name was not publicized in the US news media until her winning of the award incited violent threats from (presumably but not necessarily Japanese) right-wingers.

Multifaceted themes have been woven into almost all of her works: the racialized/ethnicized metaphor of dysfunctional families, the contradictions within the normalized bourgeois ideals of family, body, and sexuality, and the narrator's/protagonist's prevailing "sense of discord" (*iwakan*) with her surroundings, both within and outside the family. The three themes are inseparably intertwined to produce the narrator's sense of differences and discords – racial, sexual, gendered, idiosyncratic, and otherwise – from the world of habitualized relations and values.

Yu has expressed misgivings about being identified first and foremost as a writer of the so-called *zainichi* (*chōsenjin*) *bungaku* (*zainichi* (Korean) literature) on various occasions. Yet her refusal to be identified as a *zainichi* writer should not be taken too literally as her abjuration of the South Korean nationality, any more than it represents as her assimilation into the mainstream Japanese society. The author's racial and ethnic affiliation is pronounced unmistakably through her choice of the Korean reading of her surname, as well as through writings on her own extended family members. To mark this particular difference for oneself, moreover, means more than making a choice of individual preference; it is an act loaded with socio-historical implications.

For the reasons I discuss below, Yu's stories indeed reject simple readings that prioritize any one difference over another. They demonstrate the intersectionality of race/ethnicity, gender and sexuality: a notion familiar by now to everyone in the human and social sciences. As Lisa Lowe has eloquently shown, "we must always speak of more than one contradiction" (1996: 164) in countering the global forces that thrive by differentiating the laboring bodies according to race, gender, sexuality, religion and so on. Yet all too often discussion of the intersectionality of multiple structural forces organizing multiple differences is understood to be antithetical to the projects that try to address and rectify the oppressive and exploitative conditions associated with those differences. We do not seem fully to possess constructive "ways of listening" to such multiply overlapping contradictions. What seems urgently in need is not only to observe the intersectionality of differences. We need to explore the productive ways in which we can perceive those discursive practices that try to put under a single scope multiple and sometimes even contradictory forces, and show them to be equally powerful and effective in generating departures from the equilibrium maintained by those very differences.

Yu's texts – fictional writings, media opinions, and criticisms (e.g. Yu 1998) – indeed underemphasize, although never suppress, the markings of ethnicity, race, and Koreanness. And as such, they interpellate readers to produce the mainstream subject position in Japanese society which functions by disavowing the racial, ethnic, and other critical differences which organize its members. *Zainichi* scholars and writers who have been critical of Japanese society's treatment of racial minorities have invariably and understandably castigated Yu's writings as thoroughly domesticated commodities which only endorse the present condition.

My purpose here is to intervene in such hasty readings. I hope to demonstrate that, rather than dismissing it as a retreat from ethnic/racial politics, it is much more productive to read Yu's deemphasis (which is not necessarily denial or suppression) of racial or national differences as a radicalizing of critiques of normalization of bodies in modern national and bourgeois society.

Family discords, family lies

In the opening scene of "The Family Cinema," the narrator, Hayashi Sumi, a successful businesswoman who works for the marketing section of a large-scale flower company, returns to her apartment one day after work and is stunned by the invasion of her residence by her family and a film shooting crew. After many years of estrangement, the family is meeting for the first time to appear in a semi-documentary, semi-fictional film. The producer of the film is a friend of the narrator's younger sister, who used to be a popular actress in a small theater group, and now supports herself by appearing in X-rated pornographic videos and taking occasional part-time jobs. In the director's rough scenario for the whole family, the frustrated father is supposed to propose on the night of his eldest daughter's birthday that the family should live together once again in the house he owns. Resisting in vain, Sumi is forced to act along with others. Nauseated and in a daze, she observes the members of her family performing their assigned roles. But she is unable to determine whether they are acting according to the director's instructions or are exposing their true emotions. Beneath the smiling faces gathered around her birthday cake, she detects exactly the same sense of hatred the family's members held toward each other twenty years earlier.

From the outset, the mother is totally disgusted with the father's proposal to reunite the family. Instead, she is scheming to start a new business by appropriating the father's property as collateral. The mother had left the family about twenty years previously for a married man, five years younger than her, and had supported herself by working in cabarets, nightclubs, *yakitori* shops, and other entertainment businesses. To commemorate her forty-fifth birthday, she underwent a breast implant operation. She and her lover had maintained their same residence pattern over the previous two decades: he would visit her place every night, but unfailingly returned to his wife and children before midnight, and stayed over every weekend. He pretended to his wife that he needed to go on business trips.

The younger brother is a twenty-eight-year-old college student. Once praised as a genius, he one day decided to become a professional tennis player but failed. However, he does not seem to be attending any classes, nor to have any social life. He lives with the mother, who tells the narrator that her son is on the verge of madness, and that she needs to be resigned to the thought that living with him is like "keeping a pet dog, though expensive" (Yu 1997a: 38).

The father is portrayed as a wife-beater, gambler, connoisseur of expensive goods, and as the narrator remembers, a commanding patriarch whose fragile pride the family needed to pamper constantly when they used to live together. Toward the end of the story the father suggests that the whole family take a camping trip. The film crew follows the family to the campsite near a shabby outdoor mountain hot spring. The family cooks and dines at the campfire as the father had planned. Bathing together in the hot spring, the father proposes yet again that the family should live together. But the mother reveals that he has recently been fired from his high-paying job as a pinball, or pachinko parlor manager, that he will no longer be able to afford the payments on his house, and that since he would be "too proud to work as a security guard or a taxi driver" (ibid.: 45), the children can no longer rely on allowances from the father, nor on other forms of support such as health insurance coverage. The father refuses to admit that he will lose his source of income.

In the meantime, a heavy rain starts to fall and the father's outdoor plan ends in disaster. While everyone else is about to leave for a local hotel for the night, the father insists on sleeping at the campsite, inside the slanted tent. He dashes out into the rain and frantically tries to straighten the tent post, but to no avail. As the camera crew excitedly shoots the dramatic turnout of the event, the narrator watches the father in the rainstorm. And the mother's voice solemnly declares, "Sumi, once you obtain your own health insurance, it means you've found your way out of the family/household (*ie*)" (ibid.: 46).

Similar plot can be found in the portrayals of another Hayashi family in Yu's 1996 piece, *Fullhouse*. In this story a failing father builds a spectacular mansion in an attempt to reunite the ruined family, only to discover that the inhabitants are not his daughters but a homeless family with children who show signs of abuse. Where the Hayashi family in "The Family Cinema" is made up of two parents and three siblings, *Fullhouse* is about a residence inhabited by the two homeless parents, their son, daughter, and the narrator, whose name again is Sumi. *Fullhouse* begins with a scene in which the father welcomes the two daughters at the door of his brand-new house: so new that there is no water or electricity, and the smell of new paint burns the eyes and throat. From the very outset, the narrator and her younger sister are determined to declare to the father that it is impossible for them to live together.

The text is not entirely unsympathetic to the father's painful effort to attract his daughters to the new residence. The house cost fifty million yen to build, the father explains to the daughters, an amount of loan they will not be able to pay back unless they receive his life insurance payment. Overwhelmed, the narrator utters an admiring comment on the house and even says to her sister that she might stay there once in a while.

At the same time, the text remains sarcastic about the single-family residence. As she observes an inventory of newly-purchased household items, the narrator remembers the family's old house in Tokyo's Nishi district, which was practically turned into a junkyard where the father would bring back dumped electronic goods and other old junk. It was a house in which the family used to live together, which her mother left many years ago. The narrator also observes objects that are familiar to any household but utterly meaningless to her own: massive sculptures placed to decorate the house entrance, a study with built-in bookcases that do not contain a single book, a weighty golf bag no one would use, and a rice scooper inscribed with the word "love," which is thrown in randomly among other kitchen items, including three more plain rice scoopers. The narrator summarizes:

> From age 10, when mother left home, to sixteen, I went back and forth between the house in Nishi district and the condominium where mother lived with her man. In the subsequent ten years I never lived with the parents. Father might have built the house in order to regain the ties among the collapsed family; but the family has long been completed inside me.
> (Yu 1996a: 43).

About a month after her first visit, the narrator is called up by her father. When she returns to the house to her father, an unfamiliar middle-aged woman appears at the door. Interrogated, the narrator responds, "I am a member of this house." Gradually things are revealed to the narrator. The woman and her man used to own a small electronic shop, but failed in business. After having their last remaining cash stolen, the couple and their two children began living as a homeless family at the railway station. One evening, according to the woman, as they were preparing for the night in front of a department store, the narrator's father passed by and invited the family to live in his new house. It is also explained that their daughter, Kaoru, stopped talking two years earlier.

Despite the unusual circumstances, the presence of the narrator, and the occasional visits by the father, seemingly ordinary, familiar everyday scenes unfold inside the house. The two upstairs rooms are filled with children's toys and school goods; the wife leaves the house for a haircut during the day; she cooks a meal for everyone in the house; the man scolds the son to stop watching television after dinner and tells him to study his homework. The narrator, too, is quickly and irresistibly captured into playing the role of a family member. From the moment they met, the wife obtrusively expects the narrator to take care of various household chores. The narrator begins to suspect that her father has dreamed up a scenario in which his daughter, whom he knows cannot stand the family, eventually claims the house to herself to oust them.

The narrator's dilemma is described in the following words:

> As long as it is fine with father, what's the inconvenience if the family continues to live in the house? It does seem unreasonable for me, who has no desire to live here or regard it as a property to inherit, to wish the family to leave. Yet clearly a physiological sense of execration delineates dark contours outside of my consciousness. At the same time, the girl has a firm grip over my physiology. But father could not be wishing to continue to live with the family. It felt as if the house suddenly began to swell.
> (Yu 1996a: 78)

The narrator had earlier refused to live in the father's new house precisely because she did not wish to have anything to do with family matters. The new residents of the house gave her an excuse for not living there. However, although she cannot bear the way the family behaves, the narrator continues to live with them because she is erotically attracted to the daughter.

The seemingly unsolvable dilemma ends abruptly when the son makes a fraudulent phone call to the fire station. One evening, the oppressive silence that has engulfed the entire house is suddenly broken by the fire engine siren. Discovering that his son told a lie, the man savagely beats up the boy until he finally loses consciousness. The girl, who has been watching the violent father with a glaring gaze, suddenly picks up matches and sets fire to the house. The couple frantically scream and dart around the room. The remaining three inhabitants of the house, the girl, the father, and the narrator, stand aside and watch calmly as the two race all over to extinguish the fire. Once the fire is successfully put out, the man grabs the girl to slap her. It is in this final scene that the girl utters her first and last spoken words: "So, it's no longer a lie!" (ibid.: 91) The girl goes away from the house on a bicycle and disappears into the night.

"The Family Cinema" and *Fullhouse* are more than a critique of patriarchy. The undermining of fatherhood and family cannot be taken transparently as resonating, for instance, with the critique of the patriarchally organized modern Japanese *ie* (household) system which feminist historians and critics have seen as a source of women's oppression and exploitation. In this sense, the depictions of Yu's families can be taken as antithetical to the mainstream feminist criticism in Japan. Moreover, these stories do not promise any romantic communal solidarities grounded on identification as women. Yet it should also be underscored that Yu's stories expose and condemn the subsumption of unpaid domestic labor into the economy of family romance.

As in "The Family Cinema," the father in *Fullhouse*, a general manager of a successful pachinko business, is remembered by the narrator as a father who physically assaulted the mother, and who did not bring in enough regular income to support the family despite his relatively large monthly wage. At the same time, the narrator comments on her father's odd behavior with pitying amusement. He embodies every feature associated with the image of the traditional patriarch of modern invention: he is stubborn, abrupt, violent, self-infatuated, unable to communicate with the family, and pathetically attached to the daughters. Both "The Family Cinema" and *Fullhouse* unambiguously depict these fatherly traits as pathological. Yet they do not castigate patriarchy in itself as the cause of family's victimization or of the narrator's childhood trauma.

Both texts relentlessly bring into relief the often-concealed discords embedded in the history of apparently normal families. They also delineate how a family cannot function without lies and pretensions, even as it disavows mutual dishonesty in the name of truth, care, and love. Family, as portrayed in Yu's works, is that which every member, despite his or her unevenly assigned power and status – man or woman, old or young, reproductive or unreproductive, successful or unsuccessful – equally participates to uphold as an institution. It is a site where members' desire, treachery, envy, and vanity converge, clash, and are obscured.

Patriarchy is one hegemony born out of such complicitous acquiescence and participation by other members of the family.

It may be worthwhile to note that in *Fullhouse*, the daughter's aphasia suggests one possible way of not participating in such a family collusion. By refusing to speak – except the one truth she establishes – the girl in *Fullhouse* resides outside the realm of family sociality and signification. The household conversation is exchanged only among the holy trilogy, the man, woman, and their son; in contrast, the girl remains exterior to the language of lies and pretensions, as well as to the social relations of the family. Her final utterance intervenes in the realm of signification, and thereby produces a dramatic rupture onto the family-er arrangement. Between the girl and the narrator, an illicit communication unfolds beyond the established system of signs, in another realm of amorphous pleasure of bodily senses: of smell, murmur, touch, gaze, and the haunting traces of them.

Sexuality beyond ethnic family romances

In both "The Family Cinema" and *Fullhouse*, the ethnicity of the I/narrator and her family is only ambiguously marked. In the former, the family's surname is shown in an ideograph meaning "forest," and it could be read as a common Japanese name, "Hayashi," a Chinese name, or a Korean name, pronounced as "Im." In both stories, the father's occupation as a manager of a pachinko parlor, a business known to be predominated by *zainichi* Korean capital, may be identified as a distinct marker of ethnicity rather than class, but only if one subscribes to such a stereotype. The image of a violent, tyrannical and failed father, and the mother's association with work in the nightlife business certainly resonate with many of the individuals appearing in the worlds of other *zainichi* Korean writings. Yet, they, too, cannot be read as signs that exclusively denote Korean difference.

One could certainly read into Yu's stories a convergence of the Korean diaspora's historicity with narratives of a family's dispersed residence. The portrayal of the failed father and dysfunctional family can also be read as indicators of the oppressive consequences of discrimination against society's racialized others. Furthermore, when the narrator in *Fullhouse* describes her life trajectory as having moved "back and forth between the house in Nishi district and the condominium where mother lived with her man," this in-between-ness can be interpreted as indicating the postcolonial history of Korean diaspora residing in Japan. This history is one in which the position of the diasporic Koreans is constituted by both the patriarchal sovereign state of the postcolonial Korea, and Japan, with which they maintain an inauthentic yet immediate and intimate relationship. Moreover, whenever the author describes her personal history, her experience of being bullied at Japanese school is not entirely unrelated to her being a *zainichi* Korean. And because the author proclaims the I/eye-witnessed nature of her fictions, the readers inevitably project the author's ethnicity on to the characters of the stories. Finally, in *Kazoku no hyōhon* (Family Specimen) (1995), an ethnography of a variety of contemporary families including her own,

Yu fully exposes the contradictions her friends and families face as having derived specifically from the racial and ethnic difference of being Korean in the mainstream Japanese society.

Yet, according to this reading, mothers and daughters who forsake their husbands and fathers will be read only as betraying their paternally-constructed national and ethnic community. If one reads Yu's representation of family only as a metaphor of Korean national/ethnic community, and if one assumes a seamless convergence between Yu's families and the membership of Korean diaspora, women appearing in her stories, who are often forced to choose whether to live with their husbands and fathers, are given only two options: either to remain within that boundary or to abandon their membership of that collectivity.

This one-dimensional reading has another important consequence on how the sexual agency of Yu's women can be interpreted. The nationalist reading presumes women's sexuality either as reproducing the authentic members of the original community, or miscegenating to reproduce illegitimate members through their relationship with those outside the community. In either case, women's sexuality is defined by the telos of heterosexual reproductivity. To the contrary, Yu's mothers and daughters resist such a heterosexually-determined nationalist reading. In "The Family Cinema," the mother's breasts, enlarged to commemorate her forty-fifth birthday, exceed by far their reproductive instrumentality. Likewise, the narrator of *Fullhouse* is infatuated with the girl, the signification of whose body has not yet been fixed by the telos of reproductivity. The narrator's orgasmic sense is described as follows: "The sexuality inside of me is not aroused but extends horizontally" (Yu 1996a: 79). The sexuality of Yu's mothers and daughters thus cannot be subsumed by the narratives either of the conventional heterosexual familyhood or of national/ethnic family ties.

In "The Family Cinema," the narrator develops a brief relationship with an avant-garde sculptor, Fukami Seiichi. This is yet another sexual and erotic investment that cannot be reconciled with either the national/ethnic family romance or the modern bourgeois family ideology. In the following I would like to devote some time to disentangling the web of discords that the author exposes in this relationship. Where does the author wish to take the readers with the awareness of such discords and differences?

When Sumi visits Fukami in order to convey the company's request for him to produce a vase as new merchandise, she finds the renowned artist to be far from his worldly image. Fukami turns out to be a socially dysfunctional individual, who cannot converse or negotiate but simply announces his will or command. He is a man who lives in a messy room in a shabby wooden apartment building, who sleeps in a rubber float, and who likes to collect Polaroid photographs of women's naked buttocks. Fukami insists on taking a photo of the narrator's buttocks. The narrator instinctively finds Fukami to be one of the few people she can "come to terms with" (*oriau*), someone who "has no sense of reality" (*genjitsukan no nai hito*) (Yu 1997a: 47).

Whether the narrator has sexual intercourse with Fukami is left unclear. In her relationship to Fukami, insofar as the readers are informed, she is reduced to nothing but her buttocks, the thing in and of itself. Her body and the pleasure it experiences are drastically severed from the heterosexual normativity of patriarchal family reproduction. Sumi's body is chosen for neither its instrumental values nor romantic meanings attributed through the existing order of signification. In this relationship Fukami, too, is no longer a celebrated artist, but no more than "a queer old man" (*hentairōjin*) (Yu 1997a: 27). The text portrays this experience of radical objectification with a kind of *jouissance*, particularly marked by the narrator's spontaneous laugh (ibid.). Among various representations of laughter in the text, this is the only time when it appears to indicate straightforwardly a sense of simple amusement.

Yet such a pleasure, unbound by conventional ideals of romance and sexuality, only exists momentarily in the story. Even with a man like Fukami who appears to have transcended every mundane sociality and common sense, the narrator realizes that she is unwittingly made to perform a role ordinarily assigned to domestic women. Like the woman appearing in *Fullhouse*, Sumi takes care of the daily chores of cleaning and laundering. In the closing of "The Family Cinema," the narrator accidentally discovers that Fukami has other women who fulfill the same function. Leaving Fukami's apartment in a daze, she remembers her mother's words, "Finally you were able to be alone; you were able to find your way out of the family" (Yu 1997a: 48).

The mother's words can be read in two contrasting ways. Taken to be an irony, it can be interpreted that the story concludes with Sumi's realization that one can never find one's way out of a family, that complete whole which exists despite of, and because of, exclusion and collusion. This realization may indeed put her memories of the devastated family history into a relative perspective, assuring that her troubled family in its seeming "abnormality" – is not an exception. (That the deviance of the family appearing in "The Family Cinema" is far from an exception is fully explored in Yu's *Family Specimen* mentioned earlier.) According to this reading, the story only acts to restore and endorse the family as a defective yet inevitable form of social relationship. Even while it is exposing pathologies and contradictions embedded in the family as an institution, the text may well be recentering and renaturalizing it within the present social arrangements and representations.[8]

To the contrary, the mother's words can be read more productively as a positive pronouncement of the narrator's entry into a different state of sociality and consciousness. The way the narrator recalls the mother's words supports this reading. First of all, the way the mothers' words are remembered is as if they "submerged [in the narrator's mind] like an emblem branded onto a passport photo" (Yu 1997a: 48). And the sentence that follows the mother's words reads: "I pushed the gate and it opened smoothly; nobody is around; both the school yard and building were in serenity" (ibid.). It should also be noted that the position the narrator occupies in the story is not necessarily antagonistic to that of the mother. Sumi reminisces, rather favorably, as follows:

> When I became three, mother made me take piano lessons, dressed me like a French ceramic doll, and rolled my hair to create long vertical curls. But

once she realized that the actual story did not fit the happy family illustration she had dreamt of, she began working at a cabaret and plainly gave up her casting as a mother.

(Yu 1997a: 10)

Throughout the text, the moral authority tends to reside in the mother, who is portrayed as a forthright and undaunted woman, who refuses to masquerade as a "good wife and wise mother."

Given these observations, the mothers' words – "Finally you were able to be alone; you were able to find your way out of the family" – should be read in conjunction with the narrator's flight from the failed relationship with Fukami. Family is indeed a pathological social site filled with contradictions, a site where the members are always cast to perform properly their given roles, where the differences and incommensurability are disavowed in the name of love and harmony. Yet it is not merely the family as an institution that needs to be rejected. Rather, what needs to be exposed and rejected simultaneously is the work of immanent power that haunts every social relation and molds it into one like that of a family. It also works to prompt people to search for utopic redemption in the family-like relationship.

As Michel Foucault and others have convincingly shown, the regimentation and nationalizing of social bodies in modern statehood have been mutually intertwined with the normalization of modern bourgeois family values: of the idea of reproduction of healthy citizens, proper heterosexual parenting, a prolonged period of innocent, a-sexualized and passive childhood, a desirable capitalist work ethic, and so on.[9] The controlling mechanism of modern bourgeois society, above all, has worked by distinguishing normal and proper family forms from the abnormal and improper, while marking that difference in terms of nation, race, and ethnicity. It is because the place called family has been constructed in such a way as a crucial site of regimenting the modern world, a site invested with many stakes, that the task of exposing even the slightest "sense of discord" within it, as Yu's writings do, can be a most unsettling critique of the ways in which society's stability is maintained by ordering various differences, racial or otherwise.[10]

The question of racial and ethnic differences not only concerns relations among members of the existing social collectivity, such as ethnic groups or nation-state, but more fundamentally the amorphous and shifting distinctions through which power controls and organizes individuals by differentiating desirable social bodies from the undesirable. This condition of race and ethnicity may be best captured by Etienne Balibar's notion, "techno-political selection of individuals," a kind of racial stratification which does not rely upon clear markings of cultural boundedness or chromatic differences. Balibar describes this post-racist racism as follows: it is a condition:

> in which the aspect of the historical recounting of genealogical myths (the play of substitutions between race, people, culture and nation) will give way, to a greater or lesser degree, to the aspect of psychological assessment of intellectual aptitudes and dispositions to 'normal' social life (or, conversely,

to criminality and deviance), and to 'optimal' reproduction (as much from the affective as the sanitary or eugenic point of view), aptitudes and dispositions which a battery of cognitive, sociopsychological and statistical sciences would then undertake to measure, select and monitor, striking a balance between hereditary and environmental factors.

(Balibar 1991b: 26)

To view racism in this way, however, does not mean that more familiar types of race relations, cultural and biological, have ceased to exist; rather, they may very well supplement and facilitate each other. Yet, if racism is understood in this way, then the ambiguity of racial, ethnic, or national markings in many of Yu's writings can be understood as a necessary move in order to expose the issue of racism and ethnic discrimination in a most fundamental and radical manner. This move can unsettle not only the category of race and ethnicity, but other intersecting elements of power simultaneously.

One way to frustrate such workings of power, as suggested in Yu's stories, is to abandon the belief that one can ever "come to terms with" others. Thus in both "The Family Cinema" and *Fullhouse*, the narrator's/protagonist's brief sexual and erotic involvement ends unfulfilled. In order not to be fully seized by that power, one needs to withstand and carry through every sense of "discord" and incommensurable difference – racial, sexual or otherwise – at every possible moment. The very last sentence of "The Family Cinema" is suggestive in this respect. The narrator is sitting on a swing. A gust of wind swirls the sand around her heels and she feels as if being washed away by a strong tide. "In order to come to terms with the wind," the story concludes, "I rocked my body" (*watashiwa kaze to oriai o tsukerutameni karada o yurashita*) (Yu 1997a: 48). Rather than establishing a single and immobile foothold of resistance, one possible way to deal with the forces that are ceaselessly at work in recruiting individuals for yet another "family cinema," is to constantly fluctuate one's positions. In order not to be fully incorporated by those forces, if not to reject them entirely, it is necessary to shift and vacillate from one difference to another, but without disclaiming the material specificities associated with each of different positions.

In conclusion: towards a transcultural body-politics of differences

When a right-winger threatened to disturb Yu's post-Akutagawa award book signing, and when the two publishers almost canceled the event upon judging that the individual bookstores could not guarantee their customers' security, the right-winger's attack was seen as directed against Yu's Korean ethnicity. The alleged culprit repeatedly threatened her over the phone, warning her not to use the Korean reading of her surname and insisting that according to the proper Japanese reading the character for "Yu" can only be read as "yanagi" or "ryū." Yet, Yu has insisted that the incident should not be construed only in terms of

116 Lisa Yoneyama

ethnic issues. "Various organizations affiliated with South Korea wished to support me and requested me to participate in public meetings," Yu wrote, "but I declined them all with gratitude. For I fear that this criminal's disgraceful and debased (*hiretsuna*) behavior might unnecessarily incite nationalism [among ethnic Koreans] and lead the incident in wrong directions."[11] This piece, moreover, cited the Japanese constitution and declared to the public that she would "fight resolutely" against what she understood as a threat to freedom of thought and speech.

The ambiguity of ethnic and racial markings in "The Family Cinema" therefore is in large part effected by the author's autobiographical statements. In an interview with the Naoki Literary Award writer, Hayashi Mariko, Yu reiterated that she wishes that her works not to be confined within the category of "*zainichi* literature."[12] In it Yu says that she does not "possess an awareness of being a *zainichi* South Korean writer (*zainichi kankokujin sakka*)." Yu further adds:

> If I write about *zainichi kankokujin*, [my works] are framed as "*zainichi* literature." And that is what I don't like. But at the post-Akutagawa award press conference I said, "I am neither Japanese nor South Korean"; and after that when I held a separate interview with South Korean reporters, there were many voices directed at me, asking "why did you say you are not South Korean when that is your nationality?"

As I have shown, such an authorial pronouncement does not automatically indicate that concerns for racial and ethnic differences are repressed in Yu's writings. Yet trouble occurs when the mainstream Japanese readership assumes that Yu's statement represents a *zainichi* Korean's dismissal of national/ethnic differences. This was evident in the way the Japanese interviewer Hayashi received Yu's remarks. Hayashi responded, for instance, "It feels as though the fictions you write are made diminutive when summarized with words like 'discrimination'." Interestingly, in rejecting the identification as a writer of *zainichi* literature, Yu did not even once mention that she does not wish to deal with the question of "discrimination," whether it is associated with racial, sexual or other differences. Hayashi further comments:

> [You] write about your family because they are interesting; and they happened to be *zainichi* – isn't that what it is? Your novel writes about the experience of been bullied; but even that is not because you are a *zainichi*, but because [your] own aura-like thing stands out too prominently.

Perhaps Hayashi's best represents the Japanese readers' subject position effected by Yu's remarks such as these as well as by her acquiescence to her Japanese interviewer's continual dismissal of her Korean difference.

Certainly, when Yu's writings express her dismay about the right-wing threats by relying on the idea of freedom of speech, it seems as though the author has adopted a position of an unmarked, universal subject under the liberal constitution. Because the liberal constitution's universalism and disavowal of differences uphold an undifferentiated treatment of political subjects, while simultaneously disallowing policies directed at existing structural differences, the author's political pronouncement appears to be unproblematically in accordance with her own suppression of Korean difference. It also appears as if she is envisioning political activism only within the nation's constitutional terms. Yet, as readers, we might notice a profound oddity in this particular act of citing the Japanese constitution. It may well be remembered that *zainichi* are disenfranchised not only with respect to electoral rights; the nationality requirement practically bars non-Japanese residents from important public offices and high-ranking positions for national security reasons. Given the fact that all resident aliens, including the Koreans, reside outside the constitutional principles, an individual who has marked herself as *zainichi* elsewhere citing the Japanese constitution can suggest an ironic challenge, not an endorsement, to the boundary of the national political sphere.

"The Family Cinema" and *Fullhouse* do more than merely expose the contradictions and incommensurable differences that constitute the narrator's/author's family, or by extension modern bourgeois families at large. The two texts probe for clues with which to disturb such problematic arrangements. Yet, in doing so, they do not give up the question of racial and ethnic difference. Arguably, Yu's writings can be disconcerting and threatening to those who desire to maintain the stabilized boundaries of family, ethnic community, and national polity and history, for they reveal and criticize the mutual imbrications of racism and bourgeois family values.

Notes

1 *Zainichi* denotes "in Japan," and is here exclusively used to mean "Koreans in Japan." The approximately 700,000 Korean nationals who reside in Japan today are mostly descendants of those who were forcibly relocated, or obliged to leave Korea, as a result of the social and economic devastations brought about by Japan's prewar colonial and military policies, and the subsequent postwar US Cold War hegemony in the region. Japanese colonial policy during the first half of the twentieth century also imposed the Japanese language and Japanese-style family names on Koreans. After the war, Koreans were unilaterally declared non-Japanese. This collaborative US and Japanese policy confined those who (partly owing to the ensuing outbreak of the Korean War) did not return to Korea, to the unstable and disenfranchised "resident alien" status. See Lee (1981) and Kang and Kim (1989) for a succinct overview of the structural problems surrounding the Korean resident aliens in Japan. Ryang (1997) offers an analysis and descriptions of the ideology and everyday practices of *zainichi* Koreans affiliated with North Korea, an account rarely available in either Japanese or English.
2 See a *zainichi* critic, Takeda Seiji's analysis of Kim Hak-yŏng's "Frozen Lips" (Takeda 1989).
3 Pak, for instance, writes of Ōkawa Tsunekichi, a police officer who allegedly saved several Koreans from Japanese mobs in the aftermath of the 1923 Great Kantō Earthquake. (See Kyŏng-nam 1992 and 1995.) The records show that several thousand Koreans were massacred by the Japanese after the earthquake, along with a number of Chinese, Japanese socialists, and anarchists.

4 In *Yuhi*, for which she won the award, Yi Yang-ji allegorically depicts the diasporic longings for authentic ties with the lost national language and community. Yet, in *Yuhi*, the "mother tongue" painfully fails the main protagonist, a young *zainichi* college student who returns to South Korea hoping to restore her lost cultural and linguistic affiliation. Language in this story is an exclusive order of signs which prohibits rather than facilitates intercultural dialogues (Yi 1989a). See Hayes in this volume.

5 See Gordon (1995) and Yoneyama (1998). Earlier in my study on the memories of Hiroshima's atomic bombing, I explored the contradictions produced by the gap between Hiroshima City's official call for "international peace" in remembering the nuclear destruction, and the administration's reluctance to include the memories of colonized people in the public arena (Yoneyama 1995).

6 This tendency found among the commercially successful writings, of course, is not universal. See, for instance, Norma Field's discussion on the nationalism and homeland espoused by a Korean woman poet, Chung Ch'u-wŏl (Field 1993). See also Wender in this volume.

7 Li Hoe-sŏng's *Kinuta o utsu onna* (Woman Who Fulled the Clothes) best restores how the desire to restitute the lost nationhood and Koreanness is allegorized through the male narrator's longing for a lost family (Ri/Li 1972). The story moreover inscribes the mother's body with the authenticity and rootedness of Korean ethnicity and culture.

8 I am thankful to George Lipsitz for drawing my attention to the danger of Yu's work being read in this way only.

9 See especially Foucault (1985). Ann Stoler (1995) demonstrates in detail how Foucault conceptualized sexuality in its inextricable relationship to the way race has been mobilized for the production of truth in the context of modern capitalism and European imperialism.

10 It may be worthwhile considering the implications of Yu's works for a curious change in Japan's school textbook controversy. The focal points of the Ministry of Education's anxiety over the content of text books have now become family values as well as the history of war and colonialism. The official stance allowed descriptions about the Rape of Nanjing and the biological experiments of Unit 731, while censoring the description of single parenting as an alternative lifestyle.

11 From her weekly column, "Kotoba no ressun" (see Yu 1997b: 141).

12 The conversation between Yu and Hayashi is quoted from Hayashi (1997: 48). For more on Yu, see Lie in this volume.

6 Cultural identity in the work of Yi Yang-ji

Carol Hayes

The aim of this chapter is to explore cultural identity in the work of Yi Yang-ji (1955–92), a second-generation Korean writer in Japan, focusing on her individual values and sense of self and on how she positioned herself in regard to both Japanese and Korean societies. Yang-ji's work will be examined through an exploration of the identity formation of her characters, particularly in her first novel *Nabi t'aryŏng* (Grieving Butterflies), published in 1982, and the 1989 novel *Yuhi* – named after its central protagonist – which won the Akutagawa award, one of Japan's most prestigious literary awards. The chapter is divided into three sections: Yi Yang-ji's life, a literary analysis of her fictional work through an examination of the cultural identity of her characters, and her concept of ethnic and cultural identity.

Individual and group identity which merge to form cultural identity are linked by a subjective sense of belonging, for, as Iain Chambers wrote:

> Just as the narrative of nation involves the construction of an 'imaginary community', a sense of belonging is sustained as much by fantasy and the imagination as by any geographical and physical reality, so our sense of ourselves is also a labour of the imagination, a fiction, a particular story that makes sense.
>
> (Chambers 1994: 25)

Chambers argues that in the modern world there is "no uninterrupted inheritance that reaches into the present from the past, but instead bits and pieces exist in our present not as traces . . . of a unique tradition, but as elements of different histories that are continually being recomposed" (Chambers 1994: 102). These dispersed historic elements can be explored through an examination of, on the one hand, externalized forms of cultural identity such as rituals, social behavior, symbols, accepted community beliefs, and material artifacts which invest a given group, in this case Koreans in Japan, with a readily identifiable quality, and on the other hand, internalized forms where identity develops in the act of distinguishing between socially imposed roles and an individual's sense of self. Yang-ji's characters build upon these two forms – external and internal – to frame their sense of self, and an examination of this can assist our understanding of Yang-ji's own sense of cultural identity.

Yi Yang-ji's life

Yi Yang-ji was born on March 15, 1955 in Yamanashi prefecture as the eldest daughter of Yi Do-ho and O Yŏng-hŭi. Her family – her parents, two older brothers, and two younger sisters – settled in Fujiyoshida in 1959, where her father, who had arrived in Japan in 1940 at the age of fifteen, took up a job as a travelling salesperson of silk goods. Her mother was a second-generation Korean from Osaka. In 1964 Yang-ji's parents, and consequently all their children, became naturalized as Japanese, taking the name of Tanaka. Yang-ji's name was changed to Tanaka Yoshie, preserving the same characters, but now read in the Japanese way. Yang-ji believed her parents had made a conscious decision to fit into Japan to protect their children from potential discrimination, which resulted in Yang-ji suppressing her sense of self as a Korean. According to her:

> My father and mother . . . felt that to live in this land of Japan they must ingratiate themselves with Japanese culture and lifestyle, and gain the trust of the Japanese, and so they worked hard to familiarize themselves with Japanese-style living and to educate their children as Japanese. When I was nine years old, my parents became naturalized Japanese, yet I can't really blame them for that act. If somewhat unwillingly, I too automatically became naturalized, although I don't believe it made the slightest difference to the fact that I was and am Korean. My parents shouldered the heaviness of a past unknown to me, which forced them into the unnatural state termed "naturalization," giving birth to a second generation like me. It could be argued that Japan offered no other choice.
>
> (Yi 1993b: 579; all translations of Japanese materials in this chapter are mine)

Her parents' "Japanification" of their family seems to have been very successful, as Yang-ji cannot remember being discriminated against by her school friends for being a Korean. Their efforts to mesh seamlessly with mainstream Japan meant that such Korean staples as *kimch'i* were banished from the house. Even the Korean language was banned, with her parents only using Korean in heated arguments. Her parents consciously educated Yang-ji in Japanese culture, sending her to learn Japanese dancing and flower arranging, in addition to her music lessons in the *koto*. Yang-ji speaks of herself as a cheerful high-achiever who could be relied on by her teachers. However, this success at school was shadowed by a sense of despair. Her parents' relationship had deteriorated into what was to become a ten-year battle in the divorce courts. Yang-ji later came to understand that her efforts at school were actually based on an inbred fear of unpleasantness, and a desire for smooth social interaction. She found herself constantly filling uncomfortable gaps in conversation, unable to stand silences. Her home life seemed that of "small animals living in glum silence with nothing to do in a dark hole" (Yi 1993b: 584). She began to see herself and all around her as riddled with impurity. She was "inferior and spiritless with no mitigating touch of gentleness. And worse, a filthy uncivilized Korean" (ibid.). This suppressed sense of inferiority was redirected at all Koreans. On the rare occasions when she went to Osaka to visit relatives, she felt that they were "culturally backward," "dirty," and even "barbaric and uncivilized" (ibid.). This led her to reject all that was "Korean" even to the point of suppressing all conscious awareness of herself as Korean:

> Yet, I was most definitely Korean. Though I shook my head in denial and tried to hide it all the time, that self squirmed for life deep inside me. Looking back on it now, I see that I actually went out of my way to let it out, to try and grasp hold – with my own hands – of just that part of me which was so "unclean." I was completely overcome by a sense of shame; by a sense of my own ugliness. I could not but question; why had I been born? How was I going to go on living? and worse; how could I possibly go on with this impudent essence, this shamelessness exposed to all?
>
> (Yi 1993b: 585)

Tortured by her inability to balance the elements of her identity, Yang-ji even tried suicide – swallowing drugged tobacco laboriously unrolled from medicated cigarettes – but only succeeded in making herself very ill. Her inability even to take her own life made her all the more ashamed.

In 1972, in her last year of senior high school, and with only 30,000 yen in savings, she ran away to Kyoto, where she took up a menial job in a small inn. Hard though this was, it removed her from the horrors of her family home. "My salary was but a tear in a sparrow's eye. I didn't even have Sunday off. Yet in the beginning I didn't feel any lack of freedom" (Yi 1993b: 587). The following year she returned to school, entering a senior high school in Kyoto while still continuing to live and work at the inn. Yet she was still unable to overcome her embarrassment at any association with Koreans or Koreanness:

> I traveled to school by subway everyday. One morning at least ten Korean high school girls got into my carriage. They were all wearing ethnic dress – ch'ima chŏgori – and speaking loudly in Korean. Their words were those of my grandfather, still stored away somewhere deep within me. The angry sounds of my mother and father fighting resurfaced from within my subconscious. I winced. These girls were clearly Korean, but why weren't they embarrassed? Their clothing immediately identified them as Koreans, and they were talking Korean so loudly that absolutely everybody must know they were Korean. . . . I blushed red, feeling as if I had been struck in the chest. Hearing the announcement for the next station, I quickly got out – running away. . . . How could they be so courageous, so cool? And . . . how could being Korean be so natural?
>
> (Yi 1993b: 588)

Yang-ji's sense of shame and her inability to face up to her ethnicity began to change through the encouragement of her history teacher in Kyoto. Through him and her own increasingly wide reading, Yang-ji became very interested in her ethnic origins and, as her political understanding deepened, increasingly militant. This is reflected in her decision to no longer use her Japanified name of Tanaka Yoshie, but to revert to her Korean name of Yi Yang-ji, which she saw as an act of defiance against Japan and all that it represented. She consciously chose what she saw as a path of suffering, refusing the anonymity of life as a naturalized Korean in Japan, a group who, she felt, buried the sensitive spots within themselves, trying to ignore their Koreanness:

> Sometimes I lost heart wondering why I had to take issue with being Korean all the time.... My path seemed such a maze – a maze with no exit.... Yet even in the midst of all that insecurity and inner confusion – even acknowledging that I myself was a total weakling – I just could not forgive the oppression Koreans in Japan had been forced to face against their will.... Surrounded as they are by the immediate affairs of that which we call Japan, there is a clear encouragement of ethnic abandonment and the humiliation of the homeland in the assimilationist policies so skillfully incorporated into Japan's oppressive social policies. It cannot be ignored that the clear intent of these policies is to obliterate both ethnic self-awareness and any will to the future in Korean Japanese. They aim to erase that lifestyle which should rightfully be protected. Surely this is nothing but intentional humiliation!
> (Yi 1993b: 591)

In 1975 at the age of twenty Yang-ji entered Tokyo's Waseda University, only to leave after one term. She had become fascinated by the *kayagŭm*, a Korean zither similar to the Japanese *koto*, and began to learn Korean dancing. Over the next few years Yang-ji became involved in ethnic Korean political activism – largely through the Korean students group at Waseda University – focusing on the homeland and the politics of the Korean community in Japan in clear opposition to assimilation with general Japanese society. She began to associate with activists – predominantly second-generation Koreans like herself – working for rights within Japanese society, and freedom from institutionalized discrimination such as fingerprinting and being denied the right to vote. However, she began to feel a sense of self-hatred, seeing herself as a hypocrite for simply mouthing ideas and slogans imposed on her by the political leanings of those around her. Music became her only solace, and she came to feel that playing the *koto* was her only reason for living.

In 1980, at the age of twenty-five, Yang-ji went to stay in Korea for the first time, and immediately became very involved with music, not only continuing to learn the *kayagŭm* but also taking up lessons in the musical accompaniment to *p'ansŏri* [traditional Korean opera] with the living cultural treasure Pak Kwi-hŭi as her teacher. Yang-ji was also introduced to Korean folk dancing, which had a lasting impact on her. It was through this style of dancing, learnt under Kim Suk-cha, an eminent dance teacher, that she felt she was truly experiencing the spirit of her homeland.

Despite her pleasure in her music studies, Yang-ji's personal life continued to be shadowed by unhappiness. Her elder brother died suddenly of a sub-arachnoid hemorrhage at the age of 31, in October 1980, and then her second brother died, with a similar suddenness, of meningitis the following year. Both deaths placed a great strain on Yang-ji's mental stability. However she remained in Korea, pursuing the spirit of her homeland through its music and dance.

In 1982 at the age of twenty-seven, after one year at the preparatory courses, Yang-ji was admitted to the Korean literature department of Seoul National University. However, she deferred her enrolment at the same time as completing the enrolment procedures, and returned to Japan. The death of her two brothers had brought her parents' relationship to a crisis point and their bitter battle – which had gone as far as the High Court – was finally formally settled in divorce. It was in the November of this year that Yang-ji published *Nabi t'aryŏng*, a novel she had written in her lodgings in Seoul the previous year.

Yang-ji finally returned to her studies in Seoul in 1984, and graduated in 1988 at the age of thirty-three. Her undergraduate dissertation, entitled "Linkages with the world of *P'arikongju*," involved an analysis of Korean concepts of God and the afterlife in the work *P'arikongju*. (*P'arikongju* is a classical literary work – an anonymous work of oral tradition – dealing with exorcism and shamanistic beliefs.) After graduation she entered the dance department of Ewha Women's University in Seoul as a graduate non-degree research student.

Yuhi, Yang-ji's most well-known work, was published in the November 1988 issue of *Gunzō*, a Japanese literary magazine specializing in contemporary literature and literary criticism. In January 1989, Yang-ji was awarded the 100th Akutagawa award – a prestigious award for new authors, marking their successful debut on to the literary stage – for *Yuhi*. By February its Korean translation had been published.

In March 1989, Yang-ji entered the Masters program of the dance department of Ewha Women's University. Her research topic was to analyze the beauty of repetitious movements in Buddhist ceremonial dancing. In June she deferred her studies yet again and returned to Japan. The following year, 1990, she returned to her graduate studies and by 1991 completed all the credit requirements of the program.

In 1992, aged thirty-seven, she returned to Japan in January with the intention of staying for only two weeks. However her younger sister was suddenly taken ill and so she extended her stay, devoting herself to the writing of *Ishi no koe* (The Voice of the Rock). On 18 May, she developed bad cold symptoms and a high fever. As her temperature was still very high on 20 May, she was taken by ambulance to hospital, but told that she only had a cold and would recover with medication, and thus returned home. Early on the morning of 21 May, her chest hurting, she returned to the hospital to be told that she had developed pneumonia. No beds were free and so she was sent to another hospital. However, on her arrival there she had developed such advanced symptoms that they could not treat her and she was consequently returned to the intensive care unit of the first hospital, where later that evening she fell into a coma. On 22 May her family was informed that her condition had worsened and she was declared dead, of acute myocarditis, at 8:40 a.m.

Nabi t'aryŏng and *Yuhi*

In this section I will introduce to the reader two major novels by Yang-ji, *Nabi t'aryŏng* and *Yuhi*. *Nabi t'aryŏng*, Yang-ji's first novel, was published in *Gunzō* in November 1982, and was subsequently nominated for the Akutagawa award. In what is very much an autobiographical novel, Yang-ji tells the story of Aiko, a young Korean woman living in Japan. Angered by her parents' ugly divorce proceedings – in which she and her eldest brother Tetsuo have been forced to take different sides in the courtroom battles – Aiko leaves home to live and work in an inn in Kyoto: the same path followed by Yang-ji herself. The story begins when Aiko, newly returned from Kyoto, telephones her brother Tetsuo. Having heard nothing of her for the last two years, Tetsuo is both surprised and angry, but he arranges to meet her and the two drink together, avoiding all questions which cause too much pain.

The story then follows Aiko back in time to the hardships of working in the inn in Kyoto, to progress, on her return home, through her increasing political awareness of herself as a Korean and her anger at her father for having made his family become naturalized as Japanese. She sinks into a period of profound depression, becoming an alcoholic with little will to live. Her second brother Kazuo, after a sudden illness, falls into a coma, and until his death his hospital room becomes a place where the family can meet with less of the hostility of the courtroom. Aiko develops a relationship with Matsumoto, a married Japanese man twenty years her senior. In the past, Aiko has railed against both her father and brother for fancying Japanese women, sneering at their inability to associate with their own people. Yet now Aiko finds herself in the same position as the woman who had first caused the divorce proceedings to begin between her parents.

At this point in her life, Aiko discovers Korean music, and it gives her the strength to break away from Matsumoto and to follow her heart to Korea. She sets herself up in Seoul to study Korean music and dance. Even the sudden death of her eldest brother Tetsuo fails to divert her from this path.

The novel shifts quickly from scene to scene, from present to past and back to present again, yet it ends in quietness, when Aiko finally makes peace with her past. It is only this acceptance of her past which will allow her to participate in the present. Aiko finds the strength to accept her past through her dance lessons. During these lessons she has begun to feel something, to catch a certain scent in the air as she watches her teacher dancing. This scent encapsulates the very essence of her homeland. Before she can participate in the dance, however, she must first face up to her memories and reconcile the duality their repression has caused within her by setting them free:

> During the fifteen minutes while I was watching the *salp'uri* dance I was unable to draw breath. You could say I had been transfixed.

Starless, the dark leaden sky was heavy with thick clouds. With the wind cold on my cheeks I replayed my teacher's *salp'uri* in my head. Tetsuo's face flitted across my mind. Then, Kazuo's [Aiko's other brother] lying so still in the hospital. Matsumoto's face floated up next. Then everyone was there, my father, mother, and Michiko [Aiko's sister].

"Winter will come again. February will also come."

As I muttered these words, I saw the white butterflies. In the darkness behind my eyes, the white butterflies were flying as if drawing out all my memories, all my past. Relentlessly memories welled up from within me. I gasped for breath like a dying fish. My throat was parched with a burning thirst, a piercing stabbing thirst. I began to curl up into a ball, all but overcome by it all.

– Tetsuo was dead.

My left nipple began to ache.

– Kazuo's shriveled chest, his lightless eyes.

Stabbing pain shot through me. I began to pound my head with my hands. I continued my pounding in an effort to negate all these memories. But the white butterflies began to fly again. However much I hit my head and shut my eyes tight, the white butterflies continued to fly. . . . I fixed my eyes on the butterflies. . . . Never once turning my eyes from them. . . . Everytime the butterflies fluttered past they left a white trail. Following their whiteness with my eyes I began to sing.

(Yi 1993e: 58–9)

These butterflies are the "grieving butterflies" – "Nabi t'aryŏng" – which gave this novel its title. They symbolize Aiko's repressed memories, and their flight is a sign of Aiko's inability to shut them out. Only by accepting their existence, by accepting the pain they represent, can she set out on the road to the self-awareness she seeks, and only then will the healing essence of the music enfold her.

The novel moves towards its climax when Aiko receives a phone call from her sister Michiko, to tell her of Tetsuo's sudden death. Three fast shots of rice vodka fail to evoke even the slightest sense of drunkenness or forgetfulness; just an ice-cold tingle fills her head. However, as she lets loose the memories of her brother in the butterflies' flight, she senses a strong wind rising up around her, seizing hold of her body. Aiko opens the window to the first light of dawn and painstakingly cleans her room. That done, she dresses herself in the pure white *salp'uri* garments which she has laid out ready. With the newly washed *posŏn* on her feet, she draws on the long flowing skirt and high breasted over-blouse of the *ch'ima chŏgori* and takes up the long scarf-like *sugŏn* before climbing up onto the roof of her lodging. Below her, Seoul glitters in anticipation of morning, and a knife-edged cold – from out beyond the stars – cuts through her body.

The scene before me was no different from last year. No, no . . . it was different, it was just that I couldn't see it. And in ten years, even twenty, it would still continue to change – the thought wrenched a sigh from me.

My *uri nara* [homeland] was alive. Its scenery would continue to change forever, and here in its very midst, I would play the *kayagŭm*, sing the *p'ansŏri* and dance the *salp'uri*. That was the only possible way for me to live. Wherever I lived it would be no different.

The *kayagŭm* began to play a melody, as the white butterflies began to fly. I began to dance the *salp'uri* all the while following the butterflies with my eyes. Without pause, the *kayagŭm* kept up the rhythm and the *sugŏn* scarf danced in the gusting wind.

(Yi 1993e: 60)

Aiko's acceptance of her past allows her access – through the movements of her dance – to the spirit of her homeland. Her dance makes her part of the historical continuum of her people and fills her with a sense of spiritual peace. Aiko believes this spirit will now stay with her, whether in Korea or Japan, for she has succeeded in uniting the dual consciousness which had been warring within.

Yuhi was first published in *Gunzō* in November 1988. This novel – set wholly in Korea – tells of another young Japan-born Korean woman, Yi Yuhi. Like Aiko, Yuhi also travels to Korea in pursuit of the spirit of her motherland. After entering university in Japan, Yuhi becomes increasingly interested in her Korean roots, a fact she is forced to hide from her family, as her father in particular is very bitter and angry with Korea and Koreans. So Yuhi begins to study Korean on her own in secret. One day, quite by chance, she hears the music of the *taegŭm* – a transverse bamboo flute – and its melody touches a chord deep within her. Convinced this is the true sound of her homeland, Yuhi makes a pact with herself to go and study in Korea. She wishes she had had the chance to introduce this music to her father before his death, believing that then he would have understood her need to include Korea in her life (Yi 1989a: 106).

Rather than being an active student of music and dance like Aiko, Yuhi's primary goal is to master her mother tongue. As noted by Hino Keizō, a member of the 1989 Akutagawa award judging panel, this novel centers on language and its role in ethnicity. The duality at war inside Yuhi is fought between the Korean and Japanese languages:

Yuhi takes up ethnicity as a linguistic issue and delves deep into the contradictions between the two cultures of Korea and Japan. Although to date there have been novels which deal with the lack of a sense of belonging felt by Koreans in Japan – from both North and South Korea – *Yuhi* provides a high quality verbalization of the fate of Koreans as it is written from the perspective of a Korean woman who is searching for an individual path – way of life – in a Korea, which while maintaining a strong group consciousness is in pursuit of spiritual modernization.

(Hino 1989: 30)

The main focus of *Yuhi* is the failure of Yuhi's return to her motherland, as seen through her inability to settle the linguistic dispute raging within her. Yang-ji explores the shattering of the protective walls Yuhi has built up around herself to hide her brittle sense of self, and through this the shattering of the images an immigrant child draws in her mind of her homeland. The narrator is a Korean woman in her mid-thirties who tells a tale about Yuhi, the Japanese Korean student boarding in her and her aunt's home in a quiet suburb of Seoul. All the images of Yuhi in this novel are second-hand, presented through the niece's eyes. This only serves to highlight Yuhi's marginalization, as she can never speak for or define herself. From the very first line it is clear that Yuhi is the real focus, and that the first-person narrator – not even given a name – is merely a vehicle to tell Yuhi's story. Narration by the niece, peppered with her and her aunt's memories of Yuhi, allows Yang-ji to construct a narrative position which speaks for Korean natives, for the Koreans in Japan, and for Koreans resident in Japan returning to live in Korea. It serves to underline the precarious nature of displaced identity. This strategy allows Yang-ji to dispute the "fixing" which categories such as ethnicity and geography exert on the formation of identity. As Norma Field notes, "The narrative structure itself . . . attempts to enact a Resident Korean reunification with the homeland" (Field 1993: 653).

Thus, although everything is focused on Yuhi, her actions, her mind's eye, her line of vision, it is impossible for the reader to see her clearly. As seen through the niece, Yuhi has no clear identity; she seems asexual, neither male nor female, neither child nor woman: a blank slate to be filled (Yi 1989a: 34). The narrative structure of *Yuhi* reinforces the demi-monde which Yuhi herself inhabits, attempting to suppress all of her past and to recreate a new self in Korea, a mission in which she fails miserably.

Yuhi attends the same university – 'S' University (read Seoul National) – as the aunt's dead husband. Both the aunt and the niece feel some sort of link with Yuhi; the aunt feels that it was fate that brought her into their lives, on account of the link with her husband, and the niece feels she has found a soul mate whom she can help shrug off the influences of Japan and "return" to her homeland. Yuhi is even given the aunt's daughter's old room, as if she is a closer family member than the niece herself. Yet for all the welcome she has received in their home when the novel begins, Yuhi has already returned to Japan, without completing her degree, unable to stand what she sees as her own hypocrisy any longer; her search for a place within her homeland has been a failure. Yuhi's inability to find a place, to settle, to complete, is intrinsic to her personality. It is as if her lack of a place in the world prevents her from stopping in one place long enough ever to finish, she must always move on to the next spot in search of inner peace.

The novel is caught up in a web of reminiscences as the niece reviews her memories of Yuhi's arrival into their home. This focus on the past casts a sense of loss, isolation and loneliness over the novel, and exemplifies Yuhi's statelessness, the lack of a securely rooted sense of place.

The novel begins with the line: "When I hung up the phone with Yuhi, I became all flustered" (Yi 1989a: 7). This first line focuses the reader on Yuhi, of whom we still know nothing, although the title of the novel suggests her importance. It also

128 *Carol Hayes*

shows that a connection has been broken; the connection between the narrator – the niece – and Yuhi, and that this is causing mental anguish. Later it becomes clear that this break is symbolic of the cultural gulf between these two women. Yang-ji builds up suspense by showing us that the niece is unsettled, but not why. We know she is breaking with routine and going home by taxi, which is clearly a rare event. We feel her need to get home quickly and her impatience with the lights and the traffic. On her way home she shifts in and out of memory, seeming to lose any clear sense of self. Her whole being becomes "this self in the taxi," focused on the very small task of returning home. Anything else causes too much pain and allows memories of Yuhi to attack her peace of mind.

> Each time the taxi braked hard at traffic lights, Yuhi appeared in my mind's eye and then receded into the distance when the taxi started up again.
> (Yi 1989a: 7)

Further suspense is added as the niece seems to be readying herself for a plane crash. Reeling with the constant breaking of the taxi she clutches her bag and hunches over in a crash position, as if expecting the worst. She seems completely drained as if her energy has been sapped by Yuhi. Arriving home, she just stands and watches the taxi retrace its path and disappear around the corner. It is as if she is expecting Yuhi to be there waiting for her. She is alone yet: "From within my memories Yuhi's voice pierces me, pricks me from behind" (Yi 1989a: 8). Caught by this voice in her mind, she feels eyes upon her and looks around, to find; "Yuhi is standing beside me" (ibid.: 9). At first it appears as if Yuhi is actually present, but the next sentence tells us this is all in the niece's imagination. "I could clearly remember that face beside me looking up that slope of the road" (ibid.). This highlights the niece's growing inability to distinguish between present and past, her inability to see a self independent of Yuhi. After watching the taxi leave, she stands as she had six months ago, with the mental apparition of Yuhi beside her, looking up at the mountains. Absorbed by memory, the present becomes a fantasy: a deserted world with its focus Yuhi gone, leaving the connection broken.

> I turned around again, and looked up at the deserted corner up the street. It seemed as though however long I stood there no one would appear.
> Yuhi was no longer in this country.
> (Yi 1989a: 12)

Time becomes an important motif in the novel. Small moments of time take on more than their usual meaning, as at the beginning when the hands of the clock seem to catch on four as Yuhi hangs up on the niece (Yi 1989a: 7). The introductory stage of the novel is structured around moments of daily life punctuated by flashes of memory which seem to stop time. Work – memory – taxi – memory – front of house-paralyzed by memory – garden entrance – memory – living room. Through the internal monologue of narrator, the reader dips in and out of her memory:

> Surpassing my sense of the seasons . . . the pale blue sky, the scrapping of the metal patio door, etc., all serve as reminders of Yuhi rather than the season.
>
> (Yi 1989a: 12)

Memory becomes more real than the present. The niece's inability to distinguish clearly between the imagined world of memory and the real world reinforces the dislocation – the sense of misplacement – which forms a central thematic construct of the novel. The work swings between present and past, as little things: the smell of the garden; the sight of the mountain above the curve in the road; the peeling of an apple, all evoke memories of Yuhi. Thus physical descriptions of the landscape seem to parallel the narrator's mental landscape. Just as Yuhi's memory possesses the niece, the thick growth of the mountain vegetation seems to be all-enveloping, weighing down on the people below.

On her return home from work, the niece finds the house is sunk in darkness. Her aunt too has broken with routine. Today is different, Yuhi has gone and "the darkness of the inside of the house sinks into the dusk of the outside world" (Yi 1989a: 13). The niece peers into the darkness trying to understand what is missing. Her aunt has failed to switch on the outside light, failed to welcome the niece home as she always had when Yuhi was with them. Another broken precedent, it is almost as if life before Yuhi had no meaning even though she was only with them for a short six months. Yuhi's relationship with these two women becomes a microcosm of her relationship with Korea as a whole, and their house, a foil for the tension between Yuhi's inner self and the face she presents to the world:

> The smell of the first floor and the second floor were subtly different, it was as though its very strength and movement were different. And so too was the Yuhi my aunt saw downstairs and the one shown to me upstairs.
> Yes, they were entirely different.
>
> (Yi 1989a: 16)

Upstairs, Yuhi can be herself. Yet ultimately, it is in this upstairs world that Yuhi's sense of hypocrisy finally overcomes her. Downstairs with the aunt her mask is more firmly in place; only the niece – intimate with the "upstairs" Yuhi and thus looking for signs of unease – can sense it slipping.

As mentioned earlier, Hino Keizō argues that Yang-ji takes up ethnicity as a linguistic issue in *Yuhi*. The aunt talks of the relationship between upbringing and language, and how attitudes to language are often based on a deeper, more subconscious prejudice:

> Your uncle told me something before he died. Since the time of Japanese imperialism, there was strong anti-Japanese sentiment throughout the entire village where he was born in Kyŏngsang province. Many of the famous

fighters in the anti-Japanese resistance came from that province. So as he was brought up in such an environment and as his father had very strong anti-Japanese feelings, your uncle just couldn't think well of the Japanese. . . . My daughter and I were influenced by him, without even being aware of it. Somehow we just couldn't bring ourselves to like Japanese people. My daughter even made the point of not choosing Japanese as her second language at school. That might be why I feel that I understand what Yuhi is going through. That's why I feel so sad for her and why I just cannot think of her as a stranger. I can't remember when it was that I really started to think about this. . . . I don't know what fate brought Yuhi here to live in this house, but I cannot help thinking how strange it is that these two are compatriots – one hating Japan and the other hating Korea.

(Yi 1989a: 109–10)

Yuhi's upbringing, like the uncle's, traps her in a cycle of hatred. When the aunt first hears from the real estate agent that a young Korean Japanese student is looking for lodgings in her home, she worries about the social leanings of such a student, commenting:

Koreans born in Japan who come to study in Korea, seem to spend all their time fooling around near It'aewŏn [a rather rough drinking area in Seoul] and don't do even the slightest bit of study. Because the Japanese yen is so strong they're probably rather loose with their money too.

(Yi 1989a: 30)

She worries that Koreans who have lived in Japan often have political affiliations with North Korea, and thus may have dangerous ideological beliefs, yet she feels a certain obligation to help out a fellow Korean, even if she is slightly sullied by her contact with Japan.

Both the aunt and the niece find it hard to understand Yuhi's dislike– almost hatred – of Korea and the Korean language.

Yuhi noticed only the negative aspects of Korea. Since she had grown up hearing her father criticize Korea, she even hated the Korean language. But I couldn't help thinking that it couldn't be that simple. I couldn't believe that Yuhi's obsession with the Japanese language resulted only from her aversion to Korean.

(Yi 1989a: 110)

From the beginning of the novel, the niece feels suffocated and uneasy with her memories of Yuhi hidden away in her room, writing and writing "her Japanese" and refusing contact with Koreans, as when she refuses to come downstairs to watch television – Korean television. The aunt believes she has understood Yuhi's aversion to watching television, holding it to be similar to her husband's lack of desire to watch television when he was in Japan – even though it was his first experience of color television – because he hated to listen to the Japanese language. The aunt astutely notes that on Yuhi's arrival in Korea, the ideal she had drawn of her motherland in her mind suddenly disintegrated around her, and that it was that moment of disintegration which turned Yuhi against the Korean language (Yi 1989a: 109).

The mental suffocation the niece feels seems to parallel the suffocation and unease Yuhi herself feels within Korean society. Yuhi's constant moving about from lodging to lodging – she has moved eight times – is symbolic of her search for relief from this suffocation, for a spiritual space within her "homeland."

The niece feels that it is her duty – her national duty – to help Yuhi assimilate into Korean society, and consequently is frustrated that Yuhi does not try harder with her Korean:

> I never told her, but I was secretly cheering Yuhi on. In my mind, I was constantly saying to her, "It won't be much longer. If you can just overcome this pain you are feeling now, then everything will be okay. Japan is no different from Korea. What is important is to see how other people live their lives, and then to think carefully about how you want to live yours. You just need to be a little more patient, until you find your own path." I was always on her side.
> (Yi 1989a: 111–12)

The niece is particularly irritated that Yuhi only reads Japanese books; that she is constantly having books sent to her from Japan, especially considering she is a Korean linguistics major (Yi 1989a: 58). The only Korean she reads is her cramming notes for exams, and even then the niece has to go over and over the same mistakes as she helps Yuhi pass her exams. This inability to face up to the Korean language is indicative of the friction tearing Yuhi apart.

As the climax of the novel approaches, Yuhi is visibly angered by the niece commenting sarcastically on her reading only Japanese, grinding her teeth in frustrated silence. Finally the only words she can bring herself to say are "Ŏnni [elder sister] please allow me to be on my own" (Yi 1989a: 60). Thus, Yuhi's response to the niece's attack is to shut her out, and with her the Korea and Korean language that she represents:

> I can't help thinking that the Korean I hear everyone speaking – at school, in town – sounds just like the explosions of a tear gas bomb. Bitter, painful, exasperating – just the sound of it makes it hard for me to breathe. However many times I change my lodgings everyone still uses this hateful Korean. But it's okay. . . . I just go up to my room and drink coffee in silence, or sit at my desk with a pen in hand . . .but it's the sound of all those peoples' voices that I hate. The voice of their gestures, the voice of their eyes, the voice of their expressions, the voice of their bodies. . . . I can't stand any of it. I begin to burn with pain as if smothered by the tear gas exploding from the bomb.
> (Yi 1989a: 98)

The climax for Yuhi is when she can no longer confront what she sees as her own hypocrisy. One night the niece goes into Yuhi's room late at night after hearing the mournful strains of a bamboo flute. She finds a drunken Yuhi, walled into a small space between the stereo, the desk and the wall. The niece is shocked and demands: "Are you drinking? Yuhi, is this the sort of thing for a young woman to do?" Yuhi does not reply, she now seems to have lost all power of speech. Throughout the work Yang-ji uses Yuhi's ability to express herself in Korean as an emotional barometer. The more emotional she becomes, the less able she is to string a Korean sentence together. Finally she is no longer able to speak, she can only write – and then only in Japanese. In this scene, however, her response is finally wrenched from her: "I am a hypocrite. A liar!" (Yi 1989a: 82).

The first sign of this inability to control her use of Korean is seen in an earlier scene where Yuhi, on a bus with the niece, is unable to cope with the noise and vulgarity of the Korean populace. She and the niece have gone to try and buy Yuhi a desk, and have to change buses a number of times to get to the right area of Seoul. Here too Yuhi loses her ability to speak Korean. Yet her lips are moving, as she whispers something to herself over and over. Something in Japanese, the only language that offers her emotional relief. She even loses control over her body:

> Whenever the bus braked, just like an invertebrate animal Yuhi's body was thrown around, and she fell against the passengers beside her.
>
> (Yi 1989a: 66)

Yet Yuhi refuses to give up, even though her Korean has broken down to a childlike simplicity. "It was as if she had only just begun to learn Korean, she was just clumsily stringing words together" (Yi 1989a: 69). Desperately Yuhi tries to convince the niece that she can go on. " – *Ŏnni*. I go. Desk . . . want to buy" (ibid.). The niece asks herself what it is that is causing Yuhi so much distress: is it the noise, the piercing cold wind? She finally decides it is Yuhi's reaction to all that is Seoul, to the "whole landscape of Seoul" (ibid.).

Yuhi's response to the landscape of her homeland changes from an initial childlike naivete to this inability even to exist within it. This change is reflected in the linguistic breakdown of her Korean. Early in the novel, Yuhi is shown standing, looking up at the rocky mountain in front of the house and repeating the Korean word "rock" out loud, trying to get the pronunciation right. This is the first hint we have that Yuhi is not a native speaker of Korean:

> *Paui*! – Rock! I remembered Yuhi's voice. I whispered the word to myself trying to copy her pronunciation. The sound of her voice came back to me, trying so hard to pronounce *"paui"* correctly her emphasis on the "ui" had rather the opposite effect making it sound awkward.
>
> (Yi 1989a: 9)

This awkwardness with language gets worse rather than better during Yuhi's stay in Seoul.

The work of Yi Yang-ji 133

Yuhi's final confrontation with her own hypocrisy on that drunken night forces her to return to Japan, and the niece is forced to conclude the following:

> Yuhi didn't try to overcome the distance, she didn't try to come closer to this country. Instead she did the opposite, she tried to return to her Japanese.
> (Yi 1989a: 77)

Yi Yang-ji's cultural identity

In exploring Yi Yang-ji's sense of cultural identity as depicted in her literary works, the concept of diaspora is a useful tool. A diaspora is born from the relocation of a group away from its original homeland, forcing them to create an isolated ethnic community linked only through imagination and past memory with the original homeland. Diasporic social groups tend to build up a collective memory of the homeland to sustain their cultural uniqueness in their new land. Yet it is this very myth of homeland which constrains them, and a tension builds between the place of origin, the "where you are from" and the new home, the "where you are at" (Ang 1994: 5). Diasporic discourse perceived in this way attempts to provide a framework for analyzing these two points of anchorage.

Yang-ji's search for a unified sense of self can be divided into three stages, which progress along an axis of identity formation moving from "where you are from" to "where you are at." The first stage was an overtly political reassessment of her relationship with her homeland, the second a tortured self-conscious duality, and the third the siting of a proudly hybrid self in the "where she is at" of Japan.

The first stage began when Yang-ji moved to Kyoto and began to learn about the history of the Korean community in Japan and about her own family's history. She became more and more focused on her homeland and began to fight for a sense of identity as a Korean in Japan. Yet this fight took her into uneasy territory, as noted by the literary critic Kitada Sachie:

> Different from the first generation who are clearly "Korean," the second-generation Korean Japanese are born in Japan and are brought up as Japanese immersed in Japanese language and culture. Notions of homeland and their own ethnicity cannot be acquired naturally. Smiled at with pity as *panchoppari* [a very derogatory term for those seen to be Japanified-Koreans, literally "half-Japanese"] by Koreans and discriminated against by the Japanese as "second generation," these Koreans have no choice but to live *in* Japan *as* Koreans, and to fight desperately for some sense of personal identity.
> (Kitada 1987: 108–9; emphasis in the original)

Kitada goes on to argue that the pain and anger in the writing of this second generation springs from a fear of, or a shrinking away from, this *panchoppari* existence, as they search for a selfhood which is neither Korean nor Japanese.

Yu Miri, another Korean female writer born in Japan and one of the 1997 winners of the Akutagawa award, also searches for a place for herself which is neither purely Korean nor purely Japanese (see Yoneyama in this volume). In the following interview, Yu firmly positions herself in the "where you are at" placing herself clearly in and of Japanese society, yet maintaining her right to the cultural diversity she inherits from her ethnicity:

> For the people of my homeland, I am no doubt a typical *panchoppari*, and perhaps some may feel that I am living in total indifference to the origins and language of the culture of my homeland. But I believe that my plays are sited firmly in the reality of the life I live. . . . I can neither speak nor write my mother tongue. I write my plays in the language of another country. Yet I believe this makes my words dramatic. . . . If we take Japanese as an example, the current generation of Japanese under forty – including myself – cannot read works from medieval Japan . . . and the Japanese of just two hundred years ago would no doubt find it impossible to understand the conversations of Japanese youth today – just as I cannot understand Korean. In addition to all this, a great many foreign languages are inundating Japanese. Already some Japanese write sentences – in Japanese – which cannot possibly be understood without a familiarity with English.
>
> (Yu 1996b: 16–17)

Yu Miri is making a clear political statement, arguing for the right, even as a Korean Japanese, to use contemporary Japanese language, as she works to carve out a new niche for herself within Japanese society and its literature. Without denying her own "difference" she refuses to be marginalized into that limited space somewhere between Korea, the notional homeland, and Japan. She argues for more hybridity in the Japanese language, that it be allowed to take on echoes from the cultural and ethnic diversity of those who choose to use it as their creative medium.

In the case of Yang-ji, however, the first stage in her search for identity gave rise to increasing feelings of hypocrisy, as in Yuhi's case, and an inability to deny what she saw as the "Japanese" side to her character, which in turn gave rise to a tortured dualism. Yang-ji felt caught between the reality of her host society and the utopian myth of her imagined homeland. Yang-ji began to write in an attempt to gain some understanding of the duality between the Japan and the Korea within her, and her tragedy was that she rarely seemed able to find a balance between the two. The literary critic Kuroto Kazuo explores this sense of duality found in Yang-ji's work, arguing that the more Koreans in Japan become aware of themselves as "Koreans," the more they reject the "Japan" in which they were born and brought up, yet at the same time the more distant they become from the Korea which is their homeland, as they cannot unify their idealized images of Korea with its reality. Kuroto argues that Yi Yang-ji has made a transition to align herself more clearly with the "where she is at" of Japan, and that this is shown in the fact that her work does not reflect the malice which can be found in the earlier Korean writers resident in Japan (Kuroto 1987: 87–8). As Yang-ji came to see herself as being in and of Japan, she lost both her anger and the desire to revenge herself on Japan. She saw herself as living within a shadow puppet play, where her image of her homeland was like the shadow cast on the screen by the puppeteers.

Yang-ji's literary productivity was born from the space between this shadow image and the reality of her life in Japan, and her creativity fed on the emotional disparity between her own developing selfhood and the ethnic identity of Korean Japanese as a group. Writing provided her with a means of escaping from the maze in which she found herself:

> The more pleasure I gained from writing, the less I could endure the hatred growing within me. Pursuing its source, I came up against the difficult truth that this hatred arose from the "Japan" which fills the "Japanese language."
>
> I began to feel that I must re-evaluate both language and culture within me. And beyond that, I must look clearly at my rightful place within the community of Koreans in Japan. Thus, I decided to place myself on the other side of the shadow pictures, or to put it another way to throw myself into my own true country – that is into Korea.
>
> (Yi 1993c: 642)

Yang-ji choose to throw herself into her homeland in the hope that there she would overcome this duality and find a unified sense of self, and a sense of place: of belonging. Yet this very act of throwing herself into life in her "homeland" created a new set of problems. Ridding herself of all that Japan had made her was not an easy task. Korea proved too much, too invasive; just as the young Korean schoolgirls on the subway had been too much:

> I shrank away from all that fresh liveliness – the smells, conversations, words of greeting, expressions, customs etc. I could not suppress the counterattack launched by the "Japan" and its "language" from deep within me; its very smell permeated my body. . . . The paper napkins spread about and the disinfectant sprinkled around public eating areas, the dirty toilets, the chaotic streets, the incessantly swirling dust, even the voices of people passing speaking my mother tongue – all of these became harder and harder to bear. There were even times when my eyes blurred and I didn't want to read the *hangŭl* [Korean script] of my university texts.
>
> (Yi 1993c: 642)

Yang-ji oscillated between anger and despair at these two opposing camps within her, thinking "just how wonderful it would be to stay on the puppeteers side for ever, or if that wasn't possible then always on the shadow picture side" (ibid.). This is reminiscent of Yuhi's experience in Korea, which only served to reinforce her inability to fit in, forcing her to return – inevitably – to the notion of herself as more Japanese than Korean. Yuhi is unable to unite the ideal of her homeland with its reality, and consequently Yang-ji accuses Yuhi of failing to have "the courage to live" (Yi 1993a: 665). She cites Yuhi's failure in her inability to face up to reality when her hopes and ideals give way before it. Her identity is destabilized by the Koreanizing influence of the reality of the homeland and the fact that she is expected to re-ethnicize herself. However negative and hopeless reality appeared, Yuhi's only road to spiritual liberation lay in throwing herself into that very reality. Yang-ji comes to the conclusion that the conflict between her homeland and Japan can only be resolved by taking reality on its own terms, and that attaining the courage and power to confront reality is one of the fundamental problems of the human state (Yi 1993a: 663). Although much calmer, in *Nabi t'aryŏng*, Aiko also in the end comes to accept reality in its chaos and confusion.

It was through these confrontations and acceptance that Yang-ji finally found an oasis of silence:

> In behind the tone of the melody, I discovered a huge deep silence, which though silent was mankind's true and natural voice. My "mother tongue" is not in that space which is visible to the eye nor where the ears are pierced by the cacophony of sound. No, it is in a place enveloped in thick darkness, where though I quiver in fear I also find peace. . . . It is a place I come to not with my intellect but through my body – my whole body.
>
> (Yi 1993d: 645–6)

The world of dance gave her access to this place of silence. Through traditional Korean dance, Yang-ji felt that she had gained access to the ancestors who had made her existence possible. She "was able to touch the heart of the people which flowed like an underground current" through the world of imagination that was dance (Yi 1993a: 649). Music and dance gave Yang-ji access to her motherland on a more symbolic level than that introduced to her through history books at school and the politics of her fellow Korean Japanese. Such politics had only served to feed a confused hatred, and although she acknowledged the role they played in increasing her awareness of both her ethnic identity and duty, it was music and dance that filled the space between her Koreanness and Japaneseness, and which provided her with the support she sought. She found that she could finally let go of what she now saw as an imposed sense of duty to rediscover her lost ethnic awareness and just simply be:

> Through the *kayagŭm*, I was able to imagine, to picture the shape of my motherland, and through its music I developed a connection with the history of my motherland. As I pictured my own existence within the sounds loved by so many of my ancestors, I was able to overcome many of the barriers I was facing.
>
> (Yi 1993a: 657)

With the confidence gained through this musical access to the spirit of her homeland, Yang-ji found the strength to weld the pain of the two sides warring within her into the synthesis of her own personalized voice, what she referred to as her "new mother tongue," thus progressing to the third and final stage of her search for identity:

> After I entered Seoul University, I began to want to write in Japanese. I wanted to protect Japanese from Korean. I had to do whatever I could to protect it. Somehow the words one first hears from one's mother's lips – those words we call our mother tongue – are really an act of violation. . . . I write my novels in Japanese because the mother tongue which I speak and write is Japanese, yet I feel that Korean is the mother tongue of my blood. Korean is the mother tongue of my body. It is because of this I continue to dance. In a sense, my Korean dancing is my mother tongue's body and blood, while my novels in Japanese are the written word of my mother tongue . . . thus in this sense I have two mother tongues.
> (Yi 1989b: 270)

In her search for self identity Yi Yang-ji became increasingly focused on Korea, on the "where she was from." She began to look back to the homeland of her parents, to an idealized notion of "Koreanness," feeling that she must "return" to this original "Korea" to acquire "authenticity." She saw this as the only means of unifying the sense of duality which plagued her, yet her symbolic construction of "Korea" as the geographical and cultural axis of her identity resulted in feelings of inadequacy and anger. She built up a fantasy of unifying the Japan – "where she was" – with the Korea of "where she was from." It was through her writing and her music that Yang-ji worked through this fantasy and finally achieved self-empowerment, letting go of the nostalgic identification with the myth of Korea and returning to a conscious self-location in Japan, as a Korean Japanese, proud of a selfhood which was neither purely Korean nor purely Japanese. Yang-ji's process of identity formation results more from internal responses than from external political pressures. Yet this internalized response echoes the voices of other Korean Japanese. The literary critic Itō Narihiko, in his analysis of her contribution to contemporary Japanese literature, praises what he sees as an author who speaks for her generation:

> Yang-ji's newness – her contribution to Korean literature in Japan – lies in her positioning of self at a point where she cannot easily identify with her homeland nor her ethnic group, at a point where she takes a cool hard look at herself as an individual human being, yet at the same time opens up the universality of the interior of existence as a second- or third-generation Korean in Japan.
> (Itō 1995: 89)

Traditional Korean music and dance led Yang-ji into a space where she was able to coalesce her sense of Koreanness; where she finally found a sense of place and belonging, while writing provided her with a tool to examine her own identity, a way to resolve the tension between the "where she was from" and the "where she was at."

Yang-ji chose to fictionalize her search for identity in the belief that it allowed her more objectivity; that it allowed her to distance herself from her own subjective sense of self. She gives the following analysis of the novel's role in her own search for identity:

> My original motivation in depicting a Japanese-born Korean through the eyes of a Korean living in Korea, was born of an attempt to look at myself more objectively, more exhaustively. This caused me more suffering than I could have imagined possible. Yet I had invited it on myself, and this was why it took me two years to write this novel.
>
> To put it simply, I wanted to lay to rest the Yuhi inside me. For I had already realized that I would never achieve spiritual independence until I could throw off the Japanese Yuhi and rise above the Korean Yuhi. It was as if I was divided into the two parts.... Yet the blood of a Korean flowed in my veins, and the path to spiritual independence lay in an acceptance of the gradual encroachment of pain which welled up from this blood.
>
> Yuhi was unable to lean on the linguistic support which hides between the *hangŭl* "a" [Korean] and the *hiragana* "a" [Japanese] and at her wits' end had to return to Japan. But, I on the other hand, was finally able to bid farewell to that "Yuhi." To bid farewell to the Yuhi who had existed inside me, thereby gaining a new power, which gave me the strength to touch against my mother tongue again and again.
>
> (Yi 1993f: 647)

Unlike Yuhi, who had to escape, Yang-ji believed that she had overcome the weaknesses that forced Yuhi out of her homeland. She came to believe her contact with Korea taught her to see things as they were, rather than in a mythologized state. It was Korea and its people, its very air, wind, and light, which gave Yang-ji the strength to see things as they truly are, in their chaotic messy hybridity.

Yang-ji uses the image of Mount Fuji in a symbolic conclusion to this comparison between herself and Yuhi. Brought up in Fujiyoshida in the foothills of Mount Fuji, she spent her childhood looking up at the mountain. It came to represent much of her complicated attitudes to Japan. On the one hand it was an object of respect and admiration, but on the other – perhaps because of its huge implacable presence – it became a symbol of all that she hated. However much she herself suffered, the mountain remained the same, looking down at her in what she saw as amusement at the petty nature of humanity. Then as she became more interested in the politics of her ethnicity, Mount Fuji became the symbol of the militarism with which the Japanese empire invaded her homeland of Korea. The mountain then became an object she must disavow and repudiate (Yi 1993a: 663). It was only after the completion of *Yuhi* that Yang-ji finally achieved the confidence to look up at Mount Fuji with neither love nor hatred, and just accept its existence. Yuhi's tragedy was that she never managed to do this either in terms of Mount Fuji nor in terms of the Korean mountain she saw outside her bedroom window from her lodging in Seoul.

For Yang-ji the writing of this novel *Yuhi* proved a cathartic experience: a testimony to her ability to rise above the pain of the duality which plagued her. Yuhi too, wrote a testimony. During the phone call which begins the novel, Yuhi asks the niece to look for an envelope which she has left in her desk drawer. She hopes the niece will not regard it as a burden, merely a favor, telling her she can dispose of it as she likes. In the drawer is a large fat envelope containing 448 pages of Japanese: which the niece cannot read. It seems to be a diary of Yuhi's time in Korea, her testimony, her way of dealing with her pain. The niece realizes that through "the act of writing all this in Japanese, Yuhi was able to express – in the very Japanese characters – that part of herself which she did not want to show to others, exposing herself without any feeling of constraint or guilt" (Yi 1989a: 73). Yet the fact that Yuhi leaves her testimony behind her when she flees Korea is proof that she was unable to reconcile the conflicts within her. For Yang-ji, however, the novel *Yuhi* is a reconciliation, a testimony to her successful transition to spiritual independence through a synthesis of the two sides of her character.

Both *Nabi t'aryŏng* and *Yuhi* are thus very much the story of Yi Yang-ji herself. Her painful oscillation, both emotional and physical, between Japan and Korea is embodied in the lives of Aiko and Yuhi. Her personal struggle to come to terms with her own torn world, split self, and ambivalent ethnic and cultural identity was abruptly terminated by her unexpected death. However, her sense of displacement and her agony over home and homeland, the rootlessness with which she tried to grapple, and her relentless craving for home, a place to belong to, have much to offer and appeal not only to the Korean readers of Yi Yang-ji, but also to the diasporically displaced peoples of the modern world today.

Acknowledgement

I would like to thank my husband Mark Taylor for his constant support, and Sonia Ryang for her detailed advice and assistance.

7 Korean ethnic schools in Occupied Japan, 1945–52

Hiromitsu Inokuchi

The establishment of a particular sovereign state creates a corresponding "nation" (Wallerstein 1991). It follows that understanding the construction of postwar Japan's nationhood requires a close examination of the state formation that took place during the time of Allied occupation of Japan (1945–52). State formation is a series of historical processes through which various groups come together to establish a power bloc, seize the state, and build a (cultural) hegemony (see Green 1990). Hegemony here is a form of rule achieved by winning the consent of the subordinate through everyday social, cultural, and ideological practices, rather than by the direct use of force, for it is through such practices that people come to perceive and understand themselves, their social relations, and the world in particular ways: ways that in actuality serve the interests of dominant groups (see Gramsci 1971; Williams 1977 and 1983; O'Sullivan *et al.* 1994). Formal education, in playing a decisive role to sustain such hegemony, inevitably becomes a site of political struggle.

It is sometimes debated in discussions of the relation between state formation and hegemony whether the primary moment is one of force or of consent, or whether the two can be separated in reality.[1] The case of Korean ethnic schools during the Allied occupation is one that illustrates the matter very well. It is not only one in which the struggle for education, in this case for the ethnic identity of a minority population, confronted oppressors using direct force in their attempt to terminate such an education, but also one in which the oppressors (re)built and used a consensus around the idea of Japan as a single-ethnic nation. This chapter discusses the Korean ethnic school movement as it existed during the occupation period, and assesses the process of conflict and confrontation in terms of the formation of the Japanese state and its hegemony. In so doing, it looks at an important aspect of Japan's immediate postwar history, one which standard works on the period (and perhaps "Japanese postwar history" as it is usually conceptualized) have tended to overlook.

This chapter also analyzes the involvement of the United States in that process. Contrary to the image generally held of its educational policy during the occupation, that is, of bringing the "democratizing of Japanese education," the Allied Powers (mainly the United States) played a major role in the suppression of Korean ethnic schools. Under a presumption that the Koreans demanding ethnic education were "communists" – which was not entirely false but certainly a misinterpretation of their nationalist desire for freedom, including freedom of education – the occupation force effectively helped constitute Japan as the nation-state of a single-ethnic, homogeneous group, even though its population was diverse.

Japanese colonial policies in Korea

Korea became a protectorate of Japan in 1905, and in the years that followed the groundwork was laid for its annexation in 1910. Beginning in 1905, the Japanese government began to send its advisors to the Korean government with the purpose of reforming Korean society in such a way as to reflect the dominant interests of Japan. The "ordinary" school ordinance, issued in 1906 and drafted by the Japanese educational advisor, shortened the period for the completion of primary education from six years to four. It also changed the name of the public primary schools: they were now called "ordinary" schools or *futsūgakkō*, implying that no higher education was necessary for the colonized population and that four years of primary education were sufficient to prepare Koreans for Japanese rule (Komagome 1996: 80–1; Sano 1993: 17).

When Japan annexed Korea in 1910, Koreans formally became Japanese imperial subjects. The governor-general of Korea was given the authority to instate his own orders, which were to be applied specifically to Korea. Contrary to Japan's official standpoint representing Korea as an extension of Japanese domestic governance, Japan's rule of Korea made it a distinct entity under colonial rule. After the 1911 education ordinance, except for a few language classes, the language of instruction in the public primary schools (the "ordinary" schools) became Japanese, and the use of Korean was discouraged. As a result, most Koreans avoided sending their children to those schools (in the 1910s, fewer than 10 percent attended the public primary schools). Instead, they sent their children to *sŏdang*, the traditional Korean schools (Tsurumi 1984: 294–308).

Japan's colonial policies, including educational policies, ignored the autonomy of Korea and attempted to maintain a definite subjugation of Koreans *vis-à-vis* Japanese. Koreans were treated as inferior to Japanese in every aspect of life. The reaction and resistance to this marginalization generated Korean nationalism (Komagome 1996), the first nation-wide manifestation of which was the March First Independence Movement of 1919. The demand for national independence spread across the peninsula, with more than 1,500 rallies and a total of two million participants. Altogether 46,948 were arrested and 7,509 killed within three months (Kang Chae-ŏn 1986: 188–200).

Japanese rulers were threatened by the intensity of the March First Movement and launched conciliatory measures in the following years by easing restrictions on Koreans and promoting pro-Japanese Koreans in the ranks of the bureaucracy. The 1929 education ordinance instituted six years of primary education and teacher education, just as in the Japanese domestic system (Sano 1993: 20–3). In addition, a certain number of Koreans were allowed to attend the same schools attended by Japanese, whereas before Korean schools were segregated (Tsurumi 1984: 294–308). The establishment of a Korean assembly was also discussed, and the idea was supported by relatively pragmatic colonial administrators, including governor-general Saitō Makoto, although the proposal was not approved by the central government in Tokyo (Komagome 1996: 216–8).[2]

In the late 1930s, under the policy which made Koreans the emperor's subjects, or *kōminka* (Miyata 1985; see Kashiwazaki in this volume), many Japanese cultural forms, such as the worship of shrines and the use of the Japanese language, became mandatory for Koreans. During the war, the Japanese government drafted Koreans into the imperial army and navy of Japan. Japan's colonial rule never resolved the critical problem of the Japanese empire, however: the flaw in the "metal of a weld between nation and empire" (Anderson 1991: 88). The reality of the empire was that it was multiethnic, and its official slogan adopted for ruling its colonies was "Japanese as a people of multiethnic origin" (Oguma 1995); in practice, however, it relied heavily on policies that attempted to replace the languages and cultures of the colonized peoples with Japanese ones, extending an idea of the nation as a homogeneous entity.

Koreans in Japan, 1910s–45

As the First World War broke out, the demand for industrial labor in Japan increased dramatically, and Japanese industry began recruiting Koreans aggressively (Kang Chae-ŏn 1986; Weiner 1989). Most of the Koreans who migrated to the Japanese archipelago could only find jobs in the lowest stratum of the labor market, and their wages were significantly lower than those of their Japanese counterparts. Since Japanese landlords did not want to rent out properties to Koreans, they were forced to live in overcrowded and unsanitary housing, forming their own segregated ghettos (Weiner 1989: 49–98).

During the 1920s, with the increase of Korean workers, the communist orientation became more pronounced. Many Korean activists believed communism was the only way to achieve both national independence and equal treatment (Scalapino and Lee 1972). At first, Korean communists organized the Japan bureau of the Korean Communist Party. In 1928, however, following the principle of "one nation one party," the Comintern ordered the Japan bureau to amalgamate with the Japan Communist Party (JCP). By the Comintern order, the Korean workers' union, the Federation of Korean Labor in Japan, was also dissolved into the National Council of Japanese Trade Unions. Although some Korean communists were against the decision because amalgamation would undermine their nationalist cause, most Korean communists were absorbed by the JCP. Japanese communist leaders tended to reduce anti-imperialist struggle to class struggle, and they failed to apply anti-imperialist theory in the case of Korea. Also, Japanese workers tended to show discriminatory attitudes toward Korean comrades (see Smith 1998). Eventually, in the late 1920s, after many Japanese members of the JCP and the union were arrested or defected, Koreans came to have substantial influence in both the JCP and the labor movement. In the early 1930s, at the peak of the interwar communist movement, more than 10 percent of the JCP members were Koreans, most of them rank-and-file activists. They too were soon arrested, however, and the JCP and the labor movement were essentially annihilated (Weiner 1994: 165–86; Mun Kyŏng-su 1995: 176).

Outside the leftist movement, Koreans residing in Japan became a significant political block. Following the 1928 institutionalization of universal male suffrage in Japan, Korean males in Japan proper gained their voting rights (see Kashiwazaki in this volume). In the 1932 election, one Korean was elected to the House of Representatives from a district in Tokyo that had a high concentration of Koreans (he was re-elected in 1937), and voters were allowed to write his name in Korean vernacular letters. At city-level elections from 1929 to 1943, a total of 179 Koreans ran for offices, and thirty were elected (Tanaka 1974: 75–6; see Kashiwazaki, this volume).

The numbers of Koreans living in Japan increased dramatically in the early 1930s, from 298,091 in 1930 to 625,678 in 1935 (Weiner 1994). By the mid-1930s, the tendency for Koreans to settle in Japan was becoming well established. In a 1933 Osaka survey, for example, 66 percent of the heads of Korean families in Japan expressed their intention to reside permanently in Japan, and the female/male ratio had shifted from 100 to 678 in 1924 to 100 to 154 in 1938 (Mun Kyŏng-su 1995: 166–7).

The issue of education for their children arose as Koreans began settling in various parts in the Japanese archipelago. As early as 1930, the Japanese Ministry of Education clarified that the compulsory education law was equally applicable to school-age Korean children in Japan, but suggested that the law should not be strictly enforced. In its interpretation, Korean children were to be allowed to attend the public schools at the request of their parents. The proportion of children who went to elementary school in the early 1930s was very low, however, because most Korean children had to work to help their family. In 1931, only 18.5 percent of school-age Korean children attended elementary school, although the number increased to 64.7 percent by 1942 (Ozawa 1973: 71–3).

Japanese schools made no special accommodation for Korean children. In some cases, to learn the Korean language, Korean children went to after-school classes privately run by Koreans. Other Korean children (many over school-age) went to night elementary (public) school after work. In certain areas, where the students were almost exclusively Koreans, separate low-quality school buildings were built exclusively for them, because many Japanese neither wanted to study with them nor wanted to spend money on them (Ozawa 1973: 83–5).

As Japan's war spread across China, Japanese industry required more manpower. In 1938, the imperial government decided to recruit Koreans from Korea for labor in Japan, and many Koreans were forcibly taken to Japan and sent to work in mines, heavy industry, and military construction. Between 1938 and 1944, the population of Koreans in Japan jumped from 779,878 to approximately two million (Morita 1996: 71).

The United States' preparation for the occupation

In October 1942, the US Department of State began research on Japanese society with the purpose of developing policies to be practiced after the surrender of Japan. The project team, the Far Eastern Unit, was established on 23 August 1942. By October, specialists such as George H. Blakeslee (professor of international relations, Clark University), Hugh Borton (assistant professor of Japanese history, Columbia University), and Cabot Coville (a diplomat who had worked for the US Embassy in Tokyo) joined the unit. Though the project was led by Japanese specialists, its early reports included very few references to Koreans residing in Japan. They referred to the issue of Koreans in Japan only in connection with Korea's eventual independence, and they underestimated the number of Koreans living in Japan. The reports did, however, represent Koreans in Japan as economically better off than their counterparts in Korea, and noted that they should be protected from discrimination by the Japanese.

In 1944, the unit prepared a report (CAC227) specifically addressing the matter of the non-Japanese population in Japan. This report was created during a period in which the refugee issues of the European front were being discussed in other committees of the Department. The report included an item on "Koreans," with a question mark as the last item. Koreans were defined as Japanese subjects, which meant that, in legal terms, they were "enemy nationals." The report noted, however, that their status would require special consideration, because Korea in the near future would gain its independence. It also predicted the rise of Japanese hostility against Koreans in the confusion resulting from the Japanese defeat, and mentioned the need for aid to Koreans in Japan. Eventually, this report became the basis of US postwar policy in Japan (quoted in Kim T'ae-gi 1997: 32–8).

A July 1945 report issued by the State Department discussed the repatriation of Koreans in Japan. It proposed that those who remained in Japan temporarily would, upon the independence of Korea, automatically gain Korean nationality. Those who remained longer would be able to remain Japanese; or to gain Korean nationality by registering with the responsible agency of the Korean government, if they wished. In this way, Koreans in Japan were provided with a free choice of their nationality: Korean nationality for those who would eventually repatriate to Korea, and Japanese nationality for the ones who wished to remain (Kim T'ae-gi 1997: 39–42). (This did not actually happen; see Kashiwazaki in this volume.)

Along with the State Department, the Departments of War and the Navy were also concerned with the postwar occupation policy, because they were the actual administrators of the occupation. The military government section, which existed previously during the post-First World War military occupation and was re-established for the occupation of Japan, published a series of instructional materials and guides concerning the occupation. One representative series of materials, the *Civil Affairs Handbook: Japan*, was published after February 1944. In this series, Koreans in Japan were regarded simply as immigrant workers attracted to Japan by higher wages.

In 1945, the military government section provided more concrete directives in the *Civil Affairs Guide* series. One of the volumes, entitled "Aliens in Japan," recommended the elimination of any kind of discrimination against Koreans and other aliens in Japan. It also mentioned employment of competent Koreans by the occupational government. (Its authors assumed the direct governance of Japan by the Allied Powers.) The document was completed just before the surrender of Japan, and constituted the only source of direction during the early stages of the occupation (Kim T'ae-gi 1997: 45–53). In retrospect, the United States neither understood the colonial relations between Japanese and Koreans nor was really prepared for handling matters involving long-term Korean residents in Japan.[3]

Earlier policies under the occupation

After 15 August 1945, many Koreans residing in Japan rushed to the major port towns in hopes of boarding ships to Korea, only to be stranded there without sufficient food and housing because the Japanese government was preoccupied with the repatriation of Japanese from overseas. On 1 September, the Japanese government ordered the return of those Koreans who had come to Japan as forced laborers. The reason was not that the government wanted to "liberate" the Koreans, but that it feared the surplus labor force would cause social problems. In October, the government estimated – in fact, underestimated – that 40 percent of the Korean population, about 900,000, would choose to repatriate (see Kim T'ae-gi 1997).

In October, the economic and scientific section of the Supreme Commander for the Allied Powers (SCAP), in order to keep financial resources in Japan, pressured the Japanese government to restrict the amount of financial property non-Japanese could take with them when leaving Japan. Persons leaving Japan were allowed to carry only one thousand yen in cash and nothing of value, in other words no gold, silver, bonds, or jewelry. For Koreans in Japan wishing to leave, the amount was barely enough to ensure their survival in Korea, which was suffering from high inflation and food shortages. Meanwhile, on 1 November, SCAP issued a memorandum to accelerate the repatriation, including the use of US naval ships for transportation (Kim T'ae-gi 1997: 156–9; see also Wagner 1951).

While the repatriation of Koreans was urgent, the treatment of Koreans remaining in Japan posed further difficulties (Inokuchi 1996). The first US directive on the legal status of Koreans in Japan came in November 1945, when SCAP officially addressed their nationality status. In its directive, SCAP stated that Koreans, as the people of a former Japanese colony, "were to be treated as 'liberated' [i.e. non-Japanese] nationals in cases not involving military security," but that it "would be necessary to treat them as 'enemy' [i.e. Japanese] nationals in some cases," since Koreans had been Japanese imperial subjects. It was also pointed out that, if they wished, Koreans in Japan should be repatriated (Kim T'ae-gi 1997: 159–62; see also Ōnuma 1986).

The meaning of the term "liberated national" remained ambiguous and undefined, and as such, was very problematic with respect to the actual practices of the occupation administration.[4] No section in SCAP specifically dealt with the issues of Koreans in Japan. Instead, each section was left to render its own interpretation, and to implement its own policies. Thus, policies concerning Koreans in Japan were never coherent within SCAP (Kim T'ae-gi 1997: 116–20).

By March 1946, 1,340,000 Koreans had already repatriated from Japan (the official statistics recorded 940,000, but it is estimated that another 400,000 returned on their own by chartering small boats) (Morita 1955; see also Wager 1951). SCAP finally launched the official repatriation program on 16 March

1946. At that point in time, of the 640,000 registered Koreans remaining in Japan, 79 percent expressed their wish to return to Korea. By the end of the year, however, only another 83,000 had returned (which resulted in SCAP's abandoning the program) (Morita 1955). Clearly, the massive wave of repatriation was over. Moreover, some of the Koreans who had repatriated had then re-entered Japan because they could not sustain themselves in Korea.

The establishment of the League of Koreans

By October 1945, in order to protect their interests and improve their living conditions, Koreans remaining in Japan organized the League of Koreans in Japan, or, in Korean, Chaeil chosŏnin yŏnmaeng (hereafter, the league; see Ryang in this volume). The league brought together an overwhelming majority of Koreans in Japan. At first, the top of the organization included the "pro-Japanese" group, those who had collaborated with the Japanese government before the liberation of Korea, but these people were quickly excluded by the communists. Because of their subordinate position in Japanese society, many Koreans were sympathetic to communist ideas, and several important positions of the league were filled by JCP members.[5] The league's local branches, however, included many non-communists who had organized Koreans in their local areas.

At first, the major activities of the league were to assist with repatriation and to demand both compensation for Korean workers forcibly taken to Japan during the war and the fair distribution of food rations. Thus the league – originally a self-governance organization – soon became political. On 15 December 1946, in ending the repatriation program, SCAP issued a statement saying that Koreans who remained in Japan were to be regarded as Japanese nationals until the legitimate government of Korea recognized their Korean nationality. This infuriated Koreans, because they thought they deserved to be treated as "liberated people." As most Koreans saw it, they had just been liberated from Japanese colonial rule, and they did not want to be subjected to it again. The league, representing these Korean voices, demanded the revocation of the SCAP statement. SCAP changed its wording, but not its basic idea for submitting the Koreans remaining in Japan to the Japanese legal system (Kim T'ae-gi 1997: 301–11).

In December 1946, the league expressed its objection to the newly introduced capital levy tax.[6] Ten thousand marched to the premier's residence, violence broke out, and ten representative members were arrested on charges of inciting a "riot." In the end, Commander General Eichelberger of the Eighth Army decided to deport them rather than put them into Japanese prisons. This deportation indicated a significant change of occupation policy, contradicting the official policy of regarding Koreans as Japanese nationals and subjecting Koreans to the Japanese legal system.

The league also demanded voting rights for Koreans, which had been suspended since December 1945, in order to represent the interests of Koreans remaining in Japan. Since only the JCP supported the idea of Koreans' voting rights, the league became involved in the JCP's 1947 election campaign. As the JCP declared in a March 1947 document, "Ultimately, it is only Japanese proletariats or the [communist] party that can properly defend the interests of Koreans in Japan." In time, the league's communist orientation became increasingly prevalent, as exemplified by the expulsion from its executive committee of non-communist members.

The Alien Registration Law was enacted on 2 May 1947.[7] The law, which required all aliens to be photographed and registered, was intended to control illegal immigration, particularly to deport Koreans who had illegally reentered Japan. The Japanese government high-handedly attempted to apply this law to all Koreans in Japan, for the time being considering them as aliens, even though, in the official government view, they were still Japanese nationals (see Kashiwazaki in this volume). The league strongly opposed the Alien Registration Law, fearing the abuse of personal records by the police. However, as the Japanese government and SCAP showed a conciliatory attitude, the league finally agreed to have their members registered.

The league and its education

During 1946, after repatriation had passed its peak, the league's primary effort became the improvement of the livelihoods of Koreans remaining in Japan, particularly in the area of education. Already by that time, through individual and grassroots efforts, schools were being built in many places. The purpose of these schools was primarily to restore Korean culture and history and to develop Korean language proficiency, all of which had been severely suppressed under the policies of imperial Japan. There were practical reasons as well, however: the overwhelming majority of Koreans at that time were hoping to leave Japan for Korea in the near future, so knowing the Korean language was crucial. Korean younger generations, who had grown up in Japan and attended public schools, had not had the opportunity to learn Korean. Many first Korean schools, such as Kanda chōsen YMCA and Toktsuka hangŭl gakuin, had formerly been language schools.

In its second national conference in February 1946, the league decided to promote Korean education. It planned to institutionalize the elementary school system and to establish two schools for adult political leaders in Tokyo and Osaka. Overall, their educational orientation was nationalist rather than communist. Even in later years, when the Japanese conservatives and SCAP came to criticize Korean schools as communist, neither presented any evidence of communist education in Korean primary and junior high schools (Kim T'ae-gi 1997: 403).

Hundreds and thousands of Koreans made enthusiastic efforts to build their schools. The league raised money to rent, buy, or construct the buildings to house the schools. In some cases, prefectural and city governments helped with the establishment of Korean ethnic schools, by renting part of a public school building or by helping procure construction materials. In Osaka, the governor became the honorary adviser of the Korean school building committee (Yang Yŏng-hu 1985: 138). In Kobe, mayor Nakai Shōichi allowed the league to use some of the city's school buildings. As a former executive member of the league's Hyōgo office recalls:

> The issue of using parts of city school buildings was resolved soon after [our meeting], and the league was able to use parts of two school buildings in east

Kobe, and one in west Kobe. Then, when we [the league's members] gave him the written contract, the mayor generously responded, "We don't need one. You can use the buildings as long as you want, until you decide to return to your home country." We were very pleased.

(quoted in Kim Kyŏng-hwan 1988: 432)

In January 1947, the league clarified its general principles and fundamental goals of education. The general principles included phrases such as, "to set a long-term policy of education," "to achieve the improvement of the educational institutions and democratization of pedagogical contents," and "to help democratize Japanese education" (Ozawa 1973: 196-7). The fundamental goals read:

1 To teach true democracy under which all people can live a better life.
2 To foster love of our own country [Korea] with a consideration of world history.
3 To develop a unique sense of admiration for the fine arts and creative activities based on everyday life experience.
4 To develop a respect for work through everyday experience and learning.
5 To stimulate active minds for research in technology and science.
6 To facilitate the investigation of social relations between science, labor, and economic activities.

(Ozawa 1973: 196–7)

These objectives were expressed in terms of democracy rather than communism. The Korean schools reclaimed the Korean cultural heritage, and Korean language education was particularly important. The schools termed their education as "ethnic education" or *minzokukyōiku*, while it was aimed at raising a Korean national consciousness:

Ethnic education is education that actualizes the happiness of Koreans as a people. The central duty of ethnic education is to raise children who love the people, culture, and language of the homeland [Korea]. Thus, children receiving this education would risk their lives to fight against those who trample underfoot the people, culture, and language of the homeland.

(Li Dong-sun 1956: 75)

The league developed its own curriculum and educational materials, which emphasized Korean history and geography. Japanese colonialism and its assimilationist ideas were criticized, and Korean nationalism was promoted in its place.

The Korean schools were managed collectively. After the summer of 1947, the expenses of the schools were collected from the general Korean population living in each community (instead of being paid only by the parents of school children). In this way, the schools were supported not only by the committed supporters of the league, but also by the broader Korean communities. By October

1947, the league had built 541 elementary schools, seven junior high schools, twenty-two adolescent schools, and eight high schools.

Initial views toward ethnic schools

In the beginning, the Japanese Ministry of Education was not interested in, or concerned with, the issue of Korean education and schools. The ministry was preoccupied with rebuilding and restructuring the Japanese school system, and Korean schools built by Koreans' own efforts tended not to attract the attention of the Ministry of Education. Thus, the ministry allowed the building of Korean schools, though they rejected the idea of publicly funding those schools (see Kim T'ae-gi 1997).

On the other hand, in August 1946, the civil information and education section of SCAP came out against the establishment of Korean schools because it regarded the existence of a minority ethnic group as a potential source of social conflict. The issue was raised in terms of the nationality of Koreans in Japan. If Koreans were regarded as having Japanese nationality, their school-age children would be required to go to schools that met the requirements (including curriculum) of Japanese compulsory education. In other words, Korean schools would need to comply with the requirements. On the other hand, if Koreans in Japan were not Japanese nationals, their children would be able to attend any kind of school, and Korean schools did not have to satisfy the requirements. There was no clear answer to the question at that time, because SCAP itself had not yet decided the nationality issue of Koreans remaining in Japan.

However, as SCAP made its statement suggesting that Koreans in Japan should be treated as Japanese nationals (December 1946), Japan's Ministry of Education shifted its position. The treatment of Korean ethnic schools became an issue, especially after the Japanese government proclaimed a series of education laws and set curriculum standards and requirements for schools (March 1947). In April 1947, the ministry stated that Koreans residing in Japan were subject to Japanese law, and that they were obligated to have their children receive Japanese compulsory education. The ministry advised prefectural governments to consider the local contexts and to apply this instruction in a flexible manner. The ministry also allowed each prefecture to approve the establishment of new Korean schools by Koreans in Japan as elementary and secondary schools or "miscellaneous schools."[8] This indicated that the ministry acknowledged a certain degree of autonomy of Korean schools at this stage (Yang Yŏng-hu 1985: 138).

Because most of them were elementary schools, the existing Korean schools needed to be registered and approved by the prefectural educational boards. In some prefectures, such as Yamaguchi and Osaka, military government teams stationed at each site (the local administrative branch of the US Army; hereafter MGT) directly instructed the prefectural governments to enforce the registration of Korean schools and to examine the qualification of Korean schoolteachers. In the case of the Yamaguchi prefecture, the MGT suggested that if Korean schools did not cooperate in registering, the Korean individuals involved should be arrested and deported. Despite the MGT's intention, however, not many Korean ethnic schools registered themselves, since, owing to the ambiguity of the Ministry of Education's orders, the prefectural government did not take decisive action. Similar cases came up in Osaka and Kanagawa, where a large number of Koreans lived. We can see, in Kim T'ae-gi's study, that at the time some MGTs regarded Korean schools' disobedience of their policies as frustrating and unacceptable, referring to them as communists (Kim T'ae-gi 1997: 392–7).

In response to the pressure from several local MGTs, SCAP's civil information and education section directed Japan's Ministry of Education to issue an official order to the prefectural governors declaring that Korean schools should comply with all pertinent Japanese education laws. As the cabinet members discussed the draft of the order, some questioned the wisdom of forcing Japanese education on Koreans remaining in Japan. They also suspected that the order might violate the postwar constitutional rights to civil freedom. In the end, however, they approved the order, which was issued on 24 January 1948 (Kim T'ae-gi 1997: 399).

The order stated that all Korean children in Japan must attend accredited schools approved by the prefectural governments. That meant that Korean schools needed to follow the Japanese standard curriculum, and that the Korean language could only be taught as an extracurricular program. It also clarified the point that the miscellaneous schools were to be approved only as institutions of post-compulsory education, thus precluding the possibility of registering Korean schools as miscellaneous schools. The order forced a choice for Korean school-age children of going either to Japanese schools or to Korean ethnic schools accredited as formal schools. Neither case allowed for sufficient Korean teaching.

The league strongly opposed the ministry's order. In its 16 February statement, it defined Koreans in Japan as Korean nationals and claimed that instruction in the Korean language was indispensable because in the future they would return to their home country. It demanded that the Japanese government recognize the special needs of Korean schools, and that their educational autonomy be respected (Pak Kyŏng-sik 1989: 186–8). Neither the Japanese government nor SCAP offered any compromise. When the league negotiated with the education minister, Morito Tatsuo, on 19 and 20 March, Morito was being closely directed by SCAP. Morito insisted that if the closing of unregistered Korean schools was not completed before the beginning of the new school year (April), the use of force would be inevitable. Yamaguchi prefecture in southwestern Japan was the first to issue the closing order affecting unregistered Korean schools on 31 March (Pak Kyŏng-sik 1989: 188–9).

Tensions intensified as the stalemate progressed into April. The schools under the league's leadership did not accept the school closing order and continued teaching. The league organized mass demonstrations demanding the order be revoked. In Yamaguchi, in order to avoid further social unrest, the prefectural government allowed a grace period before carrying out the closing. In Hyogo prefecture, seventy-three Korean school staff were arrested for not obeying the evacuation order. In Okayama prefecture in the west of Hyogo, the local chairperson of the league was arrested because the league did not comply with the order by the due date. A mass protest of Koreans in Okayama took place, and the chairperson was finally released (Ozawa 1973: 235).

At this stage, the US Army withheld direct intervention, limiting itself to instructing the Japanese prefectural offices (Kim T'ae-gi 1997: 405). The league made another attempt to negotiate with the Japanese government. On 19 April it offered four counter proposals, stating that if the Japanese government would meet its conditions, it would register its ethnic schools as private schools. The Japanese government ignored the proposal (Pak Kyŏng-sik 1989: 190–1).

The Kobe and the Osaka incidents

In Kobe, negotiations between the league and mayor Kodera Kenkichi (who succeeded mayor Nakai) were often hindered by the mayor's arrogance (also see Wagner 1951: 71). A deputy mayor of that time recalls:

> [Mayor Kodera] flatly refused to talk about the issue of [the league's] demands. . . . Mayor Kodera always said [to the Koreans], "You don't have citizenship. Foreigners are only guests. . . . Since your country is now becoming a wonderful country, you should go back there if you don't like Japan." He trashed them with this logic.
> (Seki 1972: 119)

Kodera's view, though it was more extreme than was standard at that time, and though it was inconsistent with the official Japanese position that Koreans were Japanese nationals, was becoming dominant among Japanese. Koreans remaining in Japan were considered non-nationals and therefore had no rights for ethnic education on Japanese soil; if Koreans insisted that they should enjoy the same set of civil rights as Japanese, they would simply have to learn to be the Japanese, giving up ethnic education.

On 23 April in Kobe, police and city government workers attempted to evict Koreans from three public schools (parts of which Korean schools were using). At two schools, Koreans were forcibly evicted, but the city was not able to close the third school because of fierce protest by Korean parents. On the next morning (24 April), outraged Korean protestors and some Japanese supporters gathered around the prefectural capitol and had a mass demonstration demanding to meet the governor of Hyōgo prefecture and the mayor of Kobe. A crowd of the protestors rushed into the building and forced the governor and the mayor to have a meeting with their representatives. The prefecture and city officials finally agreed to withdraw the closing order on the Korean schools, and to allow them to continue until they were approved as special schools, which would be exempted from Japanese education laws (though there was no such category or provision). The officials also promised to release those who had been arrested in the previous protests. This was a significant victory for the supporters of Korean ethnic schools.

On the evening of the same day, however, the US military commander of the Kobe area proclaimed a state of emergency – the only time such a proclamation was issued during the Allied occupation of Japan. The primary intent of the US occupation forces was the suppression of the Koreans under the league's leadership, who were, in their view, communists not obedient to the occupation forces. The US Army and Japanese police attempted to restrain every Korean in the city. Even many Koreans who were not involved in the protests were taken to the police. (In fact, the police investigated all "strangers" on the street, and arrested all those who appeared suspicious, including Taiwanese and Okinawans.) Some of them were not released for nearly a week. Of the 1,732 who were arrested (seventy-four of whom were Japanese), some were badly tortured by the police (Pak Kyŏng-sik 1989: 94–5; Yonniyon o kirokusuru kai 1988).

Commander General Eichelberger arrived at Kobe the next day. In response to questions from the press, but with little evidence, he stated that the "rioting" of the Koreans in the area had been instigated by the communist party. In his statement to the press he said, "The behavior of Koreans was a mere act of violence, nothing but disorder. I wish I had a big ship like the Queen Elizabeth here to send all of them back to Korea" (*Kobe shinbun* 27 April 1948).

Among those arrested, thirty-nine were put on the trial. Nine (eight Koreans and one Japanese who was a member of city council and who belonged to the JCP) were sent to the military commission court. Twelve others were sent to the general military court. Another eighteen were sent to Kobe district court. Of the nine who were sent to the military commission court, five were sentenced to fifteen years of hard labor, one was sentenced to twelve years of hard labor, and another was sentenced to ten years of hard labor. The rest were judged innocent (Yonniyon o kirokusuru kai 1988: 196–9; Pak Kyŏng-sik 1989: 196). The Hyōgo league chairperson was arrested and died during his prison term (Kim Kyŏng-hae 1995).

Around the same time, similar incidents were taking place in Osaka. On April 23, 15,000 gathered in front of the prefectural capitol. When Korean (and some Japanese) protestors attempted to submit their written demands and officials refused to discuss the matter with them, a crowd of protestors rushed into the building and occupied the office. The chief of the Osaka police issued an eviction notice, and the police force was introduced to the scene. As the police cleared the building, 179 of the protestors (including nine Japanese) were arrested, twenty sustained severe injury, and 150 sustained minor injuries (Pak Kyŏng-sik 1989: 192–3).

On April 26, another 30,000 gathered in front of the Osaka capitol, and the representatives of the league had a meeting with the governor. The governor would not compromise, however, and insisted that Korean children must be sent to Japanese schools. Suddenly, a US military officer brought an order to the governor, stating that the meeting should be discontinued and that the crowd should be broken up, perhaps with the use of a fire engine and firearms. The chief of police ordered the crowd to break up in five minutes. The representatives of the league urged demonstrators to withdraw, but when a few did not follow and began to throw stones, the police began to discharge water and opened fire on the withdrawing demonstrators. A sixteen-year-old boy, Kim T'ae-il, was shot to death; a fourteen-year-old girl, Kim Hwa-sun, was badly beaten by police and suffered a severe head injury; and eight others were severely injured (Zainichi chōsenjin gakkōjiken shinsōchōsadan 1948: 17–28). Throughout this series of confrontations, forty-two were convicted and eighteen (including ten Japanese) were sentenced to one to four years of hard labor by the military court (Pak Kyŏng-sik 1989: 197).

The dissolution of the league and the closing of ethnic schools

Most of the Japanese mass media blamed Koreans for causing social disorder, in part because SCAP actively censored news reports sympathetic to the Koreans (Ozawa 1973: 244–6; see also Kim Kyŏng-hwan 1988). In the Diet, only the JCP pursued the Japanese government's responsibility (Kim T'ae-gi 1997: 415–7). The series of conflicts was settled on 3 May 1948, through the direct negotiation of the league and education minister Morito. The two parties agreed that Korean schools would follow the Japanese legal framework, registering themselves as private schools within which Korean education would be offered within the limits of the autonomy granted to private schools. While the league's demands were not fully heard, the ministry modified its position and allowed some degree of ethnic education to take place as part of compulsory education within the Japanese formal schooling system.

The reconciliation, however, did not last long, since SCAP and the Japanese government had become increasingly apprehensive of Koreans in general and hostile to the league in particular. When the Democratic People's Republic of Korea (DPRK) was established in the northern Korea (9 September 1948), the league recognized it as the legitimate government of Korea, and held a series of celebrations for the new nation all over Japan. Without providing any legitimate reason, SCAP – increasingly sensitive to communist activities – banned any display of the DPRK national flag in their celebrations. Those who did not follow the order were arrested and taken to a US military court. Some were then sentenced to be deported to South Korea (Pak Kyŏng-sik 1989: 209–13).

As Yoshida Shigeru became prime minister for the second time in October 1948, his administration put more energy into the regulation and prosecution of the illegal brewing of rice wine, which was one of the major businesses for Koreans trying to earn a living. Many Korean neighborhoods were investigated by the police, and the living conditions of Koreans worsened. In this situation, the central committee of the league came to believe that their political interests were represented only by the JCP and began to hope for a political overturning of society rather than gradual economic improvement (Kim T'ae-gi 1997: 528–49). After the one-year memorial meeting of the Kobe-Osaka incident, held on 25 April 1949, many more Koreans, including local leaders, officially joined the JCP.

In the election of January 1949, the JCP gained thirty-five seats, the most it had ever achieved. Although the Koreans could not vote, they supported the JCP's election campaign. The Yoshida administration, whose task it was to execute the US economic recovery plan, was threatened by the JCP advances, and on 4 April, backed by SCAP, it issued an order to regulate the activities of "antidemocratic" and "terrorist" organizations. Its intention was to outlaw the communists eventually, and one of the first targets was the league.

Premier Yoshida himself went so far as to write a letter to General MacArthur asking him to repatriate all Koreans in Japan to South Korea. In his letter, he consciously misrepresented the number of Koreans residing in Japan, stating that one million lived there and that half of them had entered Japan illegally. Yoshida emphasized that Koreans were harmful to Japan because many of them were engaging in criminal (or communist) activities, and because they were not contributing to the economic recovery of Japan (Tanaka 1995: 72–4).

On 9 September the Japanese government suddenly enforced its 4 April order and locked down the headquarters of the league with 500 police. The government, labeling the league as an anti-democratic, terrorist organization – the Kobe and Osaka incidents were among the major reasons the Japanese government regarded it in these terms – ordered its dissolution. Its property was confiscated, and its leaders were purged from political activities (Kim T'ae-gi 1997: 528–80; Pak Kyŏng-sik 1989: ch. 5).

With the league's dissolution, its schools were ordered to close immediately, and other Korean ethnic schools were ordered to reorganize and reapply for status as private schools. Of the latter, only three schools were approved by the Ministry of Education, and overall almost 350 Korean ethnic schools were closed (in many places by force) (Ozawa 1973: 262–7). The majority of Korean children were transferred to Japanese public schools.

Some Korean schools were simply incorporated into the Japanese public school system (for example, the Tokyo school system). In other places, where Koreans had a strong presence (such as Kobe), the prefectural governments could not shut down the schools, and Korean schools remained open as schools outside the definition established by Japanese education laws. In some Japanese elementary and secondary schools (such as in Osaka), Korean history, culture, and language were taught as extracurricular activities by Korean teachers (see Hester in this volume for the present context). In Tokyo, where the city government took over all Korean schools (twelve elementary schools, one junior high school, and one senior high school), Japanese principals were appointed and Japanese teachers replaced Korean ones. Korean teachers could only remain as contracted untenured staff (less than 25 percent of all employees), and the language of instruction became Japanese. (Ozawa 1973: 302–44).[9]

In 1952, when Japan regained its independence, all Koreans in Japan were recategorized as aliens, without being given a choice, and were no longer considered a part of the Japanese system of compulsory education. Korean children were still allowed to go to Japanese schools, but their parents were often required to sign a written consent not to complain about the education their children received in the schools. With "little reason to continue publicly funded schools for an alien population," the Tokyo city government in 1955 ended its operation of Korean ethnic schools, in spite of opposition by Koreans and Japanese supporters.

For the most part, the effort to develop Korean ethnic schools as an autonomous and legitimate part of Japanese formal schooling (as either private schools or public schools) was halted at this point.[10] After 1955, under the leadership of the general association of Korean residents in Japan, or Chongryun (which had disassociated itself from the JCP and reconstituted as an association with political allegiance to the DPRK), Korean schools were rebuilt and accredited by the Ministry of Education as miscellaneous schools (Inokuchi 1998;

Nozaki and Inokuchi forthcoming; Ozawa 1973: 345–414). As miscellaneous schools, Korean schools lost benefits enjoyed by Japanese schools, including financial assistance from the government.

State formation, educational institution, and hegemony

Benedict Anderson argues that a nation of Japanese had not existed from the earliest times; rather, it emerged during the colonial period through its experiences as a colonizer bringing official nationalism (1991: 110–11). The collapse of the empire did not hinder its process of nation-building. The early occupation period saw an exercise of power that established Japan as a single-ethnic nation even more firmly. On the one hand, it was a time of state re-formation during which Japan as an empire was abandoned and Japan as a "democratic" nation-state was institutionalized. On the other hand, the transition allowed a rebuilding of hegemony that was more clearly centered around the idea of Japan as a homogeneous nation. The suppression of Korean ethnic schools was a moment of force struck to secure the Japanese state's re-formation and its hegemony. It was also the first postwar demonstration of the idea of Japan as a single-ethnic nation-state, in that it consolidated the majority identity through the exclusion of the ethnic minority.

Since the Allied Powers decided to rule Japan indirectly, through the Japanese government as much as possible, the two governing bodies co-existed from September 1945 to April 1952. SCAP was supposed to supervise the Japanese national and prefectural governments, but the relationship between SCAP and the Japanese command systems was not always very clear. The degree of SCAP involvement in policymaking also changed throughout the occupation period. Besides, the two governing powers collaborated for different purposes and with different preoccupations and historical contexts, and those differences often resulted in tensions. SCAP was subject to the US government in Washington and there were sometimes disagreements between them. It is ironic to see that one point of their unity was the suppression of Koreans who had been colonized by the Japanese, played no significant part in the wartime hostility against the Allied Powers, and simply desired to have their own ethnic schools while remaining in Japan.

In a way, the situation faced by Koreans remaining in Japan at the beginning of the postwar era (and thereafter) can be seen as one shaped by a new form of colonialism. The right and desire to have legitimate ethnic schools be part of formal (compulsory) education were denied. Formal education was clearly recognized as a mainstay of establishing and maintaining the hegemony of dominant ideologies of the state, so the power bloc attempted to control it. Further, schools in the modern world are nationalistically organized, in that, first, schools as institutions define the proper members of the schools and, by extension, the proper members of the nation; and second, schools select, teach, and legitimize a particular kind of knowledge and render it nationalized "official" knowledge in the final analysis (see Apple 1993). These are the reasons why, from the viewpoint of the Japanese government and SCAP, Korean schools had to be destroyed, and it is why, from the Korean point of view, ethnic schools had to be defended, even at a cost of terrible loss and suffering.

Acknowledgements

I sincerely thank Yoshiko Nozaki, Judith Perkins, and Sonia Ryang for their editorial suggestions and insightful criticisms of earlier versions of this chapter. I am also grateful to Sylvan Esh for his assistance in writing this chapter.

Notes

1 Gramsci himself seems inconsistent in this respect (for further discussion see Anderson 1976; Bobbio 1979; Texier 1979).
2 Later, as the prime minister of Japan in 1932, Saitō appointed a Korean aristocrat as a member of the House of Peers for the first time. He was assassinated by ultra-nationalist army officers in the 26 February Incident of 1936 in Tokyo.
3 It might also be said that the occupational authorities' lack of perspectives on the issues of Koreans displaced by Japanese colonialism extended well beyond the boundaries of Japan itself. For example, nothing was done to help approximately 43,000 Korean laborers left stranded in the former Japanese colony of southern Sakhalin at the end of the war (see Takagi 1990). In addition, the occupation force held many Korean "comfort women" in protective custody after Japan's defeat, but did not investigate the matter as one of Japan's war crimes (see Tanaka 1996).
4 During the decision-making process in Washington, considerable dispute arose regarding the status of Koreans in Japan. The earlier drafts, created by the pro-Japanese faction (who emphasized the importance of economic recovery and stability in Japan), tended to see Koreans as an obstacle to Japanese economic recovery. This group eventually lost out to the anti-Japanese, pro-China faction, with the result that Koreans in Japan were granted a more preferable legal status. Thus, the directive was a compromise of two factions.
5 It is reported that when Korean communist Kim Ch'ŏn-hae was finally released from the prison, together with prominent Japanese communist party leaders in October, 400 Koreans (and twenty to thirty Japanese) gathered at the gate of the prison and celebrated the release.
6 *Zaisenzei* in Japanese. This was introduced as a special incidental tax in order to compensate for the economic loss suffered by heavy industry and financial institutions during the war. Since Koreans in Japan saw themselves as not responsible for the war, they claimed that they should be exempted from this tax.
7 This was actually one day before the promulgation of the new constitution. This law would be a violation of Article 14 of the new constitution, which assured Japanese nationals of equality under the law. Nevertheless, the government section of SCAP strongly promoted the enforcement of the law (Kim T'ae-gi 1997: 358–71).
8 The miscellaneous school is a category for schools whose educational credentials would not constitute a basis for higher education. They are generally skill-oriented schools such as driving schools, sewing schools, language schools and so on.
9 Some Japanese teachers working in the schools began to realize the Korean students' needs for ethnic education, and brought the issue to the second national conference of the Japan teachers' union in January 1953. The union took a position to support the establishment of public Korean ethnic schools. The union also decided to provide, as much as possible, ethnic education for Korean children in the Japanese public schools (see Nakayama 1995).
10 At this stage, seventeen public Korean schools still existed in various places in Japan. The Japanese government finally abolished all public Korean schools in 1966 (see Ozawa 1973).

8 Korean children, textbooks, and educational practices in Japanese primary schools

Eriko Aoki

More than a half century has passed since Koreans were liberated from the Japanese colonial rule. The current situation, however, indicates that Japan is far from a fair society for Korean residents, since prejudice against Koreans, largely a colonial legacy, is generally still strong among Japanese. Discrimination has been widely recorded in the areas of employment, business opportunities, marriage, schooling, and housing, let alone the systemic discrimination in the area of civil rights status which keeps Koreans in the position of second-class citizens in Japan (see for example, Min Gwan-sik 1994; Kim Ch'an-jŏng 1994; Ko Ch'an-yu 1996; Nomura 1996; Ōnuma 1986). Since being Korean carries stigma, many Koreans tend to hide their ethnic backgrounds, for example by using Japanese names in their everyday life. In order to change the situation, some Japanese, both individuals and organizations, especially in the area of education, try to encourage Korean children to appreciate their ethnic heritage. This chapter probes into obstacles and difficulties these attempts face, including some unintended consequences of well-intended support.

Nearly 90 percent of Korean children in Japan go to Japanese schools (Min Gwan-sik 1994: 44). By law every local public school must accept Korean children who live in its catchment area, if they wish to attend the Japanese school in the area. Their Japanese classmates usually do not know that they are Korean, mainly owing to their Japanese-sounding passing names. Because of the small demographic ratio of Koreans (about 0.6 percent of the entire Japanese population), in many cases a Korean child finds him or herself to be the only Korean in the class. Even if there is more than one Korean child in a class, since a Korean child rarely knows who else is a fellow Korean, each child may feel isolated from the rest and remain silent about his or her ethnic origins (Harajiri 1997: 34–5). In this chapter I shall explore complex aspects of Korean children's school life by using specific cases in Osaka prefecture, which holds the largest Korean population in Japan and is generally regarded as progressive in terms of human rights education.

In the first section I briefly discuss children's developmental psychology. This leads to the second section where I discuss school textbooks and the way in which "national language" (*kokugo*) textbooks and "social studies" (*shakaika*) textbooks influence children's formation of national identity. In the third section

I look at moral education textbooks distributed by the Osaka prefectural government. In the final section I report on a visit to a city in Osaka prefecture, where special effort is made to familiarize Korean children learning at Japanese schools with things Korean. Through these examples I hope to lay bare the reality of the limits that Korean children face in the classrooms of Japanese schools.

Children's world of discrimination

Children may seem innocent of the wrong with which the world of adults is saturated. However, they never live in a sanctuary free from the complications of the society in which adults live. Furthermore, children can sometimes treat others as cruelly as adults do, if not more cruelly. More than seventy years ago ethnologist Origuchi Shinobu witnessed such cruelty in the turmoil after the Great Kantō Earthquake of 1923. This earthquake hit the area around Tokyo and killed more than 100,000 people. Immediately after the earthquake a false rumor was spread by the Japanese authorities and the media that Koreans were setting fires, throwing poison into wells, rioting against the imperial army, killing men, and raping women (De Vos and Lee 1981a: 22; see also Weiner 1989). It is estimated that 6,000 Koreans were killed by the military, police, and civilians who were threatened by, or took advantage of, the rumor (Mizuno 1993: 15; Kuboi 1988: 89). In this scene of massacre, Origuchi witnessed a little child whipping dead Koreans and wrote a tragic poem describing the scene as "peril of my life, the terror of nirvana" (see Murai 1995).

Compared with seventy years ago, discriminations against marginalized people, including Koreans, have become covert in both official and popular discourse, owing to Japan's joining the "democratic" nations in the postwar period, its economic achievement on a global scale, recent governmental attempts at disseminating the notion of internationalization, and an increased general awareness of political correctness. However, in the classroom situation, children's cruelty towards others continues to be observed particularly through bullying of classmates. Bullying has been one of the most serious problems in Japanese schools since the late 1970s. It is sometimes so cruel that quite a few victims have committed suicide (e.g. Kawai 1996). Usually a group of children target one victim in a class. A child who is vulnerable and different from other children in any way may easily become a victim. Being an only Korean child in a class may easily induce bullying, and there was such a case where a Korean junior high school student, bullied by his Japanese peers, committed suicide (see Kim Ch'an-jŏng 1980a and 1980b).

In general, cases of cruel bullying occur not in the lower grades but in advanced grades (Kawai 1996). Reported cases of discriminatory behavior against Korean children are also found mainly among older children in advanced grades. It is reported that in the early grades of primary school, Korean children usually do not care that they are Korean, while later they tend to be embarrassed at being Korean regardless of whether they have been discriminated against because of being Korean (Kim Ch'an-jŏng 1980a and 1980b; Fukuoka and

Tsujiyama 1991: 37). Bullies seem to establish themselves by excluding some misfits as the "other." While a Japanese child who behaves discriminatorily against a Korean child might establish his or her own ethnic identity in the act of excluding others, a Korean child who is embarrassed at being Korean can develop a negative ethnic identity by way of self-negation. The act of committing suicide is deeply related to the process by which the child builds an identity: in this case in a negative way through the rejection of others, ultimately leading to the rejection of the self (Erikson 1968).

Psychological research carried out in Japanese schools points out that peers become important among children in advanced grades. They try to fit themselves to peer standards and behave so as to be approved by their peers rather than by their teachers and/or parents. Bullying can be understood as a negative form of the group-oriented behavior at this developmental stage (Fujisaki 1990: 188). Based on analysis of children's conversation, Jeffrey Parker and John Gottman point out that, from the ages of eight to twelve children aim at being accepted by their same-sex peer group; they try to avoid being rejected by the group; and they manage this social process by gossiping about others with negative evaluation (Parker and Gottman 1989: 104).

This kind of psychological development enables children to build self and identity and is interrelated to the development of abilities to categorize people. Frances Aboud suggests that children are first ego-centered and they later start emphasizing categories of people. Still later, children revert to an emphasis on individuals, viewing self and others in terms of their unique qualities (Aboud 1988: 25). Children who are involved in cruel bullying are at the second stage of cognitive development in Aboud's model.[1]

Based on research on children's racio-ethnic prejudice in the US, Canada, and the UK, Aboud points out that sorting into racio-ethnic categories and labeling often do not become accurate until the child is about seven years old. When the child becomes aware of racio-ethnicity, he or she tends to overuse it in perceptions and categorizations. This shift around the age of seven corresponds to a major shift in cognitive development. Aboud reports that the level of racial prejudice in children from the ages of four to seven is higher than in older children. Cognition concerning the physical world and the social world begins to change at this age and continues to change over the following five years (Aboud 1988: 58, 103). Jean Piaget also considers that a critical change in racio-ethnic prejudice takes place around the age of seven as children move from preoperational to concrete-operational ways of thinking and then around twelve years of age as children move from concrete operation to formal operation that enables them to deal with abstract concepts (Piaget 1932).

These psychological studies inform us that primary school children are in the midst of the process of cognitive development, which is deeply related to the development of the abilities to categorize people and to discriminate against others. Also, these studies draw our attention to the fact that small children, who are in the process of acquiring the abilities to categorize people, are likely to apply the categorization obsessively. Along with children's inaccuracy in categorization, especially in abstract categorization, their propensity to overuse socially prescribed categories and their inclination to exclude others in order to establish their own identity explain the paradox that "innocent" children can be more cruel than adults in dealing with others.

One point of difference worth noting between Aboud's model and the case of Korean children in the Japanese classroom is that the former is based on studies of children's recognition mainly of black and white peoples. The case of the relation between Korean children and Japanese children in Japan is different in that they are of the same complexion. The visible difference may be the primary reason why children in the US, the UK, and Canada display racial categorization at the much younger age of seven, while the intensified occurrence of singling out Korean children in the Japanese classroom takes place in the advanced grades of the primary school and above.

Children develop the cognitive abilities to distinguish observable attributes at an earlier stage, and then unobservable attributes later (Inagaki and Hatano 1986). From this, as for words which have physical meaning and psychological meaning, such as "bright," "hard," "sweet," and "cold," children become capable of understanding character-judging connotations of these words only in advanced grades. Before the age of seven, children apply these words only to physical objects.[2] While at the age of seven or eight, approximately 50 percent of children can apply these words to people, they cannot relate the physical meanings to psychological meanings. At around nine and ten, they become able to use them in both physical and psychological contexts, furthering their understanding of the double function of these words at the ages of eleven or twelve (Asch and Nerlove 1960; Palermo and Molfese 1972).

These observations agree with Piaget's model that children develop the abilities to operate concrete concepts from the ages of seven to twelve, and then become able to deal with abstract thoughts from the age of twelve onward (Piaget 1932). Many other researches point out that primary schoolchildren do not understand abstract concepts concerning political, social, and economic institutions such as law, community, government, and the banking system (e.g. Adelson and O'Neil 1966; Adelson *et al.* 1969; Takahashi and Hatano 1988; Kinoshita 1990). From this, we may assume that concepts such as nation, ethnicity, and state are not understood fully by children of the primary school age. In the following section, I shall consider how primary school education in Japan inspires children to grasp these concepts, by examining textbooks.

Authorized textbooks

Before the Meiji Restoration of 1868, the borders of numerous feudal states in Japan had been strictly guarded against each other. Consequently, the spoken language varied from one region to another. Furthermore, linguistic class variations were quite large (Lee Yeounsuk 1996: 47–50). This situation did not change much in the early Meiji era. Only learned people could communicate sufficiently with each other throughout Japan, by means of written Chinese. Communication

Korean children, textbooks and educational practices   161

between two people from different regions, who could not read Chinese was almost impossible. School education of the national language was introduced to make possible communication between speakers of different vernaculars.

In this multilingual situation, formal school education was imperative in order for the national standard language, *kokugo*, to emerge and be learned by every Japanese, simultaneously making them into members of the Japanese nation-state (Lee Yeounsuk 1996; Sakai 1996). Until the end of the Second World War, moral education, national language education, and national history education were designed to mould members of the Japanese empire as "babies of the emperor," with the utmost loyalty to the imperial household and the state as an entity born out of the imperial rule. Peoples in the colonies, as well as colonial immigrants in Japan, were forced to assimilate to Japanese by using the Japanese national language, deeming it as their "national" language (see Tanaka 1981). School education, especially national language education, provided an ideological stronghold for the building of a newly-emerging imperial power and the consolidation of Japan's multiethnic empire (see Kawamura 1994; Mashiko 1997).

After the end of the Second World War, the Allied occupation removed the tone of militarism and fascism from education. While the emperor system was not terminated, democracy replaced militarism and fascism based on the ideology of worshipping the emperor as the pedagogical axiom. Instead of enjoying the benefits of postwar democratization, former colonial subjects were not only not compensated for their past suffering, but also legally excluded from state benefits and welfare on the basis of the loss of Japanese nationality (see Kashiwazaki in this volume). They were also denied the rights to ethnic education (see Inokuchi in this volume).

Today, school education falls under the tight grip of the Ministry of Education. Compulsory education comprises six years of primary school and three years of junior high school. Children start their first year of compulsory education at the age of six. Textbooks are written and edited by experts and published by several publishers after passing an inspection by the ministry every three to four years (Tanigawa *et al.* 1997). Academic subjects taught in primary schools are the national language, mathematics, social studies, natural science, music, arts, physical education, moral education, and domestic technology. Through this system, schoolchildren in Japan are efficiently integrated as members of the Japanese nation-state. Academic subjects such as the national language and social studies, in particular, contribute to this integration. I shall now turn to an analysis of the contents of textbooks in these subjects.[3]

The national language

Before the Second World War, the national language played two indispensable roles, inspiring children with the militaristic ideology and enabling them to use the standardized language. For example, a story entitled "A Sailor's Mother" in a primary school textbook published in 1910 played the former role. The outline is as follows:

> At the time of the Sino-Japanese War [1894–5], a sailor who was going to serve on board the warship Takachiho was weeping while reading a letter by a woman's hand. An officer passed by and saw the sailor weeping. The officer reproached the sailor, saying what a shame for a sailor of the imperial navy to weep for his wife and children. The sailor showed the letter to the officer, and told him that he was a bachelor. The letter was from the sailor's *mother*. She complained that it was painful for her to face those caring neighbors in his *hometown* since he had not distinguished himself in military action yet. She encouraged him to die for the emperor. Reading the letter, the officer expressed his admiration for the sailor's *mother*.
>
> (quoted in Lee Yeounsuk 1996: 125–6; my italicization)[4]

The themes of "mother" and "home" were repeatedly used in textbooks so that children would consider dying for the empire as an honor, embraced by their loving "mother" and caring people in their "hometown" (Lee Yeounsuk 1996: 124–9; Akaneshobō 1974; Shibata 1980).

An example of the latter, more technical side of the national language as a tool to unify the language of the Japanese people, comes from a textbook published in 1904, which was designed for children to learn the correct distinction between two vowels, *i* and *e*, and that between two syllabic units, *su* and *shi* (Nakamura 1992: 131; Tanigawa *et al.* 1997: 31–2). Phonologically all the vernaculars in Japan's northeastern regions, which were politically, economically, and culturally peripheralized, lack these distinctions. This exemplifies that national language textbooks in the prewar period were designed to correct children's speech and to make it fit to the legitimate and standardized national language, at the same time marginalizing selective regional traits as against those of central districts such as Tokyo.

In the postwar textbooks of the national language there is no text that mentions the emperor, militarism, or nationalism except those which tell children how sad and awful the Second World War was. They continue to carry themes tinted with certain moral and social values as did the prewar textbooks. These are, however, the values of friendship, solidarity, mutual cooperation, happy school life, family, sensitivity to nature and other people, sociability, responsibility, peace-loving, tradition, internationalization, environmental protection, truthfulness, and so on. No lesson is designed to correct particular regional vernacular. On the contrary, texts in local vernacular are incorporated into current textbooks and the number of pages embracing spoken, informal forms of the Japanese language has increased.

Mass public education, the permeation of the mass media, and Japan-wide transmigration in accordance with postwar industrialization, helped by the modernization of telecommunication technology, brought about a massive high-tech communication network in the standardized Japanese, that covers both cities and the most remote areas in Japan. As long as it does not undermine the hegemony of the national language, no regional vernacular is officially repressed as an obstacle for Japan-wide communication. In some cases local languages are welcomed as varieties which may enrich the Japanese language, and the local government's tourism bureau may use distinct dialects in its pamphlet, for example.

Side by side with such a variation, in the classrooms, the national language has a solid hegemony. Before starting the first school year, children already speak vernacular, not conscious of what kind of language they are speaking. It is through primary education that children come to think that their use of language can be judged right or wrong by the standard of the national language. The hegemonic status of the national language is sustained throughout the school years by way of pedagogical discipline such as routine tests, school entrance examinations, and everyday correction in the classrooms. By learning the national language, children identify themselves as Japanese and the members of the Japanese nation. In this way, national language education operates as an efficacious state apparatus, ideologically molding people into members of the nation by penetrating their everyday lives.

It should be noted that the national language is offered to children as the only language that the Japanese possess. As such, it is never mentioned in textbooks, how similar it is to Korean, Okinawan, Chinese, and other languages in the neighboring regions of Asia and the Pacific. Japanese is taken for granted as something that is given to the Japanese on the basis of being Japanese. In this situation Korean children in Japanese schools inevitably learn the national language, standardized Japanese, as their "national" language, ironically repeating the colonial situation.

Social studies

As with the national language, social studies textbooks have gone through changes in the postwar period. Compared to textbooks published in the prewar period and up until the 1980s, recent texts are written in a friendly style, full of photographs and illustrations of good quality (Tanigawa *et al.* 1997). The first plural possessive pronoun, "our" (*watashitachino*), is repeatedly used in such phrases as "our homeroom," "our school," "our neighborhood," "our school catchment area," "our district," "our prefecture," "our country," "our nation-state," and "our national land." As children advance grades, the foci of studies are moved in this order and to the global level in the final year of primary education. Children will first register concrete topics and then gradually move toward abstract concepts.

Until 1991 the subject of social studies started from the second grade. After 1992 it was changed to start from the third grade. Third-grade textbooks start with study about the environment and geography in the children's neighborhood, leading children's interest from the school's vicinity to the school catchment areas. In Japan each local government divides its areas into many primary school catchment areas. Since it is a strict regulation that children go to the school in the catchment area where they live, all the children in a school share the same neighborhood.[5] Third-graders then move on to study the entire administrative district. They learn its geography, the role of local government, local industry, and social changes in recent decades.

Fourth-grade textbooks are similarly designed to give children an understanding about nature, industry, society, and the roles of the local government in their prefecture. They then advance to the study of diverse climates and various forms of lifestyles and occupations in Japan, divided into forty-seven prefectures. In the fifth grade, the industries and industrial structure of the Japanese nation-state are dealt with. In the last twenty or so years, topics have gradually shifted from industrialization and modernization to welfare, security, environmental protection, and cultural heritage.

Social studies textbooks for the sixth grade deal with Japanese history and the international world. While Japanese history taught at school in the prewar period started with the origin myth of Japan, the first topic dealt with in Japanese history as it is currently taught at primary school is prehistoric remains. Although these are quite different starting-points, they have in common the assumption that the community "Japan" derives from a single lineage, whose origin was the imperial family in the prewar historiography, and the myth of ethnic homogeneity in the current historiography. This effectively gives a primordial guise to the Japanese national identity.[6]

Here, it is worth looking at how Korea is dealt with in these textbooks. Descriptions concerning the political relations between Korea and Japan in the fourth or fifth century in the textbooks published by Kyōiku shuppan have changed in the following way.

The 1974 text:

> At that time [the fifth century], Yamato kingdom [in Japan] also ruled countries in the southern part of the Korean peninsula.
> (Hosoya *et al.* 1974: 16)

The 1977 text:

> In the fourth century, chiefs in Yamato [Nara prefecture] extended their power over Korea and waged a war with the army of Kōkuri [Koguryŏ in Korean; one of Korea's ancient kingdoms]. In the fifth century, they sent a messenger to the emperor of China and tried to have their rule over the southern part of Korea approved.
> (Ishii *et al.* 1977: 16–17)

The 1983 text:

> From the end of the fourth century, chiefs in Yamato started to exchange frequent visits with Korea and China. And then, in the fifth century, according to a book of history in China, they sent a messenger to the emperor of China.
> (Ishii *et al.* 1983: 22)

The 1986 text:

> According to a book of history in China, in the fifth century, the "great king" of Yamato kingdom frequently sent a messenger to the emperor of China. The purpose of sending a messenger is thought that the "great king" intended to have his rule over the southern part of Korea approved.
>
> (Ishii *et al.* 1986: 24)

Descriptions about Yamato's rule of the Korean peninsula were omitted from the 1992 and 1996 texts. Recent textbooks emphasize that in ancient times immigrants from the Korean peninsula brought advanced technology to Japan. While the textbooks before 1995 by Kyōiku shuppan describe how Toyotomi Hideyoshi, after settling civil wars in sixteenth-century Japan, *sent* his army to Korea, the present textbooks published by Kyōiku shuppan and Osaka shoseki formulate the historical incident as Hideyoshi's *invasion* of Korea. They also refer to courage and wisdom displayed by Koreans who fought back against Hideyoshi's army.

Since the 1980s, the injustice and oppression of colonial rule have been mentioned in the textbooks for primary education, by inclusion of such issues as the massacre of Koreans in the aftermath of the 1923 Great Kantō Earthquake, the forced wartime labor mobilization of Koreans, a colonial policy of changing Korean names into Japanese names, Korean comfort women recruited for the Japanese military, Korean independence movements, and so on.

Despite these historical references, social studies textbooks have neglected to mention that there are more than 650,000 Koreans living in Japan. There is only one mention of *zainichi kankokujin, chōsenjin* (Koreans in Japan) in the textbook published in 1996.[7] This omission – or neglect – renders the existing ethnic plurality invisible, as if with the end of colonial relations, Koreans ceased to exist in Japan, and Koreans lived in Japan in the past but not at present. What happens to a Korean schoolchild who reads the textbooks which refer to the standardized Japanese as "our national language" and Japan as "our nation-state," in which "her home" and "her school" exist? She may think: "My home and school are in Japan. But I am Korean. So I cannot say either 'the Japanese language is our language' or 'Japan is our country,' even though I only speak Japanese and live in Japan. Japan is the country for the Japanese people only." In the midst of her classmates learning together, she might find herself excluded from "our class."

Learning standardized Japanese not just as a language but as "our" national language, studying the Japanese state as "our" nation-state, and studying authorized Japanese history as "our" history effectively obliterate the fact that there are non-Japanese children in the classroom. Ultimately, the current Japanese education, as far as textbooks approved by the Ministry of Education are concerned, alienates Korean children not only from the Japanese society, but also from their living environments such as their home, school, and classroom. In the next section, I shall discuss moral education textbooks distributed by the Osaka prefectural government to its districts, in order to identify how the problem of the ethnonational identity of Korean children is dealt with.

Moral education: the case of the Osaka prefectural government

Osaka prefecture holds the largest Korean population among all the prefectures in Japan (around 200,000), most of whom live in Osaka city, which is the economic and political center of Osaka prefecture. Modern trading relations between Korea and Japan started after the unequal treaty agreed in 1876, which benefited Japan by way of a one-sided trading advantage over Korea. Since the late nineteenth century, merchants in Osaka have played the main role in the Japan–Korea trade. Japan exported manufactured cotton to Korea and imported rice and cheap labor from Korea. The Japanese annexation of Korea in 1910 brought about many changes to Korea. In 1922 the direct ferry line between Osaka and Cheju island in southwestern Korea was opened, which made many Cheju people migrate to Osaka (Sugihara 1986). Under the Japanese colonial rule many Koreans came to Japan, seeking jobs. The rushed industrialization in the newly emerging empire depended upon cheap labor provided by marginalized people in Japan. In Osaka, one of the largest industrial cities in Japan, Koreans, Okinawans, and disadvantaged Japanese such as Burakumin provided such labor, forming the slum area (Sugihara and Tamai 1986).[8] During the Second World War Koreans were forcibly brought to Osaka and its vicinities as laborers for military-related constructions. Koreans worked under worse conditions than Japanese (Hirakatashi kyōikuiinkai 1993).

After the war, many Korean schools were built and then destroyed by the authorities, but Korean ethnic classes for Korean children were set up in Japanese public schools in Osaka prefecture, especially in Korean-concentrated areas (Osakafu zainichi gaikokujin kyōiku kenkyūkyōgikai 1996; see Hester in this volume). As in other prefectures, however, in Osaka prefecture, most Korean children go to Japanese schools and undergo a Japanese education regardless of the neighborhoods they live in, except for a handful who go to Korean schools run by Chongryun, a Korean organization which supports North Korea.[9]

In contrast with detailed guidelines issued by the Ministry of Education on such subjects as the national language, mathematics, social studies, and natural science, moral education at primary school level is left to the local governments' decision, and it may vary from one local government to another. The scope of variation also depends on degrees of individual teachers' commitment. Osaka prefecture has distributed textbooks free of charge for moral education to its districts since 1970. While it is regarded as compulsory for the district governments to pass them to each schoolchild, their actual use in the classroom is left to each teacher's decision. These textbooks, entitled *Ningen* (Human), are compiled by Kaihōkyōiku kenkyūjo (the Institute for Buraku Liberation Education) which publishes many books on the issues of Burakumin.[10]

All the covers of the *Ningen* textbooks feature a watercolor by a child in the respective grade. The watercolors are entitled, for example, "Friends laughing together," "Friends playing music together," "A group of friends singing together," "Arm-wrestling in a classroom," and "Comrades and self-portrait filled with anger at social discrimination." Each book has ten to fifteen stories and poems with themes such as friendship, family relationships, classroom cooperation, peer relations, community-related issues, and so on. They also emphasize the necessity of understanding difference and diversity in terms of nationality, ethnicity, and social background. The *Ningen* textbooks convey anti-war messages, criticize bullying, denounce social segregation, and oppose discrimination and oppression on the basis of occupations, gender, disability, ethnicity, and nationality. They advocate resistance to oppression, in calling for an improvement in the living conditions of the oppressed.

Each volume of *Ningen* contains one story or poem concerning Korea or Koreans. In the first-grade volume, we find a poem by Tanigawa Shuntarō entitled "Konnichiwa" (Hello), which reads in part:

> On the globe,
> There are various peoples living,
> Speaking diverse languages.
> Japanese is one of them.
> Akira speaks Japanese,
> Kim Oksun in the neighboring country speaks Korean.
> (Kaihōkyōiku kenkyūjo 1997a: 20–1)

In the second grade a children's song in Korean is included, to be sung with gestures. A story in the third-grade book appeals to understand the importance for Korean children of using Korean names in order to overcome stigma. The outline of the story for the fourth grade is as follows:

> Irunamu, Korean child, and I, Japanese child, are good friends. Bumping against each other in playing soccer caused a quarrel between us. I offended him by calling him *chōsenjin* (Korean), although I did not mean to. I am really embarrassed. I want to apologize to Irunamu.
> (Kaihōkyōiku kenkyūjo 1997b: 78–83)[11]

This story is meant to encourage Japanese children to face up to the possibility of their having a discriminative view of Koreans which might be easily revealed in person-to-person contact and conflict.

The story for the fifth grade, entitled "Asukara honmyō de ikiyō" ("I Shall Live with My True Name from Tomorrow") encourages readers to understand not only such concepts as "colonization," "motherland," and "ancestral land," but also the modern and contemporary history of Japan's colonial rule of Koreans, its oppressive policy of banning Korean schools in Japan, and Korea's division into north and south. The outline is as follows:

> Kim Chun-gwan, known to his classmates by his Japanese name Kaneda, used to make every effort to conceal the fact that he was Korean. However, when his classmates visited his home, in spite of his desperate efforts to hide

168 *Eriko Aoki*

everything, including his grandmother, since she might reveal Koreanness, it became known to his classmates that he was Korean. After this incident he had a fight with one of the classmates who had visited his home, because the classmate ridiculed Koreans by mimicking how Chun-gwan's uncle had spoken to him in Japanese with a strong Korean accent. That night his father told him how courageously his grandfather, who had given him the name Chun-gwan, had resisted Japan's colonial oppression in order to be proudly Korean. His father encouraged him to use his Korean name in order to live with a pride as a Korean. Being impressed by what his father told him, he resolved that he would live with his *true* name.

(Kaihōkyōiku kenkyūjo 1997c: 70–80; my italicization)

In the book for the final grade of primary school, a detailed description is presented of how the Korean envoys, who visited Japan twelve times from 1607 to 1811, were welcomed and admired by the people in Japan. The friendly relationship between Korea and Japan in those premodern times established by the Korean envoys is shown to children as an ideal relationship which Japan and Korea should seek today.

How can these six volumes of *Ningen* be discussed in terms of a cognitive framework? In a similar manner to social studies textbooks, many stories and poems in *Ningen* are arranged according to children's cognitive development. The younger the readers, the more their cognition is restricted to the concrete and observable world. The first-grade textbook includes stories about events in such places as school, class, and home, that is, children's immediate living environment. The second grade moves on to the neighborhood, to which the third grade adds town and district. The place name Hiroshima, as a monumental city evoking peace, appears in the third grade. In the fourth grade children are expected to understand stories concerning the Osaka area, while Okinawa and the Second World War as part of peace education.[12] In the fifth grade children are directed to understand that Japan's imperialist expansion caused political injustice and Japan's modernization failed to result in socio-economic equality, creating a wide gap between poor and rich.

While up to the fifth grade most stories are set in environments familiar to children such as home, classroom, school, and neighborhood, the sixth-grade book has only three stories out of fifteen that are set in environments familiar to children, the rest being topics with abstract and politicized concepts. It introduces such words as "discriminated hamlet" (*buraku*), "human rights" (*jinken*), "social integration measures" [for Buraku liberation] (*dōwataisaku*), and "the levelers association, Suiheisha," the first liberation movement for Burakumin. These words are indispensable for explaining the Buraku liberation movement, education for which is the ultimate purpose of the compiler, Kaihōkyōiku kenkyūjo, the Institute for Buraku Liberation Education.

It is obvious that the institute puts the strongest emphasis on the final volume, which is designed to concentrate readers' attention upon the issues of Burakumin. The texts incorporated there suggest to children that the issues of Burakumin may represent all the issues of categories or groups of oppressed people. Thus, the poor, those people with certain occupations, and those living in certain places in the stories that children have already read in the earlier volumes, may be retrospectively understood as Burakumin. It is suggested that the issues of other categories of oppressed people such as women, the disabled, and Koreans in Japan should be comprehended, derivatively and metaphorically, by applying inferences from the issues relating to Burakumin.

What do *Ningen* books tell a Korean child? *Ningen* volumes teach children to act for human rights as a member of the Japanese nation. They try to raise children's consciousness of being Japanese, while not clarifying what non-Japanese people living in Japan can do for their own human rights. On the one hand, *Ningen* texts suggest that discrimination against Koreans in Japan should be comprehended in connection to Burakumin issues, and emphasize that children must speak up as *Japanese nationals* against such discrimination and oppression. On the other hand, in dealing with Korean issues, *Ningen* texts give priority to cultivating national/ethnic identity among Korean children, thereby somewhat placing Korean children outside the tenets of human rights issues in Japan, as if Japanese children and Korean children have different moral missions on the basis of their separate ethnicities.

Ningen texts undoubtedly play an important role in drawing attention to the situation in which Korean children are placed in their class, while school textbooks authorized by the Ministry of Education completely ignore the existence of Korean children in Japanese schools. Nevertheless, what *Ningen* offer to a Korean child is the opportunity to live proudly as a Korean with a Korean name, appreciating the Korean traditional culture and language. This reflects as much the essentialism of the Japanese national subject as that of the Korean national subject; national identity is taken for granted as a point of departure for Korean children. However, the problem that Korean children face in the Japanese classrooms is not how essentially to understand themselves as Koreans as such, but rather, how to live through the diverse parameters of their identity, carving out their existential location as Korean children born and raised in Japan. For example, as long as the Japanese in general are discriminatory against Koreans, declaring one's "true names" can be stressful for a Korean child and it may isolate the child from Japanese peers, who are going through the cognitive developmental process of labeling others (Fujisaki 1990: 180; see also Hamamoto 1995). Although *Ningen* try to disclose the oppressive structure of the Japanese society, which the Ministry of Education does not clarify, they still leave untouched a set of complex questions faced by Korean children in Japanese schools: questions pertaining to an identity that does not necessarily presuppose membership of a nation-state, and a sense of belonging that cannot be secured through an affiliation with a nation-state. As such, *Ningen* operate within the limits of nation-state boundaries, and fail to deal with identities that go beyond and against them.

Korean children in the community: the case of Hirakata city

Hirakata city, located in the northeast area of Osaka prefecture, has a population of about 400,000 (Hirakatashi 1996).[13] It has grown tenfold over the last forty years, reflecting its location which is convenient for commuting to both Osaka and Kyoto cities. The city consists of various areas: old villages, comparatively new residential areas, old town areas, newly developed town areas, farm areas, and industrial areas, together with wet-rice fields, vegetable fields, and forests (Hirakatashi kyōikuiinkai 1997). Condominiums and houses are being constructed and sold at a relatively reachable cost. Overall, there is neither a slum nor any extremely poor neighborhood.

Koreans with either South Korean nationality or North Korean political orientation, and with Japanese permanent residence, number about 2,000 in the district, making the district's proportion of Koreans to Japanese a little lower than the national average (Wada 1993; Hirakatashi 1996). There is no distinctly Korean neighborhood comparable to those found in Osaka city, such as Ikaino. Koreans in Hirakata tend to run self-employed businesses. Most Koreans use Japanese names (Hirakatashi tabunken 1997). In addition to the branches of Korean organizations such as Mindan and Chongryun, sympathetic to South Korea and North Korea respectively, there is a voluntary society of Korean mothers, Ŏmŏni no kai or "mothers' society."

Some Koreans in Hirakata regard Korean neighborhoods in Osaka city as different worlds. A woman in her early forties, whose grandfather came from southeastern Korea and who grew up in Hirakata and graduated from a high school run by Chongryun, talked about the Korea town in Osaka city as follows:

> The Korea town is a different world to me. I remember a strong cultural shock that I experienced when I first visited my senior high school classmate who lived there. People there spoke to each other in the Cheju dialect, which sounded totally different from the Korean language that I learned at school. I almost could not stand the smell of food filling the whole streets. Since then I have visited there many times. But whenever I go there I still feel nervous as though I am walking in a foreign country.

There is an interesting parallel between this woman's account and the attitude of Hirakata Koreans *vis-à-vis* Koreans in Osaka city before the Second World War. A 1930 newspaper article wrote that Koreans in Kitakawachigun, which covered Hirakata and its vicinity, were antagonistic towards Koreans in Osaka city. Because of the economic stagnation, many Koreans in Osaka city had lost their jobs and come to the area looking for work. Koreans in Hirakata feared the loss of their own jobs to the newcomers, and decided to establish the society of Kitakawachi Korean laborers in order to secure their living (*Asahi shinbun,* 13 June 1930). Before the Second World War approximately 3,000 Koreans lived in Hirakata, working in military-related construction. Newspaper articles reported how successfully Koreans in Hirakata had been incorporated as "children of the emperor" by means of several organizations for assimilation, including Sōaikai and Kyōwakai (Wada 1993: 147; see Kashiwazaki in this volume for assimilation).

Today, except a handful of children who go to a primary school run by Chongryun in Osaka city, almost all Korean children in Hirakata go to Japanese schools in their respective catchment areas. Most of them use their Japanese names instead of their Korean names (Hirakatashi tabunken 1997). In the schools it is "invisible" that they are Korean.[14]

Earlier in this chapter, I pointed out that Korean children in Japanese schools are not likely to be encouraged to identify themselves as Korean in the ordinary course of primary education. Such is the predominant situation in Hirakata. We have seen that *Ningen* encourage them to come out as Koreans by using their Korean names as their true names. However, *Ningen* tend not to be used as teaching materials for moral education in Hirakata, because only forty-five minutes are allocated for moral education each week, and priority has been given to peace-loving and anti-war education. Also, the very small proportion of Korean children contributes to the lack of attention to Korea-related issues in classroom discussion.

There is no obvious Buraku area in Hirakata.[15] However, the Hirakata board of education has a special section for dealing with issues concerning Buraku and those concerning human rights, including those of Koreans in Japan. The main activity to which the section is assigned is consciousness-raising in terms of human rights issues. It often organizes seminar series, the topics of which are Burakumin, Koreans in Japan, women, the disabled, and the elderly.

In 1997, Hirakata teachers who had been involved in education to raise consciousness of the issues of Burakumin organized the Hirakatashi tabunka kyōseikyōiku kenkyūkai or the Hirakata group for research on multicultural education (hereafter, the research group) in order to deal with the issues of Korean children and children who had recently come from abroad, for example from China, South America, and Southeast Asia. These children have rapidly increased in number recently. The research group encourages Korean children to use their Korean name at school and provides Korean children with events at which they can meet fellow Korean children.

One of these events is a summer school, in which Korean children, their parents, teachers, the research group members, Korean mothers of Ŏmŏni no kai, members of the Korean YMCA in Osaka city, and a representative of the Hirakata board of education take part. Every year it is held at the beginning of the school summer vacation, around 20 July, in a camping park near Hirakata city. The aim of the school is to give an opportunity to Korean children to meet people and encounter the culture of "their own ethnicity/nationality." The first thing children do in the school is to make a nameplate of their Korean names, which they wear throughout the school. The activities consist of playing traditional Korean games and sports, learning how to play Korean musical instruments, performing Korean dance and music, and speaking a few Korean words that they learn in the summer school.

Ŏmŏni no kai, another pivotal organization running the summer school, has nineteen members. Except for one member, who came from Korea twelve years ago and was married to a Japanese man, they are second- or third-generation Korean mothers. Most of them cannot speak Korean at all. They usually use their Japanese names in their everyday life. The majority hold South Korean nationality, although some of them want to be naturalized. In their meetings that I was allowed in, they talked frankly about the issues of nationality, various experiences, education of their children, how to tell their children about Korean ethnicity/nationality, and so on. In the summer school, they use their Korean names and try to project their Koreanness on many levels, mainly to provide a model for their children.

In 1998 the summer school met from 19 to 20 July, with twenty-five participants consisting of Korean students of various levels from kindergarten to senior high school. From the organizers' side, a total of fifty adults participated including Korean mothers, YMCA members, Japanese teachers, and representatives of local education authorities of various levels.

Although the summer school is designed with a certain agenda on the part of the adults, upon reading children's past comments it appears that for them it is primarily an occasion when they enjoy playing together with other kids whom they do not meet in their own schools (Samāsukūru jimukyoku 1997). These activities are, so to say, annual rituals, where Japanese organizers and Korean mothers and members of the Osaka Korean YMCA do their best to give great opportunities for Korean children, and children in turn enjoy participation. However, there seems to be a fundamental problem: no Japanese children are invited to join, nor are they even informed of such an event during the summer vacation. Even if Korean children were to have a great time in the summer school, in the fall they go back to their Japanese school, again as invisible Koreans, with almost no one to share their memories of the summer. In this way, the summer school eventually reinforces the ethnic segregation and isolation of Korean children in the classroom during the normal term time. The summer school, as such, represents the adults' attempt, with a dose of political correctness and ethnic essentialism, to make children appreciate their ethnic heritage. This is not to say that there is anything wrong with it in itself. However, the lack of systematic year-long follow-up measures renders the summer school a kind of vacuum where children experience Koreanness out of the context of their everyday school life. Despite the good intentions of the organizers, Korean children in Japanese schools are again left without clear guidance on how to cope with their complex identity.

Concluding remarks

Schools are arenas for power games, an opportunity for various collective agents to gain resources for the future in the form of children. Children are not supposed to become agents of the games, since they are still minors. Not only the general public, but also parents, are tacitly excluded from the school. Parents are not supposed to visit and stay at their children's school even for short periods, except on particular occasions decided by the school. It seems that it is hard even for teachers to act as individual persons in a school. Ultimately, collective agents influence the educational practices in the classroom in a top-down sequence, from the Ministry of Education to the city educational authorities. This influence is paralleled by the interventions of co-existing political organizations such as the Buraku Liberation League and teachers' unions.

In the primary education currently practiced in Japan, the Ministry of Education and its policies ultimately dominate the classroom. In the eyes of the Ministry of Education, Korean children do not exist in primary schools, while prefectural and city-level education authorities, and even conscientious teachers, often fail to address the highly complex set of identity issues Korean children face, owing mainly to their fundamentally nation-state-oriented pedagogical vision. The victims of this are children of foreign heritage, and in particular Korean children, who are caught between their colonial past and the postcolonial politics waged between the nation-states. At the same time this situation disadvantages the majority of Japanese children, by depriving them of the opportunities to meet their Korean classmates, learn about their situation, and become friends beyond the narrow confines of the nation-states.

Acknowledgements

I am deeply grateful to the Ōmŏni no kai, Hirakatashi tabunken, Osaka shigaiken, Hirakatashi kyōikuiinkai, Osakafu kyōikuiinkai, and organizers and participants of the 1998 summer school. I would like to thank Sonia Ryang for her critical comments and helpful advice. I wish also to thank Kathleen Kato for her patient help in correcting my English. Many thanks are also due to my children and their friends.

Notes

1 The three-step shift seems to be incorporated in the related areas of social development, moral development, and sex role development. Moral judgments by very young children are ego-centered, depending on their preferences. Later they are tied to social rules, and finally they are based on personally evaluated principles (Kohlberg 1976). Similarly the way one views one's sex role and prescribes sexually appropriate behavior changes with age. Initially, children define appropriate behavior in terms of what they want to do. Later they rely on social stereotypes about males and females to determine their appropriate behavior. Still later, children begin to differentiate within these two gender categories, until they finally realize that an individual can be more flexible than stereotypes allow (Block 1973).
2 The word "sweet" can be an exception (Asch and Nerlove 1960).
3 For this, I deal with the national language textbooks published by Mitsumura tosho, a company that held the largest share in Japan, 60.8 percent, in publication and distribution of national language textbooks in 1997; with the social studies textbooks published by Kyōiku shuppan, holding the second largest share, 24.7 percent; and with books published by Osaka shoseki which held the third largest share of 17.5 percent in the social studies textbooks market in 1997. Tokyo shoseki held the largest share of the social studies textbooks market in 1997 (Tanigawa et al. 1997: vi).
4 All translations from Japanese materials in this chapter are mine.
5 This applies to public education only.

6 After the Second World War, Japanese history textbooks became a topic of controversy. As a most recent comprehensive source on this in English, see Hein and Selden (1998).
7 In textbooks prior to 1996, Koreans in Japan were placed in the category of "foreigners in Japan." The 1996 textbook states: "We must also try to solve [the problem arising from] the social discrimination and prejudice against the Ainu and Koreans in Japan (*zainichi kankokujin, chōsenjin*)" (Itō *et al.* 1996: 11).
8 The term *buraku* means a hamlet or a section of a village and *min*, people. Burakumin refers to the people who live in particular hamlets outside villages where the Japanese majority live. Burakumin have their historical origin in the ancient Japan. In feudalistic Japan from the early seventeenth century to the late nineteenth century, the four-caste system was introduced, dividing the population into warriors, peasants, artisans, and merchants. Burakumin were placed outside this system as outcastes, and they physically lived outside the districts where other people lived, working in limited occupations such as leather production. The outcast status was formally abolished in 1890, incorporating Burakumin as members of the newly-emerging Japanese nation-state, but the discrimination against them persists in severe form even today.
9 See Ryang (1997: Chs. 1 and 2) for Chongryun schools.
10 The Institute for Buraku Liberation Education is affiliated with the Buraku kaihō dōmei, or Buraku Liberation League. It is the largest and the most powerful liberation organization for Burakumin in Japan (see Hanami 1995).
11 The word *chōsenjin* literally means "Korean people" or "Koreans." In the process by which Koreans have been marginalized in Japan throughout the colonial and postcolonial periods, the word has acquired a derogatory connotation. "Irunamu" is a Korean name in an alphabetized Japanese notation. The Korean pronunciation is "Ilnam."
12 At the end of the Second World War, Okinawa became a battlefield. Many people, including children, the aged, and women, were killed. See Suzuki and Oiwa (1996).
13 Hirakata city falls under the jurisdiction of Osaka prefecture, though Osaka city has autonomy *vis-à-vis* prefectural government. Although the same name "city" is used, Osaka city and Hirakata city denote different scopes of political authorities.
14 I was told that quite a few Korean children themselves did not know that they were Koreans until the fifth grade or later (personal communication).
15 I received this information from an official of the Hirakata board of education. He also told me that although there was no Buraku, it did not necessarily mean that people did not discriminate against the Burakumin.

9 Kids between nations
Ethnic classes in the construction of Korean identities in Japanese public schools

Jeffry T. Hester

Every Wednesday afternoon, after school has been let out, twenty or so first- through sixth-graders gather in a third-floor classroom of Tohan primary school in Osaka. These are children of Korean heritage. Most of them have Korean nationality, though there are a few whose family has naturalized, or who are the offspring of an "international marriage" between a Japanese and a Korean. These mostly third- and fourth-generation Koreans in Japan gather, under the guidance of a third-generation Japan-born Korean *sŏnsaengnim* (teacher), to sing songs in Korean, learn something of the Korean writing system, called *hangŭl*, study Korean folk tales, history and geography, practice Korean folk dance and music, and learn and become acclimated to hearing their own Korean names.

Most of these children have two names: a Korean name that continues to be recorded in a family register kept in a local government office somewhere in the southern half of Korea, and a Japanese name that their parents and teachers usually call them, and by which they know themselves. The family registration system, the two names, the children's very presence in Japan, are legacies of Japan's colonial rule of Korea. The objective of the class in which they have gathered, as conceived by those responsible for its direction, in essence, is to undo some of what Japan's colonial policy and subsequent assimilation policies have done. The objective is to build a Korean identity among these children.

Focusing on *minzokugakkyū* or "ethnic classes," this chapter aims to shed some light on the processes and strategies involved in these efforts to construct Korean identities within the context of the Japanese school and Japanese society.[1] I begin with a very brief sketch of the historical process in which Japanese colonial leaders sought to eradicate a Korean national identity and thereby rendered elements of identity formation processes, such as language and names, subject to political struggle. Following a discussion of the development of a system of ethnic classes in Osaka, I offer a more fine-grained look at the workings of one such ethnic class. The approach followed in this class seeks to cultivate among students a Korean identity through the construction of symbolic boundaries that mark a Korean national culture and differentiate it from a Japanese national culture.

There is no consensus among those of Korean heritage in Japan, however, as to how Korean heritage should be presented and how the categorical ascription of "Korean" should be negotiated in everyday life. These issues are framed by the configurations of power in the Japanese community and society within which Koreans live and strategize for their own and their children's future, as well as by generational processes of assimilation. They suggest the difficulty, within the discursive field of the Japanese nation-state, of locating a stable "Koreanness" that does not affirm the principles of national belonging by which Koreans themselves have faced exclusion in Japanese society.

Historical roots of ethnic education for the recovery of a Korean national subjectivity

Education is a key site for the construction of national identities, for inculcating the categories and sentiments that bind people in an "imagined community" (Anderson 1991) of the nation. The nation-state builders of modern Japan after the Meiji Restoration of 1868 recognized this. With Western educational systems as models, in 1872 the Ministry of Education adopted the first detailed plan for a centralized national system of mass education for Japan (Marshall 1994: 32–50). While the Japanese educational system has gone through several permutations since the Meiji period (1868–1912), it continues to serve as a central institution for the formation of national subjects, by which the discourse of the nation is incorporated as aspects of the cognitive, emotional, and moral orientations of experiencing selves.[2] An ongoing process, national subject-making unfolds through the symbolic mediations of a national imaginary comprising language, history, and geography. Before leaving primary school, a Japanese child, through the study of "the national language" (*kokugo*), of maps and memory sites, of great heroes, and by learning to recognize the symbolic markings of national distinctiveness, has come to a basic understanding of the historical, geographic, and moral contours of Japan, an imagined community to which she or he belongs in an ineffable but unmistakably special way (see Aoki in this volume).

Ethnic education for Koreans in Japan emerged, not out of state policy, but out of opposition to the colonial forms of government which the Japanese state imposed upon Koreans. It is a result of a series of historically imbricated social movements of resistance to colonial and postwar attempts to assimilate Koreans to a Japanese national consciousness, while relegating them to an inferior social position (see Inokuchi in this volume). Colonial education policy aimed to construct among Koreans an identification with the Japanese state, through an identification with the Japanese nation, while maintaining the structural inferiority of Koreans within the empire. In its most radical form in the colony, expressed in a series of measures launched in 1937 known collectively as the *kōminka undō* (imperial subjectification campaign), Japanese assimilation policy amounted to an all-out effort to forcibly "Japanize" the entire Korean population. Along with the obligation to swear loyalty to the Japanese emperor and worship at Shinto shrines, these measures included the *sōshikaimei* (name-changing) campaign, based on an ordinance implemented from 1940 requiring Koreans to adopt a Japanese-style "family" (as opposed to Korean "clan") naming system (Chou 1996: 55–61; see also Kashiwazaki in this volume).[3] The *kokugo* (national language) movement aimed to completely replace the use of the Korean language by Japanese in the colony (Chou 1996: 50; Dong 1973: 160). In Japan itself, similar measures were put in place through a program of *kyōwa* (harmony) education. This education was aimed at inculcating Korean children in Japan with, as set forth in the policy guidelines of one primary school, "self-awareness as Japanese children." Korean children in Japan were to be induced to feel "to the depths of their hearts, 'we are Japanese, we are children of Japan'" by transplanting "the germ of the Japanese spirit" (Ozawa 1973: 87).[4]

In the aftermath of war, with many Koreans in Japan finding immediate repatriation an unfeasible or undesirable option, Koreans established a nationwide system of schools to teach the Korean language and other subjects oriented to the cultivation of an autonomous Korean national subjecthood. When Koreans were ordered to bring this national system of schools into conformity with Japanese educational regulations, they resisted fiercely. This resistance, centering around mass demonstrations in Osaka, Kobe, and elsewhere in April 1948 (see Inokuchi in this volume), led to the exchange of a memorandum between the Ministry of Education and Korean representatives on 5 May 1948 which allowed for the possibility of some Korean curricular content within the bounds of Japanese educational law. In Osaka, a separate memorandum was signed on 4 June 1948, based on the principles of the 5 May memorandum, which provided, *inter alia*, the basis for the establishment of extracurricular ethnic classes within Osaka's public school system (Yang Yŏng-hu 1994: 87–8).

The resistance of Koreans to the efforts of the Japanese authorities, backed by the Occupation powers, to close Korean schools has come to be known as the April 24 education struggle (*Yonniyon kyōikutōsō*). It is central to the collective memory of those involved in the ethnic education movement who view their goal as the cultivation of Korean national subjects. The struggle is commemorated annually through public meetings and other activities. "The spirit of 4.24" refers to the refusal of Koreans to submit to state pressures to assimilate, and to their self-reliant efforts toward the recovery of an autonomous Korean subjectivity. As Inokuchi (this volume) describes, however, the accommodations reached in mid-1948 concerning ethnic education for Koreans were not to last. By November 1949, nearly all Korean schools nationwide had been ordered to close (Ozawa 1973: 262).

Through these measures, the Japanese authorities drastically curtailed the opportunities for Korean children to receive education in Korean and in Korea-related subjects. In Osaka, forty-one Korean schools were ordered closed, forcing nearly 10,000 students into the Japanese educational system. With 10,000 Koreans already enrolled in Japanese public schools in Osaka, this left the education of some 20,000 Korean children in the charge of the Osaka prefecture board of education (Ozawa 1973: 295; Ri Yu-hwan 1971: 210–2).

The development of Osaka's ethnic classes

Bearing distinct traces of origins in political struggle and compromise across time and place, ethnic education in Osaka's public schools is undertaken within a dual structure. The two types of classes are the so-called "memorandum-based" and the "1972-type" ethnic classes. They are distinguished on the basis of their respective historical origins, sources of finance, and the employment status of the instructors. While similar in their aims and activities, these classes, products of bottom-up struggle, do not operate under a uniform curriculum. Differing philosophies among instructors result in somewhat different approaches in practice.

Memorandum-based ethnic classes

"Memorandum-based ethnic classes" (*oboegaki minzokugakkyū*) are those launched in some thirty-three schools in 1950, based upon the memorandum of understanding exchanged between the governor of Osaka and Korean representatives on 4 June 1948, authorizing the hiring of Korean teachers to teach Korean language, culture, and history on an extracurricular basis in schools under prefectural jurisdiction. For a variety of reasons, not least among them the frustration and alienation resulting from the inhospitality with which the ethnic instructors and their classes were received by their Japanese colleagues, by the mid-1970s two-thirds of the ethnic instructor posts had become vacant. With their vacancy, prefectural authorities simply allowed the classes themselves to lapse.

Appeals over several years to the Osaka prefecture board of education to increase the number of instructors and improve their working conditions fell on deaf ears. With three more instructors scheduled to retire in March 1985, a movement was hurriedly put into motion to pressure the board to ensure the hiring of successors to incumbent ethnic instructors. Without action, the system was in danger of collapse. In March 1986, the board agreed to recognize the continuation of the ethnic classes under its jurisdiction, based upon the 1948 memorandum, and to the replacement of incumbent instructors (Ko Ch'an-yu 1996: 133–5). Thus, the number of such ethnic classes is now frozen at eleven (seven in Osaka city and four elsewhere in the prefecture). These are funded by the prefecture and are taught by full-time instructors who are formally integrated within each school's structure for dealing with issues relating to foreign students.

"1972-type" ethnic classes

If the prefecture-funded ethnic classes were the outcome of struggles by Koreans to ensure a degree of access to ethnic education, the ethnic classes founded since 1972 are the results of collaborative efforts by Japanese teachers of conscience and Korean students, parents, and young activists. These classes, of which there are now nearly seventy within Osaka city, receive some funding from the city. Funding for instructors, however, only began in 1992. Prior to that, instructors worked on a volunteer basis. Many still do, as remuneration, based on an hourly wage, is restricted to one or two person-hours a week per school. Instructors of these classes are not part of the school staff, and so have no formal input into decision-making on foreign student issues.

The launching of these classes through educational activism represented a turning point in progressive education in Japan. In the postwar era, the Japanese educational arena has been a site of often fierce political contestation. A progressive element, primarily based in the Japan Teachers' Union, has resisted authoritarian tendencies within the educational bureaucracy to use education for statist goals. Though not always unified, they have sought to present an alternative vision of a more democratic future for Japan.

As concerns the issue of education for Koreans, in the 1950s, with the resuscitation of an autonomous ethnic school system under the umbrella of Chongryun as an organization of "overseas nationals" of the Democratic People's Republic of Korea (DPRK) (see Ryang 1997), the Japan Teachers' Union adopted a position supporting Koreans' right to autonomous education. This position is summarized in the slogan, "Bring Korean children to the gates of the ethnic schools" (Inatomi 1988: 33–4). With the Japan Teachers' Union emphasizing support for autonomous Korean education, and in a social context of deep-seated prejudice against Koreans from which educators were hardly exempt, a strategy for addressing the problems of Korean children actually sitting in Japanese classrooms went undeveloped. This finally changed in the early 1970s with a series of incidents that signaled a profound need to reorient educational philosophy and practice concerning Korean children.

In April 1971, a spark was ignited which compelled teachers to confront the position of Koreans within Japanese public education, when the Osaka middle school principals' conference released a pamphlet on its previous year's research. In a few brief pages in a section on "the situation of foreign students," the conference put on display a prejudice toward Koreans that, while not uncommon at the time, was not generally committed to print.[5] In the pamphlet, Korean children were characterized as "selfish," "calculating," "impulsive," "lacking a sense of guilt," "sexually precocious," and prone to "telling lies with indifference." At the same time, the pamphlet makes virtually no mention of the historical or social context of the Korean presence in Japan (Kim Yŏng-hae 1996: 189–93).

Once made public, the pamphlet caused a furor. The issue was widely reported in newspapers. Ethnic organizations issued statements of protest. And Japanese teachers met to denounce the attitudes expressed in the pamphlet and to construct strategies to counter them. To further these aims, teachers formed a committee to consider the education of Koreans in Japanese schools. This committee, which has been key to the development of ethnic education in Osaka's public schools, eventually gave birth in 1983 to a nationwide organization, the National Council for Research on Education for Koreans in Japan (Kishino 1985: 44–5; Ko Ch'an-yu 1996: 149).

This incident took place in a context of increasing sensitivity to problems of discrimination among Japanese educators. The origin of anti-discrimination education in Japan lies in the movement to promote the integration of Japan's former outcast group, the Burakumin, a movement which has demonstrated significant political effectiveness in this area. After nearly a half-century of social activism, in 1969, this movement secured the passage of the Law on Special Measures for Integration (*dōwa*) Projects which provided for funding at all levels of government for projects to improve the living conditions and social position of

Burakumin (Neary 1997). Major aims of the law included provisions in the area of education to improve the achievement levels of Burakumin students in schools, and to promote sensitivity to issues of discrimination among non-Burakumin. Along with this institutionalization of anti-discrimination in government policy, the movement for Buraku liberation also attracted non-Burakumin activists. Among them were dedicated teachers, some of whom moved into Burakumin communities as an act of solidarity, and better to understand the conditions of daily life of this historically oppressed group.

Located in Osaka's Nishinari ward, Nagahashi primary school is situated in the midst of Japan's largest Burakumin community. Not uncommon for Buraku areas, there is also a significant population of Koreans in the area, making up some 20 percent of Nagahashi's students. Nagahashi was one of the first schools designated for special supplementary classes for Burakumin children. Around 1970, Korean children in the school began to express their sense of injustice that Burakumin children received special attention from which they were excluded. At a staff meeting that year, it was agreed that "education that leaves out Koreans may be 'integration education' (*dōwakyōiku*), but it is not 'liberation education' (*kaihōkyōiku*)" (Kishino 1985: 52).

Groping toward a positive response to the needs of Koreans, teachers at the school began talking in class about Korean–Japanese relations, the meaning of using an ethnic name, and the historical background to the presence of Koreans in Japan. Korean students then created a Korean study club within the school's club activities, and began to clamor for a Korean instructor to be invited to the school (Kishino 1985: 53–4). Negotiations with the Osaka city board of education for support were initially promising, and the school launched its first ethnic class in November 1972 with Korean ethnic instructors. They finally failed, however, when city authorities cancelled promised assistance. Various pressures on the school and on the board, and bureaucratic trepidation at becoming involved in "north-south" political conflicts among Koreans in Japan, are cited among the reasons (Inatomi 1988: 36–8). Taking matters into their own hands, teachers at Nagahashi began teaching an ethnic class themselves, with the aid of tape-recorded Korean language and songs. With students continuing to demand "real" Korean teachers, in late 1973 young Koreans dedicated to the cause of ethnic education were contacted and given charge of the class (Kishino 1985: 55).

The developments at Nagahashi demonstrated that even in the face of a recalcitrant educational bureaucracy, ethnic education can be provided with the cooperation of dedicated Korean instructors. Similar volunteer-based ethnic classes began to spring up elsewhere in Osaka, slowly in the 1970s and gaining momentum in the 1980s. A bilateral agreement signed by representatives of the Republic of Korea and Japan in 1991 included an undertaking by the Government of Japan regarding extracurricular ethnic education activities. Following this up, the Ministry of Education instructed all prefectural boards of education that they "not restrict opportunities for Korean children to study Korean language, Korean culture, etc., on an extracurricular basis" (cited in Tokuhara 1998: 26). While stopping short of concrete support, these words brought recognition for ethnic classes into the realm of national education policy. More than half the ethnic classes in Osaka were initiated during the 1990s (Minsokkyō 1997: 21).

Combining the two types discussed above, there are now ethnic classes or clubs operating in over 100 public primary and middle schools within Osaka prefecture. This is only a fraction of Osaka's compulsory education facilities, however, and about half of the Korean students in Osaka's public schools still lack access to school-based ethnic education (Minsokkyō 1997: 32).

Approaches to ethnic education

Korean parents in Osaka generally have three choices when deciding where their child should be educated.[6] Chongryun runs a nationwide system of schools. In the vicinity of the primary school I discuss below, there are Chongryun primary and middle schools within easy biking distance. Around 12 percent of Korean children in Osaka attend such schools. Most parents, however, balk at the political slant of the DPRK-oriented education offered, the schools' marginality to mainstream Japanese society and the implications this holds for their child's future, or the financial costs. The two Mindan-affiliated schools in Osaka, which receive support from the ROK, unlike the Chongryun facilities, offer a curriculum that meets the Ministry of Education's standards for full accreditation. The approved Japanese curriculum is combined with electives in Korean subjects, and most teachers are Koreans with full teaching credentials. Students use their Korean ethnic names within the schools. Not quite 4 percent of Osaka's Korean youngsters attend one of these two schools. This leaves about 85 percent of Korean parents in Osaka who send their children to Japanese public schools (1996 figures from Minsokkyō 1997: 32).

These three different educational settings offer students quite distinct kinds of identity-forming experiences, suggesting the variety of positions among Korean parents concerning how best to negotiate questions of ethnic consciousness in the context of strategizing for their children's futures in Japan. Even among Korean parents whose children attend Japanese public schools, there is no consensus as to what ethnic education should be (or if it is even necessary) and what sorts of identification should be fostered in their children.

Japanese educators, of course, have responsibility for both Japanese and Korean children. The activists among them, who, as discussed above, were instrumental in expanding the space for ethnic education within Japanese schools from the early 1970s, generally take as their task the integration of Korean children into Japanese society *as* Koreans. This involves a three-pronged approach, which has been codified in Osaka's guidelines for the education of foreign children (see Osakashi 1998; Osakafu 1998). The three elements are: first, raising the ethnic self-awareness of foreign students and instilling in them a pride in their ethnic heritage. This is work to be done with Korean children, for which ethnic classes are indispensable settings. Second is cultivation of a respect for human rights and "international understanding." This is work primarily for the regular classroom, and is focused on the majority Japanese children. Third is fostering solidarity between Japanese and foreign children, based on mutual respect. This is a version of the process of "group formation" whereby values such as teamwork, cooperation, dedication to group goals and sensitivity to others are cultivated. These are values consistently stressed in Japanese educational practice (Lewis 1995; Peak 1991; Rohlen and LeTendre 1996).

Having Korean students use their ethnic names is central to achieving these aims. The theory behind the teachers' practice may be summarized as follows. Echoing an approach developed early in the Buraku liberation movement, embracing rather than trying to hide a status that has been stigmatized works to neutralize the stigma. Efforts to hide that status, as the use of a Japanese-style name by Koreans is thought by many to be, only serve to legitimize the stigma and further its internalization.[7] It is the stigmatization and discrimination that should be struggled against, not the identity.[8] Thus, use of Korean names can help free Korean children from the stigma and the discrimination that stems from it as well as from the psychic burden of concealing their heritage (goal 1). For promoting respect for human rights (goal 2), Japanese students must develop the capacity to acknowledge and respect difference. This capacity can only be fostered if Korean students themselves assert a positive identity as Koreans through a consistent use of a Korean name, the most readily available marker of ethnic distinctiveness. Solidarity (goal 3) is only possible with mutual respect which, again, must include acknowledgement and respect of difference.

In the following I would like to turn to an examination of the concrete practices of ethnic education in one public primary school in Osaka, in order to explore the work undertaken to construct Korean national subjects, along with some of the difficulties faced and resistances evoked.

Cultivating Korean subjects in the Toraji ethnic class

Tohan primary school is located on the eastern edge of Osaka city, just outside of the railway loop line that encircles the central city's core.[9] It lies in a mixed residential/commercial/light-industrial zone where houses often double as shops or small family-operated factories. The area was developed out of agricultural land beginning around the time of the First World War. Koreans, settling in the area in significant numbers from the 1920s, have played an important role in this development. The area now contains Japan's largest Korean population.

The Korean population itself is residentially clustered so that, in an extreme case, in one school district (the catchment area for one primary school), the proportion of Koreans is 70 percent, while in the neighboring district the proportion is around 10 percent. At Tohan, about 20 percent of the students are Korean, a figure that has been gradually declining over the past several years. The absolute number of students has been falling throughout Japan because of declining birth rates. The fall in the proportion of Koreans, however, arises from the accelerating pace of both naturalization and marriage to Japanese among Koreans. This in turn has given rise to a greater number of children of

Japanese nationality who can trace Korean heritage through one or both parents.[10]

The ethnic class at Tohan is a "1972-type" class, established early in the history of the movement. In the midst of the rising consciousness of problems of discrimination in Japanese society, a young activist Japanese teacher became the prime instigator of the ethnic class. It was founded, with little initial support from the administration or even Korean parents, out of an educational practice that holds efforts to combat discrimination as central to a teacher's mission. Long and careful persuasion finally convinced a number of Korean parents of the value of the endeavor. A few years into its operations, those involved in the class decided to give it the name "Toraji ethnic class," after the balloon flower which figures in a well-loved Korean folk song.

Initiation into the ethnic class

The ethnic class entrance ceremony for 1997 was held on a bright, warm April afternoon, the first Wednesday of the school year. Two girls and four boys, first-graders all, were scheduled to join. These six were among the forty or so six-year-olds who had over the previous few days been ritually welcomed into the school and into their own classes, becoming Tohan students and first-graders. Now they were to be inducted into yet another social group, this one marked off by the imagined boundaries of the nation.

The ceremony was to take place in the "Toraji room," a classroom at the end of a third-floor hallway given over exclusively to the activities of the ethnic class. The room was equipped with low desks at which three little or two big kids could sit comfortably directly upon the thinly carpeted floor. A baby grand piano stood by the door. Most of the decorations in the room were displays of things the kids had made. Prominent among these were eight larger-than-lifesize full-body crayon self-portraits of children, covering most of the inside wall, upon which the eyes, nose, lips, ears, and tongue were labeled in the Korean *hangŭl* script. On the front wall, on one side of the blackboard, was a large map labeled *"uri nara"* ("our country"), depicting the Korean peninsula. Next to this was a chart of the *hangŭl* script. On the back wall was the "name board," a bulletin board upon which name slips with each kid's Korean name written in *hangŭl* were hung. A small bookshelf on the windowed side of the room contained a few Korean picture books, an album of photographs of one of the class's recent ethnic festivals, and a display of some Korean cultural artifacts, including a female doll dressed in the native *ch'ima chŏgori* costume and small replicas of a mask and a drum, made in class. The room overlooked the school's sports field from three stories up. Before class and during breaks, kids often shouted down to their classmates playing kick-ball on the sports field below.

The layout and equipping of the classroom reflects the purpose of its use and the strategy of the instructors: the classes need to be enjoyable for kids, and they should promote a positive association with things Korean. Solidarity, mutual identification among the children as Koreans is a central aim. In the Toraji room, there are no one-person desks that confine and individualize and work to channel youthful energy into concentration on texts. Kids sit on the floor, and places are not assigned. The low tables are easily shoved aside to make an open space. There is an easy movement from the study of Korean characters to singing songs to banging out rhythms on instruments which give the ethnic class a less regimented character than the regular school classes.

Just before three o'clock, the room was arranged for the induction of the new kids. Some twenty children were sitting on the carpeted floor behind the rows of low desks. Most were in their school uniforms, though two or three were in street clothes. As they have been trained to do so that it is now second nature, the children had sorted themselves into grade order, with the youngest children sitting in the front and the oldest in the back. Also present were three teachers, the three ethnic instructors, Mrs Yasuda of the foreign parents association, two or three other mothers, and the school principal.

On the chalkboard across the front wall of the room, the heading "Toraji ethnic class opening ceremony" had been written in large, neatly drawn characters, with "Toraji" in *hangŭl* and the rest in ideographic Japanese *kanji* characters, topped with *furigana*, Japanese phonetic script, to indicate the readings. Underneath this, the order of the ceremony had been written in a combination of *kanji* characters, the Japanese *kana* syllabic characters, and *hangŭl*:

1 Introductory greetings
2 Introduction of new students
3 Introductory greetings by the principal
4 Mothers' greetings
5 Greetings by current students
6 Greetings by the teachers [*sonsennimu*].

Within this, "greetings" was written "*insa*" in *hangŭl*, as was the word for "mother," "*ŏmŏni*." The word for "teacher," "*sŏnsaengnim*" (here referring to the ethnic instructors) on the other hand, was written in the Japanese *katakana* syllabary characters, conventionally used for rendering transliterations of foreign words, as "*sonsennimu*," with some of the characters written smaller than the rest in an attempt visually to represent a pronunciation closer to the Korean original.[11] *Sonsennimu* is a public title attached to the instructors' names used by the Japanese staff at the school as well as by the children and their mothers. Rendering it in Japanese *katakana* makes it accessible to all.

The ceremony began with Kang Mi-jeong, the principal ethnic instructor, asking the currently enrolled kids to stand and perform their greetings, as they do before the start of every class. First, facing the instructor standing at the front of the room, they intoned in unison, "*Sŏnsaengnim, annyŏnghashimnikka. Yŏrŏbun, annyŏnghashimnikka*" (How are you, Teacher? How are you, everyone?).

Kang Mi-jeong, a third-generation Korean, is a veteran instructor. Like many ethnic instructors a product of Japanese education, she used her Japanese name all the way through high school. Influenced by an elder sibling, she became active in the movement promoting democracy in South Korea, which led her to the ethnic consciousness movement and her work with the ethnic class. A vibrant, energetic woman, with no shortage of experience with children, she is imminently up to the challenge of holding the attention of a roomful of first- through sixth-graders. Along with her responsibility for the ethnic class, she holds a steady job and continues to be active in Korea-related political issues.

Moving on to the second item on the ceremonial agenda, Mi-jeong invited the entering first-graders, two girls and four boys, to the front of the room to face the others. All but one little girl were dressed in the standard uniform of short brown pants for boys, dress for girls, and white short-sleeved shirts. They had yet to absorb the training that has made kids in the higher grades so adept at the ceremonial form: sitting stiffly, face forward; standing with chest out, arms clasped behind the back; the brisk response to commands to sit, stand, or move. These little ones freely exhibited their feelings through their bodies, fidgeting, or standing calmly, or shyly trying to hide behind the woman who was about to become their new teacher.

Mi-jeong asked of them, "Those who are able to cooperate, please try. I don't know all of your names, so when I call them, raise your hand. And say 'ye' when you do." "*Ye*" is a Korean interjection of affirmation, acknowledging understanding of a command, corresponding to "Here!" in this case. In their regular Japanese classrooms, these kids are being taught to say "*hai*" in these circumstances.

Mi-jeong read from the list that she had prepared in cooperation with the Japanese teacher in charge:

"O Hwa-mi?"

A little girl answered, "*Ye.*"

"Mun Geon-soo-*kun*?" Mi-jeong affixed the Japanese "*kun*," often added to the names of boys and young men when used by superiors or equals.

"*Ye.*"

"Kim Ho-su?"

"*Ye.*"

"Pak Shin-il-*kun*?"

"'Zat me? [*Ore*?]" answered the barrel-chested youngest son of Mrs Arai.

Mi-jeong moved on.

"Kim Haeng-ja?"

This little girl was clinging to Mi-jeong from behind, peaking out at her audience and smiling broadly, shyly. Mi-jeong smiled, repeated her name, and snuck a look at her, but Haeng-ja remained silent.

Finally, "Noguchi Yumiko?"

The little girl, offspring of a third-generation Korean mother and Japanese father, answered a sprightly "*Ye!*"

Four of these kids have older siblings who are either in or have graduated from the ethnic class. While most respond to their Korean names, none of the five of Korean nationality regularly uses her or his ethnic name outside of the ethnic class. "We look forward to seeing you all next week," said Mi-jeong, completing the second item on the agenda.

Moving on, Mi-jeong introduced the principal of Tohan primary. In his brief remarks, he urged the students to have fun in the class. His presence was a sign of his personal support of the class, but also of the degree to which it has come to be recognized within Osaka's educational system. After Mrs Yasuda, an officer of the foreign parents' association, made brief remarks, it was the turn of the representative of the current students. This was a bright fifth-grade girl, called Mun An-gi within the ethnic class. She welcomed the new students and, exercising her new social role of *senpai*, an older, more experienced person now beginning to bear responsibility for the guidance of those now starting upon the same path, bid them, "Please ask us anything at all if you don't understand."

Mi-jeong then introduced the other instructors. Chang Hyun-p'il comes during periods of special need, such as in the weeks before performances. In a gendered division of labor, he takes charge of running the kids through their practice for the *t'aekwŏndo* martial arts demonstration. Ri Sook-ja, the 22-year-old daughter of a second-generation Korean mother and Korea-born father, runs the class when Mi-jeong cannot come. When they divide the class, Sook-ja usually takes the younger children. She is proficient in piano and takes charge of teaching songs to the kids. Sook-ja asked the inductees to call her "Sook-ja *sŏnsaengnim*." Similarly, Mi-jeong is called "Mi-jeong *sŏnsaengnim*" by children and parents alike.

After Mi-jeong made her own introductory remarks, Mrs Yasuda presented a gift to each new member of the class: a colorful, playfully drawn map of Korea (the whole undivided peninsula), and a chart of the Korean *hangŭl* characters, printed respectively on the two sides of a hard sheet of plastic.

After Ms Okamura, the young teacher responsible for coordinating foreign student affairs, including liaising between the school and the ethnic class, made her brief remarks, the ceremony came to an end. Mi-jeong thanked everyone for coming and reminded the kids of the time to come to class the following week. While some people moved into the hallway, Ri Sook-ja sat at the piano and began to play the *Hangŭl Song*. The younger children hung by Sook-ja's side. The ones who had learned the song a year or two earlier sang along with her:

Ka Na Ta Ra Ma Pa Sa A
Cha C'ha K'a T'a P'a Ha
Hangŭl vowels A Ya Ŏ Yŏ O Yo U Yu Ŭ I
Let's have fun learning hangŭl!

Responding to Korean sounds

Mi-jeong was unable to attend the first regular session of the ethnic class, so Sook-ja was left to run it by herself. Each class session begins with the same ritual: the kids' greetings in Korean. A student is chosen to lead this, and this time Sook-ja chose a third-grader called Pyong-su. He shouted out the greetings. The littlest kids, of course, were not expected to know. This was one of the items that they would begin to be taught on this day.

Sook-ja then moved the class into the main lesson for the day, teaching the basic greetings and the commands "stand at attention" (*ch'aryŏ*), "stand up" (*ilŏsŏ*), and "sit" (*anja*), in Korean.

First she asked them all to stand up. Then she asked, "What does it mean, *ch'aryŏ*?" An older boy answered in Japanese.

"*Ki o tsuke* (Attention)!"

Sook-ja and the older kids, in an exaggerated motion, threw their shoulders back and put their arms stiffly at their sides. She then went through the other two commands, *anja* and *ilŏsŏ*. She put the first-graders through the paces, asking the others to check that they responded correctly to each command. "Sit!" "Stand!" "Sit!" "Stand!" "Stand!" Delighted laughter broke out as a couple of the kids were tricked flat onto their bottoms by Sook-ja's last command.

She then turned to the greetings. She told the first-graders to join in as they all repeated "How are you?" together.

"*Sŏnsaengnim, annyŏnghashimnikka.*" The first-graders stumbled through it the first time, but they would pick it up quickly imitating their more experienced classmates.

She corrected their posture: "You're greeting the teacher, so bow your head." Then they sounded the mutual greeting among students:

"*Yŏrŏbun, annyŏnghashimnikka.*"

Going back over the lesson to see how well the kids had remembered it, Sook-ja asked, in the earthy Osaka dialect spoken in this area, "What do you do when I say *ch'aryŏ*?" Pak Shin-il, the youngest child, and eldest son, of five siblings, and always ready to take the stage, spun around. In quick imitation, the other first-graders spun around. Then Sook-ja spun, and the older kids. Now everyone had spun and, with much laughter, a couple of the littlest kids flopped to the floor. Shin-il, entertaining himself and his fellows, had given a new meaning to the Korean *ch'aryŏ*.

At around 3:15 p.m., the older kids came in and tossed their heavy rucksacks on to the floor in the back of the room. After they got settled, Sook-ja announced that they would do the greetings again. Ignoring a collective groan of protest, Sook-ja assigned two fifth-grade boys to lead. One of the fifth-graders pulled out from the podium some "yellow cards," modeled after the system in soccer to warn a player he has committed an egregious foul. Soccer had become hugely popular among young boys with the introduction of Japan's professional "J-League." "Anyone who gets three of these will have to clean the room," Sook-ja warned the kids. "And that won't be easy, you know. This room is dirty!" The two fifth-graders watched the younger kids carefully as they all went through the greetings once again. When one boy was not properly joining in, one of the fifth-graders shot his hand into the air and, displaying the card, shouted in Japanese, "*Ierō kādo!*" ("Yellow card"). No one, ultimately, was rejected.

Dismissing the younger children, Sook-ja was now alone with the upper-grade students. She gathered them all in a circle around a desk in the front of the room. There were three girls and four boys present, all fifth-graders. One fourth-grader would join later. Attendance is not compulsory, and sixth-graders generally have the lowest participation rate because of *juku* (private school) activities for personal development (such as piano and martial arts) and for academic study.

Sook-ja wanted to ask the students what they would like to do in the class for the upcoming year. Giving the students a say in what activities they will pursue is both a way to gear activities toward those they will most enjoy, and a way of involving them more actively in the class by giving them some responsibility for its direction. This strategy does not always have the hoped-for results.

"So what would you like to do?"

"Unicycle!" chimed in Kwan Mi-shil. This activity has become very popular among older primary school girls. They even stage "synchronized unicycle" performances.

"You can do that anywhere," Sook-ja explained. "What would you like to do inside the Toraji ethnic class?" The conditions on what can be undertaken in the class remained unspoken, but the kids were reminded of the boundaries of what constitute "ethnic activities."

The kids were not inspired to make further suggestions. Sook-ja continued, "Okay, we've got the sports meet coming up in June. Toraji performs every year, right? This year, I think we should do *p'ungmul*."

The *p'ungmul* piece the upper-grade students would perform during the lunch break at the annual school sports meet is a type of Korean folk performance of integrated music and dance performed with a standard set of percussion instruments. The performance involves a series of several separate rhythms. The players move in a procession, with the type of movement – walking, skipping, kicking in place, running – changing with the rhythm.

With the performance coming up in only a few weeks, there was little choice but to begin rehearsal immediately. The first step was to choose instruments. For the sports meet, there was to be only one *kkwaenggwari* player, in order that this small hand-held bronze gong not overwhelm the other instruments. Four kids volunteered to play this lead instrument, which sets the tempo and signals the changes in tempo and rhythm. "Whoever plays *kkwaenggwari* will have to practice hard," Sook-ja warned. "If you make a mistake, you'll throw everyone else off." Undaunted by this responsibility, the four tossed a few quick rounds of *janken* (the Japanese "paper-scissors-rock" game) to choose the player. The winner was Mun An-gi who, with this, strengthened her leadership role in the class.

One fifth-grade boy was a transfer student, new to the school and the class. Sook-ja asked him if he would like to try the *puk*, the barrel drum beaten with a single stick. This instrument is technically less difficult than either the *kkwaenggwari* or the *changgo*, the hourglass drum beaten with two sticks. "Sure," he responded shyly. Sook-ja looked at the Japanese name on his school name tag and asked what his Korean name was. Some Japanese "passing" names that Koreans use contain obvious clues to the original Korean name. This one did not. The boy hesitated, then replied without much confidence, "Cho."

"What's the character?"

"I dunno."

Next, a *ching* player had to be chosen. This is the large deep-voiced gong that lays down the basic beat in *p'ungmul*. The two outgoing boys who had earlier led the group in the greetings thrust their hands into the air. A round of *janken* left the smaller of the two boys, Mrs. Arai's son, as the *ching* player. The remaining two girls opted for *changgo*, while the other boys chose the *puk*.

"Okay. Go get your instruments." The seven kids rushed in a mass to the storage room next door and returned in a cacophony of clashes, clangs, thumps and ta-ta-ku-ta's. Sook-ja took up a *changgo* that one of the girls had brought for her. She orally called out the rhythm that the *changgo* were to follow. Don-ta-don-tatata! Then for the puk: ton/ton-ton/ton-ton/ton-ton-click!: ending with a smart crack of the thick wooden stick on the wooden rim of the drum.

Sook-ja then turned to Mun An-gi to work on the complex rhythms beaten out on the *kkwaenggwari* with a felt-tipped wooden mallet. Proper play demands a quick wrist and a coordination of beating with damping accomplished by the hand holding the gong. Sook-ja taught her one of the signals that will lead the group into a new rhythm. Having practiced several of the different *p'ungmul* rhythms for each instrument, Sook-ja had the kids put them together. Considering this was the first practice of the year, they made a creditable effort. Four-twenty rolled around, and the kids' fatigue was showing. Sook-ja had them put their instruments away and dismissed the class.

Learning names

When I arrived on the following Wednesday, only four or five kids had shown up. So had Mi-jeong, who was in discussion with Sook-ja at the front of the room. They greeted me with a hearty *annyŏnghaseyo* and continued their conference.

A group of older kids came in. Pak Che-wŏn called out to Mun An-gi, "Mun An-gi, U-NA-GI!," punning on the resemblance of her name to the Japanese word for a type of eel, a culinary delicacy. An-gi hit back with "Che-wŏn, CHA-WAN!," twisting his name into the Japanese word for rice bowl. There was no meanness, but rather a playful affection in this interchange. In fact, the kids rarely use their ethnic names to refer to one another. Both An-gi and Che-wŏn are called by their Japanese names outside the ethnic class, and this is what is written on their school name tags: "Fumimoto Yasuko" and "Arai Takeo," respectively.

Mi-jeong began the class. To signal, and settle, the twenty-four or so kids who had by now assembled, Mi-jeong counted down from 10 in Korean: "*Yŏl! Ahop!* I don't mean '*aho*,' you know!" Mi-jeong made a preemptive punning reference to the Japanese *aho*, a usually lighthearted "stupid" in the Osaka dialect. She continued, slowing down as she approached "one": "*Hana* . . . Good!" The kids had been listening intently. When she finished, a rare, conspicuous silence reigned. But only for a moment.

Greetings completed, Mi-jeong launched into the first lesson, again introducing the first-graders to the class and to their own ethnic Korean names. One at a time, she wrote the *kanji* characters for the name of each new member on the blackboard. Underneath these she wrote it again in *hangŭl* and in the Japanese *hiragana* script to approximate the pronunciation.

After she finished writing Kim Ho-su's name on the board, Mi-jeong called out for him. "Is Ho-su-*kun* here?" After just a moment's hesitation, the bright little boy with "Kanemitsu Hirohide" written in *hiragana* on his school name tag cried out a confident "*Hai!*"

"For '*hai*,' we say '*ye*,'" Mi-jeong corrected. "One more time. *Tashi hanbŏn*. Ho-su-*kun*?"

"*Ye!*"

"Okay," Mi-jeong addressed all the other students, "From tomorrow, everyone call him 'Ho-su.' What a great name!"

After writing the characters for Pak Shin-il's name, Mi-jeong called out for the boy. "Is Shin-il here?" The subject of her query closed his eyes tightly, making an exaggerated, squished-up face. Mi-jeong called again. This time Shin-il covered his eyes with his hands, like the monkey who sees no evil. With Shin-il maintaining his defiant, clowning silence, Mi-jeong moved on. She called upon a little girl called Kim Haeng-ja, who is otherwise known to herself and her classmates as Kanemura Sachiko. As Mi-jeong was writing a *hiragana* "*ki*" followed by a much smaller *hiragana* "*mu*," she explained, "When you say *kim*, make sure you shut your mouth tight. *Kim*. Not *kimu*." Mi-jeong then told the kids a little more about Haeng-ja. "She has a fine older sister, an *ŏnni*. For older sister, we say *ŏnni*." Haeng-ja exhibited a little stage-shyness facing the class, but managed a clear "*ye*" when called upon. Mi-jeong further explained, "Haeng-ja's father is from South Korea, while her mother is Japanese. To understand the culture of both sides, she's joined Toraji. Please become a great friend to her!"

After all the first-graders were introduced, Mi-jeong introduced three other students – second-, fourth-, and fifth-graders – who were new to the ethnic class. When the second-grader had some confusion about the use of '*ye*,' a third-grade veteran of the class spoke up in his defense, "*Sŏnsaengnim*, when we're suddenly told to say '*ye*,' it's hard!" Mi-jeong let this comment slide by. Having introduced eight new students, Mi-jeong asked the other students to give them a round of applause.

She next practiced the Korean commands with the first-graders. Wrapping up this basic practice, Mi-jeong then discussed the ethnic class's role in the upcoming sports meet. After discussion with some of the mothers, it had been decided that all Toraji members would be given an opportunity to participate in the ethnic class's lunch-break performance during the meet. While the *p'ungmul* performance would be restricted to upper-grade students, all members would be able to join in on a demonstration of the Korean martial art, *t'aekwŏndo*. Participation in the latter was not obligatory, however, and the instructors gave kids a chance to decline. One third-grade boy shouted out, "Is Kanemitsu-*kun* gonna do it?," using Ho-su's in-school Japanese "passing" name. "Yeah, I'm gonna," Ho-su, by now crawling under the piano, called back.

Before dismissing the younger kids, Mi-jeong asked one of the fifth-graders to lead the final greetings:

"*Sŏnsaengnim, annyŏnghi kashipshio* (Teacher, go in peace)."

"*Yŏrŏbun, annyŏnghi kashipshio* (Everyone, go in peace)."

Performing Korean

Over the few short weeks before the sports meet, while the younger children consolidated their competence in greetings and commands, practiced writing their Korean names in *hangŭl*, and rehearsed their part for the *t'aekwŏndo* demonstration, the older kids continued their *p'ungmul* rehearsals.

Carrying the responsibility for the performance's success on her shoulders, and frustrated by the complexity and variety of rhythms and the limited time she had to practice them, Mun An-gi broke down in tears one afternoon. Her good friend Kwan Mi-shil put her arms around her in a comforting embrace, while Sook-ja offered encouragement: "Fight on! Don't give up. It'll be fine." Once settled down, she did continue: with her tear-stained cheeks, a picture of resolve. Mi-jeong called for an extra rehearsal for the Saturday before the sports meet on Sunday.

Korean kids participate in the sports meet like their Japanese classmates. Dressed in uniform blue shorts, white shirts and sneakers, they partake of a full day of relay races and other team competitions as well as choreographed cheering performances. Participation is universal. The only relevant lines of demarcation, other than grade, are the "red" and "white" teams into which the whole student body is divided, marked by the color of the students' hats. Parents also turn up in great numbers.

Halfway through the sports meet, with about thirty minutes remaining of the lunch break, the kids of Toraji gathered in the ethnic class room. With the room crowded with several mothers, and some Toraji graduates, all girls, now attending the nearby junior high, Mi-jeong gave the kids a pep talk and oversaw last-minute preparations. "You don't have to feel any pressure. It's no big deal if you fail. What's important is that you do your best." This time, it was Mi-shil's turn to cry. An-gi helped strap her into her *changgo*.

The *p'ungmul* performers were ten in all. Because there was no time for a costume change between the *p'ungmul* and the *t'aekwŏndo* demonstration, the performers dressed in their white *t'aekwŏndo* gis, festooned with red, blue, and yellow ribbons across their chests and tied in the back with big bows, for a reasonable facsimile of the *paji chŏgori* usually worn.

To the cue of An-gi's *kkwaenggwari*, the Toraji *p'ungmul* troupe walked onto the sports field encircled by an audience of perhaps 300 classmates, parents and school staff. The performance went fine. There was about thirty seconds of unplanned silence in the middle, when An-gi forgot a rhythm, but an impromptu conference with her fellow troupe members got the procession back on track. The *t'aekwŏndo* performance also went fine, board-breaking and all. Having successfully performed as Koreans in front of the assembled community, the Toraji kids rushed off to remove their gis and reappear in the Tohan athletic uniform.

Back into their blue shorts and white shirts, An-gi and Mi-shil were both in the first after-lunch event, a pom-pommed cheer choreographed to the theme song of the popular children's cartoon, "Crayon Shin-chan."

Over the course of the year, the children would study more Korean (the names of animals and the sounds they make; objects found in a classroom), sing songs, learn a little Korean history and geography, and rehearse for their Korean cultural festival, held at the school annually now for about fifteen years, and participate, with fellow Korean primary school children from their own and the adjacent ward of Osaka, in an all-Korean sports meet. With their parents, they would have a *yakiniku* (Korean barbecue) picnic and a Korean cuisine cooking class, with mothers, children, and Japanese teachers joining in to make *kimbap* (rice and vegetables rolled in dried seaweed) and *hwachŏn p'achŏn* (fried rice cakes).

Kids in the discursive web of the nation

Having "the same faces" as Japanese, as Mi-jeong once observed, and having reached primary-school age being called by Japanese-style names, Korean kids first come to Tohan primary school from a position, in most cases, of invisibility as Koreans – not only to others but to themselves. Meeting each week in a room of their own, the kids of the Toraji ethnic class are taught to make distinctions between what belongs to the national imaginary of Japan and what to that of Korea, and which of these properly belongs to them. Within an environment in which "Koreanness" is foregrounded and given a morally positive valence, Mi-jeong, Sook-ja, and the other instructors provide the kids with a series of oppositions through which a national or ethnic affiliation can be identified. Many of these are materially-mediated: sounds, of the Korean language, of Korean rhythms and timbres; objects, including the shapes and colors of traditional Korean dress, musical instruments, masks and other performance props, the shapes of *hangŭl*; and the smells, tastes, and textures of Korean food. Then there are minimum elements of a Korean behavioral repertoire, such as greetings. Consistent use of kin terms in Korean mark the moral boundaries of kinship and the obligations it implies with the sounds of national affiliation.

Central to the task of creating Korean subjects out of children well on the road to "Japanization," great pains are taken to bring the kids to a positive association with things Korean and to a positive experience of their classmates as fellow Koreans. With occasional breaks for purely "fun" activities, ample emphasis is placed on activities, such as performances, that are made rewarding through hard work and team play. The collective activities of the class enable a grounding of the experience of Koreanness in concrete social interactions with other members of the ethnic class. With *p'ungmul*, as we have seen, the children are made to rely upon one another in a coordinated effort to successfully "perform Korean." In this and other "high-stakes" performances requiring dedicated preparation and done in front of an audience, collective action is bound with the adhesive of emotional intensity to the experience of being "Korean." Thus, in the ethnic class, cognitive, categorical elements are invested with emotional and moral value and these elements are foregrounded to frame collective social experience. This is nothing other than the process of creating national subjects.

In the case of the Toraji ethnic class, however, this is undertaken within the context of the Japanese school and Japanese community, where the process of creating *Japanese* national subjects moves on inexorably. Thus, the children's experiences in the ethnic class, as I have attempted to sketch above, are but a moment in the processes of identification which situate the children as historical subjects. Yet, even this hour or so per week in the class, as a sort of "crash course" in the principles of national symbolic boundary marking, can work powerfully to help organize and make intelligible the differences that the categorical ascriptions "Japanese" and "Korean" carry in Japanese society.

How should the differences in "national culture" that are addressed in the ethnic class best be understood? With constant exposure to a great variety of mass media and popular culture, Korean and Japanese children, in many ways, have more in common with one another than they do with their Korean or Japanese parents. There may be more or less difference in certain domestic customs, such as food preferences or domestic rites concerning ancestors. These, of course, also differ among those of the same national heritage.

The most meaningful differences are not located in any residual differences that could be described in terms of "Korean" or "Japanese" cultural content, but arise from the symbolic mobilization of "the nation" to elicit political loyalty and identification. Korean heritage signifies a difference in "origin" which is difficult to accommodate in the grand narrative of the Japanese nation, rendering Koreans' full belonging problematic. Legal instruments, such as the nationality and alien registration laws, and bureaucratic practice, are used to contain this difference, so that Japan-born, native Japanese-speaking descendants of former imperial subjects are now third-, fourth-, and fifth-generation foreigners. The cost of Japanese nationality, meanwhile, is cultural and political assimilation so as not to disturb the equation of nationality and ethnonational identity (see Kashiwazaki in this volume).

In the ethnic class, differences in historical positioning *vis-à-vis* national narratives are transformed into a language of cultural difference, keeping intact criteria for belonging which originate out of the discursive power of the national narrative. Both the Korean instructors and their Japanese supporters in the school promote these kinds of symbolic alignments, which have become institutionalized in state educational policy for promoting "international understanding" and mutual respect between "Japanese and foreign students."

Both the Korean instructors and the supportive Japanese teachers, I am convinced, have undertaken their work out of love for the children and hopes for their health and happiness. Both see an identification with a Korean heritage as key to a positive self-image among the children. This is what will allow them to "be who they are," and be recognized as "who they are." The emphases of Korean instructors and the Japanese teachers differ, however, with the former seeking to create, or at least plant the seeds of, a Korean national subjectivity among the children, in a sort of "self-essentialization" toward the creation of an historical subject referencing a politically agentive Korean nation. The Japanese side, on the other hand, emphasizes the goal of eliminating the stigma heretofore attached to the status of "Korean," so that Koreans' pursuit of happiness as foreigners in Japanese society not be hindered by either self-loathing or discrimination. In practice, there seems to be little conflict in these different emphases.

Given the broader agenda of the educational system in the creation of national subjects, this approach of aligning heritage, "culture," and identity is not surprising. The symbolic, pedagogical and institutional resources with which educators have long worked are reoriented toward a goal of justice and human rights. It is not the only possibility, however, and it is not given uniform support by Korean parents. Most parents, in fact, resist calls to have their children use their ethnic Korean names outside of the ethnic class, as well as the more implicit suggestions that they themselves do so. Some parents resent the exclusion of Japanese children from the ethnic class and the goal of creating a Korean "we" against a Japanese "they" which the practice is designed to facilitate. Most, in short, seek a mode of being which does not require the foregrounding and consistent public presentation of national heritage as their most salient identity. While valuing those elements of their lives and personal relationships that they identify as Korean, they reject the requirement inhering in the identification process to construe Japanese-marked elements as a "constitutive outside" (Hall 1996d: 3). They consider these elements to be part of who they are.[12]

The reception of "foreigners" in Japanese society has changed vastly since the colonial period and the 4.24 educational struggle of 1948. The sight of a *p'ungmul* procession of Korean kids moving through an audience of Japanese students and parents on the grounds of the central community institution of the Japanese school is evidence enough of that. Beginning with activist Japanese teachers and other progressives, the notion of "living together" (*kyōsei*) with cultural difference based on "international understanding" has been incorporated into policy at all levels of government. In contrast to the colonial approach of "harmony" (*kyōwa*), in which differences ascribed to national heritage were stigmatized and designated worthy of erasure, in the practice of *kyōsei*, such differences are (re)constructed and positively accentuated.

What has not changed is the foregrounding of heritage, "blood," filiation and symbolically marked cultural elements as salient boundaries in social relations. In a fine recent work, Tessa Morris-Suzuki (1998) traces the still continuing processes by which notions of race, culture, gender, and so on, have been put to use in the discursive construction of a distinctive, bounded, homogeneous Japanese nation. It is within this context that, by inducing Korean kids to experience and display their "Koreanness," ethnic classes help children organize and give positive meaning to a socially recognized difference that would otherwise be an even greater source of confusion and psychic burden. They also organize difference in a way generated by, and made sensible through, this discourse of the nation.

Acknowledgements

I am indebted to Sonia Ryang and Aihwa Ong for helpful comments and suggestions on earlier versions of this chapter. I also wish to thank Elizabeth Herskovitz, Peta Katz, Margery Lazarus, Diane Tober, and Sandra Hyde for useful suggestions, and YoomiJa Hyun for sharing with me some of the data of her study of an ethnic class in Osaka. The staff of the pseudonymous Tohan primary school, and especially the children, parents, and instructors of what I call the Toraji ethnic class, accepted my intrusions with grace and kindness, for which I remain most grateful.

Notes

1 Embedded in a logic in which race, language and culture are intricately linked, the term *minzoku* is notoriously tricky to render in English. Shifting with context, the term overlaps with the English semantic fields covered by such terms as "folk" (or the German "Volk") or "nation" or "ethnic group," or sometimes "tribe" (see Morris-Suzuki 1998: 32 and ch. 5 passim; Field 1993: 645). Throughout this chapter, I have translated *minzokugakkyū* as "ethnic class." The reader will note, however, that the semantic ground covered by the term *minzoku* in the context discussed in this paper has shifted between 1950, when *minzokugakkyū* were first established, and today, and even now shifts with the point of view of the speaker. Questions concerning what are the criteria that unite Koreans as a *minzoku*, whether Koreans in Japan do, or should, belong to it and what moral obligations that belonging might entail – that is, what constitutes a *minzoku* – are issues fundamentally contested among Koreans in Japan.
2 See Ong (1996) for an ethnographic account of "cultural citizenship" as a process of "subjectification and cultural performance" (1996: 750) among Asian immigrants in the United States.
3 Korean names, however, continued to be recorded in all public records in order to allow the continued social control of Koreans as a subordinated group (Eckert *et al.* 1990: 318).
4 All translations from the Japanese in this chapter are my own.
5 In Japanese educational parlance, issues concerning Koreans are usually covered under the term "foreign students." Until the recent increase in non-Korean foreign children in Japanese schools, the policies for foreign students were targeted at Koreans.
6 Of the 498,477 public primary school students in Osaka prefecture, 8,293 are legally Korean "foreign students," and make up 1.7 percent of total primary school students. Total primary school students in Osaka city, included within the above, amount to 129,752, of which 5,001 are Korean "foreign students," making up 3.9 percent of the city's public primary school students (May 1997 figures from Yonniyon Hanshin kyōikutōsō 50 shūnenkinen jigyōkai 1998: 40). Korean "foreign students" include those of Republic of Korea nationality and those registered as *chōsen* (Korean), the category, not technically a nationality, for those Koreans in Japan at the end of the Second World War and their descendants who have not taken ROK or some other nationality (see Kashiwazaki in this volume; Ryang 1997: 120-4). Figures for Korean "foreign students" do not include children of Koreans who have naturalized and most children of marriages between Koreans and Japanese (see note 10 below).
7 A dissenting view is offered by Hamamoto (1995). An ethnic Korean who goes by her Japanese name, Hamamoto suggests that adopting a Korean name in order to "recover" a Korean identity amounts to a denial of the "Japanese" aspects of Koreans in Japan which they have acquired by virtue having grown up and been educated in Japanese society, and merely promotes the essentialism upon which discrimination against Koreans in Japan is based. I thank Sonia Ryang for calling this reference to my attention.
8 Noguchi, to whose work on this point I am indebted, calls this the "pride strategy," and traces its origins to the 1922 declaration of the levelers' society (Suiheisha) which began the Buraku liberation movement (1996: 167-8).
9 The following is based on fieldwork undertaken from March 1993 to May 1994, with the support of a Japan Foundation Dissertation Fellowship, and from April to August

1997. The events described largely took place in the spring of 1997. Tohan primary school and Toraji ethnic class are fictitious names. I have assigned pseudonyms to those involved with the school and the ethnic class depicted herein.

10 Under the revised nationality law of 1984, children of a Japanese and non-Japanese parent are allowed the choice of either parental nationality up to the age of twenty-two. For such children living in Japan, however, until a choice is made, the non-Japanese nationality is considered "latent" and the children are considered to be Japanese. This is not to be confused with "dual nationality," as the choice of a non-Japanese nationality entails the obligation to renounce Japanese nationality, and *vice versa* (Moriki 1995: 234–44).

11 The Japanese syllabary is a blunt tool for representing a sound system with complex consonant combinations. Reducing the size of the *"mu"* symbol is an attempt to suppress the tendency of a native Japanese speaker to affix a vowel at the end of what should be a bilabial stop, as in the Korean honorific marker, *nim*.

12 These observations are based upon my interviews with Korean parents and on listening in on their discussions among themselves. Fukuoka and Kim present interesting survey data revealing that only around 20 percent of their sample of eighteen- to thirty-year-old Koreans in Japan used their Korean ethnic names with greater frequency than they used Japanese-style names, with the figure for their parents only slightly higher (1997: 78–9).

10 Ordinary (Korean) Japanese

John Lie

For any reflective individual, the question of identity is at once inevitable and irresolvable.[1] It is inevitable because a thinking person cannot but ponder on existential questions, such as "who am I?" or "where do I come from?" It is irresolvable because there is no permanently satisfactory answer. Reflections on an answer may provoke new questions: what does it mean to be a member of group *x* or to have an attribute *y*? Any answer must also resist the pull of time. If time, and its inevitable concomitant, experience, should affect, perhaps even alter, one's sense of self (here I use this to be interchangeable with the concept of identity), then one should presumably be chary of considering any answer as definitive. Furthermore, any response that has pretensions of being a workable answer is perforce short, or essentialist: I am x, y, and perhaps z. If an answer were to include twenty-six, or perhaps 260, characteristics, then it wouldn't presumably be satisfactory. For example, a woman might identify herself as *au fond* Korean Japanese.[2] In any sustained reflection on her identity, however, she would be remiss if she were to neglect any number of family roles – daughter, sister, and so on – or work roles: professor, bureaucrat, and so on. That the question may be irresolvable of course makes it no less inevitable, and perhaps all the more urgent.

Given the inevitable complexity and flux of an individual identity, it is puzzling to encounter expressions of ethnic fundamentalism: the notion that one's ethnic background should disclose profound, or at least meaningful, truths about one's self or identity. The urge for a simple and fixed notion – heightened undoubtedly by the desire for scientificity – is no less urgent among social scientists. Consider in this regard the straitjacket of an (ethnic) identity offered in perhaps the most sustained social-scientific work in English on Korean Japanese (Lee and De Vos 1981). For example, George De Vos and Changsoo Lee (1981b: 365) characterize Korean Japanese thus: "They tend to feel more conflict about committing themselves to any purpose." But several pages earlier, the authors (ibid.: 358) assert that: "Koreans in Japan have responded to their present conditions by an ethnic consolidation not dissimilar . . . to . . . the black American population." Elsewhere, they define Korean Japanese identity in the following fashion: "The maintenance of Korean identity invariably implies some conflict over assumption or avoidance of responsibility and guilt" (ibid.: 367). One would have thought that the previous sentence could apply to virtually any group. Beyond contradictory assertions and banal generalizations, De Vos and Lee (ibid.: 375) note: "The family relationships themselves become bonds of aggressive displacement, of mute frustration, and of inescapable ignominy. The family is not a haven but a place of alienation." One may, following the British poet Philip Larkin (1988: 180) – "They fuck you up, your mum and dad/They may not mean to, but they do" – regard family alienation as a common human condition, but its specific attribution to Korean Japanese seems problematic at best.

In this paper, I hope to elaborate, if ever so briefly, my skepticism regarding efforts to seek a simple, similar, and constant sense of the self, or personal identity, among Korean Japanese. Any sustained reflection on personal identity reveals discontinuity and difference; ethnic, or group, identity cannot be reduced to simple and static essences. I illustrate my argument by considering some recent narratives by Korean Japanese writers. Although these narratives may provide insights into Korean Japanese and Japanese society, Korean Japanese ethnicity cannot capture the flux and heterogeneity of individual identities.

Personal identity

Since John Locke's classic discussion in *An Essay Concerning Human Understanding*, the prevailing Western understanding of personal identity has emphasized the psychic unity and temporal continuity of individual consciousness. As Locke (1975: 342, 344) wrote: "*personal Identity* consists, not in the Identity of Substance, but...in the Identity of *consciousness* . . . Nothing but consciousness can unite remote Existences into the same Person." In Locke's view, the faculty of memory underpins the unity and continuity of personal identity. These themes of sameness and continuity underlie, for example, Erik Erikson's (1985: 142) influential formulation of personal identity in *Childhood and Society*: "this sense of identity provides the ability to experience one's self as something that has continuity and sameness, and to act accordingly." The occasional crises – the threats of difference and discontinuity – are categorized as "identity crisis," and mark the important but infrequent biographical stages of an individual life course (Erikson 1958).

In contradistinction to the emphasis on continuity and sameness, David Hume and Thomas Reid, among others, counter Locke's confident and commonsensical account, arguing instead for the indefinable and impermanent nature of personal identity. For Hume (1978: 259): "The identity, which we ascribe to the mind of man, is only a fictitious one." Rather than a unitary entity, he (ibid.: 253) envisions it as "a kind of theatre, where several perceptions successively make their appearance; pass, re-pass, glide away, and mingle in an infinite variety of postures and situations. There is properly no *simplicity* in it at one time, nor *identity* in different." Rather than Locke's continuity and homogeneity, Hume suggests discontinuity and heterogeneity in the constitution of identity.

The Humean view, although not as popular as the Lockean view, finds adherents especially among the most self-conscious of people, writers. In John Keats'

(1990: 418-19) letter of 27 October 1818 to Richard Woodhouse, we learn that: "As to the poetical Character itself . . . it has no self. . . . A Poet . . . has no Identity." This is because the poet is constantly "filling some other Body." The intimation of a fluctuating and multiple self becomes the commonsense of literary modernism (Joyce and Woolf, for instance). By the late twentieth century, it is not uncommon to read various expressions of difference and discontinuity in personal identity. Jorge Luis Borges, extending Keats's theme, notes in "Borges and I":

> It is to my other self, to, Borges, that things happen. . . . But I recognize myself much less in the books he writes than in many others or in the clumsy plucking of a guitar. . . . I cannot tell which one of us is writing this page.
> (Borges 1995: 4–5)

In a slightly different vein, Bernard Malamud (1979: 20) writes in *Dubin's Lives*: "There is no life that can be captured wholly; as it was. Which is, to say that all biography is ultimately fiction. What does that tell you about the nature of life, and does one really want to know?"

To be sure, I do not wish to exaggerate the themes of diversity and discontinuity in personal identity. There are well-defined mental illnesses at the respective extremes: multiple-personality disorder and amnesia. However, the Lockean confidence in a relatively fixed and homogeneous identity seems misplaced.[3] In any case, if I can cast enough doubt on the continuity and sameness of personal identity, then the ground for being skeptical about the existence of a static and simple group identity should be all the more cogent.

Social identity

Let us consider "simple" societies. In what Émile Durkheim influentially categorized as societies of mechanical solidarity, he (1984: 84–5) postulated that the basis of solidarity is the sameness among members: "The individual consciousness . . . is simply a dependency of the collective type . . . [I]ndividuals resemble one another . . . [T]he individual personality is absorbed into the collective personality."

Even the simplest societies, however, have a fair degree of heterogeneity and diversity, which confounds Durkheim's assertion of mechanical solidarity. Given the inevitable existence of role differentiation – such as gender and generation – we find in the seemingly "simplest" societies a source of identity differentiation: one is a "Big Man," husband, father, son, brother, hunter, and so on. And, as Godfrey Lienhardt observes, a sense of individuality is omnipresent. If nothing else, the ontological separation of each individual offers a potent source of more or less well-articulated individuality. Writing of the Dinka – presumably a "simple" society – Lienhardt notes:

> though all clansmen are equivalent in certain situations – in blood feud, for example – this clanship does not diminish the individuality of its members

by making them mere units or cells of the larger organization.... Rather it adds something to each individual, as (on a rather shaky analogy) a strong sense of belonging to an Oxford college does not diminish the individuality of its members.

(Lienhardt 1985: 155)

Although collective identities exist – as they do in all social situations – this should not imply their ready identification with constituent individuals. In addition, Eric Wolf (1982), among others, alerts us to the inevitability of temporal change and of contact with the outside world for even the most isolated, "simple" societies.

If considerable diversity of identities exists in "simple" societies, then the case is even more compelling for contemporary complex societies. Personal identity, as I have suggested, is complex and in constant flux, and provides a poor foundation for a homogeneous and static group identity. Group identity also presumes not only heterogeneity but also historicity.[4] The simple, static essences are chimerical.

Korean Japanese identity

Why should we expect perhaps a million people of Korean descent in Japan to exhibit a considerable degree of a common ethnic identity? What more can we say than that they share the category of Korean descent and their cultural citizenship in Japan? And how important should these factors be in the personal definition of contemporary Korean Japanese?

Needless to say, the question is socio-historically specific. In a strictly racially stratified – or caste – society, as was largely the case in imperial Japan, the fact of Korean descent emerged as a master signifier with potent social consequences (see e.g. Weiner 1994; Nishinarita 1997). For example, the over two million Koreans in the main Japanese islands (*naichi*, or inland) were racial inferiors, who were in turn segregated from their Japanese counterparts in living and working arrangements. Japanese workers often lynched Koreans who crossed the ethnic barrier, and sought higher-waged jobs reserved for Japanese nationals. Virtually all Koreans in *naichi* were, moreover, Korean-born and reared. They faced varying levels of difficulty in speaking Japanese, and were excluded from Japanese social and cultural life. In imperial Japan, therefore, the category of Korean descent denoted a distinct group of people whose sense of self and identity, albeit variegated, evinced no overlap with ethnic Japanese.

In the very late twentieth century, there are still significant barriers in terms of employment, marriage, and civic participation for Korean Japanese. However, they do not constitute a uniformly inferior group. Furthermore, many of them are second-, third-, and even fourth-generation Japanese residents who are culturally Japanese. By "cultural Japanese," I mean to highlight that they grew up speaking Japanese, watching Japanese television, playing with Japanese children, attending Japanese schools, and so on, such that virtually the sole source of social differentiation from ethnic Japanese is the fact of Korean descent. Even in the case of those who have attended and still identify with the North Korea-affiliated schools and organization, the overwhelming cultural influence is often no different from that of other Japanese children. As the ideological control of North Korea-affiliated schools wanes, the fact of cultural Japanese-ness becomes all the more inescapable (Ryang 1997: 198).

Needless to say, given the pervasive prejudice and discrimination against people of Korean descent in Japan, the fact of Korean descent has a significant impact on Korean Japanese identity. Many Korean Japanese belong, for example, to ethno-political organizations (Gohl 1976: 122–31). However, the fact of Korean descent does not, at least for most second-, third-, or fourth-generation Korean Japanese, imply familiarity with the Korean language or culture, and offers no obvious differentiation from their Japanese counterparts. The fact of Korean descent, in other words, no longer determines or dominates the individual identity of Korean Japanese. Other social conditions, such as economic or regional background, vary tremendously. What unites Son Masayoshi, the Bill Gates of Japan, and a homeless, and socially faceless, Korean Japanese man? Or consider regional diversity: a Korean Japanese man who grew up in Tokyo writes of Korean Japanese in Osaka as people "who are clearly a different species, an alien cultural group" (Chŏng A-yŏng 1997: 87). When he first went to Ikaino (a Korean area in Osaka), he wondered whether he was still in Japan.

Thus, ethnicity in and of itself cannot in any sense predict the concrete contours of individual identity. Let me put it another way. I do not doubt, for example, that the experiences of Korean Japanese may shed a great deal of light on the nature and extent of mainstream Japanese prejudice and discrimination against people of Korean descent. However, I do question whether the fact of Korean descent has a determining impact on the sense of self, or personal identity, of culturally Japanese people of Korean descent. The fact of Korean descent is a factor – and it can become the dominant factor for some people – but only one among many factors in the personal identity constitution of Korean Japanese. And the sense of identity may change dramatically for any individual over her or his life course. We should therefore not expect a great degree of homogeneity among Korean Japanese.

Personal narratives

Let me present some recent narratives by Korean Japanese. I consider narratives in part because some scholars consider them to be the very way in which identities are constituted and constructed. The philosopher Mark Johnson (1993: 11), for example, argues: "Narrative is not just an explanatory device, but is actually constitutive of the way we experience things" (see *inter alia* Polkinghorne 1988; Kerby 1991; and Cave 1995). They offer, at the least, a rich repository of the ways in which people make sense of themselves, which are, after all, the very stuff of identity. Novelists and memoirists, most impressively, attempt to capture a life – a sense of the self – out of a welter of historical residues, social backgrounds, personal experiences, and considered reflections by narrating. We are *homo narrans*.

In focusing on three narratives, my intention is not to generate a random sample. They are exemplary not in the sense of expressing a statistical mode, or of being the best and the most noble expressions of Korean Japanese people, but rather because they record and represent individual experiences without excessive recourse to preconceived categories or received formulas.

Hwang Min-gi (1993)

Hwang grew up in a poor area of Osaka notable for its high concentration of Koreans. Living in a tenement house (*nagaya*) in an area that can be characterized as an ethnic enclave, his family and their neighbors experienced a strong sense of community, remarkably devoid of a sense of victimization or of what some social scientists call the culture of poverty. He is critical of Japanese intellectuals for being poverty tourists, who render the Korean neighborhood to be a site of otherness. For him, the area is simply where he grew up and for which he has fond memories.

Hwang's sense of Korean identity is flickering and nebulous. When a person with a Korean surname is accused of a crime, he apprehends a sense of crisis among adults. Teachers in his school appear to know the real (Korean) names of Hwang and his friends, even though they use Japanese names (*tsūmei*). Although the four heroes of his childhood are Korean Japanese – "Queen" Misora Hibari (singer), "Emperor" Kaneda Masaichi (baseball star), "Don" Yanagawa Jirō (a local *yakuza* boss), and "Japan's brilliant star" Rikidōzan (wrestling star) – they are not explicitly identified as being of Korean descent. It is difficult to discern whether they are heroes because of their Korean ethnicity, or because they are able to succeed in "ordinary" Japanese society in spite of their ethnicity.

The dominant motif of Hwang's memoir is the territorial struggle between a local gang (*gurentai*) and an expanding *yakuza* organization. The confrontation of gangs ironically underscores the significance of Korean descent for him and his friends. The special attraction of an outlaw life is that: "In *bōryokudan* [gang organization], it doesn't matter whether one is Japanese or Korean. Whoever has power wins." Indeed, the fact of Korean descent marks the lives of Hwang and his friends. One boyhood acquaintance "returns" to North Korea, another commits suicide (possibly over the breakup of a relationship, which may have been due to his Korean descent), and yet another joins a *yakuza*.

Hwang is, then, unquestionably Korean Japanese. Growing up in an ethnic neighborhood, he experiences Korean and Japanese people and cultures. He is, in his recollection, far from special, however. As a child, he "did not have any special characteristic." He was neither physically powerful nor intellectually brilliant. His childhood is characterized by experiences of boyhood solidarity: jokes and pranks. Meditations on Korean Japanese identity remain peripheral.

Kyō Nobuko (1987)

Neither poor nor surrounded by Korean Japanese, Kyō grew up in Yokohama with virtually no knowledge of the Korean language and very little familiarity with Korean culture. Celebrating the New Year's Day with her Japanese husband, she can only count the Korean-style rice cake and a diluted form of ancestor worship as marks of her Korean descent. She cannot, for example, answer questions about Korean culture that her Japanese mother-in-law asks her. She cannot, for that matter, eat "authentic" (and spicy) Korean food.

Kyō's narrative enhances her individuality by differentiating her from Japanese and other Korean Japanese. On the one hand, she constantly bemoans the ignorance of the Japanese public. Her Japanese husband, for example, knows very little about Korean Japanese despite his interest in Korean culture. On the other hand, she feels distant from other Korean Japanese she meets, especially those who are proud of their "ethnicity" (*minzoku*). In a meeting with other Korean Japanese young people, Kyō remarks that she "could not get used to the idea of pondering over her identity with everyone else." "My way is not to raise my voice in protest or to live quietly without saying anything. I don't want to pretend to be Japanese, or to emphasize my ethnicity. I want to live ordinarily in Japan as 'resident South Korean in Japan' (*zainichi kankokujin*)." She goes so far as to regard her group as a "new species of humanity," despite her alienation from many other Korean Japanese.

Although Kyō's inquiry into the meaning of being Korean Japanese (more accurately, resident South Koreans in Japan; *zainichi kankokujin*) dominates her narrative, she is remarkably untroubled and light-hearted in her reflection. She is aware that some Korean Japanese consider marrying a Japanese to be tantamount to betraying her people, but she hesitates only briefly when she decides to marry her Japanese husband. At one point, she regards the difference in their nationality as something akin to being of different height, or of one person looking better clothed in green.

In fact, however, Kyō's lighthearted reflections mask rather serious problems of being Korean Japanese. Although she claims that she was never bullied in school, she bypasses the simple fact that she used a Japanese name (*tsūmei*) when she attended Japanese schools. At one point, when her classmate suspects that she may be of Korean descent, Kyō lies about being "mixed-blooded" (*hāfu*) of Korean father and Japanese mother. She finds herself in trouble when she must confront the authorities without the alien registration card which she is required by law to carry at all times. Her desire to become a teacher is dashed when she realizes that non-Japanese nationals cannot become teachers. She faces employment discrimination despite her stellar academic record as a graduate of the prestigious Law Faculty at the University of Tokyo.

The numerous contradictions of Kyō's narrative are perhaps most acute when she expresses her desire to live "normally" (*futsū*). If nothing else, her Tokyo University diploma makes her even more distinct from ordinary Japanese people than the fact of her Korean descent. She nonetheless insists on her identity as a not particularly exceptional individual. As in the title of her book, she is an "ordinary Korean Japanese," although she considers herself to be quite different from other Korean Japanese college students.

Yu Miri (1997c)

Yu's narrative begins in doubt and ends with an explicit recognition of the fictive character of the past. She was born into a family of secrets; she is not sure of her father's age or whether her mother was born in Japan. She characterizes her parents' past as a "dark tunnel," which is closed on both ends by "silence." Her family life, which is a constant theme in her plays and stories, is tempestuous – a father who is violent, a mother who runs away with another man – but she acknowledges that she is loved by her parents, even incurring her sister's jealousy. Although she played with the popular Rikachan dolls (the Japanese equivalent of Barbie dolls) and liked insects, her childhood was marked by her exclusion from group life. Other children bullied her from early on, the first time in kindergarten when she came with a different hairstyle. In part she blames herself for being unable to endure group life. "I was conceited and I thought that I was a chosen person. . . . I thought that I was special." At the same time, however, bullying seems inextricable from her Korean ancestry. "For me, bullying and *kimch'i* [a Korean staple which her mother made and sold for a time] are somehow linked."

Yu characterizes herself as a runaway (*tōbōsha*), as someone who flees not to hide but simply to run away. She is embarrassed by her aunt, whom one of her friends mistakes for a beggar. She is ashamed of her meager lunch. She avoids school by playing hooky, and becomes a delinquent. The desire to flee culminates in Yu's attempts to run away from home and also to kill herself. After she is expelled from her school, she thinks of emigrating to the United States.

Although she finds friends from time to time, she feels closer to dead writers than to any living people. "I was closer to the dead than to the living. In my bag were books by Nakahara Nakaya [poet] and Dazai Osamu [novelist], and I could only talk easily with the dead. The living inevitably hurt me, but the dead forgave, and cured me." Indeed, her memory recounts the story of a neighbor who molests her as a child, and other acts of inhumanity and betrayal.

Yu writes her memoir in part through a motivation to bury her past. The desire is a long-standing one. When she moves from her elementary school, her homeroom teacher gives her an antique music box and a handkerchief. She buries them, because: "I wanted to change, to become a different person. I didn't need souvenirs." But she also writes because she wants to create her own "reality." She writes seriously in part because she was bullied as a child: "It was my 'story.' If I am not careful, I would be forsaken by reality, and diverge from the world. I needed to write to fill the void." She closes by noting that: "everything is a fact, everything is a lie." Her memoir is a "sedimentation of words." (For more on Yu, see Yoneyama in this volume.)

The search for the least common denominators

These disparate narratives are, of course, recognizably Japanese: not only in the (not necessarily trivial) sense that they are written in Japanese, but also in the more significant sense that they presume broad familiarity with Japanese culture.

But what in fact unite them beyond their Japanese provenance? Most powerfully, I think, we can glean the ferocity of the state-sanctioned exclusion of people of Korean descent from public life. The pervasiveness of public exclusion seeps into various spheres of social life, including bullying at school. But the reception of public exclusion is far from uniform. Hwang does not mention being bullied, and Kyō claims not to have been bullied. Although Yu is convinced that bullying and her Korean ancestry are intertwined, she is far from certain that her Korean descent explains completely her exclusion from group life as a child.

Indeed, it is not uniformity but diversity that marks the three narratives. Consider the question of ethnic identity. Although Kyō's narrative struggles with the question of identity, her search and answer are far from the norm. She feels alienated from those passionate about Korean Japanese causes. Hwang, in contrast, is keenly aware of Korean descent, having grown up in a neighborhood full of Korean Japanese. Yet he does not probe deeply into the question of his ethnic identity. In a different way, Yu's sense of self literally makes her a character from a play, endowed with certain propensities, such as the desire to flee, but unmarked by her ethnic heritage or Japanese racism.

Hwang and Kyō both regard themselves as "ordinary." However, they are far apart in their upbringing and in their outlook. Kyō, despite her well-adjusted and "ordinary" upbringing, finds herself to be different from her fellow Korean Japanese university students. Yu is conscious of her difference and her alienation from group life.

Recall De Vos and Lee's assertion regarding the family alienation of Korean Japanese (1981b: 375). Yu appears to be a paradigmatic case; her life seems to buttress De Vos and Lee's argument. However, the narratives of Hwang and Kyō do not fit very well into their scheme.

If we consider the impact of Korean or Japanese culture, then we again find no obvious uniformity. In Hwang's world, Korean and Korean Japanese cultures and events appear here and there. In contrast, Kyō grew up ignorant of Korean culture, although she later spent time in South Korea (Kyō 1990). Yu grew up playing with Rikachan dolls and communicating with dead Japanese writers, such as Dazai.

In spite of their shared background as Korean Japanese, then, we find little convergence. Surely, we can seek their differences in part in their divergent backgrounds: gender, region, class, and so on. These social differences exist alongside the different courses and contours of their individual lives.

I wish to suggest that the divergence goes well beyond these three narratives. Surveys reveal a considerable diversity of Korean Japanese opinions on various questions of ethnic identity (Fukuoka and Kim 1997). Other narratives do not take us any closer to convergence (Fukuoka and Tsujiyama 1991). As I have suggested, this should not be surprising. Although the wrestling star Rikidōzan assiduously sought to "pass" as Japanese, the baseball star Harimoto Isao proudly proclaimed his Korean background (Yamamoto 1995). While Yi Chŏng-ja (1994) expresses Korean Japanese identity through the classical Japanese poetic form of *tanka*, other Korean Japanese writers avoid the question altogether. Among the latter, some, such as Ijūin Shizuka, do not hide their Korean descent, while others do. While some Korean Japanese writers explore the historical legacy of Japanese imperialism (e.g. Yun Kŏn-ch'a 1997), others wish to move beyond talking about the past (e.g. Lee Seijaku 1997: 10).

The search for the least common denominators of Korean Japanese identity is futile. Although certain common questions are raised, they are answered in distinct ways. Furthermore, to the extent that there are common concerns, they teeter on becoming rather generic to all human beings.

If we can identify Korean Japanese essences, they reside in the two terms of their category – Korean descent and Japanese livelihood – and in the persistence of Japanese discrimination which does not allow people of Korean descent to be legitimately Japanese. The dominant belief in Japanese monoethnicity stipulates that to be Japanese means inevitably to be ethnic Japanese (Lie, forthcoming). *Pace* Kyŏ's title, then, it is impossible to be an "ordinary" (Korean) Japanese. Given that hybridity and heterogeneity have no places in the dominant Japanese discourse on Japanese identity, the fact of Korean descent renders necessary for Korean Japanese their individual and collective struggles for a viable place and identity in contemporary Japanese society. That Korean Japanese sometimes struggle together does not mean, however, that we should expect the emergence of a simple, static, and homogeneous ethnic identity.

Conclusion

In summary, it is well-nigh impossible to look for salient common denominators among Korean Japanese writers, beyond the very facts of their Korean descent and their lives in Japan. Needless to say, their lives reflect in various ways the persistence of Japanese racism against Korean Japanese, but it would be difficult to conclude that the ethnic experience leaves consistent marks on individual identities and lives.

Korean Japanese personal narratives tell us a great deal about the place and the time in which the writers lived. They also provide insights into Korean Japanese as a social group. However, the usual social-scientific approach – to use social backgrounds or factors as the independent variables, and individuals and their identities as the dependent variables – does not work very well. As we have seen, personal narratives resist simple, reductionist, and essentialist characterizations.

Perhaps we should query instead the urge to encapsulate the other – although the same urge may be found in the efforts to essentialize one's own group or oneself – into a simple and static receptacle. The search for certainty in something as complex, confused, and changing as personal identity seems misplaced. The endeavor, which probably belongs more properly in the realm of the aesthetic or the spiritual, finds social scientists out of their depth, seduced as they might be by the goal and deluded as they might be about their effectiveness. Gustave Flaubert was right to emphasize our limitations:

> Whereas the truth is that fullness of soul can sometimes overflow in utter

vapidity of language, for none of us can ever express the exact measure of his needs or his thoughts or his sorrows; and human speech is like a cracked kettle on which we tap crude rhythms for bears to dance to, while we long to make music that will melt the stars.

(Flaubert 1993: 180)

Acknowledgement

I wish to thank Aya Ezawa, Norma Field, Sonia Ryang, and Mark Selden for their helpful comments.

Notes

1 By "identity," I refer loosely to "personal identity," or the sense of self, and focus in this paper on "ethnic identity" in particular. I am not raising a deep philosophical question of identity: the one and the many, form versus matter, and so on (see e.g. Williams 1995). Rather, I am joining a conversation replete with category mistakes and semantic confusions (e.g. Schrag 1997: 34–5). For example, Cornel West (1995: 15) fancifully defines identity as "fundamentally about desire and death. How you construct your identity is predicated on how you construct desire, and how you conceive of death." The ensuing discussion (Rajchman 1995: 21–31) does a wonderful job of deepening the confusion, thereby keeping readers warm but in the dark.

2 The category for people of Korean descent in Japan is highly contested. The conflicting allegiances to the two Koreas, the different sense of one's place in Japan (temporary versus permanent, for example), and other concerns weigh heavily in the choice of a proper nomenclature. Perhaps the most common term in Japan in the 1990s is *zainichi kankokuchōsenjin* (resident South and North Koreans in Japan). I use the term "Korean Japanese" because the two essential characteristics of this group are that they are of Korean descent and that they live, and most likely will continue to live, in Japan.

3 In this regard, Arnold H. Modell writes:

> The self endures through time as a sense of identity, yet consciousness of self is always changing. The self derives its sense of coherence from within, yet at the same time depends on the appraisals of others, who can either support or disrupt the self's continuity. The self is paradoxical: it is an enduring structure and at the same time nearly coterminous with an ever-changing consciousness. Furthermore, the private self supports a relative self-sufficiency, whereas from another perspective the self is not at all autonomous but can be seen as vulnerable in its dependence upon others for a sense of coherence and continuity.
>
> (Modell 1993: 3)

A non-trivial synthesis of Locke and Hume is necessary.

4 The distinction between the personal and the social can be drawn as that between the imaginary and the symbolic (see e.g. Milner 1983). The former refers to attributes or properties, the latter refers to belonging to, or membership in, a larger entity.

Bibliography

Books and journal articles

Abelmann, Nancy and Lie, John (1995) *Blue Dreams: Korean Americans and the Los Angeles Riots*, Cambridge, Mass.: Harvard University Press.
Aboud, Frances (1988) *Children and Prejudice*, Oxford: Blackwell.
Adelson, Joseph and O'Neil, Robert (1966) "Growth of Political Ideas in Adolescence: The Sense of Community," *Journal of Personality and Social Psychology* 4: 295–306.
Adelson, Joseph, Green, Bernard, and O-Neil, Robert (1969) "Growth of the Idea of Law in Adolescence," *Developmental Psychology* 1: 327–33.
Akaneshobō (ed.) (1974) *Kodomo no koro sensō ga atta* (I experienced a war in my childhood), Tokyo: Akaneshobō.
Akiba Junichi (1960) "Soshōnōryoku no junkyohō narabini chūkyō shihaichiiki ni sekikan o yūsuru iwayuru chūgokujin no zokujinhō" (Proper Law for the Lawsuit and the *Lex Domicilii* of the Chinese Person Who Belongs to the Areas under the Jurisdiction of the People's Republic of China), *Juristo* 195: 60–1.
Alcoff, Linda (1988) "Cultural Feminism Versus Post-Structuralism: The Identity Crisis in Feminist Theory," *Signs* 13, 3: 405–36.
An Une, Murai Osamu, Watanabe Naomi, Asada Akira, and Karatani Kōjin (1994) "Sabetsu to bungaku" (Discrimination and Literature), *Hihyō kūkan* II, 2: 6–33.
Anderson, Benedict (1991) *Imagined Communities: Reflections on the Origin and Spread of Nationalism*, London: Verso.
Anderson, Perry (1976) "The Antinomies of Antonio Gramsci," *New Left Review* 100: 5–78.
Ang, Ien (1994) "On Not Speaking Chinese: Postmodern Ethnicity and the Politics of Diaspora," *New Formations* 24, Winter 1994: 1–18.
Apple, Michael (1993) *Official Knowledge*, New York: Routledge.
Arendt, Hannah (1966) *The Origins of Totalitarianism*, New York: Harcourt, Brace and World.
Asch, Solomon and Nerlove, Harriet (1960) "The Development of Double-Function Terms in Children: An Exploratory Investigation," in Bernard Kaplan and Seymour Wapner (eds) *Perspectives in Psychological Theory: Essays in Honor of Heinz Werner*, New York: International Universities Press.
Association Fighting for the Acquisition of the Human Rights of Koreans in Japan (1979) *Koreans in Japan (Ethnic Minority Problem): A Report Presented to the Division of Human Rights of the United Nations*, Kitakyūshū: Association Fighting for the Acquisition of the Human Rights of Koreans in Japan.
Bakhtin, Mikhail (1981) *The Dialogic Imagination*, Austin: University of Texas Press.
Balibar, Etienne (1991a) "The Nation Form: History and Ideology," in Etienne Balibar and Immanuel Wallerstein, *Race, Nation, Class: Ambiguous Identities*, London: Verso.

—— (1991b) "Is There a 'Neo-Racism'?," in Etienne Balibar and Immanuel Wallerstein, *Race, Nation, Class: Ambiguous Identities*, London: Verso.
Bauböck, Rainer (1994) *Transnational Citizenship: Membership and Rights in International Migration*, Aldershot: Edward Elgar.
Behar, Ruth and Gordon, Deborah (eds) (1995) *Women Writing Culture*, Berkeley: University of California Press.
Bhabha, Homi (1994) *The Location of Culture*, London: Routledge.
Bisharat, George (1997) "Exile to Compatriot: Transformations in the Social Identity of Palestinian Refugees in the West Bank," in Akhil Gupta and James Ferguson (eds) *Culture, Power, Place: Explorations in Critical Anthropology*, Durham: Duke University Press.
Block, Jeanne (1973) "Conception of Sex-Role: Some Cross-Cultural and Longitudinal Perspectives," *American Psychologist* 28: 512–26.
Bobbio, Norberto (1979) "Gramsci and the Conception of Civil Society," in Chantal Mouffe (ed.) *Gramsci and Marxist Theory*, London: Routledge and Kegan Paul.
Borges, Jorge Luis (1995) "Borges and I," in Daniel Halpern (ed.) *Who's Writing This?*, Hopewell: Ecco Press.
Bourdieu, Pierre (1991) *Language and Symbolic Power*, Cambridge: Polity Press.
Brubaker, Rogers (1992) *Citizenship and Nationalization in France and Germany*, Cambridge, Mass.: Harvard University Press.
Castles, Stephen and Miller, Mark J. (1993) *The Age of Migration: International Population Movements in the Modern World*, New York: Guilford Press.
Cave, Terence (1995) "Fictional Identities," in Henry Harris (ed.) *Identity*, Oxford: Oxford University Press.
Chambers, Iain (1994) *Migrancy, Culture, Identity*, London: Routledge.
Chang Myŏng-su (1995a) "Tokyo chōsen kōkōsei Sin Sŏn-ŏn o osotta higeki" (A Tragedy that Assaulted the Tokyo Korean High School Student, Sin Sŏn-ŏn), *Bessatsu takarajima* 221: 77–83.
—— (1995b) "Kikokujigyō wa 'jindōshugi' toiu na no tsuihōseisaku datta!?" (Was Repatriation an Exclusion Policy in the Name of Humanitarianism!?), *Bessatsu takarajima* 221: 94–106.
Chee, Choung-Il (1983) "Japan's Post-War Mass Denationalization of the Korean Minority in International Law," *Korea and World Affairs* 7: 81–113.
Chŏng A-yŏng (1997) "Tokyokei chōsenjin ga mita! Konnamon arimasuka in Osaka" (According to Koreans in Tokyo: What's Happening in Osaka?), *Horumon bunka* 7: 86–95.
Chong Ch'u-wŏl (1984) *Ikaino/onna/ai/uta* (Ikaino/Woman/Love/Poems), Osaka: Burēn sentā.
—— (1985) "Mun Konbun ŏmŏni no ningo" (Mun Kon-bun *Ŏmŏni's* Apple)," *Shinnihon bungaku* 450: 14–30.
—— (1986) *Ikaino taryon* (Ikaino Lament), Tokyo: Shisō no kagakusha.
—— (1987) *Saran he/aishite imasu* (Sarang hae/I Love You), Tokyo: Kage shobō.
Chŏng Yŏng-he (1994a) "Tsuki wa dotchini deteiru o megutte" (On *Tsuki wa dotchini deteiru*), *Gekkan kazoku* 98: 7.
—— (1994b) "Nihonjin to hinihonjin tono riaritii – gyappu koso ga mondai" (What is at Issue is the Gap Between Japanese and non-Japanese in Terms of the Perception of Reality), *Gekkan kazoku* 99: 7.
—— (1996) "Aidentitī o koete" (Beyound Identity), in Inoue Shun, Ueno Chizuko, Ōsawa Masachi, Mita Munesuke, and Yoshimi Shunya (eds) *Sabetsu to kyōsei no shakaigaku* (Sociology of Discrimination, and Co-Existence), Tokyo: Iwanami shoten.
Chou, Wan-yao (1996) "The Kōminka Movement in Taiwan and Korea: Comparisons and

Interpretations," in Peter Duus, Ramon H. Myers, and Mark Peattie (eds) *The Japanese Wartime Empire*, Princeton: Princeton University Press.

Çinar, Dilek (1994) "From Aliens to Citizens. A Comparative Analysis of Rules of Transition," in Rainer Bauböck (ed.) *From Aliens to Citizens: Redefining the Status of Immigrants in Europe*, Aldershot: Avebury.

Clifford, James (1994) "Diasporas," *Cultural Anthropology* 9, 3: 302–38.

Cumings, Bruce (1981) *The Origins of the Korean War vol. I: Liberation and the Emergence of Separate Regimes 1945–1947*, Princeton: Princeton University Press.

—— (1990) *The Origins of the Korean War vol. 2: The Roaring of the Cataract, 1947–1950*, Princeton: Princeton University Press.

—— (1997) *Korea's Place in the Sun: A Modern History*, New York: Norton.

de Certeau, Michel (1984) *The Practice of Everyday Life*, Berkeley: University of California Press.

De Vos, George and Lee, Changsoo (1981a) "Koreans and Japanese: The Formation of Ethnic Consciousness," in Changsoo Lee and George De Vos (eds) *Koreans in Japan: Ethnic Conflict and Accommodation*, Berkeley: University of California Press.

—— (1981b) "Conclusions: The Maintenance of a Korean Ethnic Identity in Japan," in Changsoo Lee and George De Vos (eds) *Koreans in Japan: Ethnic Conflict and Accommodation*, Berkeley: University of California Press.

Dong, Wonmo (1973) "Assimilation and Social Mobilization in Korea: A Study of Japanese Colonial Policy and Political Integration Effects," in Andrew C. Nahm (ed.) *Korea Under Japanese Colonial Rule*, Kalamazoo: Center for Korean Studies, Western Michigan University.

Dummett, Ann and Nicol, Andrew (1990) *Subjects, Citizens, Aliens and Others: Nationality and Immigration Law*, London: Weidenfeld and Nicolson.

Durkheim, Émile [1893] (1984) *The Division of Labor in Society*, New York: Free Press.

Duus, Peter (1995) *The Abacus and the Sword: The Japanese Penetration of Korea, 1895–1910*, Berkeley: University of California Press.

Eckert, Carter, Lee, Ki-baik, Lew, Young Ick, Robinson, Michael, and Wagner, Edward (eds) (1990) *Korea Old and New*, Seoul: Ilchokak.

Egawa Hidefumi and Sawaki Yoshirō (1958) "Heiwajōyaku ni yoru chōsen no dokuritsu no shōnin to chōsenkokuseki o shutokushita nihonjin no hani" (On the Independence of Korea by the Peace Treaty and the Scope of Japanese Nationals Who Acquired Korean Nationality), *Jurisuto* 161: 66–7.

Erikson, Erik (1958) *Young Man Luther*, New York: Norton.

—— (1968) *Identity: Youth and Crisis*, New York: Norton.

—— [1950] (1985) *Childhood and Society*, New York: Norton.

Field, Norma (1993) "Beyond Envy, Boredom, and Suffering: Towards an Emancipatory Politics for Resident Koreans and Other Japanese," *positions* 1, 3: 640–70.

Flaubert, Gustave [1857] (1993) *Madame Bovary*, New York: Knopf.

Foucault, Michel (1985) *History of Sexuality, vol. One: An Introduction*, New York: Vintage.

Fujisaki Machiyo (1990) "Gakkō to seikatsu" (School and Life), in Mutō Takashi *et al.*, *Hattatsu shinrigaku nyūmon I* (An Introuction to Developmental Psychology I), Tokyo: Tokyodaigaku shuppankai.

Fukuoka Yasunori and Kim Myŏng-su (1997) *Zainichi kankokujin seinen no seikatsu to ishiki* (Life and Consciousness of Korean Youth in Japan), Tokyo: Tokyodaigaku shuppankai.

Fukuoka Yasunori and Tsujiyama Yukiko (1991) *Hontō no watashi o motomete* (In Search of True Self), Tokyo: Shinkansha.

Giddens, Anthony (1990) *The Consequences of Modernity*, Cambridge: Polity Press.

Gilroy, Paul (1990) "It Ain't Where You Are From, It's Where You Are At. . . . The

Dialectics of Diasporic Identification," *Third Text* 13, Winter 1990: 3–16.
—— (1993) *The Black Atlantic: Modernity and Double Consciousness*, Cambridge, Mass.: Harvard University Press.
Gluck, Carol (1985) *Japan's Modern Myth: Ideology in the Late Meiji Period*, Princeton: Princeton University Press.
Gohl, Gerhard (1976) *Die koreanische Minderheit in Japan als Fall einer "politisch–ethnischen" Minderheitengruppe*, Wiesbaden: Otto Harrassowitz.
Gordon, Avery (1995) "The Work of Corporate Culture: Diversity Management," *Social Text* 44: 3–30.
Gramsci, Antonio (1971) *Selections from the Prison Notebooks*, New York: International Publishers.
Green, Andy (1990) *Education and State Formation: The Rise of Education Systems in England, France, and the USA*, New York: St Martins Press.
Hall, Stuart (1990) "Cultural Identity and Diaspora," in Jonathan Rutherford (ed.) *Identity: Community, Culture, Difference*, London: Lawrence and Wishart.
—— (1992) "The West and the Rest: Discourse and Power," in Stuart Hall and Bram Gieben (eds) *Formations of Modernity*, Cambridge: Polity Press.
—— (1996a) "When Was 'The Post-Colonial'? Thinking at the Limit," in Iain Chambers and Lidia Curti (eds) *The Post-Colonial Question: Common Skies, Divided Horizon*, London: Routledge.
—— (1996b) "New Ethnicities," in David Morley and Kuan-Hsing Chen (eds) *Stuart Hall: Critical Dialogues in Cultural Studies*, London: Routledge.
—— (1996c) "What Is This 'Black' in Black Popular Culture?," in David Morley and Kuan-Hsing Chen (eds) *Stuart Hall: Critical Dialogues in Cultural Studies*, London: Routledge.
—— (1996d) "Who Needs 'Identity'?," in Stuart Hall and Paul du Gay (eds) *Questions of Cultural Identity*, London: Sage.
—— (1997) "The Spectacle of the 'Other,'" in Stuart Hall (ed.) *Representation: Cultural Representations and Signifying Practices*, London: Sage.
Halliday, Jon and Cumings, Bruce (1988) *Korea: The Unknown War*, London: Viking.
Hamamoto Mariko (1995) "Hito wa ikanishite mizukara ga umaresodatta basho de ihōjintariuruka: Zainichi chōsenjin no nanori no mondai" (How Could a Person Be a Foreigner in Her Own Place of Birth?: A Question of the Declaration of Ethnic Names of Koreans in Japan), in Nakauchi Toshio and Nagashima Nobuhiro *et al.*, *Shakaikihan – tabū to hōshō* (Social Norm: Tabu and Reward), *Sōsho: Umu, sodateru, oshieru – tokumei no kyōikushi* (Series: Birth, Rearing, Teaching: the Anonymous History of Education), Tokyo: Fujiwara shoten.
Hammar, Tomas (1990) *Democracy and the Nation State: Aliens, Denizens and Citizens in a World of International Migration*, Aldershot: Avebury.
Hanami, Makiko (1995) "Minority Dynamics in Japan: Towards a Society of Sharing," in John Maher and Gaynor Macdonald (eds) *Diversity in Japanese Culture and Language*, London: Kegan Paul International.
Hara Masaru (1996) "Kokusaikekkon to kika" (International Marriage and Naturalization), *Minji geppō* 51, 6: 3–6.
Harajiri Hideki (1997) *Nihon teijū korian no nichijō to seikatsu: Bunkajinruigakuteki apurōchi* (The Daily Lives and Livelihood of Koreans Permanently Living in Japan: An Anthropological Approach), Tokyo: Akashi shoten.
Harvey, David (1990) *The Condition of Postmodernity*, Oxford: Blackwell.
Hayashi Eidai (1989) *Kesareta chōsenjin kyōseirenkō no kiroku* (The Erased Document of Forced Labor Mobilization of Koreans), Tokyo: Akashi shoten.

212 Bibliography

Hayashi Mariko (1997) "Mariko no iwasete gomen!" (Mariko's "Sorry, but I must say it!") 78, *Shūkan asahi* March 1997: 48–52.

Hayata Yoshirō (1965) "Chūgokujin, chōsenjin no hongokuhō no kettei" (On Defining the *Lex Domicilii* of Chinese and Koreans), *Bessatsu jurisuto* 4: 206–7.

Hein, Laura and Selden, Mark (eds) (1998) *Textbook Nationalism, Citizenship, and War: Comparative Perspectives, Bulletin of Concerned Asian Scholars* 30, 2.

Hino Keizō (1989) "Shinise bungakushō 100 kaime – yorokobi ikkyo yonin – Akutagawa/Naoki" (The 100th Anniversary of the Established Literary Awards, Akutagawa and Naoki – Four Recipients' Sudden Joy), *Asahi shinbun* 13 January 1989.

Hirakatashi (1996) *Hirakata tōkeisho* (Statistics of Hirakata), Hirakata: Hirakatashi.

Hirakatashi kyōikuiinkai (ed.) (1993) *Zainichi chōsenjin no rekishi: Hirakata deno horiokoshi no tameni* (History of Koreans in Japan: For Digging up Their History in Hirakata), Hirakata : Hirakatashi kyōikuiinkai.

—— (1997) *Watashitachino machi Hirakata* (Our Town Hirakata), Hirakata: Hirakatashi Kyōikuiinkai.

Hirakatashi tabunken (Hirakatashi tabunka kyōseikyōiku kenkyūkai) (1997) *1997 nendo tabunka kyōseikyōiku kenkyūkatsudō kadai* (Research Themes for Multicultural Education in 1997), Hirakata: Hirakatashi tabunka kyōseikyōiku kenkyūkai jimukyoku.

Hiroyama Shibaaki (1955) "Minsen no kaisan to chōsensōren no keisei ni tsuite" (Dissolution of Minjŏn and Emergence of Chongryun), *Kōan jōhō* 22: 5–11.

"Hitosashiyubi no jiyū" henshūiinkai (1984) *Hitosashiyubi no jiyū* (Freedom of the Index Finger), Tokyo: Shakai hyōronsha.

Hosoya Toshio *et al.* (1974) *Shakai 6 jō* (Social Studies part 1 of volume 6), Tokyo: Kyōiku shuppan.

Hume, David [1740] (1978) *A Treatise of Human Nature*, Oxford: Oxford University Press.

Hwang Min-gi (1992) "Rikidōzan densetsu" (The Legend of Rikidōzan), *Oruta* 1: 49–57.

—— (1993) *Yatsura ga naku maeni* (Before They Cry), Tokyo: Chikuma shobō.

Inaba Toshio (1975) "Kika to kosekijō no shori" (Naturalization and the Administration of Family Registry), *Koseki* 357: 1–7.

Inagaki Kayoko and Hatano Giyoo (1986) "Gijinka ni yoru ruisui no kōyō to genkai" (Effects and Limits of Guessing by Personification Employed by Children), in *Nihon kyōikushinrigakkai dai 28 kai sōkai happyō ronbunshū*, Fukuoka: Nihon kyōikushinrigakkai dai 28 kai sōkai junbiiinkai.

Inatomi Susumu (1988) *Mugunfa no kaori* (The Fragrance of the Rose of Sharon), Tokyo: Aki shobō.

Inokuchi, Hiromitsu (1996) "The Finger-Printing Rejection Movement Reconsidered," *Japanese Society* 1: 77–105.

—— (1998) "An Examination of 'Internationalization' from the Perspective of Korean Residents in Japan," *Global Connection* 6, 2: 2–6.

Inoue Masutarō (1956) *Zainichi chōsenjin kikokumondai no shinsō* (The Facts about Repatriation of Koreans in Japan), Tokyo: Nihon sekijūjisha.

Ishii Motosuke *et al.* (1977) *Shakai 6 jō* (Social Studies part 1 of volume 6), Tokyo: Kyōiku shuppan.

—— (1983) *Shakai 6 jō* (Social Studies part 1 of volume 6), Tokyo: Kyōiku shuppan.

—— (1986) *Shakai 6 jō* (Social Studies part 1 of volume 6), Tokyo: Kyōiku shuppan.

Itō Mitsuharu *et al.* (1996) *Shakai 6 ge* (Social Studies part 2 of volume 6), Tokyo: Kyōiku shuppan.

Itō Narihiko (1995) *Jihyō toshite no bungaku: 1984–1995* (Literature as the Sign of the Times: 1984–1995), Tokyo: Ocha no mizu shobō.

Iwabuchi, Koichi (1994) "Complicit Exoticism: Japan and its Other," *Continuum* 8, 2:49–82.
—— (1998) "Pure Impurity: Japan's Genius for Hybridism," *Communal/Plural: Journal of Transnational and Crosscultural Studies* 6, 1: 71–86.
Jameson, Fredric (1995) *Postmodernism: Or, the Cultural Logic of Late Capitalism*, Durham: Duke University Press.
Johnson, Mark (1993) *Moral Imagination: Implications of Cognitive Science for Ethics*, Chicago: University of Chicago Press.
Kaihōkyōiku kenkyūjo (1997a) *Ningen 1* (Human 1), Tokyo: Meiji tosho shuppan.
—— (1997b) *Ningen 4* (Human 4), Tokyo: Meiji tosho shuppan.
—— (1997c) *Ningen 5* (Human 5), Tokyo: Meiji tosho shuppan.
Kajita Takamichi (1996) "Gaikokujin sanseiken" (Voting Rights of Resident Foreigners), in Miyajima Takeshi and Kajita Takamichi (eds) *Gaikokujinrōdōsha kara shimin e* (From Foreign Workers to Citizens), Tokyo: Yūhikaku.
Kaneko, Ann (1995) "In Search of Ruby Moreno," *AMPO Japan-Asia Quarterly Review* 25, 4/26, 1: 66–70.
Kang Chae-ŏn (1986) *Chōsen Kindaishi* (Modern History of Korea), Tokyo: Heibonsha.
Kang Chae-ŏn and Kim Tong-hun (1989) *Zainichi kankokuchōsenjin: Rekishi to tenbō* (Koreans in Japan: History and Future Perspectives), Tokyo: Rōdō keizaisha.
Kang Sang-jung (1988) "Hōhō toshite no 'zainichi' – Yang T'ae-hoshi ni kotaeru" ('Zainichi' as Method – In Response to Yang T'ae-ho), in Iinuma Jirō (ed.) *Zainichi kankuchōsenjin – sono nihon ni okeru sonzaikachi* (Resident Koreans: The Value of Their Existence in Japanese Society), Tokyo: Kaifūsha.
Kaplan, Caren (1996) *Questions of Travel: Postmodern Discourses of Displacement*, Durham: Duke University Press.
Karatani, Kojin (1993) *Origins of Modern Japanese Literature*, Durham: Duke University Press.
Katō Norihiro, Ōnuma Yasuaki, Watanabe Hiroshi, and Satō Shinichi (1990) "Wareware nihonjin no jimeisei o ikani kaitaisuruka" (How to Deconstruct the Self-Evidence of Our Japaneseness), in Ōnuma Yasuaki (ed.) *Kokusaika: Utsukushii gokai ga umu seika* (Internationalisation: Fruits of Beautiful Mutual Misunderstanding), Tokyo: Tōshindō.
Kawai Hayao (ed.) (1996) *Ijime, kokoro no kagaku tokubetsukikaku* (Bullying: Special Issue on Science of Human Mind), Tokyo: Nihon hyōronsha.
Kawamura Minato (1994) *Umi o watatta nihongo: Shokuminchi no "kokugo" no jikan* (The Japanese That Went Across the Ocean: The "National Language" Classes in the Colonies), Tokyo: Seitosha.
Keats, John (1990) *John Keats (Oxford Authors)*, Oxford: Oxford University Press.
Kerby, Anthony Paul (1991) *Narrative and the Self*, Bloomington: Indiana University Press.
Kim Byŏng-sik (1959a) "Kunan to konkyū no donzoko ni aegu zainichi chōsenjin no seikatsujittai" (The Reality of Poverty and Hard Livelihood of Koreans in Japan) 1, *Chōsen mondai kenkyū* 3, 2: 21–30.
—— (1959a) "Kunan to konkyū no donzoko ni aegu zainichi chōsenjin no seikatsu jittai" (The Reality of Poverty and Hard Livelihood of Koreans in Japan) 2, *Chōsen mondai kenkyū* 3, 3: 41–60.
Kim Ch'an-jŏng (1980a) *Boku mō gamandekinaiyo* (I Cannot Stand It Any Longer), Tokyo: Ikkōsha.
—— (1980b) *Zoku boku mō gamandekinaiyo* (I Cannot Stand it Any Longer: Second series), Tokyo: Ikkōsha.
—— (1994) *Zainichi toiu kandō* (Residing in Japan Is Exciting), Tokyo: Sangokan.
Kim Ch'ang-saeng (1982) *Watashino Ikaino: Zainichi ni totteno sokoku to ikoku* (My Ikaino: Homeland and Foreign Country as Seen by *Zainichi*), Nagoya: Fūbaisha.

―― (1985) "Zainichi chōsenjin no kurashi/seikatsu" (Resident Koreans' Daily Life), in Kim Yong-gwŏn and Yi Chŏng-yang (eds) *Zainichi kankokuchōsenjin: Wakamono kara mita iken to omoi to kangae* (Resident Koreans: The Opinions, Feelings, and Thoughts of Young People), Tokyo: Sanichi shobō.

―― (1987) "Akai mi" (The Red Fruit), *Mintō* 3: 256–76.

Kim Dŏk-hwan shi no gaitōhōsaiban o shiensuru kai (1990) *Igyora! (Ganbare!): Tokkansan no shimonsaiban (Igyŏra!* [Win!]: Tokkansan's Fingerprinting Trial), Tokyo: Shinkansha.

Kim Il Sung (1972) *Chongryun ilkundŭl gwa chaeiltonp'odŭl ege jusin Kim Il Sung wŏnsu ŭi kyosi* (The Teachings of Marshal Kim Il Sung given to Chongryun Workers and Koreans in Japan), Tokyo: Chongryun chungang sagim wuiwŏnhoe.

Kim Kyŏng-hae (1995) "4.24 kyōikutōsō" (The April 24 Educational Struggle), *Horumon bunka* 5: 183–96.

Kim Kyŏng-hwan (1988) "4.24 kyōikutosō no omoide" (The Memory of the April 24 Educational Struggle), in Kim Kyŏng-hae (ed.) *Zainichi chōsenjin minzokukyōiku yōgotōsō shiryōshū* (Collected Documents on the Struggle to Defend Korean Ethnic Education in Japan), vol. 1, Tokyo: Akashi shoten.

Kim Si-jong (1975) "Ikaino shishū" (Ikaino poems) 1, *Sanzenri sōkangō*, February 1975: 183–93.

Kim T'ae-gi (1997) *Sengo nihonseiji to zainichi chōsenjin mondai* (Postwar Japanese Politics and the Issue of Koreans in Japan), Tokyo: Keisō shobō.

Kim U-sŏng (1994) "Yun no machi kara no shuppatu, soshite hikari e" (Departure from *Yun no machi* and towards *Hikari*), in Wan koria fesutibaru jikkōiinkai (ed.) *Wan koria* (One Korea), Osaka: Tōhō shuppan.

Kim Yŏng-dal (1990) *Zainichi chōsenjin no kika* (The Naturalization of Koreans in Japan), Tokyo: Akashi shoten.

―― (1991) "Dainijitaisenchū no chōsenjin senjidōin ni tsuite" (On Wartime Mobilization of Koreans During World War II), in Sengo hoshō mondai kenkyūkai (eds) *Zainichi kankokuchōsenjin no sengohoshō* (Postwar Compensation for Koreans in Japan), Tokyo: Akashi shoten.

―― (1996) "Hoshō: Kaisetsu to tōkei no hosoku" (Supplement: Commentary and Addition to Statistics), in Morita Yoshio, *Sūji ga kataru zainichi kankokuchōsenjin no rekishi* (The History of Resident Koreans Illustrated by Statistics), Tokyo: Akashi shoten.

Kim Yŏng-dal and Takayanagi Toshio (eds) (1995) *Kitachōsen kikokujigyō kankei shiryōshū* (Collected Documents on the Repatriation to North Korea), Tokyo: Shinkansha.

Kim Yŏng-hae (1996) *Honmyō wa minzoku no hokori* (Real Names Are the Nation's Pride), Osaka: Midorikawa shobō.

Kinoshita Yoshiko (1990) "Shakaiteki ninchi" (Social Cognition), in Mutō Takashi *et al.* (eds.) *Hattatsu shinrigaku nyūmon I* (An Introduction to Developmental Psychology I), Tokyo: Tokyodaigaku shuppankai.

Kishino Junko (1985) *Jiritsu to kyōzon no kyōiku* (Education for Independence and Co-Existence), Tokyo: Hakujusha.

Kitada Sachie (1987) "'Zainichi' suru 'ba' no imi" (The Meaning of the '*Zainichi*' Space'), *Mintō* 1: 107–14.

Ko Ch'an-yu (1996) *Kokusaikajidai no minzokukyōiku* (Ethnic Education in the Age of Internationalization), Osaka: Tōhō shuppan.

Kobayashi Tomoko (1994) "GHQ no zainichi chōsenjin ninshiki ni kansuru ichi kōsatsu: G-2 minkan chōhōkyoku teikihōkokusho o chūshin ni" (A Study of GHQ's Perspective on Koreans in Japan: Evidence from G-2 Intelligence Agency Regular Reports), *Chōsenshi kenkyūkai ronbunshū* 32: 165–92.

Kohlberg, Laurence (1976) "Moral Stages and Moralization: The Cognitive–Developmental Approach," in Thomas Lickona (ed.) *Moral Development and Behavior*, New York: Holt, Rinehart and Winston.

Komagome Takeshi (1996) *Shokuminchi teikoku nihon no bunkateki tōgō* (The Cultural Integration of the Colonial Empire Japan), Tokyo: Iwanami shoten.

Kondō Atsushi (1996) *"Gaikokujin" no sanseiken: Denizunshippu no hikakukenkyū* (Voting Rights of Foreigners: A Comparative Study of Denizenship), Tokyo: Akashi shoten.

Kondo, Dorinne (1996) "The Narrative Production of 'Home,' Community, and Political Identity in Asian American Theater," in Smadar Lavie and Ted Swedenburg (eds) *Displacement, Diaspora, and Geographies of Identity*, Durham: Duke University Press.

Kōseishō engokyoku (1968) *Hikiage to engo 30 nen no ayumi* (Thirty Years of Repatriation and Its Assistance), Tokyo: Gyōsei.

Kristeva, Julia (1986) "Women's Time," in Toril Moi (ed.) *The Kristeva Reader*, Oxford: Oxford University Press.

Ku Wŏn-ho (1960) "P'yŏnji" (Letter), in Tokyo chosŏn chunggogŭp hakkyo (ed.) *Choguk ŭi p'um anesŏ: Kwiguk haksaeng p'yŏnjijip* (In the Bosom of the Fatherland: Letters from the Repatriated Students), Tokyo: Tokyo chosŏn chunggogŭp hakkyo.

Kuboi Norio (1988) *Nyūmon chōsen to nihon no rekishi* (Introduction to the History Between Korea and Japan), Tokyo: Akashi shoten.

Kuroto Kazuo (1987) "Zainichi chōsenjin bungaku no genzai" (Zainichi Korean Literature Today), *Mintō* 1: 86–97.

Kuwata Saburō (1959) "Iwayuru kitachōsenjin no otto ni taisuru rikonseikyū no junkyohō" (Proper Law for Divorce Cases in Which the Husband Is Assumed to Be a North Korean), *Jurisuto* 189: 72–4.

—— (1960) "Nikka heiwajōyaku 10 jō no kaishaku, chūgokujin ni okeru hongokuhō no tekiyōmondai" (Interpretation of Article 10 of the Sino-Japanese Peace Treaty and the Question of the *Lex Domicilii* of the Chinese), *Jurisuto* 203: 83–4.

Kyō Nobuko (1987) *Goku futsū no zainichi kankokujin* (An Ordinary South Korean in Japan), Tokyo: Asahi shinbunsha.

——(1990) *Watashi no ekkyōressun: Kankoku hen* (My Lesson for Transnationalism: South Korea), Tokyo: Asahi shinbunsha.

—— (1994) "Kono yo no dokonimo nai kotoba o sagashitai" (Looking for a New Way of Representing Koreanness in Japan), in Li Bong-u (ed.) *Tsuki wa dotchini deteiru o meguru nisan no hanashi* (A Couple of Stories Around *Tsuki wa dotchini deteiru*), Tokyo: Shakai hyōronsha.

Kyŏng-nam (Pak Kyŏng-nam) (1992) *Pokkari tsuki ga demashitara* (When the Moon Shines Bright), Tokyo: Sangokan.

—— (1995) *Watashino sukina Matsumotosan* (Mr Matsumoto I So Like), Tokyo: Sangokan.

Larkin, Philip [1971] (1988) "This Be the Verse," in Philip Larkin, *Collected Poems*, London: Marvell Press.

Lee, Changsoo (1981) "The Legal Status of Koreans in Japan," in Changsoo Lee and George De Vos (eds) *Koreans in Japan: Ethnic Conflict and Accommodation*, Berkeley: University of California Press.

Lee, Changsoo and De Vos, George (eds) (1981) *Koreans in Japan: Ethnic Conflict and Accommodation*, Berkeley: University of California Press.

Lee Seijaku (1997) *Zainichi kankokujin sansei no mune no uchi* (Inner Thoughts of a Third-Generation Korean in Japan), Tokyo: Sōshisha.

Lee Yeounsuk (1996) *"Kokugo" to iu shisō* (The "National Language" as Ideology), Tokyo: Iwanami shoten.

Lewis, Catherine C. (1995) *Educating Hearts and Minds: Reflections on Japanese*

Preschool and Elementary Education, New York: Cambridge University Press.
Li Dong-sun (1956) *Nihon ni iru chōsen no kodomo* (Korean Children in Japan), Tokyo: Shunjusha.
Li Sang-t'e (1993) "Tsuki wa dotchini deteiru: Nan no hakken mo nai eiga" (There is no New Finding in *Tsuki wa dotchini deteiru*), *Minkenkyō News* 35: 22.
Lie, John (forthcoming) "The Discourse of Japaneseness and Foreign Workers," in Michael Douglass and Glenda Roberts (eds) *Japan and Global Migration*, London: Routledge.
Lienhardt, Godfrey (1985) "Self: Public, Private. Some African Representations," in Michael Carrithers, Steven Collins, and Steven Lukes (eds) *The Category of the Person: Anthropology, Philosophy, History*, Cambridge: Cambridge University Press.
Locke, John [1689] (1975) *An Essay Concerning Human Understanding*, Oxford: Oxford University Press.
Lowe, Lisa (1996) *Immigrant Acts: On Asian-American Cultural Politics*, Durham: Duke University Press.
Lowitz, Leza and Aoyama, Miyuki (1995) *Other Side River: Free Verse*, Berkeley: Stone Bridge Press.
Maher, John and Macdonald, Gaynor (eds) (1995) *Diversity in Japanese Culture and Language*, London: Kegan Paul International.
Malamud, Bernard [1977] (1979) *Dubin's Lives*, London: Chatto and Windus.
Marshall, Byron (1994) *Learning to Be Modern: Japanese Political Discourses in Education*, Boulder: Westview Press.
Mashiko Hidenori (1997) *Ideorogī toshiteno "nihon": "Kokugo" "nihonshi" no chishiki shakaigaku* ("Japan" as Ideology: Sociology of Knowledge of the "National Language" and "National History"), Tokyo: Sangensha.
Massey, Doreen (1994) *Space, Place, and Gender*, Minneapolis: University of Minnesota Press.
Matsuda Toshihiko (1995) *Senzenki no zainichi chōsenjin to sanseiken* (Prewar Koreans in Japan and Their Voting Rights), Tokyo: Akashi shoten.
Matsumoto Kunihiko (1988) "Zainichi chōsenjin no nihonkokuseki hakudatsu" (The Deprivation of Japanese Nationality from Koreans in Japan), *Hōgaku* 52, 4: 111–45.
McClintock, Anne (1992) "The Angel of Progress: Pitfalls of the Term 'Post-Colonialism,'" *Social Text* 31/32: 84–98.
Milner, Jean-Claude (1983) *Les Noms Indistincts*, Paris: Editions du Seuil.
Min Gwan-sik (1994) *Zainichi kankokujin no genjō to mirai* (Present and Future of Koreans in Japan), Tokyo: Hakuteisha.
Minsokkyō (Minzokukyōiku sokushinkyōgikai) (1997) *Minzokukyōiku wa mirai o hiraku* (Ethnic Education Will Open up the Future), Osaka: Minzokukyōiku sokushinkyōgikai.
Mitchell, Richard H. (1967) *The Korean Minority in Japan*, Berkeley: University of California Press.
Miyata Setsuko (1985) *Chōsenminshū to "kōminka" seisaku* (The Korean People and the Policy of "Making Them into the Emperor's Subjects"), Tokyo: Miraisha.
—— (1990) "*Sōshikaimei* ni tsuite" (On *sōshikaimei*), *Rekishi hyōron* 486: 46–62.
—— (1992) "*Sōshikaimei* no jisshikatei" (The Enforcement Process of *sōshikaimei*), in Miyata Setsuko, Kim Yŏng-dal, and Yang T'ae-ho, *Sōshikaimei* (Creating Japanese-Style Names and Reforming Korean Names), Tokyo: Akashi shoten.
Miyata Setsuko, Kim Yŏng-dal, and Yang T'ae-ho (1992) *Sōshikaimei* (Creating Japanese-Style Names and Reforming Korean Names), Tokyo: Akashi shoten.
Miyoshi, Masao and Harootunian, Harry (eds) (1989) *Postmodernism and Japan*, Durham: Duke University Press.
Mizuno Naoki (1993) "Shokuminchi shihai no jitsuzō" (The Reality of the Colonial Rule),

in Hirakatashi kyōikuiinkai (ed.) *Zainichi chōsenjin no rekishi: Hirakata deno horiokoshi no tameni* (History of Koreans in Japan: For Digging up Their History in Hirakata), Hirakata: Hirakatashi kyōikuiinkai.

—— (1996) "Zainichi chōsenjin, taiwanjin sanseiken 'teishi' jōkō no seiritsu" (The Stipulation of the Suspension of Voting Rights Held by Resident Koreans and Taiwanese) 1, *Sekai jinkenmondai kenkyūsentā kenkyū kiyō* 1: 43–65.

—— (1997) "Zainichi chōsenjin, taiwanjin sanseiken 'teishi' jōkō no seiritsu" (The Stipulation of the Suspension of Voting Rights Held by Resident Koreans and Taiwanese) 2, *Sekai jinkenmondai kenkyūsentā kenkyū kiyō* 2: 59–82.

Modell, Arnold (1993) *The Private Self*, Cambridge, Mass.: Harvard University Press.

Moriki Kazumi (1995) *Kokuseki no arika: Bōdāresujidai no jinken towa* (The Place of Nationality: Human Rights in the Borderless Age), Tokyo: Akashi shoten.

Morita Yoshio (1955) *Zainichi chōsenjin shogū no suii to genjō* (Changes in and the Current Situation of the Treatment of Koreans in Japan), Tokyo: Hōmu kenshūjo.

—— (1968) "Senzen ni okeru zainichi chōsenjin no jinkōtōkei" (Prewar Demography of Koreans in Japan), *Chōsen gakuhō* 48: 63–77.

—— (1996) *Sūji ga kataru zainichi kankokuchōsenjin no rekishi* (The History of Resident Koreans Illustrated by Statistics), Tokyo: Akashi shoten.

Morris-Suzuki, Tessa (1995) "Becoming Japanese: Imperial Expansion and Identity Crises in the Early Twentieth Century," paper presented at the Ninth Biennial Conference of the Japanese Studies Association of Australia.

—— (1998) *Re-inventing Japan*, Armonk: M. E. Sharpe.

Mun Kyŏng-su (1995) "Zainichi chōsenjin ni totteno 'sengo'" (The Meaning of the 'Postwar Time' for Koreans in Japan), in Nakamura Masanori, Amakawa Akira, Yun Kŏn-ch'a, and Igarashi Takeshi (eds) *Kako no seisan* (Clearing the Past), Tokyo: Iwanami shoten.

—— (1996) "Kōdo keizai seichōka no zainichi chōsenjin" (Koreans in Japan under Japan's High Economic Boom), in Kang Chae-ŏn et al., *"Zainichi" wa ima* (What "Zainichi" Are Now), Tokyo: Seikyū bunkasha.

Murai Osamu (1995) *Nantōideorogī no hassei* (The Genesis of the "Southern Islands" Ideology), Tokyo: Ōta shuppan.

Nakamura Kikuji (1992) *Kyōkasho no shakaishi* (Social History of Textbooks), Tokyo: Iwanami shoten.

Nakayama Hideo (ed.) (1995) *Zainichi chōsenjin kyōikukankei shiryōshū* (Collected Documents on the Education of Koreans in Japan), Tokyo: Akashi shoten.

Narige Tetsuji (1964a) "Zainichi chōsenjin oyobi chūgokujin ni tekiyōsubeki hongokuhō" (The *Lex Domicilii* to be Applied to Koreans and Chinese in Japan) 1, *Minji geppō* 19, 7: 81–96.

—— (1964b) "Zainichi chōsenjin oyobi chūgokujin ni tekiyōsubeki hongokuhō" (The *Lex Domicilii* to Be Applied to Koreans and Chinese in Japan) 2, *Minji geppō* 19, 8: 17–49.

Neary, Ian (1997) "Burakumin in Contemporary Japan," in Michael Weiner (ed.) *Japan's Minorities: The Illusion of Homogeneity*, London: Routledge.

Nishibe Susumu, Mishima Hiroshi, Hwang Min-gi, and Kyō Nobuko (1996) "Sōshitsu no jidai narebakoso" (Let's Talk about the Age of Loss), *Ronza* 2, 9: 30–41.

Nishino Rumiko (1992) *Jūgunianfu: Moto heishitachi no shōgen* (Army Prostitutes: Testimonies of Former Soldiers), Tokyo: Akashi shoten.

Nishinarita Yutaka (1997) *Zainichi chōsenjin no "sekai" to "teikoku" kokka* (The World of Koreans in Japan and the Imperial State), Tokyo: Tokyodaigaku shuppankai.

Noguchi Michihiko (1996) "Burakusabetsu no genjōninshiki no zure to kaihō no senryaku" (Gaps in the Perception of Buraku Discrimination and Strategies for Liberation), in Yagi Tadashi (ed.) *Hisabetsusekai to shakaigaku* (Sociology and the World of the Discriminated), Tokyo: Akashi shoten.

Bibliography

Nomura Susumu (1996) *Korian sekai no tabi* (Journey to Korean Communities Around the World), Tokyo: Kōdansha.

Norman, E. Herbert (1973) *Japan's Emergence as a Modern State*, Westport: Greenwood Press.

Nozaki, Yoshiko, and Inokuchi, Hiromitsu (forthcoming) "The Korean Ethnic Education Movements in Japan: An International Perspective for the Education of Immigrant and Ethnic Minority Students," *Social Education*.

Nyūkoku kanrikyoku (1964) *Shutsunyūkoku kanri to sono jittai* (Immigration Control and Its Reality), Tokyo: Hōmushō.

—— (1976) *Shutsunyūkoku kanri – sono genkyō to kadai* (Immigration Control: Current Situation and Future Tasks), Tokyo: Hōmushō.

Ochi Michio (1994) "Senjutsu toshiteno *Tsuki wa dotchini deteiru*" (*Tsuki wa dotchini deteiru* as a Strategy to Laugh off Discrimination), *Takarajima* 30, March 1994: 106–15.

Ogawa Masaaki (1985) "Zainichi gaikokujin no shakaihoshō hōseijō no jōkyō" (The Legal Status of Resident Aliens in the Social Security System), *Hōritsu jihō* 57, 5: 43–55.

Oguma Eiji (1995) *Tanitsu minzoku shinwa no kigen* (The Origin of the Myth of the Homogeneous Nation), Tokyo: Shinyōsha.

—— (1998) *"Nihonjin" no kyōkai* (The Boundaries of the Japanese), Tokyo: Shinyōsha.

Okamoto Masakiyo (1990) "'Shukkoku, kikoku no kenrisengen' to teijūgaikokujin no kyojūkoku ni kaeru kenri" ('Declaration of the Rights for Departure and Re-entry' and the Rights for Resident Aliens to Return to the Country of Residence), *Hōritsu jihō* 62, 7: 34–40.

Ong, Aihwa (1996) "Cultural Citizenship as Subject–Making," *Current Anthropology* 37, 5: 737–62.

Ong, Aihwa and Nonini, Donald (eds) (1997) *Ungrounded Empires: The Cultural Politics of Modern Chinese Transnationalism*, London: Routledge.

Ōnuma Yasuaki (1978) "Shutsunyūkoku kanri hōsei no seiritsukatei" (The Process of the Establishment of the Immigration Control System) 1, *Hōristu jihō* 50, 4: 89–96.

—— (1979a) "Zainichi chōsenjin no hōtekichii ni kansuru ichi kōsatsu" (A Study of the Legal Status of Resident Koreans in Japan) 1, *Hōgaku kyōkai zasshi* 96, 3: 266–315.

—— (1979b) "Zainichi chōsenjin no hōtekichii ni kansuru ichi kōsatsu" (A Study of the Legal Status of Resident Koreans in Japan) 2, *Hōgaku kyōkai zasshi* 96, 5: 529–96.

—— (1979c) "Zainichi chōsenjin no hōtekichii ni kansuru ichi kōsatsu" (A Study of the Legal Status of Resident Koreans in Japan) 3, *Hōgaku kyōkai zasshi* 96, 8: 911–80.

—— (1979d) "Shutsunyūkoku kanri hōsei no seiritsukatei" (The Process of the Establishment of the Immigration Control System) 14, *Hōritsu jihō* 51, 5: 100–6.

—— (1980a) "Zainichi chōsenjin no hōtekichii ni kansuru ichi kōsatsu" (A Study of the Legal Status of Resident Koreans in Japan) 4, *Hōgaku kyōkai zasshi* 97, 2: 192–269.

—— (1980b)"Zainichi chōsenjin no hōtekichii ni kansuru ichi kōsatsu" (A Study of the Legal Status of Resident Koreans in Japan) 5, *Hōgaku kyōkai zasshi* 97, 3: 279–330.

—— (1980c) "Zainichi chōsenjin no hōtekichii ni kansuru ichi kōsatsu" (A Study of the Legal Status of Resident Koreans in Japan) 6, *Hōgaku kyōkai zasshi* 97, 4: 455–536.

—— (1986) *Tanitsu minzoku shakai no shinwa o koete* (Beyond the Myth of Single-Ethnic Society), Tokyo: Tōshindō.

—— (1992) "Interplay Between Human Rights Activities and Legal Standards of Human Rights: A Case Study on the Korean Minority in Japan," *Cornell International Law Journal* 25: 515–33.

Osakafu (1998) "Zainichi kankokuchōsenjin mondai ni kansuru shidō no shishin" (Guidelines for Approaching Issues Regarding Koreans in Japan), in Yonniyon Hanshin kyōikutōsō 50 shūnenkinen jigyōiinkai (ed.) *Shinno kyōseishakai wa minzokukyōiku no hoshōkara!* (The True Society of Co-Existence Comes after Ethnic Education Is

Guaranteed!), Osaka: Yonniyon Hanshin kyōikutōsō 50 shūnenkinen jigyōiinkai.
Osakafu zainichi gaikokujin kyōiku kenkyūkyōgikai (1996) *21 seiki o tenbōsuru tabunka kyōseikyōiku no kōsō* (The Plan for Multi-Cultural Education for the 21st Century), Yao: Osaka zainichi gaikokujin kyōiku kenkyūkyōgikai.
Osakashi (1998) "Osakashi gaikokuseki jūmin shisaku kihonshishin – kyōseishakai no jitsugen o mezashite" (Osaka City's Fundamental Guidelines for Measures Regarding Foreign Residents), in Yonniyon Hanshin kyōikutōsō 50 shūnenkinen jigyōiinkai (ed.) *Shinno kyōseishakai wa minzokukyōiku no hoshōkara!* (The True Society of Co-Existence Comes after Ethnic Education Is Guaranteed!), Osaka: Yonniyon Hanshin kyōikutōsō 50 shūnenkinen jigyōiinkai.
O'Sullivan, Tim, Hartley, John, Saunders, Danny, Montgomery, Martin, and Fiske, John (1994) *Key Concepts in Communication and Cultural Studies*, London: Routledge.
Ozawa Yūsaku (1973) *Zainichi chōsenjin kyōikuron* (On the Education of Koreans in Japan), Tokyo: Aki shobō.
Ōta Junichi (1987) *Onnatachi no Ikaino* (Women's Ikaino), Tokyo: Shobunsha.
Pae Jang-jin (Chair), Kim Ch'ang-saeng, Cho Pak, Ch'ae Hyo, Kang Na-mi, Chŏng Yun-hŭi, and Chŏng Tae-sŏng (1987) "Zainichi bungaku wa korede iinoka" (Resident Korean Literature: Is This Good Enough?), *Mintō* 1: 56–85.
Pak Ch'un-sŏn (1994) *Kitachōsen yo, jūsatsushita ani o kaese!* (North Korea Must Return My Brother Whom It Executed!), Tokyo: Za masada.
Pak Kyŏng-sik (1989) *Kaihōgo zainichi chōsenjin undōshi* (The History of Korean Social Movement in Japan after the Liberation), Tokyo: Sanichi shobō.
—— (1992) "Taiheiyōsensōchū ni okeru chōsenjinrōdōsha no kyōseirenkō ni tsuite" (On Forced Recruitment of Korean Laborers During the Pacific War), in Pak Kyŏng-sik, *Zainichi chōsenjin, kyōseirenkō, minzokumondai* (Koreans in Japan, Forced Labor Recruitment, National Questions), Tokyo: Sanichi shobō.
Pak Kyŏng-sik, Yamada Shōji, and Yang T'ae-ho (eds) (1993) *Chōsenjin kyōseirenkō ronbunshūsei* (Collected Essays on Forced Labor Mobilization of Koreans), Tokyo: Akashi shoten.
Pak Sun-ja (1960) "P'yŏnji" (Letter), in Tokyo chosŏn chunggogŭp hakkyo (ed.) *Choguk ŭi p'um anesŏ: Kwiguk haksaeng p'yŏnjijip* (In the Bosom of the Fatherland: Letters from the Repatriated Students), Tokyo: Tokyo chosŏn chunggogŭp hakkyo.
Palermo, David and Molfese, Dennis (1972) "Language Acquisition from Age Five Onward," *Psychological Bulletin* 78: 409–28.
Parker, Jeffrey and Gottman, John (1989) "Social and Emotional Development in Relational Context: Friendship Interaction from Early Childhood to Adolescence," in T. Berndt and G. W. Ladd (eds) *Peer Relationships in Child Development*, New York: Wiley.
Patterson, Orlando (1997) *The Ordeal of Integration: Progress and Resentment in America's "Racial" Crisis*, Washington, D.C.: Civitas.
Peak, Lois (1991) *Learning to Go to School in Japan: The Transition from Home to Preschool Life*, Berkeley: University of California Press.
Piaget, Jean (1932) *The Moral Judgement of the Child*, London: Kegan and Paul.
Polkinghorne, Donald (1988) *Narrative Knowing and the Human Sciences*, Albany: SUNY Press.
Rajchman, John (ed.) (1995) *The Identity in Question*, London: Routledge.
Rekishigaku kenkyūkai (ed.) (1990) *Senryōseisaku no tenkan to kōwa: Nihon dōjidaishi* (Shifting Occupation Policies and Peacemaking: Contemporary History of Japan), vol. 2, Tokyo: Aoki shoten.
RENK henshūbu (ed.) (1997) "Kita kara no tegami" (A Letter from the North), *RENK* 13: 43–50.

Ri Kaisei (Li Hoe-sŏng) (1972) *Kinuta o utsu onna* (The Woman Who Fulled Clothes), Tokyo: Bungei shunjusha.

Ri Yu-hwan (1971) *Zainichi kankokujin rokujūman* (600,000 Koreans in Japan), Tokyo: Yōyōsha.

Rohlen, Thomas and LeTendre, Gerald (1996) "Conclusion: Themes in the Japanese Culture of Learning," in Thomas Rohlen and Gerald LeTendre (eds) *Teaching and Learning in Japan*, New York: Cambridge University Press.

Rueschemeyer, Dietrich and Evans, Peter (1985) "The State and Economic Transformation: Toward an Analysis of the Conditions Underlying Effective Intervention," in Peter Evans, Dietrich Rueschemeyer, and Theda Skocpol (eds) *Bringing the State Back In*, Cambridge: Cambridge University Press.

Rushdie, Salman (1981) *Imaginary Homelands: Essays and Criticism 1981-1991*, London: Penguin.

Rutherford, Jonathan (1990) "A Place Called Home," in Jonathan Rutherford (ed.) *Identity: Community, Culture, Difference*, London: Lawrence and Wishart.

Ryang, Sonia (1992) "Indoctrination or Rationalization?: The Anthropology of 'North Koreans' in Japan," *Critique of Anthropology* 12, 2: 101-32.

—— (1997) *North Koreans in Japan: Language, Ideology, and Identity*, Boulder: Westview Press.

—— (1998) "Inscribed (Men's) Bodies, Silent (Women's) Words: Rethinking Colonial Displacement of Koreans in Japan," *Bulletin of Concerned Asian Scholars* 30, 4: 3–15.

—— (Forthcoming) "Takamure Itsue ni okeru ai to shokuminchi" (Love and Colonialism in Takamure Itsue's Feminism), in Sonia Ryang (Ryō Jun), *Shokuminchi, zainichi, feminizumu ni kansuru rekishi, bunkajinruigaku ronbunshū* (Historical and Anthropological Essays on Colonialism, Koreans in Japan, and Feminism), Kyoto: Shōraisha.

Safran, William (1991) "Diasporas in Modern Societies: Myths of Homeland and Return," *Diaspora* Spring 1991: 83–99.

Sai Yōichi (1993) "Interview with Sai Yōichi," *Eiga shinbun* 102: 1–3.

—— (1994) *Sai Yōichi no sekai* (The World of Sai Yōichi), Tokyo: Nihon terebi hōsōmō.

Sai Yōichi, Yang Sŏg-il, Chŏng Wi-sin, and Li Bong-u (1994) "Kokkyō o koetara oretachi no jidaidatta" (Our Time Has Come When We Overcome National Borders), in Li Bong-u (ed.) *Tsuki wa dotchini deteiru o meguru nisan no hanashi* (A Couple of Stories Around *Tsuki wa dotchini deteiru*), Tokyo: Shakai hyōronsha.

Sakai Naoki (1996) "Shizansareru nihongo/nihonjin" (The Still-Born Japanese Language and Japanese), in Sakai Naoki, *Shizansareru ihongo/ihonjin* (The Still-Born Japanese Language and Japanese), Tokyo: Shinyōsha.

Samāsukūru jimukyoku (ed.) (1997) *Dai 17 kai samāsukūru kansōbunshū* (The Collected Comments of the 17th Summer School), Hirakata: Samāsukūru jimukyoku.

Sano Michio (1993) *Kindainihon no kyōiku to chōsen* (Korea and the Education in Modern Japan), Tokyo: Shakai hyōronsha.

Scalapino, Robert A. and Lee, Chong-sik (1972) *Communism in Korea*, vol 1, Berkeley: University of California Press.

Schrag, Calvin O. (1997) *The Self after Postmodernity*, New Haven: Yale University Press.

Scott, Joan (1995) "Multiculturalism and the Politics of Identity," in John Rajchman (ed.) *The Identity in Question*, London: Routledge.

Seikatsujittai chōsadan (1959a) "Kyōtoshi Nishijin, Kashiwano chiku chōsenjin shūdan kyojūchiiki no seikatsujittai" (Survey of Living Conditions of Koreans Concentrated in Nishijin and Kashiwano Aareas of Kyoto City), *Chōsen mondai kenkyū* 3, 2: 31–42.

—— (1959b) "Ōsakashi Senbokugun chōsenjin shūdan kyojūchiiki no seikatsujittai" (Survey of Living Conditions of Koreans Concentrated in Senboku County of Osaka

City), *Chōsen mondai kenkyū* 3, 1: 25–34.
Seki Toyoo (1972) *Tōi hi no kiroku* (The Memory of the Distant Past), Kobe: Kobe shuppan insatsu.
Sekigawa Natsuo (1992) *Taikutsu na meikyū: "Kitachōsen" towa nandattanoka* (A Dull Labyrinth: What Was "North Korea" for Us?), Tokyo: Shinchōsha.
Shibata Michiko (1980) "Sensō ga unda kodomotachi" (Children Born by the War), in *Bessatsu jinseidokuhon*, Tokyo: Kawade shobō shinsha.
Shohat, Ella (1992) "Notes on the 'Postcolonial,'" *Social Text* 31/32: 99–113.
Shohat, Ella and Stam, Robert (1994) *Unthinking Eurocentrism: Multiculturalism and Media*, London: Routledge.
Skocpol, Theda (1985) "Bringing the State Back In: Strategies of Analysis in Current Research," in Peter Evans, Dietrich Rueschemeyer, and Theda Skocpol (eds) *Bringing the State Back In*, Cambridge: Cambridge University Press.
Smith, W. Donald (1998) "Koreans in Interwar Japan: Militant Workers or an Obstacle to Working-Class Organization?," paper presented at the Association for Asian Studies Annual Conference, Washington D.C.
Sollors, Werner (1986) *Beyond Ethnicity: Consent and Descent in American Culture*, New York: Oxford University Press.
Song Jong-ch'ŏl (1960) "P'yŏnji" (Letter), in Tokyo chosŏn chunggogŭp hakkyo (ed.) *Choguk ŭi p'um anesŏ: Kwiguk haksaeng p'yŏnjijip* (In the Bosom of the Fatherland: Letters from the Repatriated Students), Tokyo: Tokyo chosŏn chunggogŭp hakkyo.
Sŏng Mi-ja (1995) *Zainichi nisei no haha kara zainichi sansei no musume e* (From the Second-Generation Korean Mother to the Third-Generation Daughter), Tokyo: Banseisha.
Song Yŏn-ok (1993) "Osaka ni okeru zainichi chōsenjin no seikatsu: 1945 izen" (The Lives of Resident Koreans in Osaka Before 1945), in Hirakatashi kyōikuiinkai (ed.) *Zainichi chōsenjin no rekishi: Hirakata deno horiokoshi no tameni* (History of Koreans in Japan: For Digging up Their History in Hirakata), Hirakata: Hirakatashi kyōikuiinkai.
Soysal, Yasemin (1994) *Limits of Citizenship: Migrants and Postnational Membership in Europe*, Chicago: University of Chicago Press.
Spivak, Gayatri (1987) *In Other Worlds: Essays in Cultural Politics*, London: Methuen.
—— (1988) "Can the Subaltern Speak?," in Cary Nelson and Lawrence Grossberg (eds) *Marxism and the Interpretation of Culture*, London: Macmillan.
Spivak, Gayatri and Gunew, Sneja (1993) "Questions of Multiculturalism," in Simon During (ed.) *The Cultural Studies Reader*, London: Routledge.
Stoler, Ann (1995) *Race and Education of Desire: Foucault's History of Sexuality and the Colonial Order of Things*, Durham: Duke University Press.
Sugihara Kaoru and Tamai Kingo (eds) (1986) Taishō/Osaka/Suramu (The Taisho Period, Osaka, the Slum). Tokyo: Shinpyōsha.
Sugihara Tōru (1986) "Zaihan chōsenjin no tokōkatei" (How Koreans Came to Osaka), in Sugihara Kaoru and Tamai Kingo (eds) *Taishō/Osaka/Suramu* (The Taishō Period, Osaka, the Slum), Tokyo: Shinpyōsha.
Suzuki, David and Oiwa, Keibo (1996) *The Japan We Never Knew: A Journey of Discovery*, Toronto: Stoddart.
Suzuki Yūko (1992) *Jūgunianfu, naisenkekkon* (Army Prostitutes and Japan-Korea Marriage), Tokyo: Miraisha.
Takagi Kenichi (1990) *Saharin to nihon no sengosekinin* (Sakhalin and Japan's War Responsibility), Tokyo: Gaifūsha.
Takahashi Keiko and Hatano Giyoo (1988) "'Kinyūseido' no rikai ni okeru gogainen" (Mistaken Concepts in the Understanding of 'Banking System'), in *Nihon kyōikushinrigakkai dai 30 kai sōkai happyō ronbunshū*, Naruto: Nihon kyōikushinrigakkai dai 30

kai sōkai junbiiinkai.
Takeda Seiji (1989) "Kurushimi no yurai" (Where the Pain Comes From), in Takeda Seiji, *Yume no gaibu* (The Outside of Dream), Tokyo: Kawade shobō shinsha.
Takeda Seiji, Kang Sang-jung, and Katō Norihiro (1995) "Zainichi surukoto e no shiza" (A Perspective of Residing in Japan), *Shisō no kagaku* 28, May 1995: 54–78.
Takeuchi Yasuhiro (1985) "Hirakareta gengo o kakutokusuru tameni: Chong Ch'u-wŏl 'Mun Konbun ŏmŏni no ningo' ga shisasuru mono" (In Order to Attain More Open Language: The Implications of Chong Ch'u-wŏl's "Mun Kon-bun *Ŏmŏni's* Apple"), *Shinnihon bungaku* 456: 15–25.
Tameike Yoshio (1959) "Chōsenjin no hongokuhō toshite tekiyōsubeki hōritsu – hokusenhō no tekiyōmondai o chūshin toshite" (The *Lex Domicilii* of Koreans in Japan – With Attention to the Question of Applying the North Korean Law), *Minshōhō zasshi* 40, 4: 591–608.
Tanaka Hiroshi (1974) "Nihon no shokuminchi shihaika ni okeru kokusekikankei no keii" (A Historical Survey on the Voting Right and the Compulsory Military Service of the Formosan and Korean Peoples under the Japanese Colonization), *Aichi kenritsu daigaku gaikokugogakubu kiyō* 9: 61–96.
—— (1985) "Gaikokujin no kyōiku kōmuin shikaku sono mondai to haikei" (Qualifications Required of Foreigners to Work in Public Educational Sector), *Hōritsu jihō* 57, 5: 37–42.
—— (1991) *Zainichi gaikokujin* (Resident Foreigners in Japan), Tokyo: Iwanami shoten.
—— (1995) *Zainichi gaikokujin, shinpan* (Resident Foreigners in Japan: New Edition), Tokyo: Iwanami shoten.
Tanaka Katsuhiko (1981) *Kotoba to kokka* (Language and the State), Tokyo: Iwanami shoten.
Tanaka Toshiyuki (1996) "Naze beigunwa jūgunianfu mondai o mushishitanoka [jō]" (Why the US Occupation Ignored the Issue of Comfort Women for the Japanese Military [part 1]), *Sekai* October 1996: 174–83.
Tani Tomio (1996) "Minzokukankei no shakaigakuteki kenkyū no tameno oboegaki: Osakashi kyū Ikaino/Motogi chiiki o jirei toshite" (Thoughts for Sociological Research on Ethnic Relations: The Example of the Former Ikaino/Motogi Districts in Osaka), in Komai Hiroshi (ed.) *Nihon no esunikkushakai* (Japan's Ethnic Society), Tokyo: Akashi shoten.
Tanigawa Shuntarō, Saitō Jirō, and Satō Manabu (1997) *Konna kyōkasho ari?: Kokugo to shakaika no kyōkasho o yomu* (What Kind of Textbooks Are They?: Reading National Language and Social Studies Textbooks), Tokyo: Iwanami shoten.
Tashiro Aritsugu (1969) "Koseki to kokuseki tono kankei ni tsuite" (On the Relationship Between Household Registry and Nationality) II, *Koseki* 284: 2–14.
Tashiro Aritsugu, Yoshida Kazuo, and Hayashida Satoshi (1969) "Kyōtsūhō 3 jō 3 kō to heiekihō tono kankei" (The Relationship Between the Common Law Article 3 Item 3 and the Conscription Law), *Koseki* 271: 2–15.
Tatsumi Nobuo (1966) "Nikkan hōteki chii kyōtei to shutsunyūkoku kanri tokubetsuhō" (The Japan–ROK Legal Status Agreement and the Special Provision for the Immigration Control Act), *Hōritsu jihō* 38, 4: 59–67.
"Teijūgaikokujin nokosareta mondai" (Resident Aliens and Remaining Issues) (1990) *Sekai* 544, August 1990: 102–17.
Texier, Jacques (1979) "Gramsci, Theoretician of the Superstructures," in Chantal Mouffe (ed.) *Gramsci and Marxist Theory*, London: Routledge and Kegan Paul.
Tokuhara Yumiko (1998) *Zainichi chōsenjin o meguru kyōiku: Osakashi Ikunoku no A shōgakkō o jirei toshite* (Education for Koreans in Japan: The Case of "A" Primary School in Ikuno Ward, Osaka City), unpublished Master's thesis in linguistics and culture, Faculty of Language and Culture, University of Osaka.
Torres, María de los Angeles (1995) "Encuentros Y Encontronazos: Homeland in the Politics and Identity of the Cuban Diaspora," *Diaspora* 4, 2: 211–38.

"Tōshindai no zainichi chōsenjin" (Unwrapping the Reality of Resident Koreans in Japan) (1993) *Spa!* 10 November 1993: 116–21.
Tsuboe Senji (1949) *Zainihon chōsenjin no gaikyō* (The Outline of Koreans in Japan), Tokyo: Hōmushō.
Tsuboi Toyokichi (1957) *Zainichi chōsenjinundō no gaikyō* (The Outline of the Movement of Koreans in Japan), Tokyo: Hōmu kenkyūjo.
Tsurumi, E. Patricia (1984) "Colonial Education in Korea and Taiwan," in Ramon H. Myers and Mark R. Peattie (eds) *The Japanese Colonial Empire, 1895–1945*, Princeton: Princeton University Press.
Ueno Chizuko (1998) "'Jūgunianfu' mondai o megutte" (On the 'Comfort Women' Issue), in Ueno Chizuko, *Nashonarizumu to jendā* (Nationalism and Gender), Tokyo: Seitosha.
Utsumi Aiko (1991) "Naze chōsenjin ga senpan ni nattanoka" (Why Koreans Became Japan's War Criminals?), in Sengo hoshō mondai kenkyukai (eds) *Zainichi kankokuchōsenjin no sengohoshō* (Postwar Compensation for Koreans in Japan), Tokyo: Akashi shoten.
van den Bedem, Ruud (1994) "Towards a System of Plural Nationality in the Netherlands: Changes in Regulations and Perceptions," in Rainer Bauböck (ed.) *From Aliens to Citizens: Redefining the Status of Immigrants in Europe*, Aldershot: Avebury.
Volosinov, V. N. (1986) *Marxism and the Philosophy of Language*, Cambridge, Mass.: Harvard University Press.
Wada Haruki (1992) *Kin nissei to manshū kōnichi sensō* (Kim Il Sung and the Anti-Japanese War in Manchuria), Tokyo: Heibonsha.
Wada Yoshihisa (1993) "Zainichi chōsenjin to Hirakata" (Koreans in Japan and Hirakata), in Hirakatashi kyōikuiinkai (ed.) *Zainichi chōsenjin no rekishi: Hirakata deno horiokoshi no tameni* (History of Koreans in Japan: For Digging up Their History in Hirakata), Hirakata: Hirakatashi kyōikuiinkai.
Wagner, Edward (1951) *The Korean Minority in Japan: 1904–1950*, New York: Institute of Pacific Relations.
Wallerstein, Immanuel (1991) "The Construction of Peoplehood: Racism, Nationalism, Ethnicity," in Etienne Balibar and Immanuel Wallerstein, *Race, Nation, Class: Ambiguous Identities*, London: Verso.
Weil, Simone (1978) *The Need for Roots: Prelude to a Declaration of Duties Toward Mankind*, New York: Ark.
Weiner, Michael (1989) *The Origin of the Korean Community in Japan 1910–1923*, Atlantic Highlands: Humanities Press International.
—— (1994) *Race and Migration in Imperial Japan*, London: Routledge.
—— (ed.) (1997) *Japan's Minorities: The Illusion of Homogeneity*, London: Routledge.
West, Cornel (1995) "A Matter of Life and Death," in John Rajchman (ed.) *The Identity in Question*, London: Routledge.
Williams, Bernard (1995) "Identity and Identities," in Henry Harris (ed.) *Identity*, Oxford: Oxford University Press.
Williams, Raymond (1977) *Marxism and Literature*, Oxford: Oxford University Press.
—— (1983) *Keywords*, Oxford: Oxford University Press.
Wolf, Eric (1982) *Europe and the People Without History*, Berkeley: University of California Press.
Xenos, Nicholas (1993) "Refugees: The Modern Political Condition," *Alternatives* 18: 419–30.
Yamamoto Tetsumi (1995) *Hokori: Ningen Harimoto Isao* (Dignity: A Man Harimoto Isao), Tokyo: Kōdansha.
Yamawaki Keizō (1994) *Kindainihon to gaikokujinrōdōsha* (The Modern Japan and Foreign Workers), Tokyo: Akashi shoten.

Yang Sŏg-il (1981) *Takushī kyōsōkyoku* (Taxi Crazy Rhapsody), Tokyo: Chikuma shobō.

Yang T'ae-ho (1988) "Kyōzon/kyōsei/kyōkan – Kang Sang-jungshi eno gimon" (II) (Shared Existence/Shared Lives/Shared Feelings – Questions for Kang Sang-jung (II)), in Iinuma Jirō (ed.) *Zainichi kankokuchōsenjin – sono nihon ni okeru sonzaikachi* (Resident Koreans: The Value of Their Existence in Japanese Society), Tokyo: Kaifūsha.

—— (1992) "'Sōshikaimei' no shisōteki haikei" (The Ideological Background of 'Sōshikaimei'), in Miyata Setsuko, Kim Yŏng-dal, and Yang T'ae-ho, *Sōshikaimei* (Creating Japanese-Style Names and Reforming Korean Names), Tokyo: Akashi shoten.

Yang Yŏng-hu (1985) "Zainichi chōsenjin shijo no kyōikumondai" (Problems Pertaining to the Education of Korean Children in Japan), in Isomura Eiichi, Ichibangase Yasuko, and Harada Tomohiko (eds) *Kōza: Sabetsu to jinken, 4, Minzoku* (Series on Discrimination and Human Rights, vol. 4, Ethnic Groups), Tokyo: Yūzankaku.

—— (1994) *Sengo Osaka no chōsenjin undō: 1945–1965* (The Postwar Korean Movement in Osaka: 1945–1965), Tokyo: Miraisha.

Yi Chŏng-ja (1994) *Furimukeba nihon* (When I Turned Around, There Was Japan), Tokyo: Kawade shobō shinsha.

Yi Yang-ji (1989a) *Yuhi*, Tokyo: Kōdansha.

—— (1989b) "Zainichi bungaku o koete" (Beyond *Zainichi* Literature), *Bungakukai* 43, 3: 264–84.

—— (1993a) "Watashi ni totte no bokoku to nihon" (What My Motherland and Japan Mean to Me), in *Yi Yang-ji zenshū* (Collected Works of Yi Yang-ji), Tokyo: Kōdansha.

—— (1993b) "Watashi wa chōsenjin" (I Am a Korean), in *Yi Yang-ji zenshū* (Collected Works of Yi Yang-ji), Tokyo: Kōdansha.

—— (1993c) "Bokoku de kurashite yonkagetsume" (Four Months in My Homeland), in *Yi Yang-ji zenshū* (Collected Works of Yi Yang-ji), Tokyo: Kōdansha.

—— (1993d) "'Hyōgo no toshi' Souru eno kenokan" (My Hatred for Seoul, That 'City of Slogans'), in *Yi Yang-ji zenshū* (Collected Works of Yi Yang-ji), Tokyo: Kōdansha.

—— (1993e) *Nabi t'aryŏng* (Greiving Butterflies), in *Yi Yang-ji zenshū* (Collected Works of Yi Yang-ji), Tokyo: Kōdansha.

—— (1993f) "Kotoba no tsue o motomete" (Searching for a Linguistic Walking Cane), in *Yi Yang-ji zenshū* (Collected Works of Yi Yang-ji), Tokyo: Kōdansha.

Yi, Yong Yo (1995) "Maintaining Culture and Language: Koreans in Osaka," in John Maher and Gaynor Macdonald (eds) *Diversity in Japanese Culture and Language*, London: Kegan Paul International.

Yoneyama, Lisa (1995) "Memory Matters: Hiroshima's Korean Atom Bomb Memorial and the Politics of Ethnicity," *Public Culture* 7, Spring 1995: 499–527; republished in 1997 with corrections in Laura Hein and Mark Selden (eds) *Living with the Bomb: American and Japanese Cultural Conflicts in the Nuclear Age*, Armonk: M. E. Sharpe.

—— (1998) "Bunka to iu tsumi" (A Sin Called Culture), in Kajiwara Kageaki *et al.* (eds) *Iwanamikōza bunkajinruigaku* (Iwanami's Series on Cultural Anthropology), vol. 13, Tokyo: Iwanami shoten.

Yonniyon o kirokusuru kai (ed.) (1988) *4.24 Hanshin kyōikutōsō* (The April 24 Osaka-Kobe Educational Struggle), Osaka: Burēn sentā.

Yonniyon Hanshin kyōikutōsō 50 shūnenkinen jigyōiinkai (ed.) (1998) *Shinno kyōseishakai wa minzokukyōiku no hoshōkara!* (The True Society of Co-Existence Comes after Ethnic Education Is Guaranteed!), Osaka: Yonniyon Hanshin kyōikutōsō 50 shūnenkinen jigyōiinkai.

Yoshida Mitsuo (1993) "Koseki kara mita 20 seiki shotō Souru no 'hito' to 'ie'" ('Person' and 'Household' in Household Registries in the Early Twentieth Century Seoul), *Chōsen gakuhō* 147: 25–119.

Yoshino, Kosaku (1992) *Cultural Nationalism in Contemporary Japan: A Sociological Inquiry*, London: Routledge.
Yu Miri (1993) *Sakana no matsuri* (The Fish Festival), Tokyo: Hakusuisha.
—— (1995) *Kazoku no hyōhon* (Family Specimen), Tokyo: Asahi shinbunsha.
—— (1996a) *Furuhausu* (Fullhouse/The Full House), Tokyo: Bungei shunjusha.
—— (1996b) *Mado no aru shotenkara* (From the Bookshop with a Window), Tokyo: Kadokawa shoten.
—— (1997a) "Kazoku shinema" (The Family Cinema), *Gunzō* December 1997: 7–48.
—— (1997b) "Kotoba no ressun" (The Language Lesson), *Shūkan asahi* March 28, 1997: 141.
—— (1997c) *Mizube no yurikago* (A Cradle on the Riverside), Tokyo: Kadokawa shoten.
—— (1998) *Kamen no kuni* (The Land of Masks), Tokyo: Shinchōsha.
Yun Jŏng-ok *et al.* (1992) *Chōsenjinjosei ga mita "ianfumondai"* (The "Comfort Women Issue" Seen by Korean Women), Tokyo: Sanichi shobō.
Yun Kŏn-ch'a (1992) *"Zainichi" o ikiru towa* (To Live as "Zainichi"), Tokyo: Iwanami shoten.
—— (1997) *Nihon kokuminron* (On the Japanese Nation), Tokyo: Chikuma shobō.
Zainichi chōsenjin gakkōjiken shinsōchōsadan (1948) "Zainichi chōsenjin gakkōjiken no shinsō" (The Truth about the Korean Schools Incident), in Kim Kyŏng-hae (ed.) *Zainichi chōsenjin minzokukyōiku yōgotōsō shiryōshū* (Collected Documents on the Struggle to Defend Korean Ethnic Education), vol. 1, Tokyo: Akashi shoten.
Zainihon chōsenjin sōrengōkai (1989) *Sokoku no futokoro ni idakarete – zainichi chōsenjin no kikoku jitsugen 30 shūnen* (In the Bosom of the Fatherland: The Thirtieth Commemoration of Repatriation of Koreans from Japan), Tokyo: Zainihon chōsenjin sōrengōkai.

Newspapers

Asahi shinbun (Asahi daily), nationwide daily newspaper in Japanese.
Chosŏn sinbo (Korea daily), a Korean newspaper published by Chongryun.
Kobe shinbun (Kobe daily), a Japanese newspaper distributed in the Kobe area.
Kyoto shinbun (Kyoto daily), a Japanese newspaper distributed in the Kyoto area.
Osaka shinbun (Osaka daily), a Japanese newspaper distributed in the Osaka area.

Official documents

Hōmunenkan (The Ministry of Justice Annual) yearly published, Tokyo: Hōmushō.
Konintōkei: Jinkō dōtai tōkei tokushu hōkoku (Marital Statistics: A Special Report on Vital Statistics) (1987) Tokyo: Kōseishō.
Shutsunyūkoku kanri tōkeinenpō (Immigration Control Statistics) yearly published, Tokyo: Hōmushō.

Index

Aboud, F. 159–60
Ainu 99
Akutagawa award 103, 105, 115, 119, 123, 124, 126, 134
Alien Registration Law 4, 21, 24, 74, 84, 91, 99, 147
amnesia 69
An, Une 67
Ang, I. 63
anti-fingerprinting movement 28, 75, 76, 79, 84, 91, 98, 100
Antonio Maceo Brigade 50
Arendt, H. 49
assimilation 2, 13, 14, 17, 19, 20, 26, 27, 29, 49, 63, 69, 72, 77, 79, 122, 170, 175, 176, 193

Bakhtin, M. 80, 88–9
Balibar, E. 114
Borges, J. 199
Bourdieu, P. 57
Buraku kaihō dōmei 57, 173
Burakumin 57, 99, 166, 168–9, 171, 179–80

Chambers, I. 60, 119
Chejudo 76, 77, 81, 166
Chŏng, Yŏng-he 65, 67
Chongryun 5, 6, 8, 25, 26, 28, 29, 32, 78, 170; collective identity 42; exclusion from Japanese society 49; schools 5, 36, 44, 49, 94, 154, 166, 170, 179, 181; self-definition 36; visitors to North Korea 40, 41–3; *see also* North Korea
Clifford, J. 50
Cold War 5, 6, 25, 39, 41, 44

colonialism 2, 3, 17, 21, 63, 98, 100, 105, 148, 155
comfort women 3, 59, 165

de Certeau, M. 48
De Vos, G. 197
denizen 14, 15, 16, 29
deportation 27, 33, 38, 60, 146, 150
diaspora 6, 48, 63, 104, 105, 111, 112, 133
discrimination 2, 5, 10, 36, 42, 57, 58, 60, 61, 66, 74, 77, 93, 95, 98, 100, 104, 105, 111, 115, 120, 122, 144, 157, 158, 167, 169, 179, 182, 183, 193, 201, 203, 206
Durkheim, E. 199

Erikson, E. 198

Field, N. 79
Flaubert, G. 206–7
Foucault, M. 114

Giddens, A. 48
Gilroy, P. 63
Gordon, A. 105
Gottman, J. 159
Great Kantō Earthquake 18, 158, 165
Great East Asian Coprosperity Sphere 3, 17

Hall, S. 51, 55, 70
Hammer, T. 14, 29
Harvey, D. 75, 76, 90
Hayashi, Mariko 116
Hino, Keizō 126, 129
homogeneity 16, 27, 70, 164
household registration 2–3, 4, 17–18, 19, 26–7

Hume, D. 198

identity 8, 9, 28, 51, 61, 64, 65, 70, 75, 76, 77, 78, 98, 134, 136, 172–3, 181, 182, 194, 197; cultural 6, 133, 139; displaced 127; ethnic 1, 7, 8, 9, 20, 29, 63, 139, 159; ethnonational 13, 29, 165, 193; Korean Japanese 135, 200–1; national 8, 41, 46, 52, 72, 157, 164, 169; national/cultural 63; national/ethnic 169; negative 93–4, 159; personal 198–9; resident Korean 89, 91
Immigration Control Law 28
Immigration Control Order 22
intermarriage between Koreans and Japanese 6, 28, 61, 175
International Covenants on Human Rights 6, 28, 39
Itō, Narihiko 137

Jackson, J. 75
Jameson, F. 75
Japan: Allied occupation 4, 9, 14, 20–1; Communist Party 26, 35–6, 142, 146–7, 152, 153–4; insensitivity to the cultural difference of Koreans 68–9; media taboo 56–8; Ministry of Education 5, 9, 143, 149, 153–4, 161, 165, 166, 171, 172–3, 176, 177, 180, 181; Ministry of Justice 26, 27, 39, 92; multiethnic empire 2, 27, 142, 161; Nationality Law 4, 22, 33; obliteration of its colonial past 57; Red Cross 34–5, 38; Teachers' Union 179

Kaneko, A. 66
Kang, Sang-jung 77–8
Keats, J. 198–9
Kim, Chi-ha 83
Kim, Dŏk-hwan 92–3
Kim, Hak-yŏng 104
Kim, Hwa-sun 152
Kim, Il Sung 2, 34, 36, 37, 43, 45, 62
Kim, Jong Il 45
Kim, Si-jong 76
Kim, T'ae-gi 150
Kim, T'ae-il 152
Kim, U-sŏng 61
kimch'i 38, 77, 80, 81, 120

Kitada, Sachie 133
Kondo, Dorinne 48
Korea; partition 4, 5, 13, 22, 24, 25, 32, 39; reunification 24, 28, 35, 36, 62, 96, 97; University 40, 41, 44, 46
Korean War 4, 20, 25, 32, 33, 34, 35
Kuroto, Kazuo 134
Kyō, Nobuko 70. 104
Kyōwakai 19, 170

language: aphasia 111; and Yi Yang-ji's ethnic identity 135; and *Yuhi* 126–7, 129–33; derogatory 67; in the colonies 141–2; instruction of Korean language in Japanese schools 180; multilinguality 160–1; national language 157, 161–3, 165, 166, 176–7; "new mother tongue" 137; novelistic 88–9; of first generation Koreans as living language 84–5; postwar instruction of Korean language 150, 154; women's speech 82–3
Larkin, P. 198
League of Koreans 5, 24, 35, 146; and the Japanese Communist Party 146–7; and the Japanese Ministry of Education 150; education program 148; the 4.24 education struggle 151–3; the dissolution of 153–4
Lee, Changsoo 197
Lee, Seijaku 60–1
Li, Bong-u 68
Li, Hoe-sŏng (Ri Kaisei) 85, 103
Li, Sang-t'e 66, 67
Lienhardt, G. 199
Locke, J. 198
Lowe, L. 106

Manchuria 2
Malamud, B. 199
March First Independence Movement 141
Massey, D. 76, 90
Mindan 6, 8, 22, 24–6, 29, 35, 38, 78, 96, 170, 181; *see also* South Korea
Minjŏn 35–6
Mintōren 78, 92
Miyata, Setsuko 3
modern: bourgeois family 112, 114, 117; Habermasian 98; Japanese fiction 79; nation-state 49, 91, 98, 114; society 107

modernist 98
modernity 47, 48, 49, 85, 77
modernization 77
Morris-Suzuki, T. 69

Nakada, Tōichi 71
name: adoption of Japanese name under colonialism 19; appropriation of a slandered name 58; Japanese reading/pronunciation of Korean names 56, 58, 59, 103, 111, 189; learning the ethnic name 171, 185, 189–90; using Japanese name in public 84, 157, 171, 184, 203; using Korean name in public 100, 133, 167–8, 169, 171, 180, 182
nationalism 3, 7, 10, 14, 24, 25, 34, 35, 36, 63, 99, 100, 101, 116, 141, 148, 155, 162
naturalization: criteria 26; in Germany 15; increase of 29, 182; statistics 6, 26; the Justice Ministry policy 27; Yi Yang-ji's 120; *see also sōshikaimei*
North Korea 4, 8, 10, 13, 24, 26, 32, 59, 62, 94, 170; economic crisis 43; education funds 36; family reunion trip to 39–43; Foreign Ministry 34; nationality 25; nationality law 22; overseas nationals 8, 25; Red Cross 34, 35; repatriation to 34–5; *see also* Chongryun, repatriation

Okinawa 2, 168
Okinawan 99, 152, 163, 166
Ōnuma, Yasuaki 24
Origuchi, Shinobu 158

pachinko 5, 99, 104, 108, 111
Pak, Ae-ja 91
Pak, Ch'un-sŏn 43
Pak, Kyŏng-nam 104
Park, Jung Hee 39
Parker, J. 159
patriarchy 104, 110, 111, 113
place: and space 48–9, 75–6; politics of 90
Piaget, J. 159, 160

Rhee, Syngman 35, 38
repatriation: decline in number of repatriates to North Korea 38–9; of Japanese 34, 145; of Koreans 21, 32–7, 41, 44, 50, 51, 144, 145, 146; payment for repatriates' well-being 45; political meaning of the term 38; news on repatriates 43–4
repatriationism 24, 28, 32–9, 41
Ri, Kaisei (Li Hoe-song) 85
Rikidōzan 58, 202, 205
Rutherford, J. 51

Sai, Yōichi 56, 61, 62, 66
Saitō, Makoto 142
SCAP (Supreme Commander for the Allied Powers): ambiguous policies toward Koreans 21, 145–6; and Korean schools 149–50; and San Francisco Treaty 22; and the League of Koreans 146; anti-Communism 23; armed suppression of Koreans 152; ban on North Korean flag's display 153; military court 152, 153; proclamation of the state of emergency 151; relation to the Japanese government 155; repatriation policy 145; *see also* the League of Koreans
school: and the modern nation-state 155; bullying 158, 203, 205; catchment area 157, 163, 171, 182; colonial ordinances 141; early postwar Korean schools 147, 177; Japanese schools and Korean parents 93, 194; Ministry of Education and Korean schools 149–50; miscellaneous schools 149, 150, 154–5; of the League of Koreans 148–9; prewar enrolment of Korean children in Japan 143; textbooks 9, 160–5; the 4. 24 educational struggle 151–3, 177, 194; *see also* Chongryun schools, Japan Ministry of Education
Scott, J. 100
shamanism 77, 81, 85, 123
Shohat, E. 73
Sōaikai 19, 170
Son, Masayoshi 201
sōshikaimei 2–3, 19–20, 26, 176
South Korea 4, 5, 6, 7, 10, 13, 32, 35, 38, 59, 62, 91, 96, 153, 185, 190, 205; diplomatic normalization with Japan

4, 22, 25, 28, 32–3, 39; nationality 25, 28, 39–40, 106, 116, 170, 172; Nationality Law 22, 33; Overseas Nationals Registration Law 22; *see also* Mindan

Stam, R. 73

Takeuchi, Yasuhiro 88–9
Tanigawa, Shuntarō 167
Tashiro, Aritsugu 26, 29
theater: Asian American 48; Seishun Gogatsutō 105; Tokyo Kid Brothers 105
tokenism 68, 170

UN Refugee Convention 6, 28, 39

writing and literacy: and sexual satisfaction 97; as empowerment 95; as resistance 86

Xenos, N. 49

Yang, Sŏg-il 56, 66
Yang, T'ae-ho 78
Yang, Yŏng-ja 91
Yi dynasty 3
Yoshida, Shigeru 153–4

zainichi 59, 65, 68, 71, 72–3, 77–9, 83, 99, 103–6, 116

CPSIA information can be obtained
at www.ICGtesting.com
Printed in the USA
BVHW072106141218
535670BV00006B/41/P